BATMAN VS. SUPERMAN

THE GREATEST BATTLES

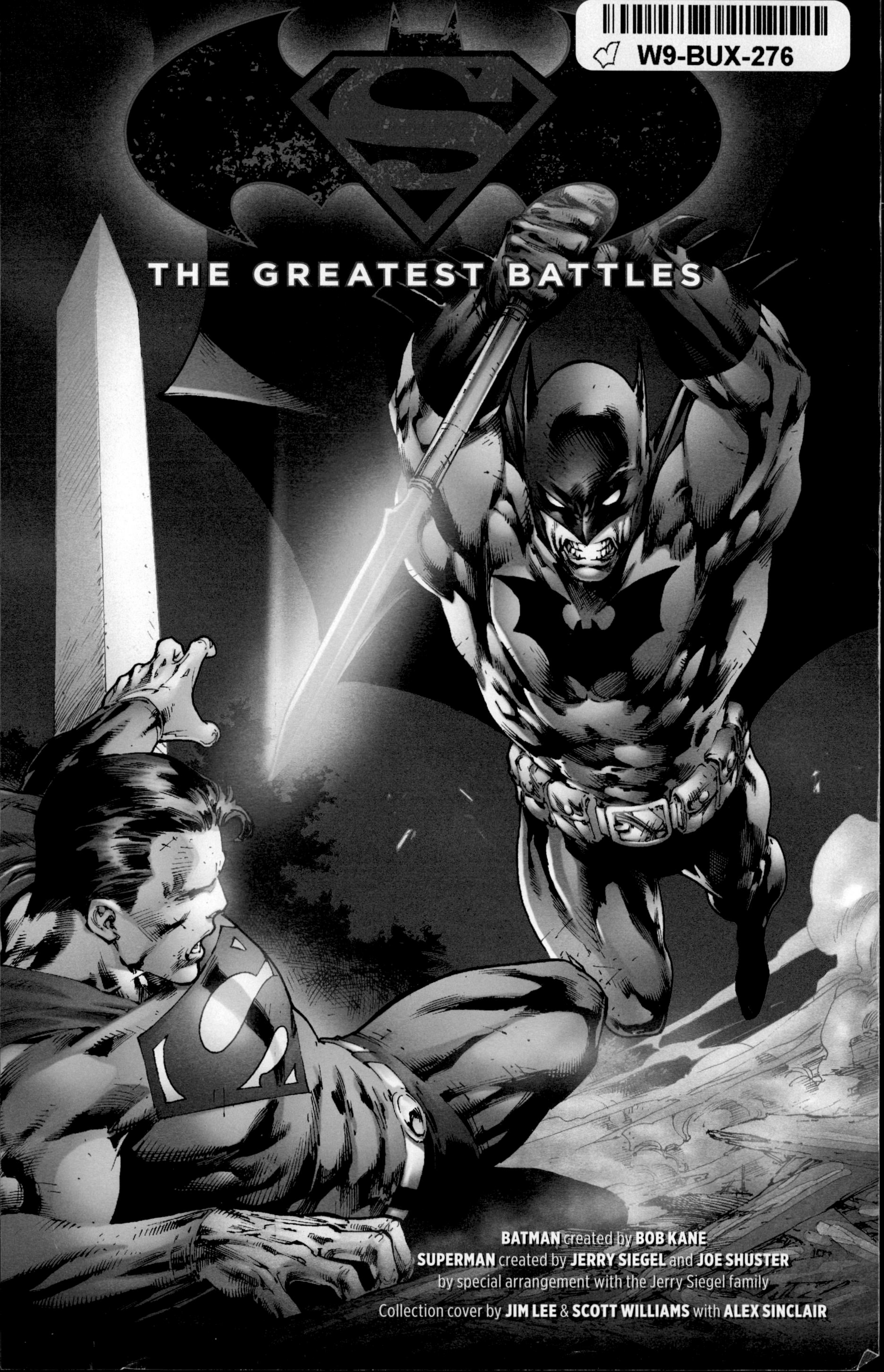

BATMAN created by **BOB KANE**
SUPERMAN created by **JERRY SIEGEL** and **JOE SHUSTER**
by special arrangement with the Jerry Siegel family
Collection cover by **JIM LEE** & **SCOTT WILLIAMS** with **ALEX SINCLAIR**

DICK GIORDANO
DENNY O'NEIL
BOB SCHRECK
EDDIE BERGANZA
MARK DOYLE
Editors – Original Series

REX OGLE
Associate Editor – Original Series

MORGAN DONTANVILLE
ADAM SCHLAGMAN
MATT HUMPHREYS
Assistant Editors – Original Series

ROBIN WILDMAN
Editor

JEB WOODARD
Group Editor – Collected Editions

CURTIS KING JR.
Publication Design

BOB HARRAS
Senior VP – Editor-in-Chief, DC Comics

DIANE NELSON
President

DAN DIDIO and JIM LEE
Co-Publishers

GEOFF JOHNS
Chief Creative Officer

AMIT DESAI
Senior VP – Marketing & Global Franchise Management

NAIRI GARDINER
Senior VP – Finance

SAM ADES
VP – Digital Marketing

BOBBIE CHASE
VP – Talent Development

MARK CHIARELLO
Senior VP – Art, Design & Collected Editions

JOHN CUNNINGHAM
VP – Content Strategy

ANNE DEPIES
VP – Strategy Planning & Reporting

DON FALLETTI
VP – Manufacturing Operations

LAWRENCE GANEM
VP – Editorial Administration & Talent Relations

ALISON GILL
Senior VP – Manufacturing & Operations

HANK KANALZ
Senior VP – Editorial Strategy & Administration

JAY KOGAN
VP – Legal Affairs

DEREK MADDALENA
Senior VP – Sales & Business Development

JACK MAHAN
VP – Business Affairs

DAN MIRON
VP – Sales Planning & Trade Development

NICK NAPOLITANO
VP – Manufacturing Administration

CAROL ROEDER
VP – Marketing

EDDIE SCANNELL
VP – Mass Account & Digital Sales

COURTNEY SIMMONS
Senior VP – Publicity & Communications

JIM (SKI) SOKOLOWSKI
VP – Comic Book Specialty & Newsstand Sales

SANDY YI
Senior VP – Global Franchise Management

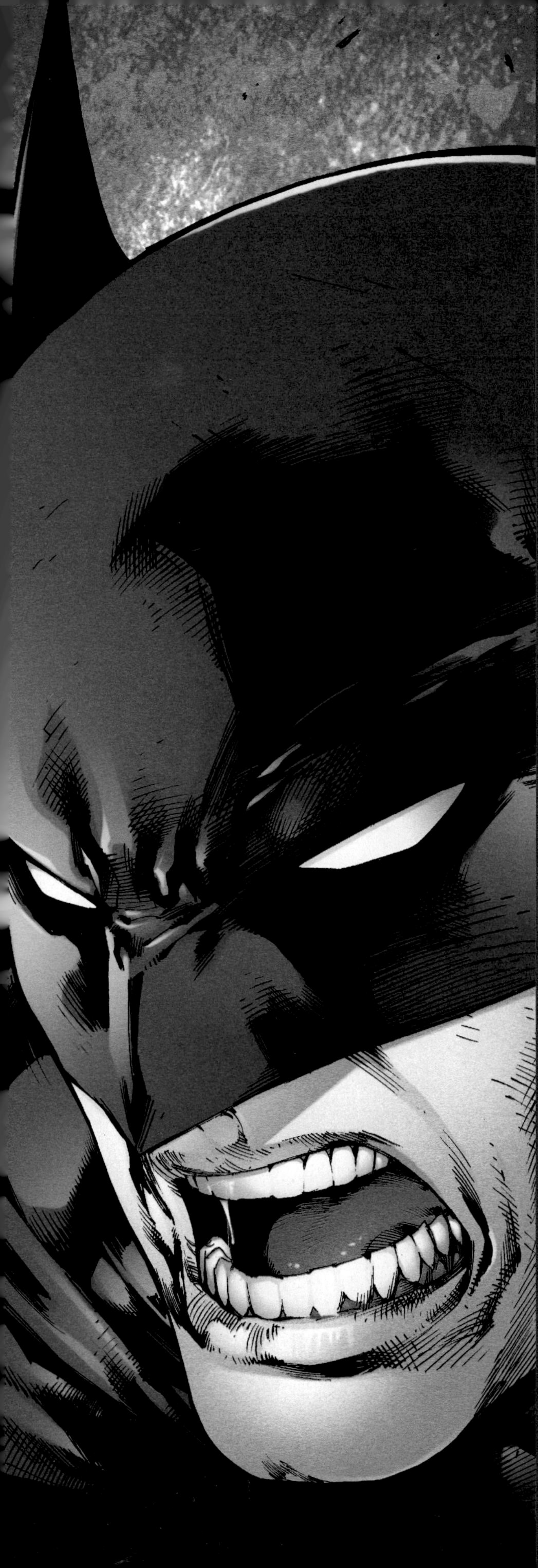

TABLE OF CONTENTS

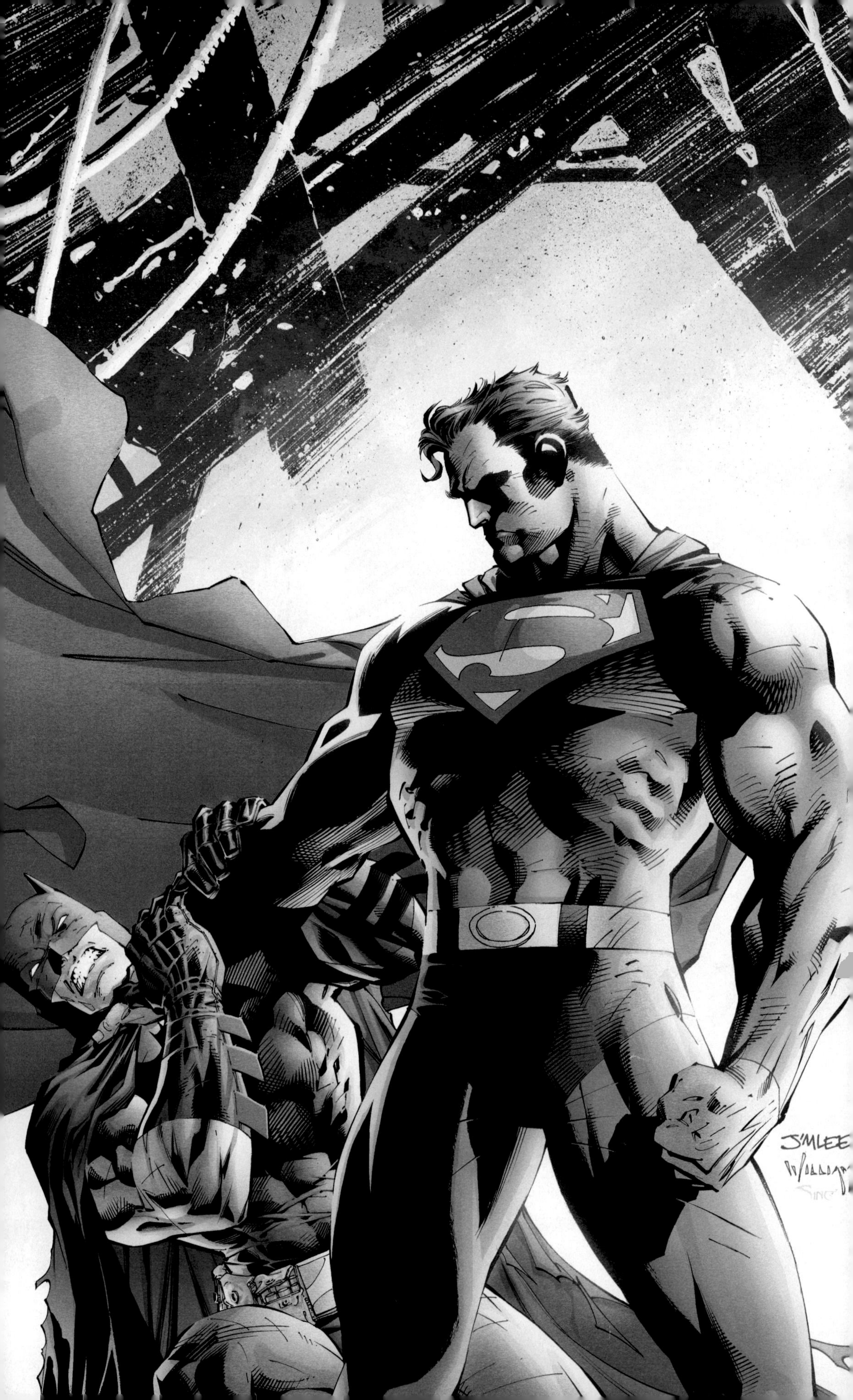

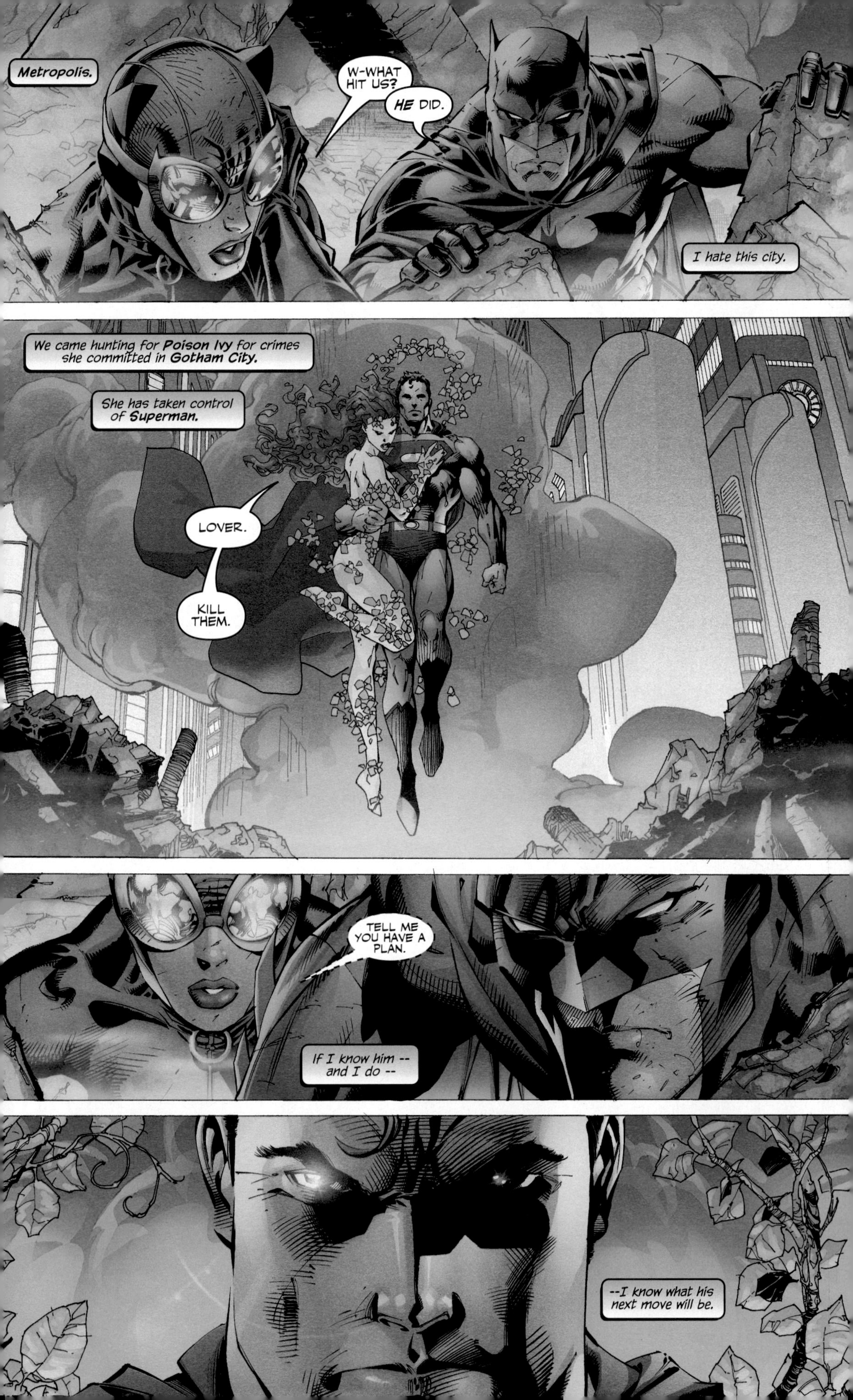

Metropolis.
W-WHAT HIT US?
HE DID.
I hate this city.
We came hunting for Poison Ivy for crimes she committed in Gotham City.
She has taken control of Superman.
LOVER.
KILL THEM.
TELL ME YOU HAVE A PLAN.
If I know him -- and I do --
--I know what his next move will be.

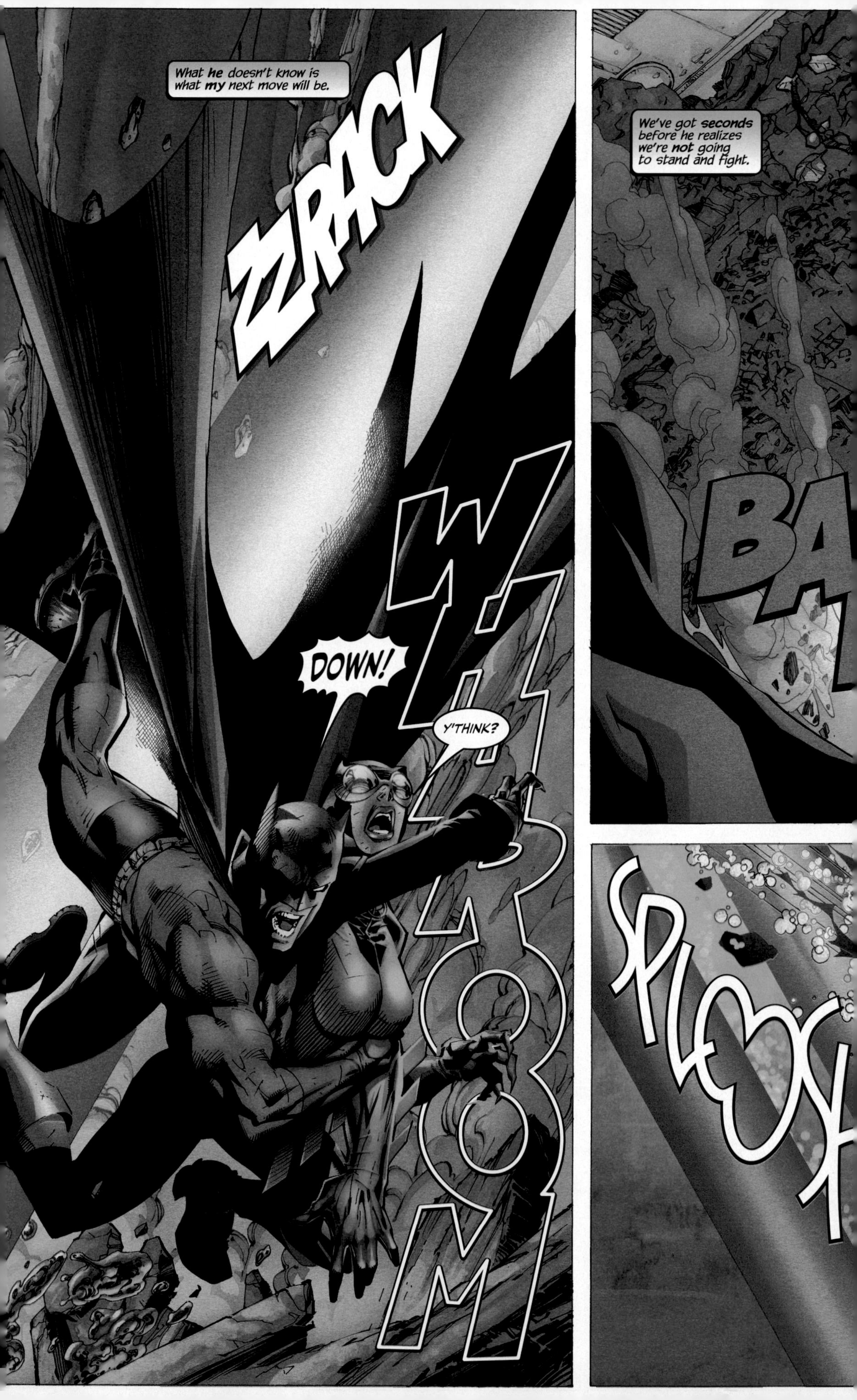
What he doesn't know is
what my next move will be.
ZZRACK
DOWN!
Y'THINK?
WHOOM
We've got seconds
before he realizes
we're not going
to stand and fight.

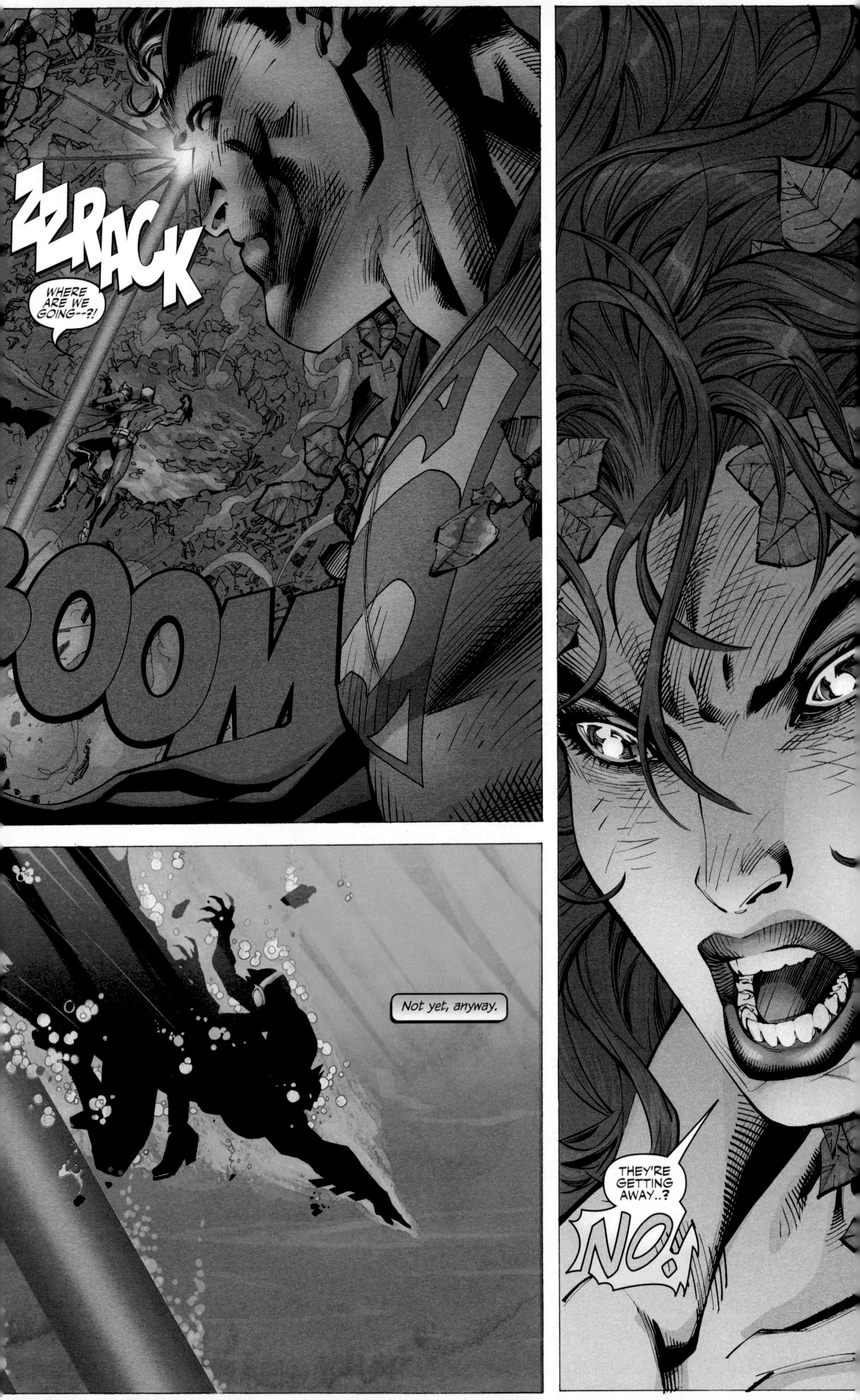
ZZRACK
WHERE ARE WE GOING--?!
BOOM
Not yet, anyway.
THEY'RE GETTING AWAY..?
NO!

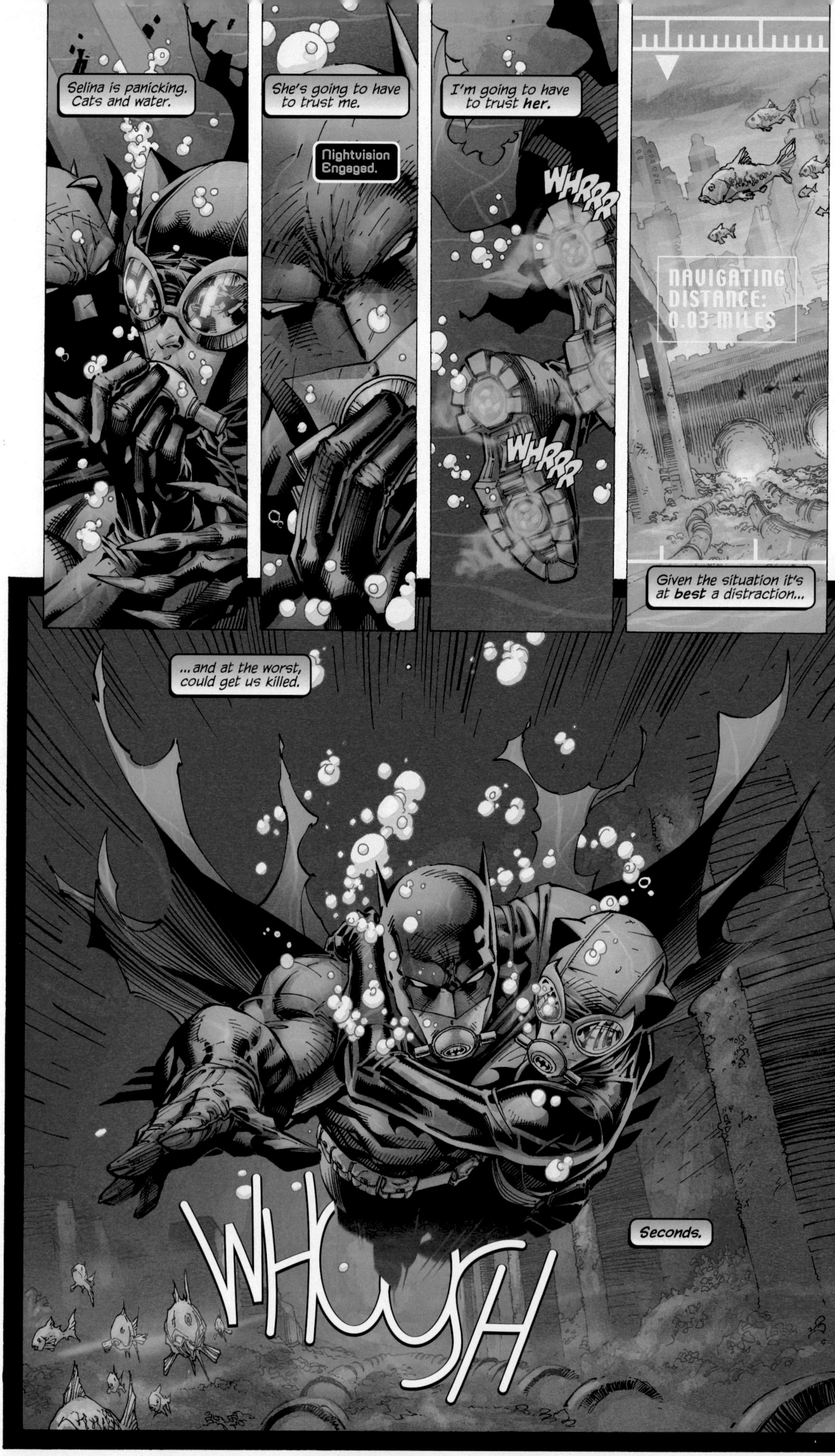
Selina is panicking. Cats and water.
She's going to have to trust me.
Nightvision Engaged.
I'm going to have to trust her.
WHRRR
WHRRR
NAVIGATING DISTANCE: 0.03 MILES
Given the situation it's at best a distraction...
...and at the worst, could get us killed.
WHOOSH
Seconds.

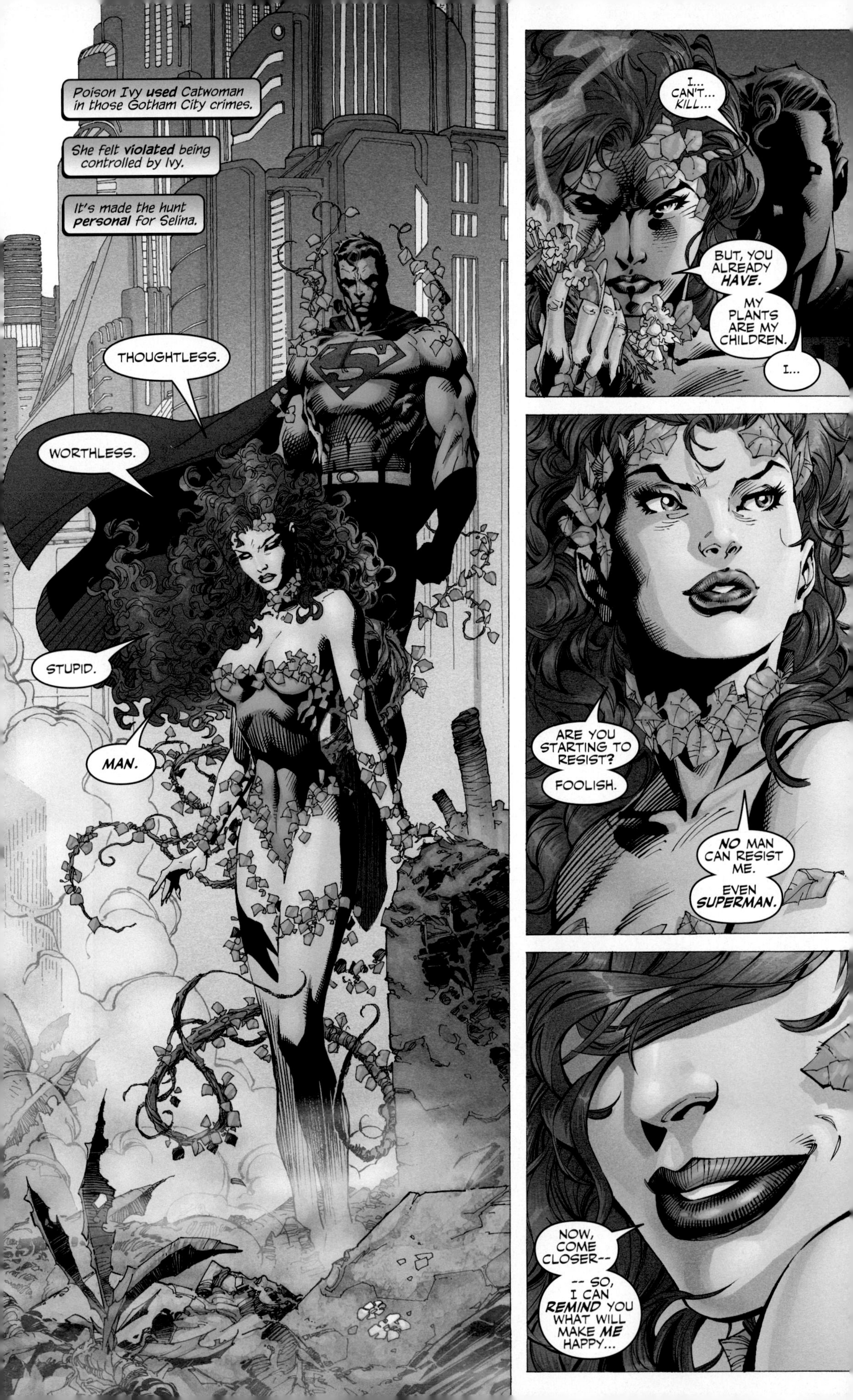

Poison Ivy **used** Catwoman in those Gotham City crimes.
She felt **violated** being controlled by Ivy.
It's made the hunt **personal** for Selina.
THOUGHTLESS.
WORTHLESS.
STUPID.
MAN.
I... CAN'T... KILL...
BUT, YOU ALREADY **HAVE.**
MY PLANTS ARE MY CHILDREN.
I...
ARE YOU STARTING TO RESIST?
FOOLISH.
NO MAN CAN RESIST ME.
EVEN **SUPERMAN.**
NOW, COME CLOSER--
-- SO, I CAN **REMIND** YOU WHAT WILL MAKE **ME** HAPPY...

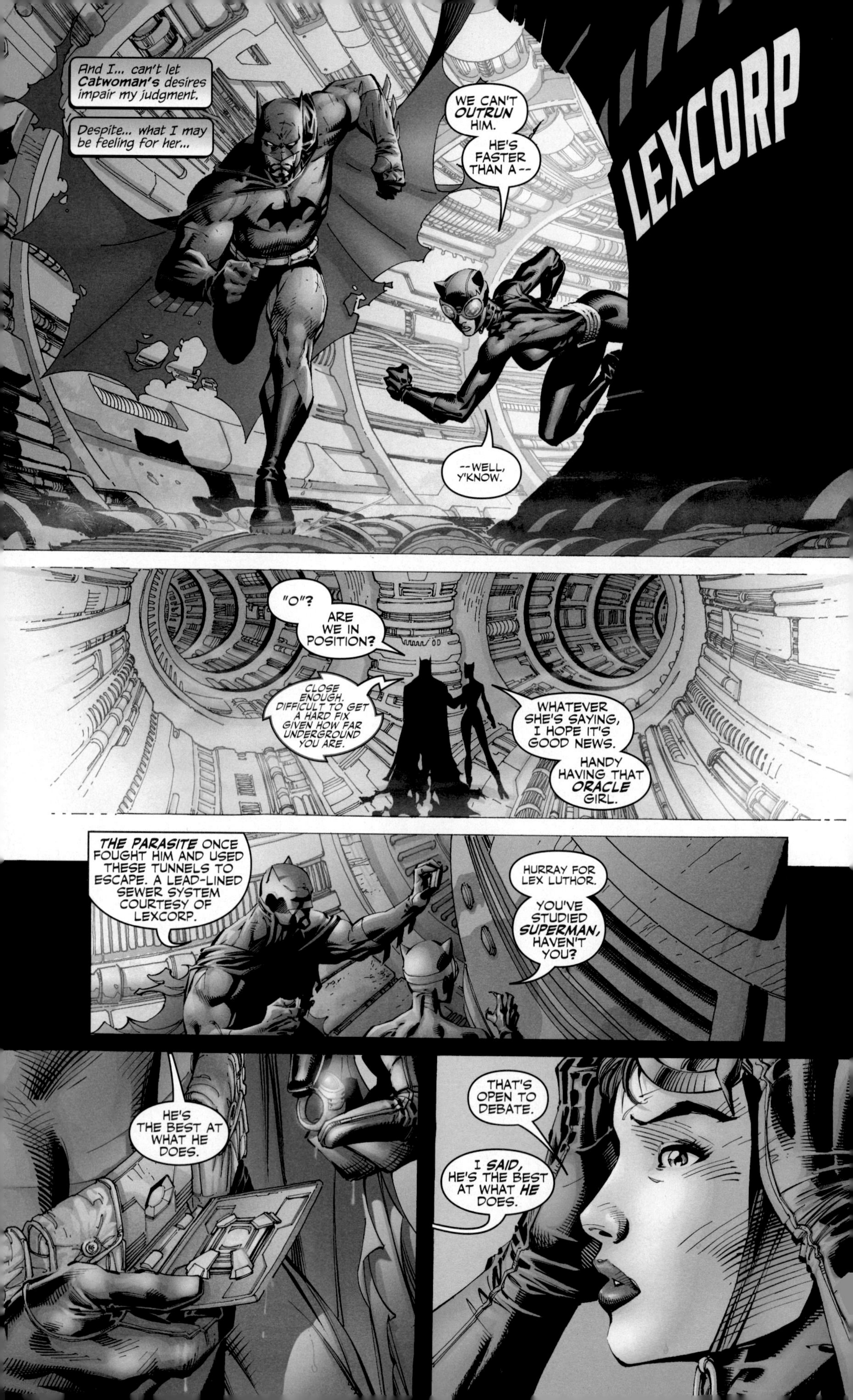

And I... can't let Catwoman's desires impair my judgment.
Despite... what I may be feeling for her...
WE CAN'T OUTRUN HIM.
HE'S FASTER THAN A--
LEXCORP
--WELL, Y'KNOW.
"O"? ARE WE IN POSITION?
CLOSE ENOUGH. DIFFICULT TO GET A HARD FIX GIVEN HOW FAR UNDERGROUND YOU ARE.
WHATEVER SHE'S SAYING, I HOPE IT'S GOOD NEWS.
HANDY HAVING THAT ORACLE GIRL.
THE PARASITE ONCE FOUGHT HIM AND USED THESE TUNNELS TO ESCAPE. A LEAD-LINED SEWER SYSTEM COURTESY OF LEXCORP.
HURRAY FOR LEX LUTHOR.
YOU'VE STUDIED SUPERMAN, HAVEN'T YOU?
HE'S THE BEST AT WHAT HE DOES.
THAT'S OPEN TO DEBATE.
I SAID, HE'S THE BEST AT WHAT HE DOES.

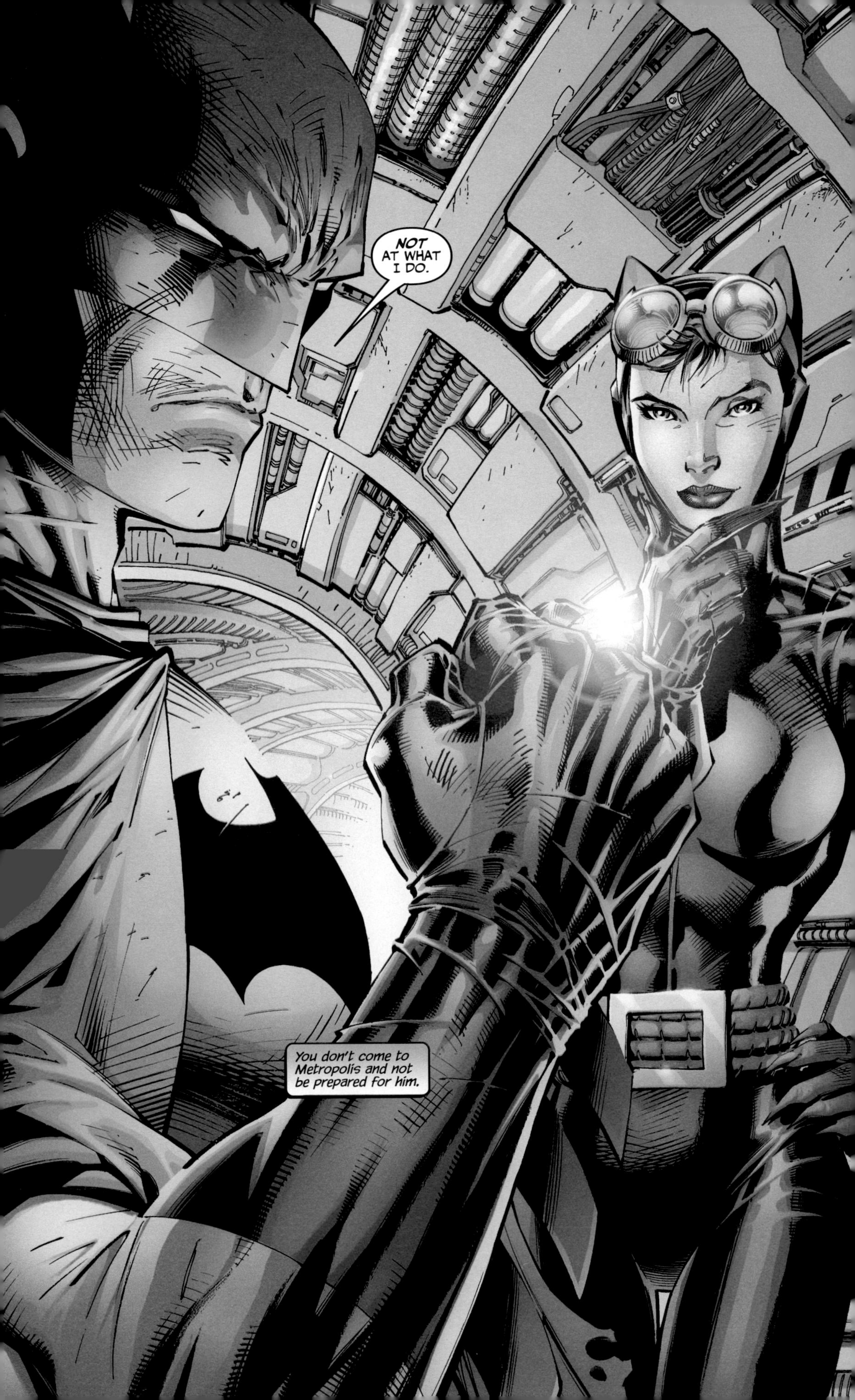
NOT AT WHAT I DO.
You don't come to Metropolis and not be prepared for him.

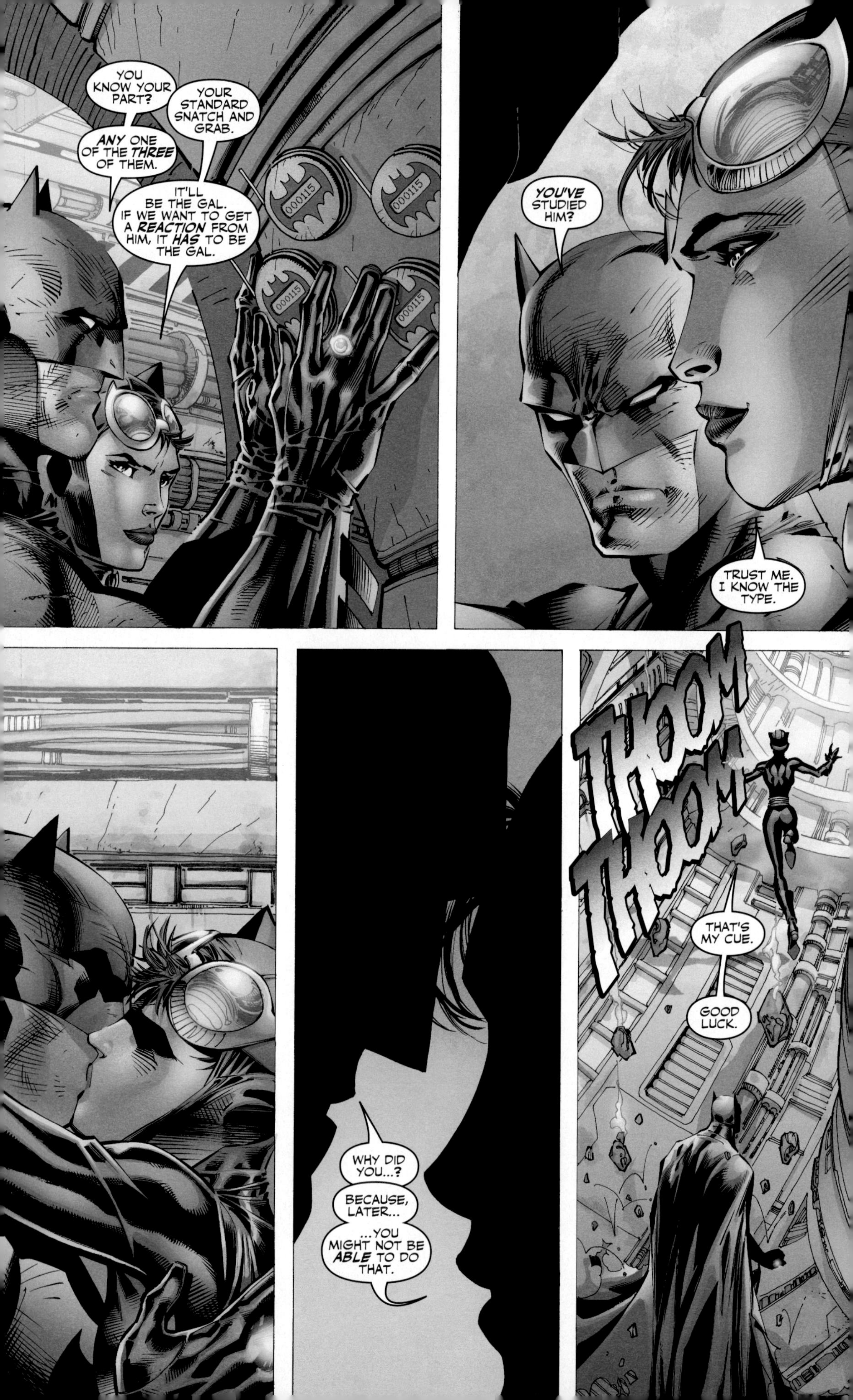
YOU KNOW YOUR PART?
YOUR STANDARD SNATCH AND GRAB.
ANY ONE OF THE THREE OF THEM.
IT'LL BE THE GAL. IF WE WANT TO GET A REACTION FROM HIM, IT HAS TO BE THE GAL.
000115
YOU'VE STUDIED HIM?
TRUST ME. I KNOW THE TYPE.
WHY DID YOU...?
BECAUSE, LATER...
...YOU MIGHT NOT BE ABLE TO DO THAT.
THOOM THOOM
THAT'S MY CUE.
GOOD LUCK.

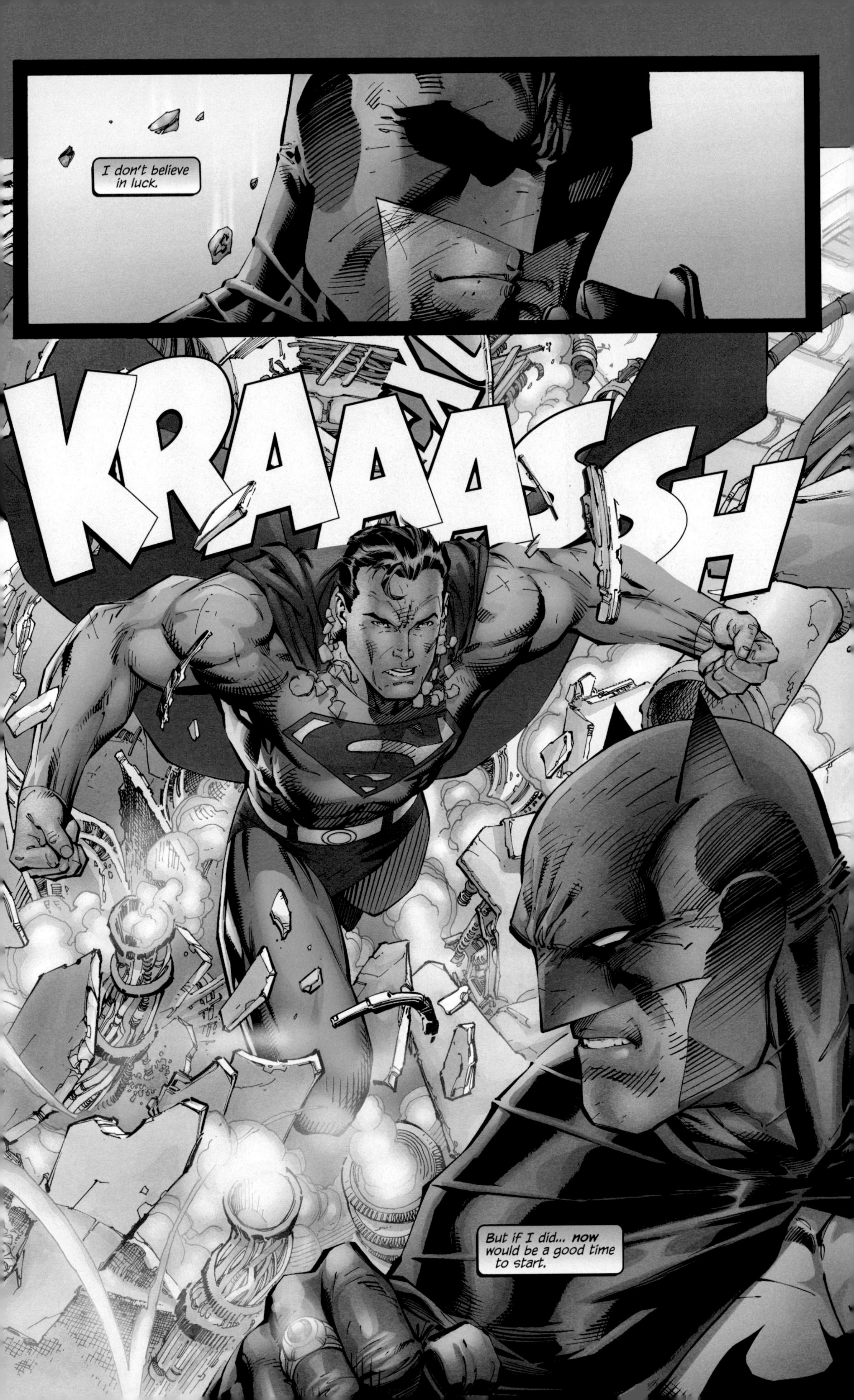
I don't believe in luck.
KRAAASH
But if I did... now would be a good time to start.

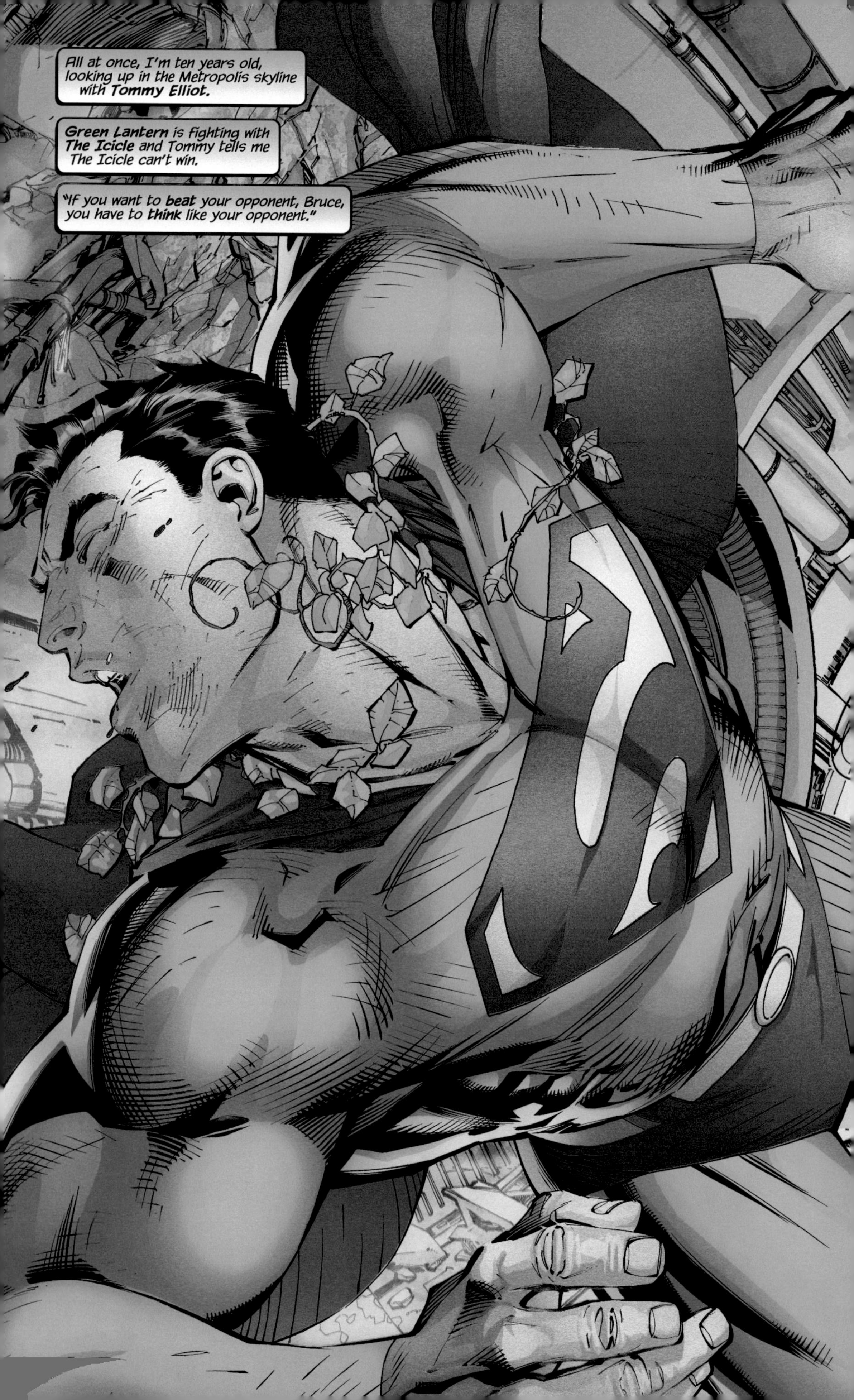
All at once, I'm ten years old, looking up in the Metropolis skyline with Tommy Elliot.
Green Lantern is fighting with The Icicle and Tommy tells me The Icicle can't win.
"If you want to beat your opponent, Bruce, you have to think like your opponent."

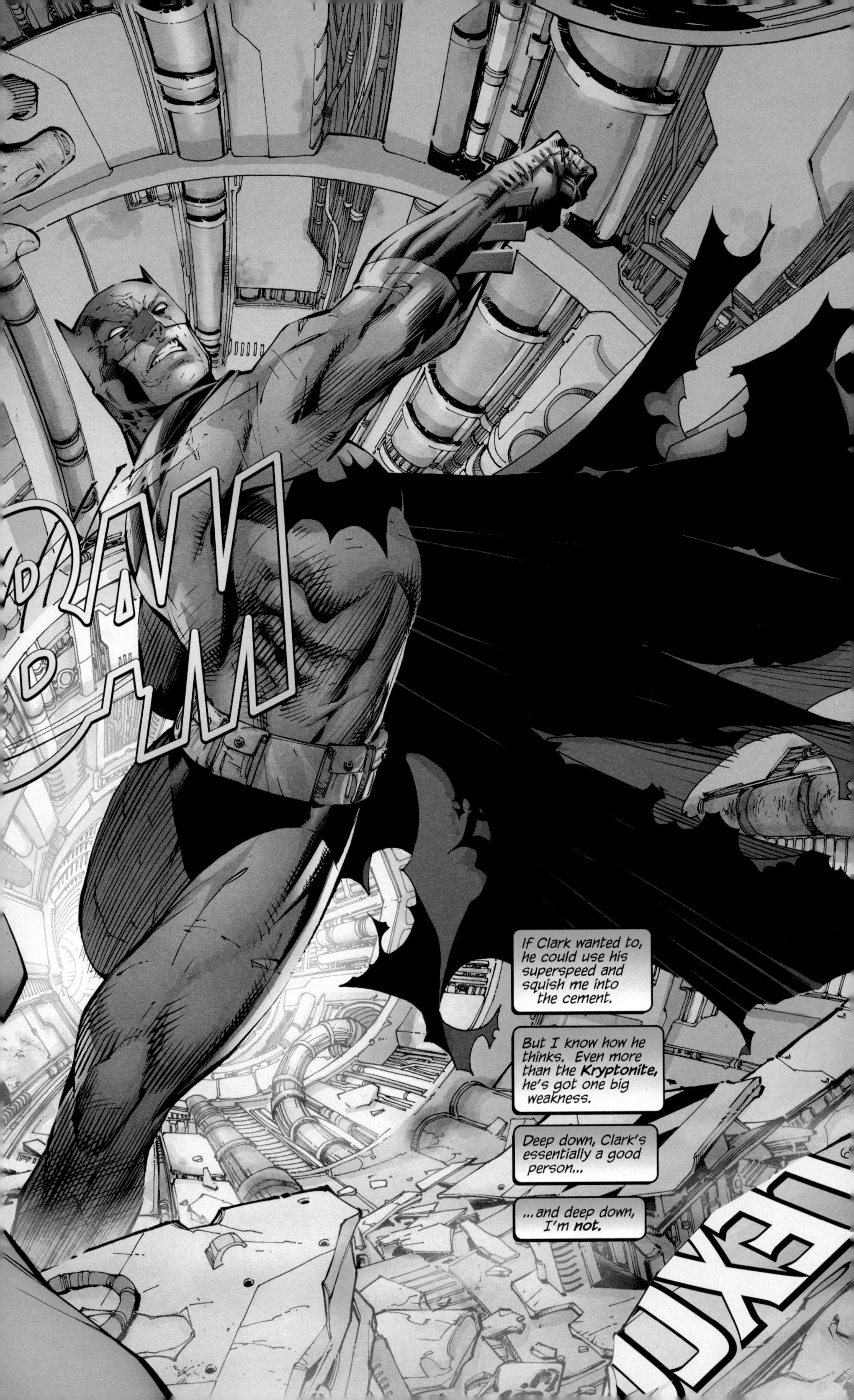

If Clark wanted to, he could use his superspeed and squish me into the cement.
But I know how he thinks. Even more than the **Kryptonite,** he's got one big weakness.
Deep down, Clark's essentially a good person...
...and deep down, I'm **not.**

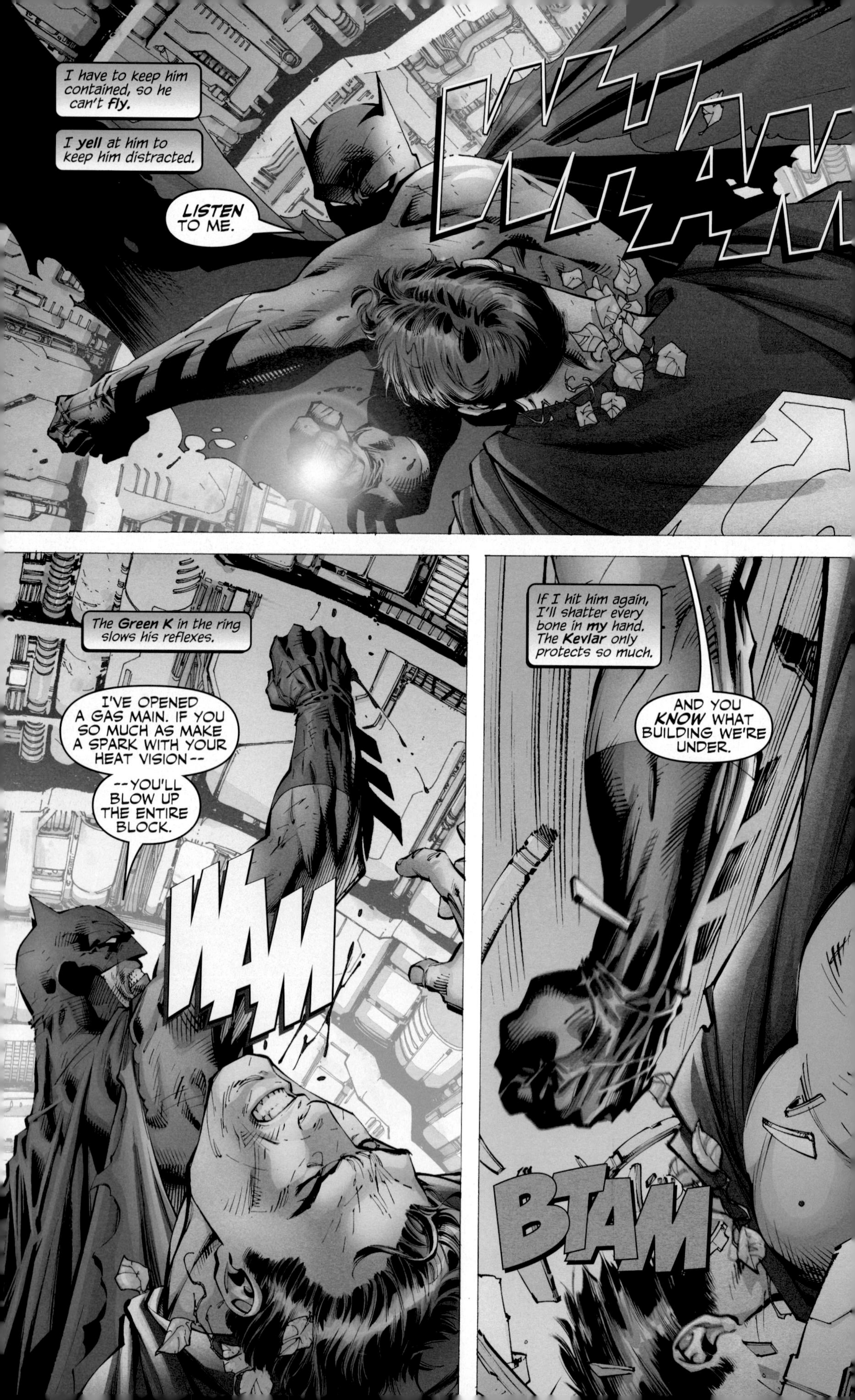

I have to keep him contained, so he can't fly.
I yell at him to keep him distracted.
LISTEN TO ME.
The Green K in the ring slows his reflexes.
I'VE OPENED A GAS MAIN. IF YOU SO MUCH AS MAKE A SPARK WITH YOUR HEAT VISION--
--YOU'LL BLOW UP THE ENTIRE BLOCK.
WAM
If I hit him again, I'll shatter every bone in my hand. The Kevlar only protects so much.
AND YOU KNOW WHAT BUILDING WE'RE UNDER.
BTAM

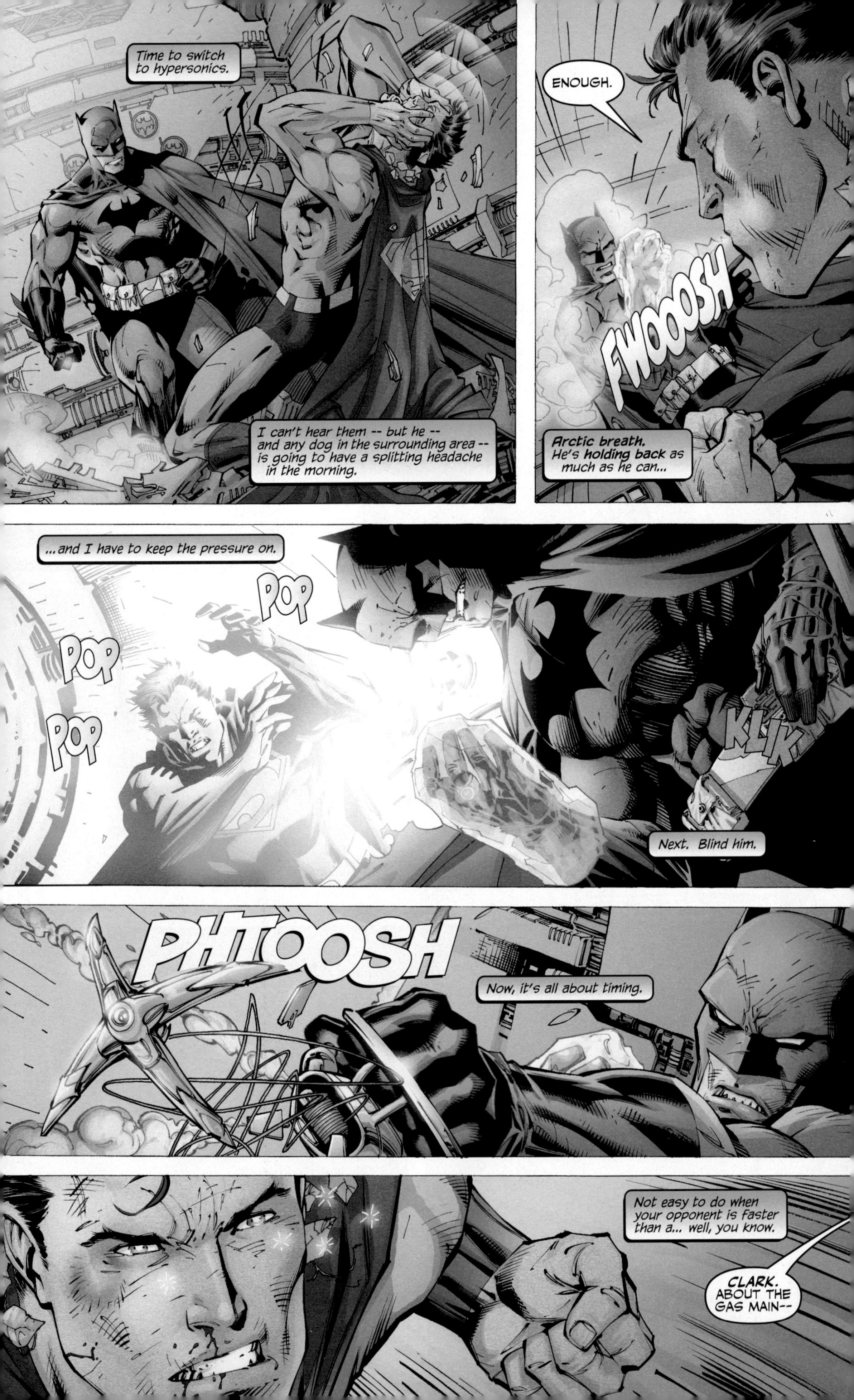

Time to switch to hypersonics.
I can't hear them -- but he -- and any dog in the surrounding area -- is going to have a splitting headache in the morning.
ENOUGH.
FWOOOSH
Arctic breath. He's holding back as much as he can...
...and I have to keep the pressure on.
POP
POP
POP
KLIK
Next. Blind him.
PHTOOSH
Now, it's all about timing.
Not easy to do when your opponent is faster than a... well, you know.
CLARK. ABOUT THE GAS MAIN--

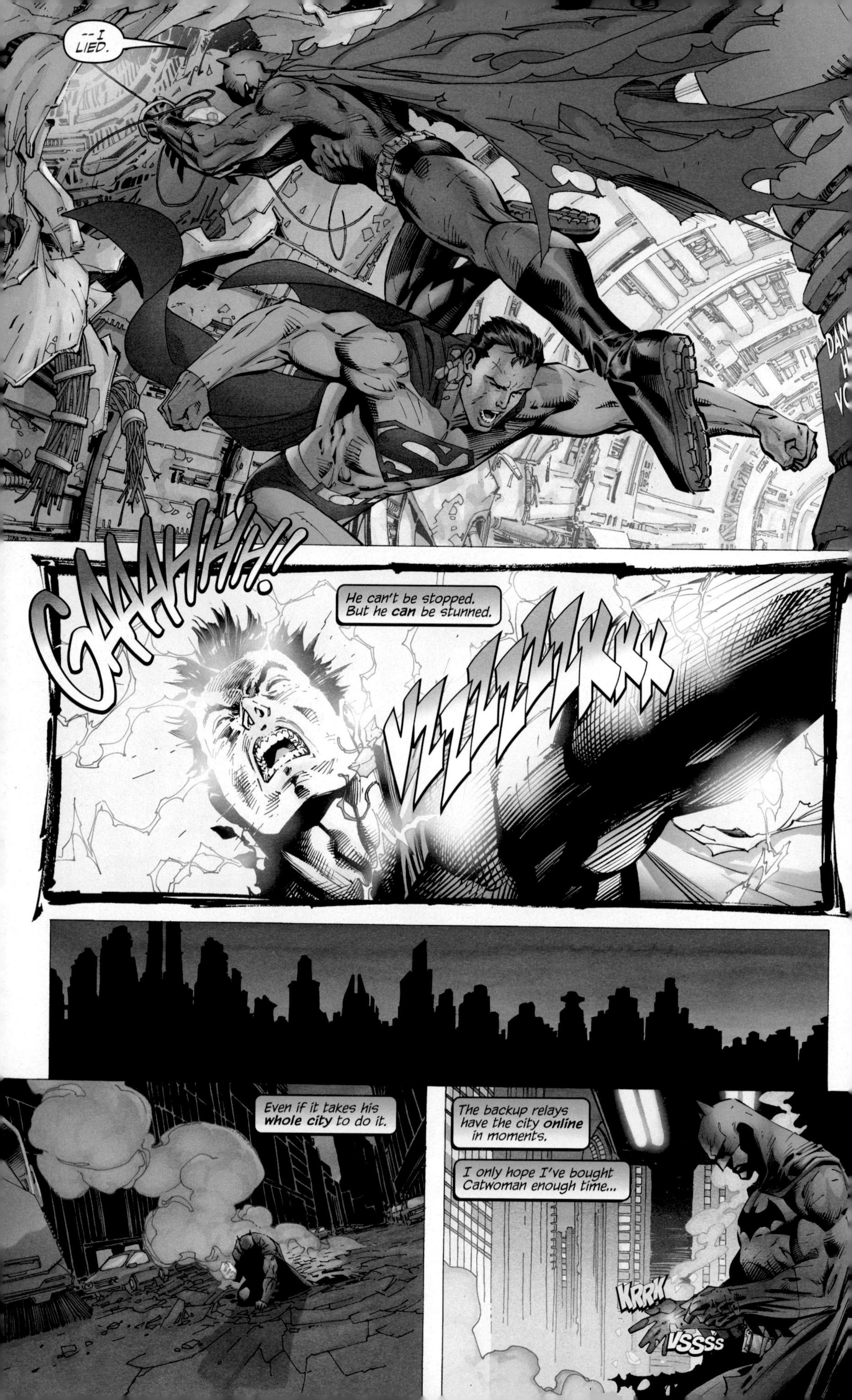
--I LIED.
GAAHHH!!
He can't be stopped. But he **can** be stunned.
Even if it takes his **whole city** to do it.
The backup relays have the city **online** in moments.
I only hope I've bought Catwoman enough time...
KRRK
VSSSS

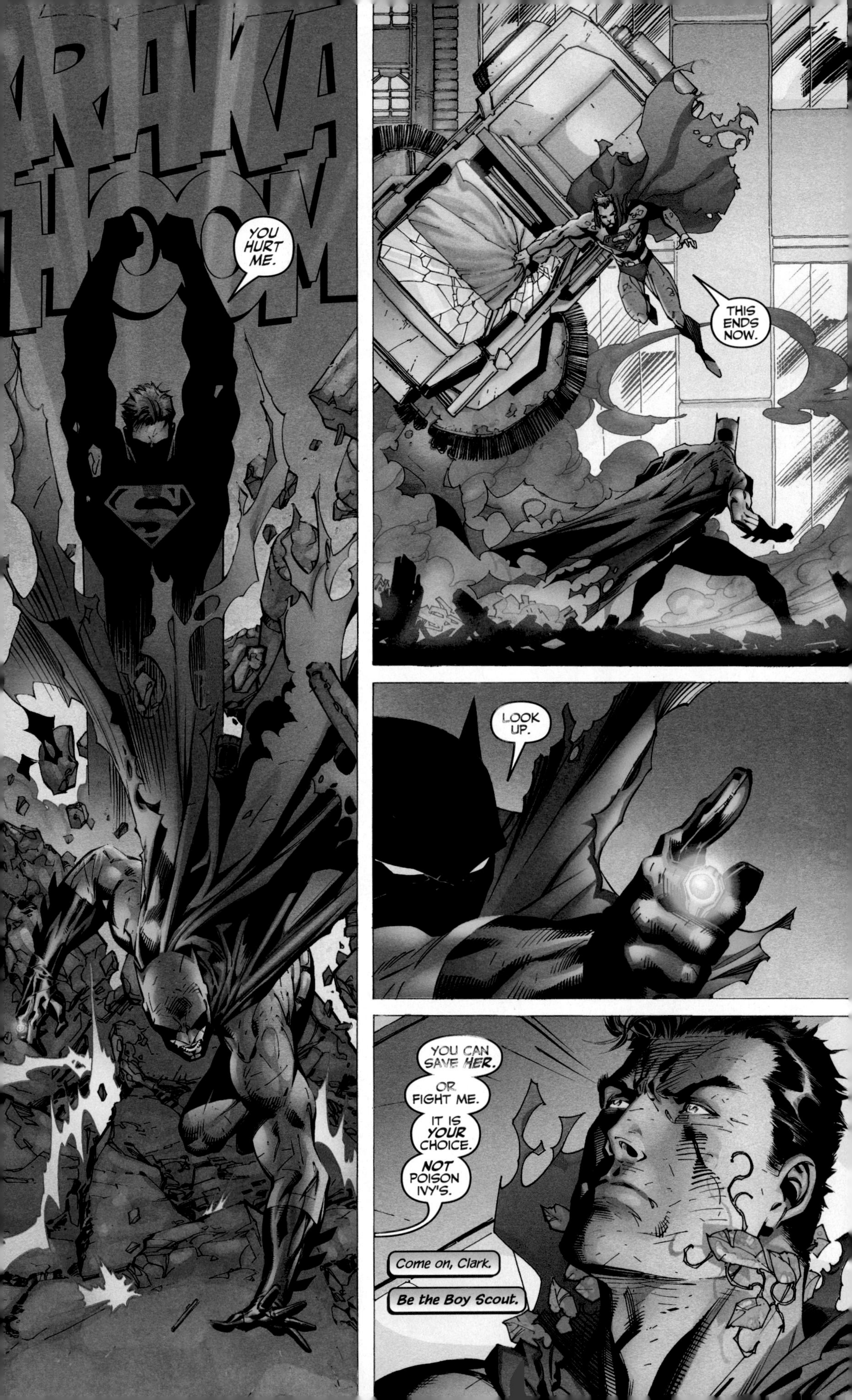

KRAKA-THOOM
YOU HURT ME.
THIS ENDS NOW.
LOOK UP.
YOU CAN SAVE *HER*.
OR FIGHT ME.
IT IS *YOUR* CHOICE.
NOT POISON IVY'S.
Come on, Clark.
Be the Boy Scout.

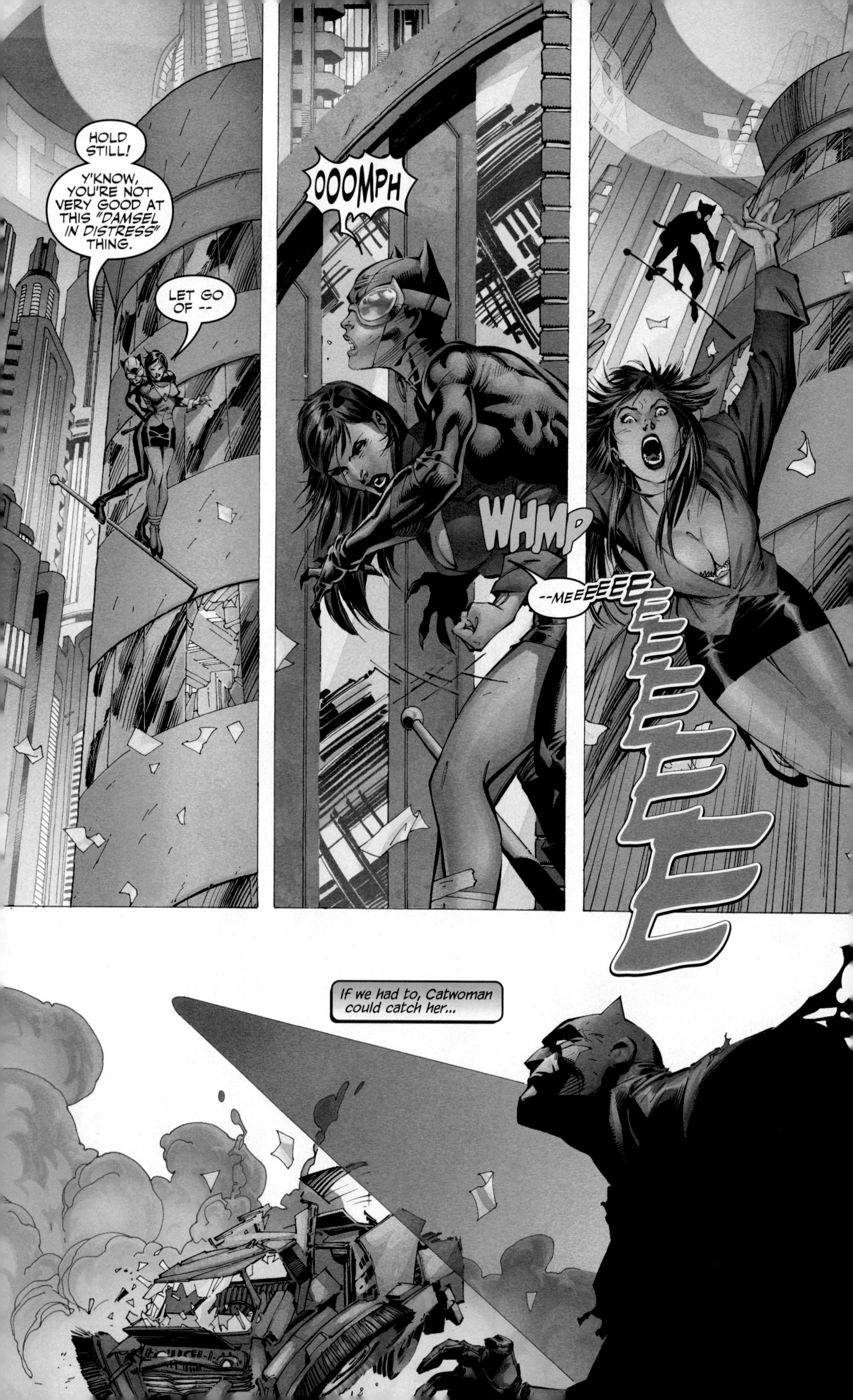
HOLD STILL!
Y'KNOW, YOU'RE NOT VERY GOOD AT THIS "DAMSEL IN DISTRESS" THING.
LET GO OF --
OOOMPH
WHMP
--MEEEEEEEEEEEEEEE
If we had to, Catwoman could catch her...

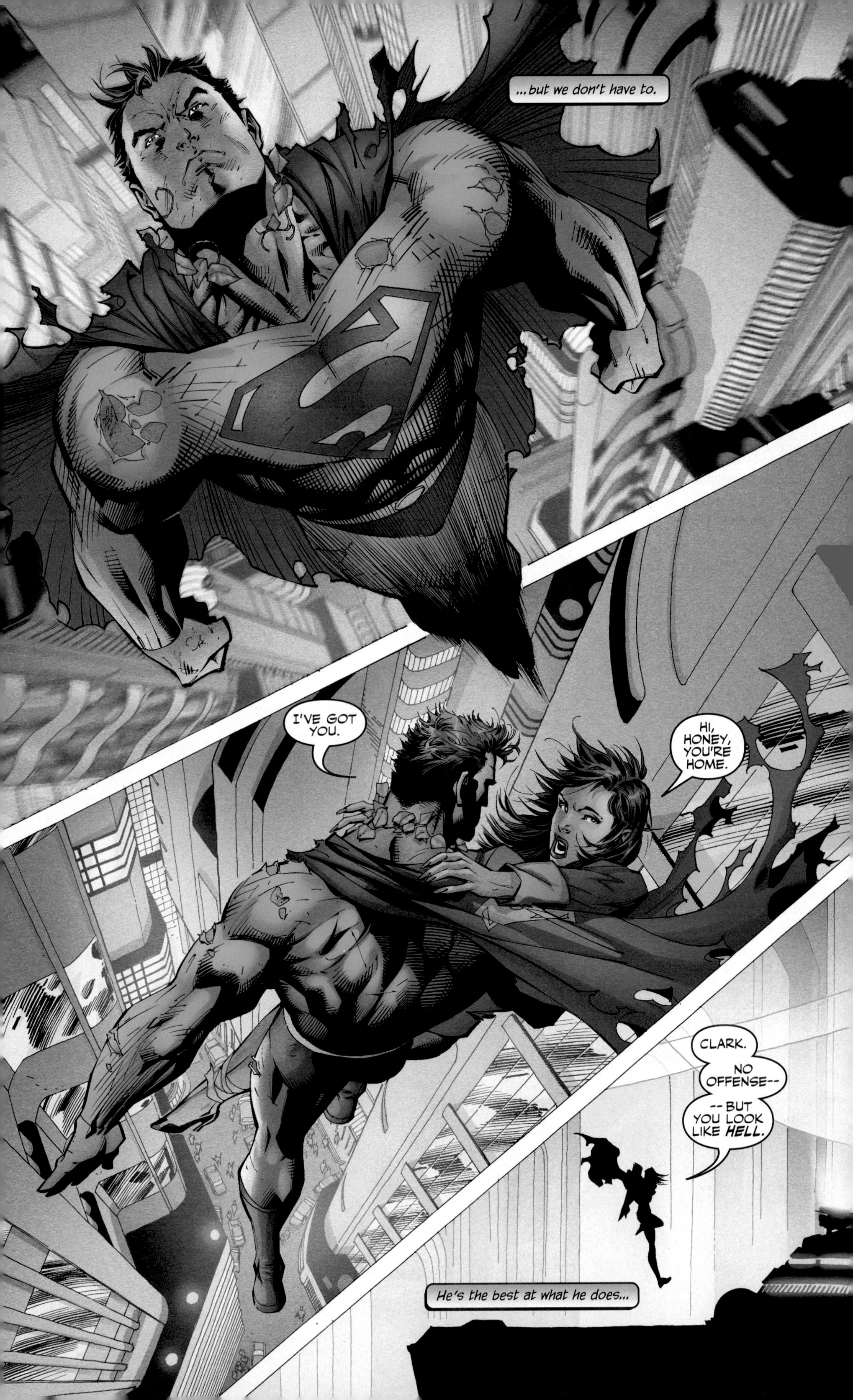
...but we don't have to.
I'VE GOT YOU.
HI, HONEY, YOU'RE HOME.
CLARK.
NO OFFENSE--
-- BUT YOU LOOK LIKE *HELL*.
He's the best at what he does...

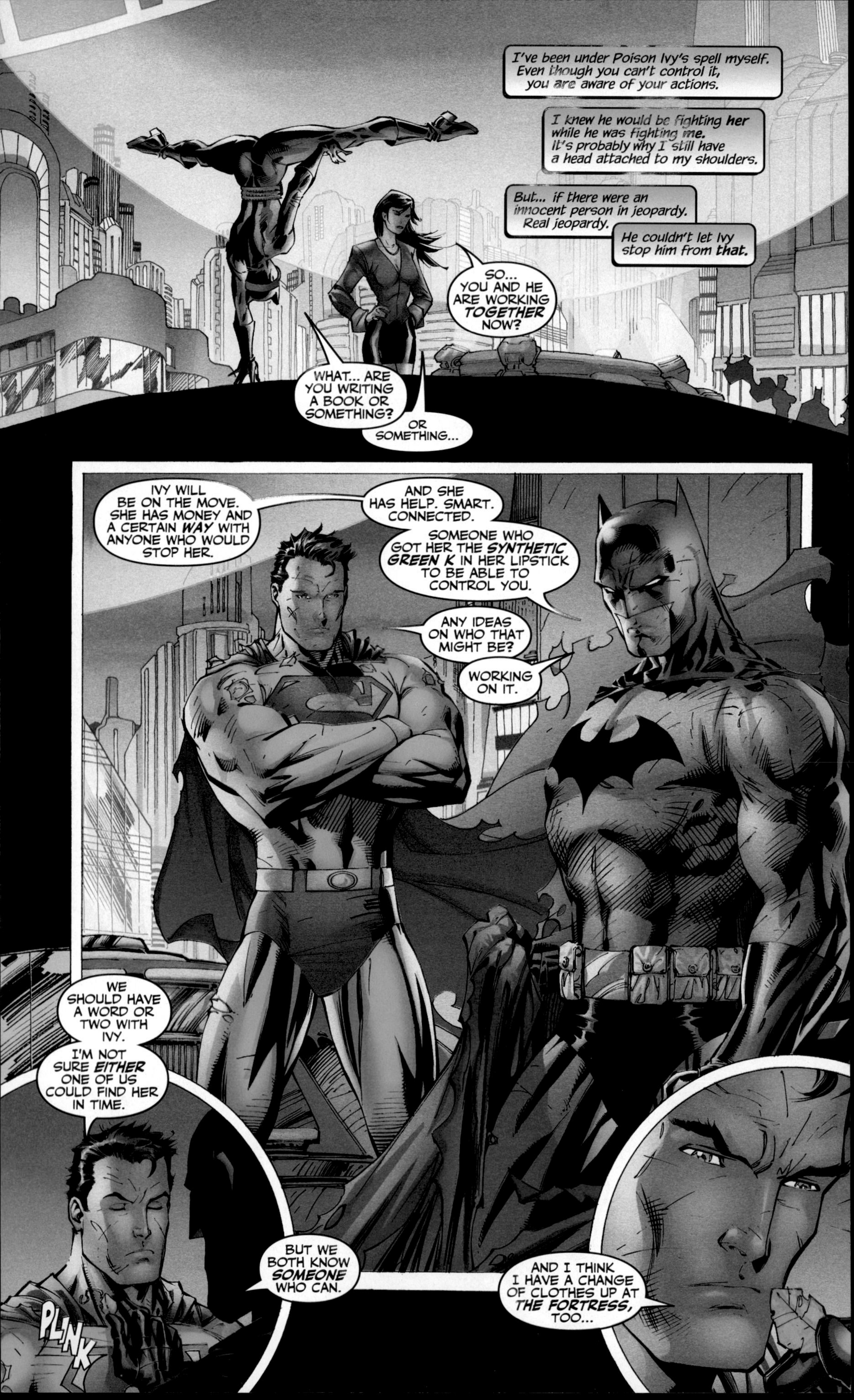

I've been under Poison Ivy's spell myself. Even though you can't control it, you are aware of your actions.
I knew he would be fighting her while he was fighting me. It's probably why I still have a head attached to my shoulders.
But... if there were an innocent person in jeopardy. Real jeopardy.
He couldn't let Ivy stop him from that.
SO... YOU AND HE ARE WORKING TOGETHER NOW?
WHAT... ARE YOU WRITING A BOOK OR SOMETHING?
OR SOMETHING...
IVY WILL BE ON THE MOVE. SHE HAS MONEY AND A CERTAIN WAY WITH ANYONE WHO WOULD STOP HER.
AND SHE HAS HELP. SMART. CONNECTED.
SOMEONE WHO GOT HER THE SYNTHETIC GREEN K IN HER LIPSTICK TO BE ABLE TO CONTROL YOU.
ANY IDEAS ON WHO THAT MIGHT BE?
WORKING ON IT.
WE SHOULD HAVE A WORD OR TWO WITH IVY.
I'M NOT SURE EITHER ONE OF US COULD FIND HER IN TIME.
BUT WE BOTH KNOW SOMEONE WHO CAN.
PLINK
AND I THINK I HAVE A CHANGE OF CLOTHES UP AT THE FORTRESS, TOO...

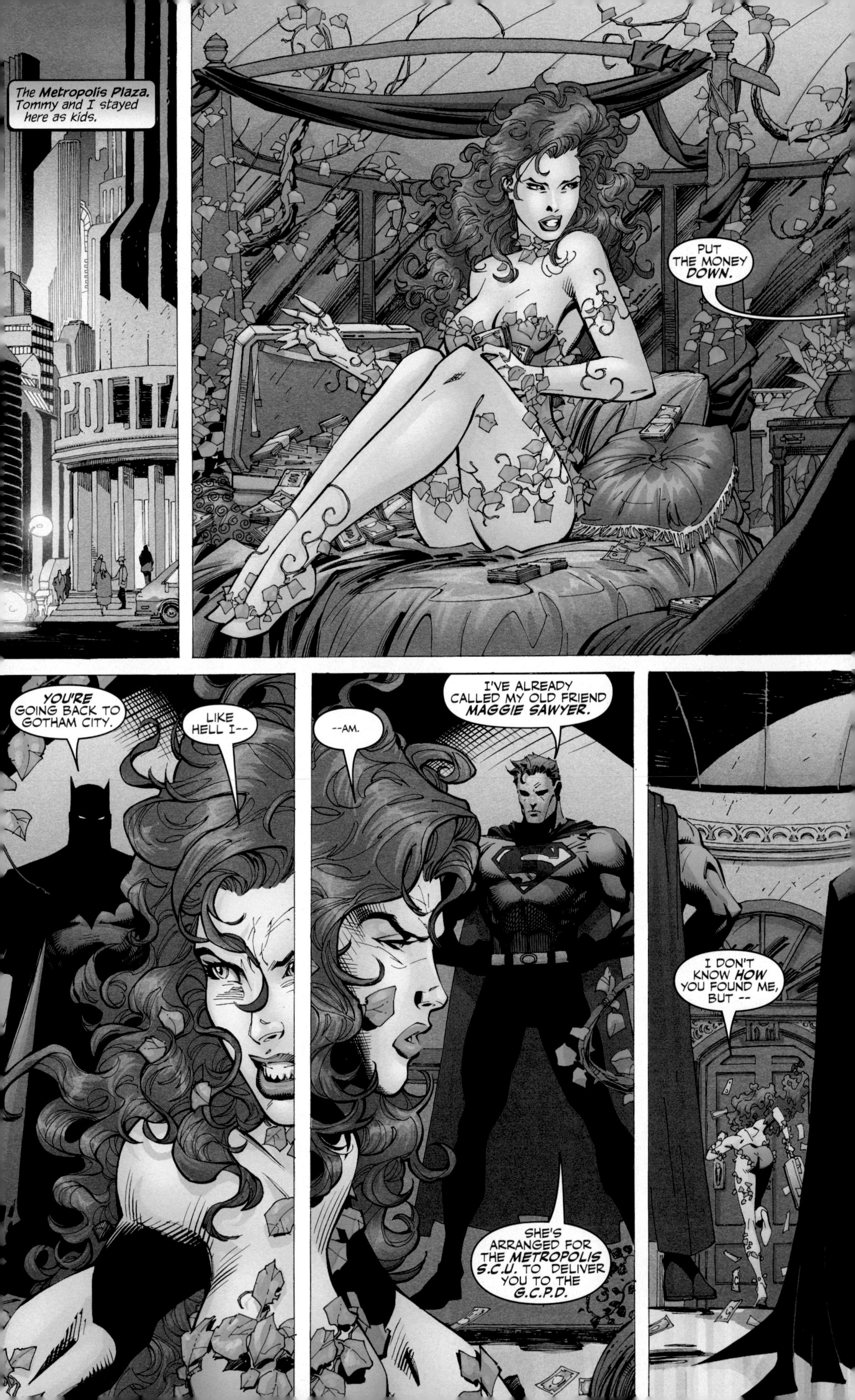

The **Metropolis Plaza.** Tommy and I stayed here as kids.
POLITA
PUT THE MONEY ***DOWN.***
YOU'RE GOING BACK TO GOTHAM CITY.
LIKE HELL I--
--AM.
I'VE ALREADY CALLED MY OLD FRIEND ***MAGGIE SAWYER.***
SHE'S ARRANGED FOR THE ***METROPOLIS S.C.U.*** TO DELIVER YOU TO THE ***G.C.P.D.***
I DON'T KNOW ***HOW*** YOU FOUND ME, BUT --

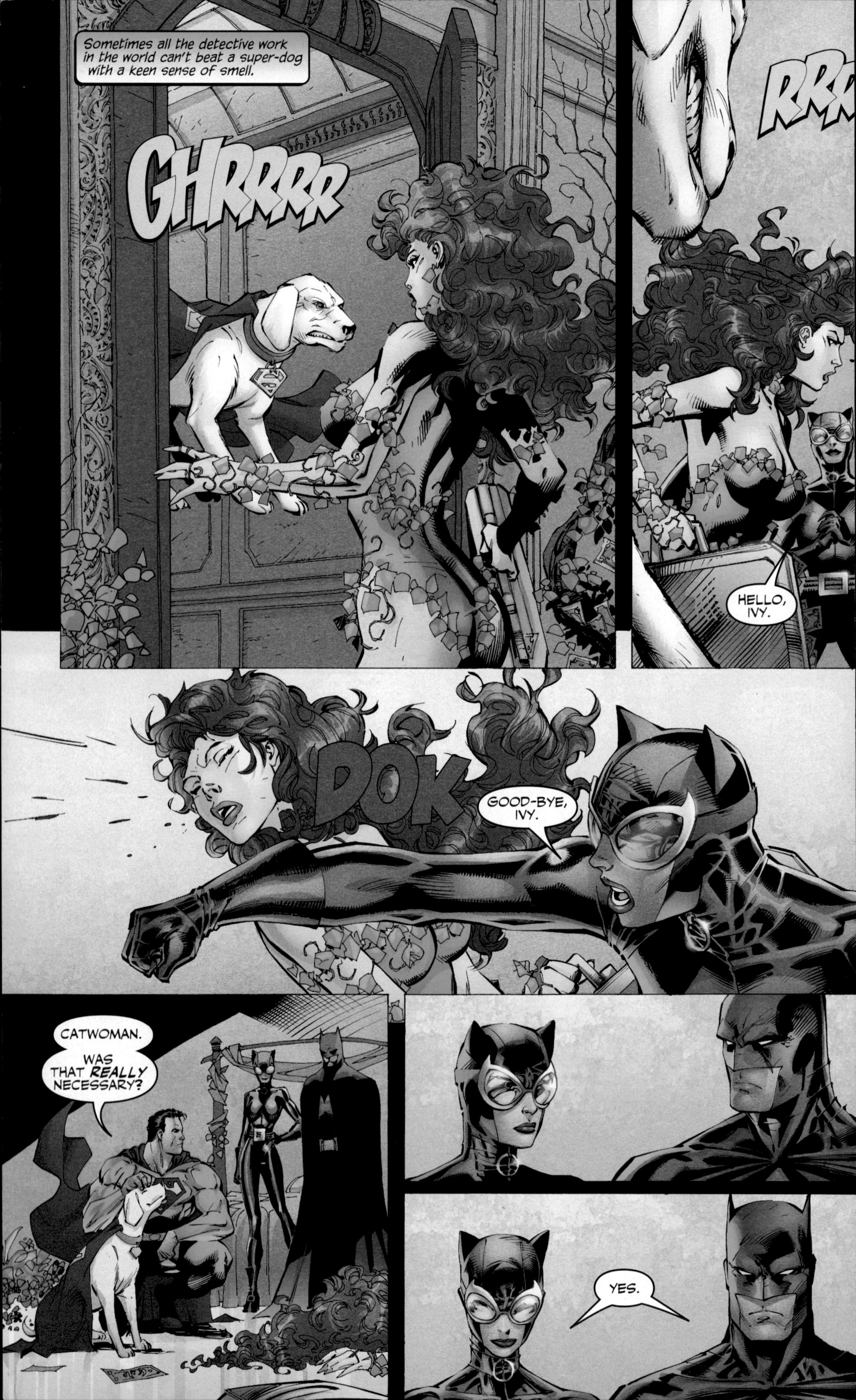
Sometimes all the detective work in the world can't beat a super-dog with a keen sense of smell.
GHRRRR
RRR
HELLO, IVY.
DOK
GOOD-BYE, IVY.
CATWOMAN.
WAS THAT REALLY NECESSARY?
YES.

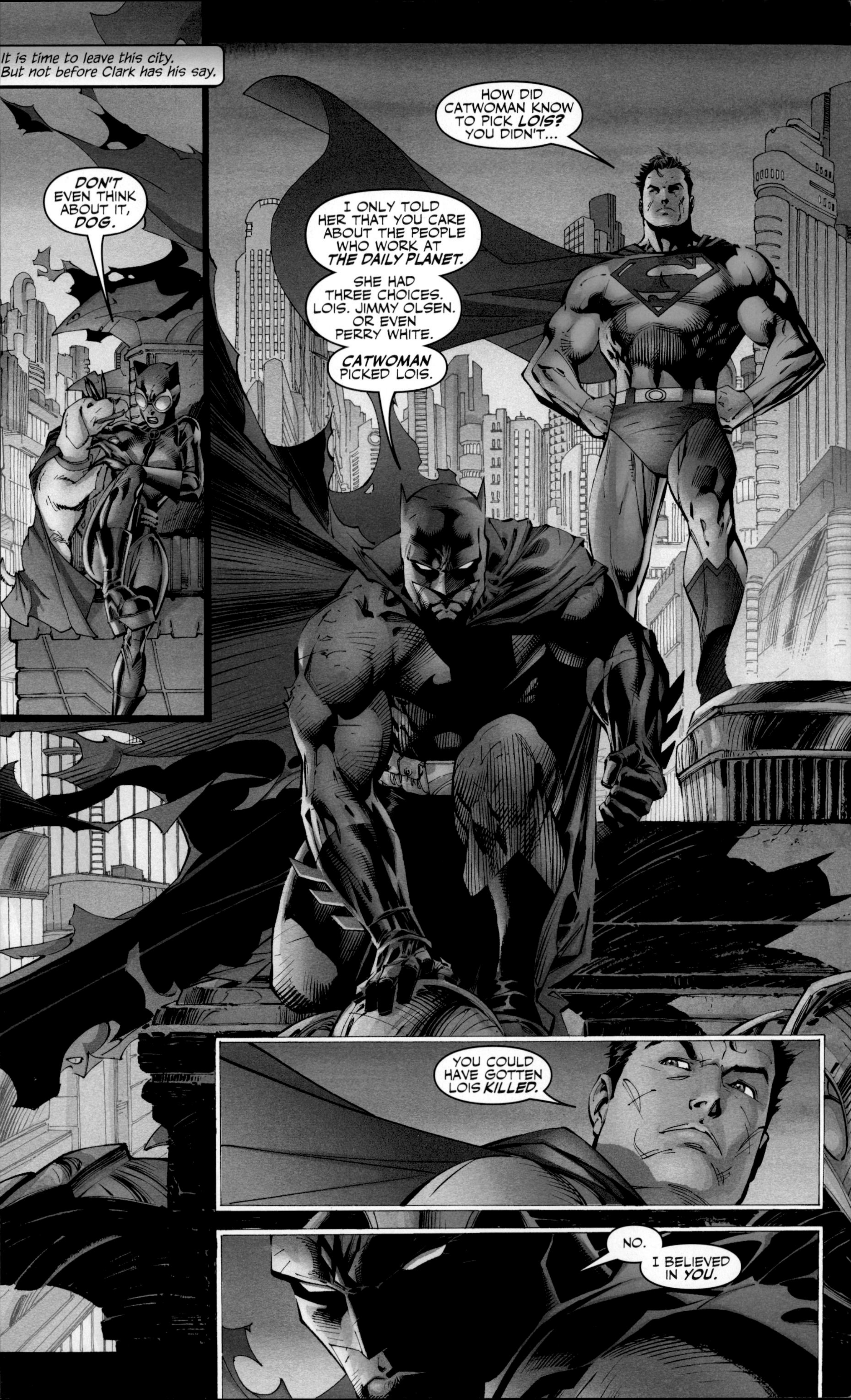
It is time to leave this city. But not before Clark has his say.
HOW DID CATWOMAN KNOW TO PICK LOIS? YOU DIDN'T...
I ONLY TOLD HER THAT YOU CARE ABOUT THE PEOPLE WHO WORK AT THE DAILY PLANET.
SHE HAD THREE CHOICES. LOIS. JIMMY OLSEN. OR EVEN PERRY WHITE.
CATWOMAN PICKED LOIS.
DON'T EVEN THINK ABOUT IT, DOG.
YOU COULD HAVE GOTTEN LOIS KILLED.
NO.
I BELIEVED IN YOU.

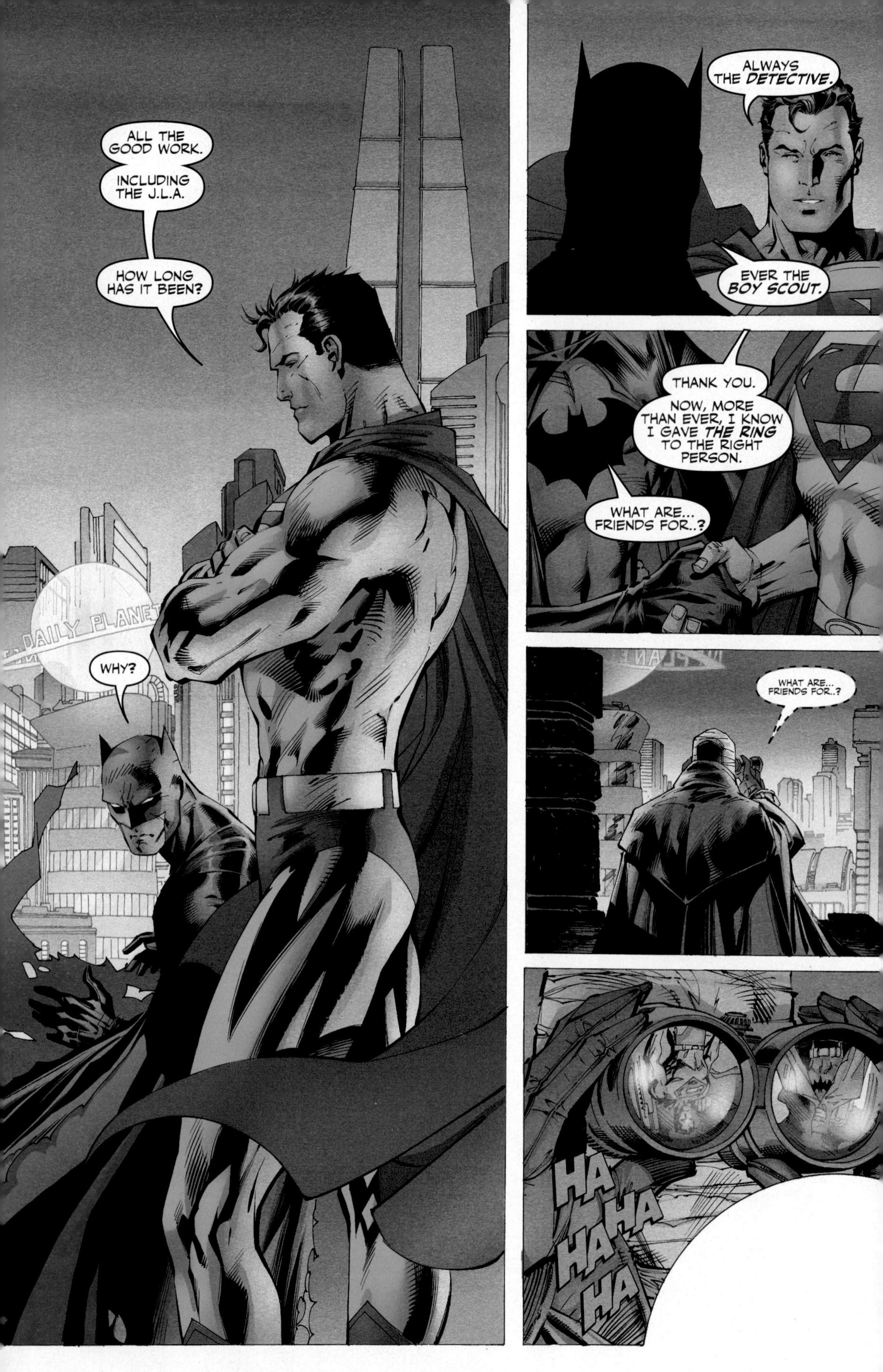
ALL THE GOOD WORK.
INCLUDING THE J.L.A.
HOW LONG HAS IT BEEN?
WHY?
ALWAYS THE DETECTIVE.
EVER THE BOY SCOUT.
THANK YOU.
NOW, MORE THAN EVER, I KNOW I GAVE THE RING TO THE RIGHT PERSON.
WHAT ARE... FRIENDS FOR..?
DAILY PLANET
WHAT ARE... FRIENDS FOR..?
HA HA HA HA HA HA HA HA

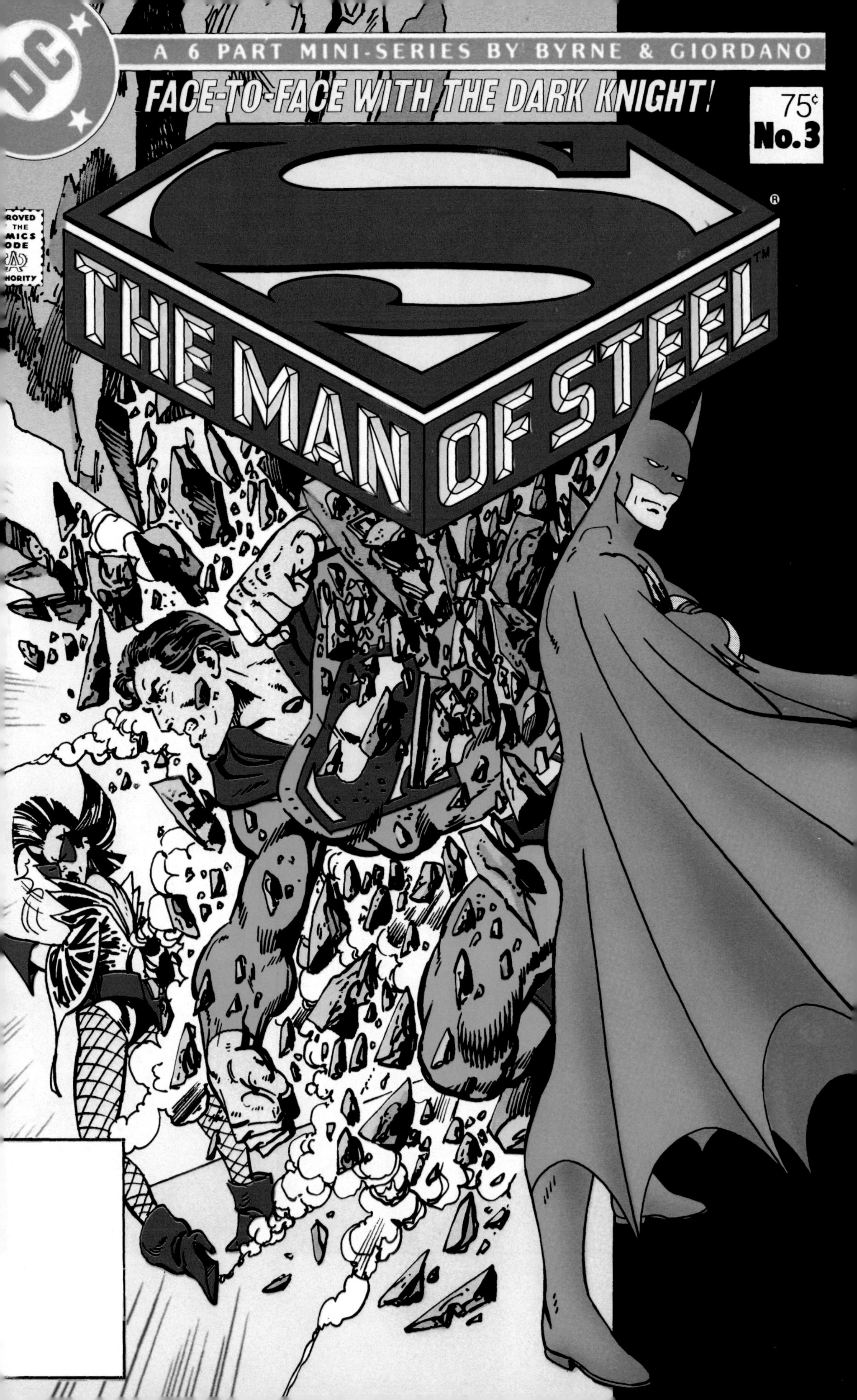
A 6 PART MINI-SERIES BY BYRNE & GIORDANO
FACE-TO-FACE WITH THE DARK KNIGHT!
75¢
No.3
THE MAN OF STEEL

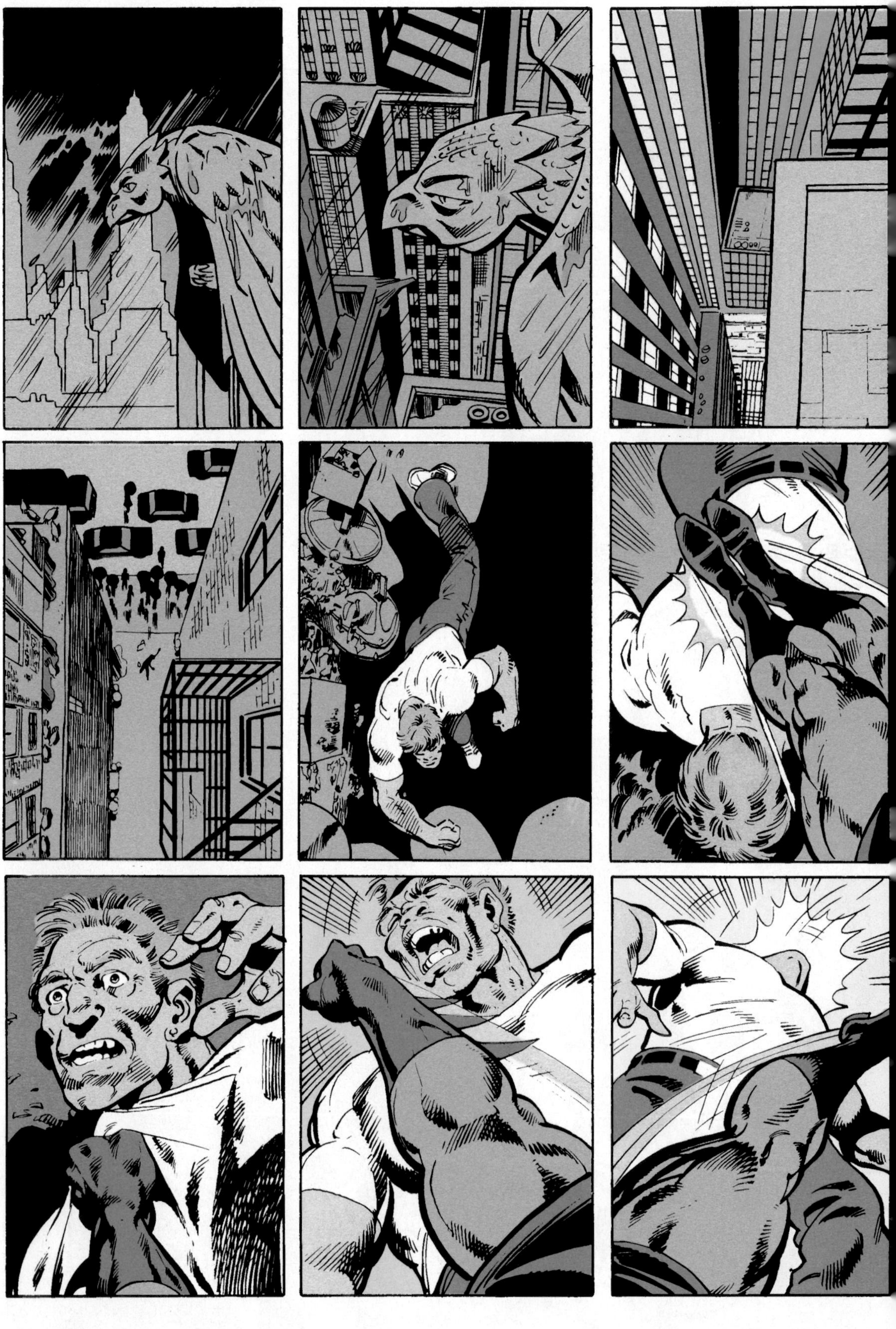

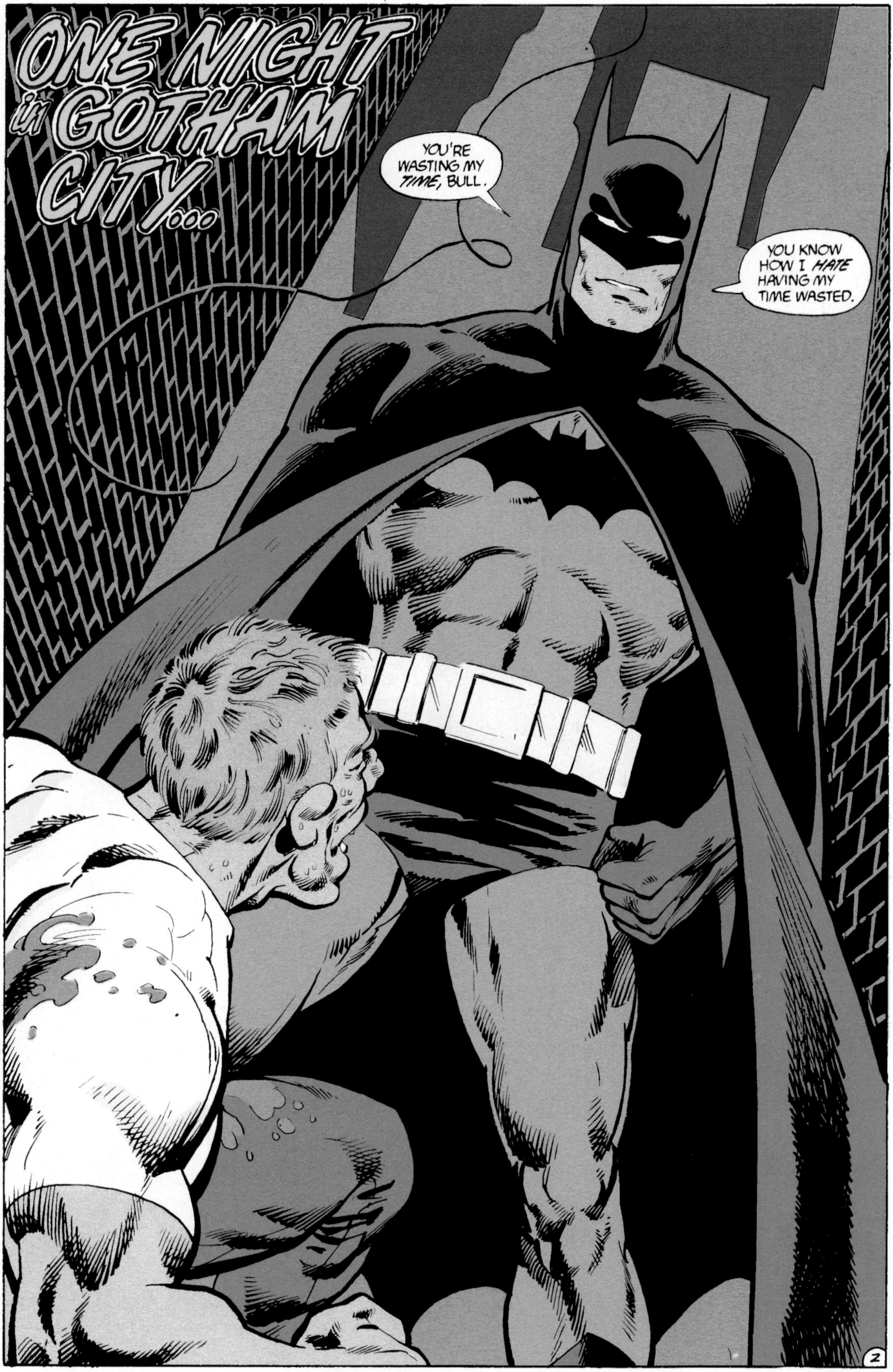
ONE NIGHT in GOTHAM CITY...
YOU'RE WASTING MY *TIME*, BULL.
YOU KNOW HOW I *HATE* HAVING MY TIME WASTED.

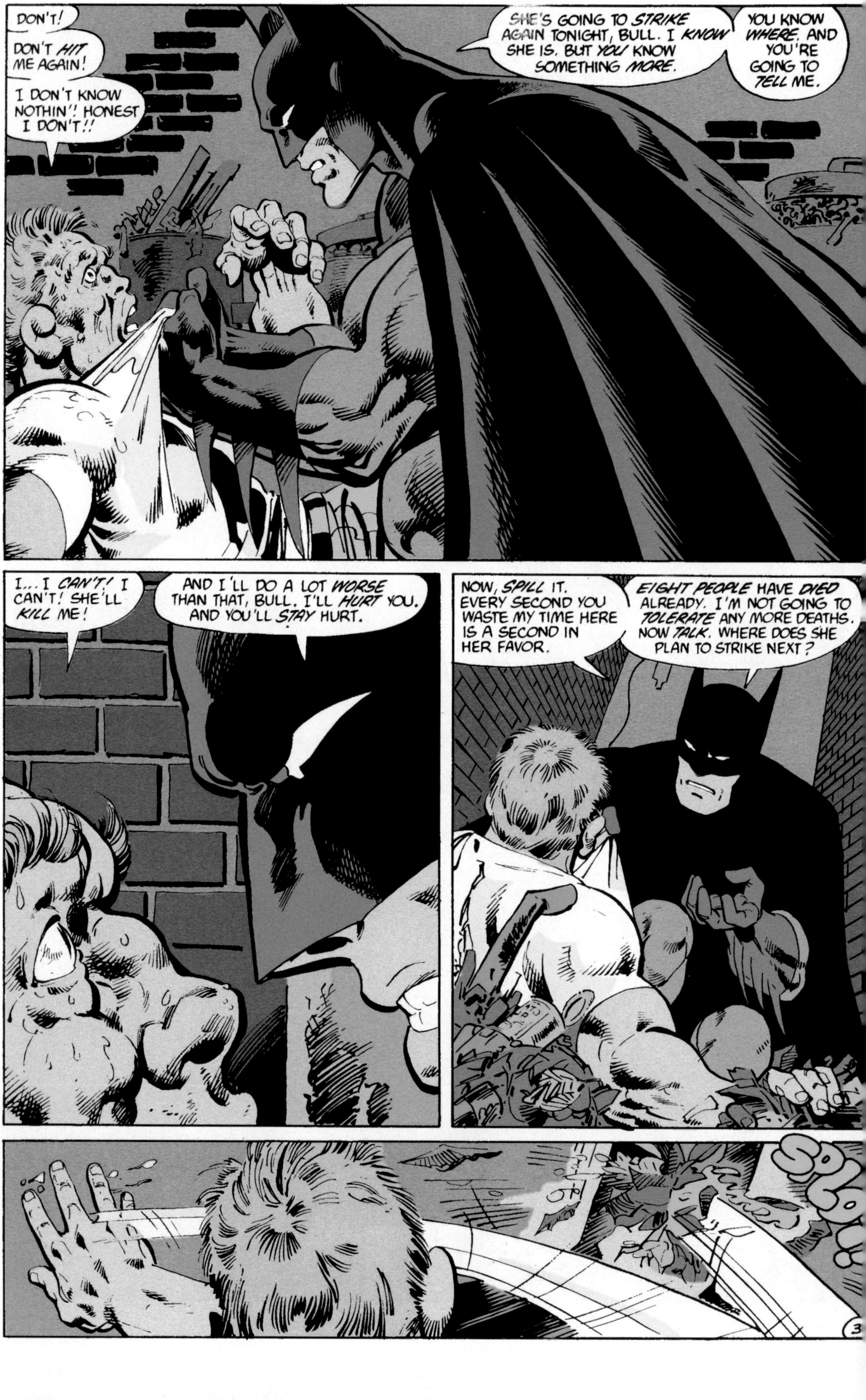
DON'T!
DON'T HIT ME AGAIN!
I DON'T KNOW NOTHIN'! HONEST I DON'T!!
SHE'S GOING TO STRIKE AGAIN TONIGHT, BULL. I KNOW SHE IS. BUT YOU KNOW SOMETHING MORE.
YOU KNOW WHERE. AND YOU'RE GOING TO TELL ME.
I... I CAN'T! I CAN'T! SHE'LL KILL ME!
AND I'LL DO A LOT WORSE THAN THAT, BULL. I'LL HURT YOU. AND YOU'LL STAY HURT.
NOW, SPILL IT. EVERY SECOND YOU WASTE MY TIME HERE IS A SECOND IN HER FAVOR.
EIGHT PEOPLE HAVE DIED ALREADY. I'M NOT GOING TO TOLERATE ANY MORE DEATHS. NOW TALK. WHERE DOES SHE PLAN TO STRIKE NEXT?

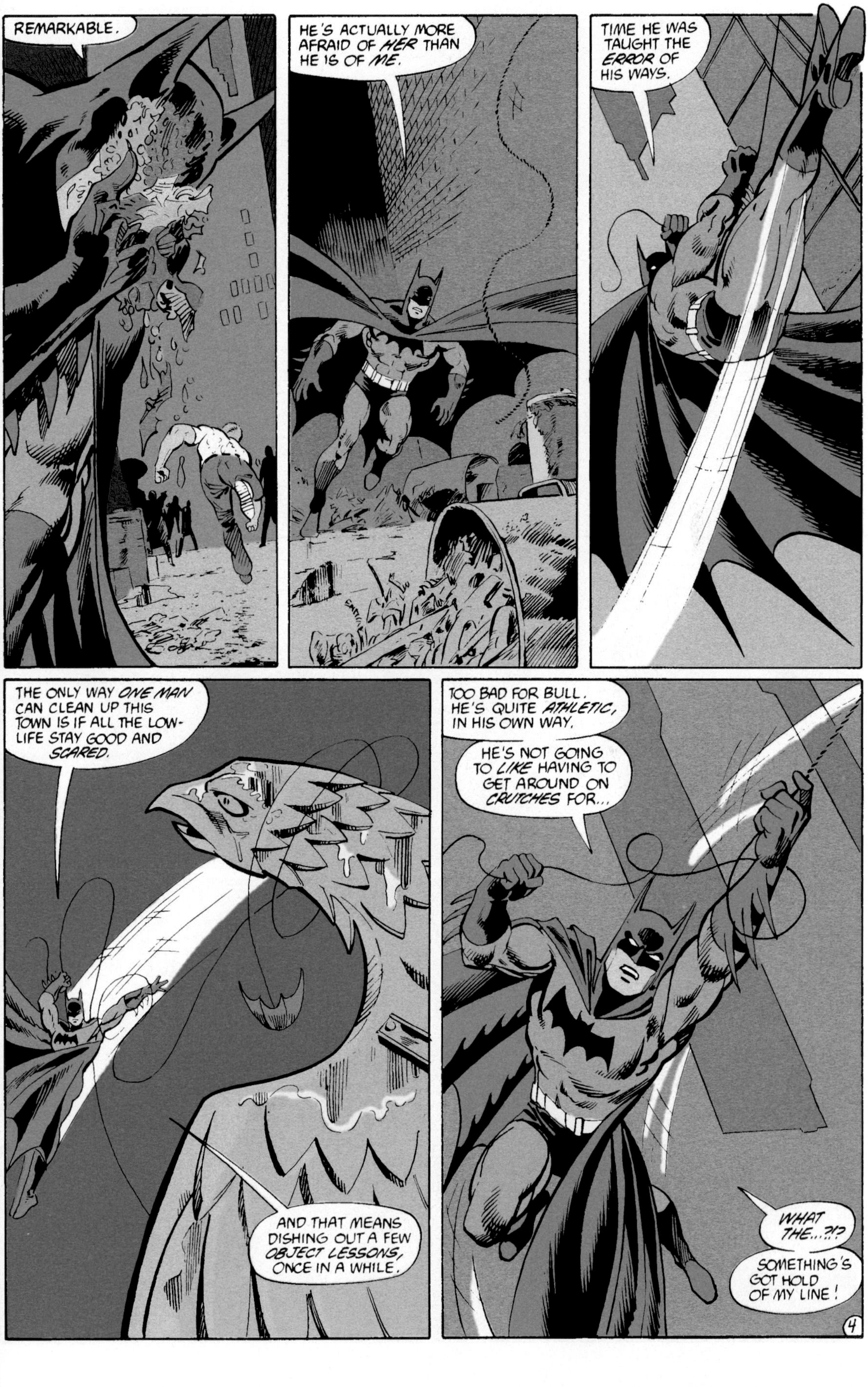
REMARKABLE.
HE'S ACTUALLY MORE AFRAID OF HER THAN HE IS OF ME.
TIME HE WAS TAUGHT THE ERROR OF HIS WAYS.
THE ONLY WAY ONE MAN CAN CLEAN UP THIS TOWN IS IF ALL THE LOW-LIFE STAY GOOD AND SCARED.
AND THAT MEANS DISHING OUT A FEW OBJECT LESSONS, ONCE IN A WHILE.
TOO BAD FOR BULL. HE'S QUITE ATHLETIC, IN HIS OWN WAY.
HE'S NOT GOING TO LIKE HAVING TO GET AROUND ON CRUTCHES FOR...
WHAT THE...?!?
SOMETHING'S GOT HOLD OF MY LINE!

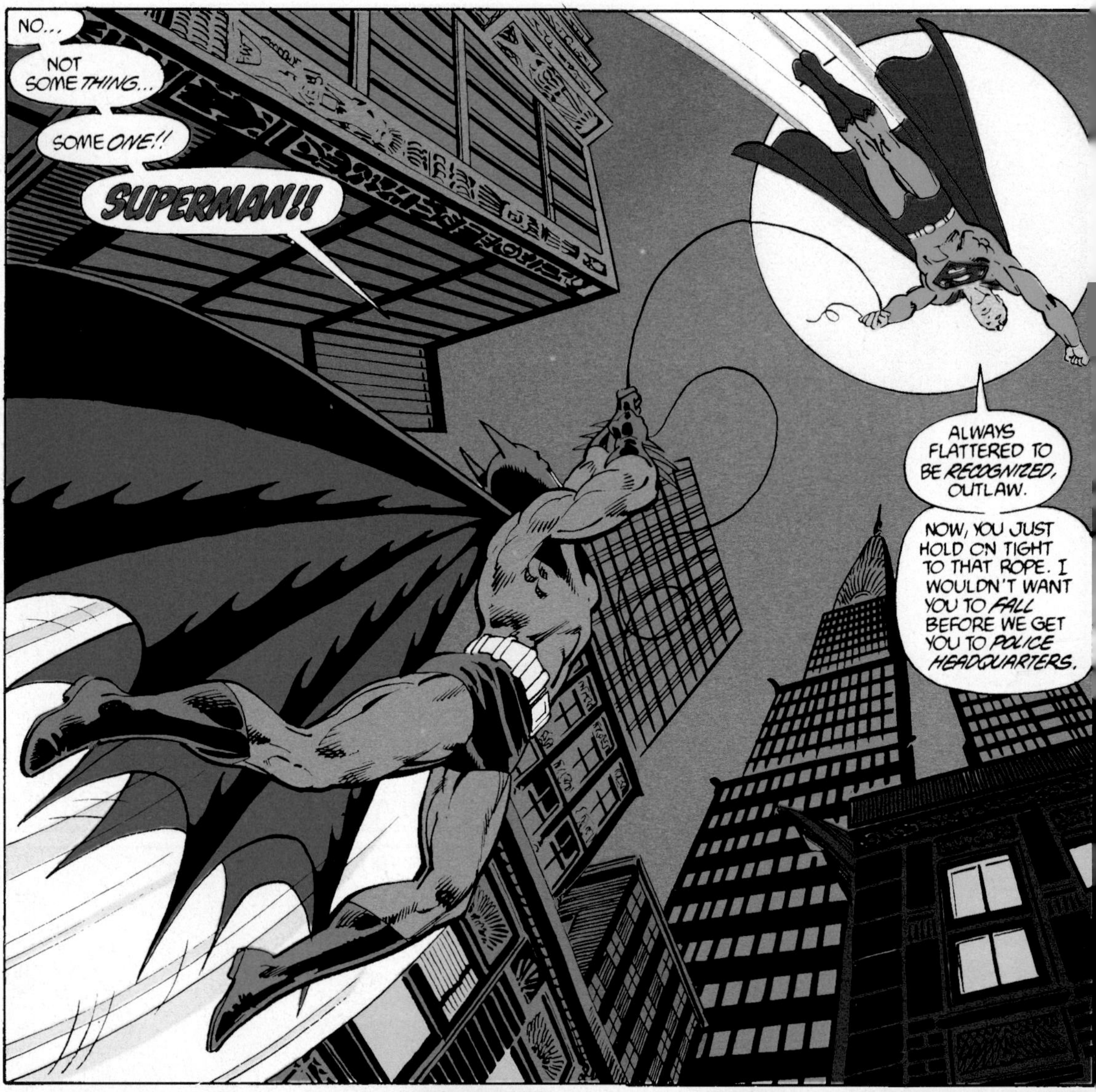
NO...
NOT SOME THING...
SOME ONE!!
SUPERMAN!!
ALWAYS FLATTERED TO BE RECOGNIZED, OUTLAW.
NOW, YOU JUST HOLD ON TIGHT TO THAT ROPE. I WOULDN'T WANT YOU TO FALL BEFORE WE GET YOU TO POLICE HEADQUARTERS.

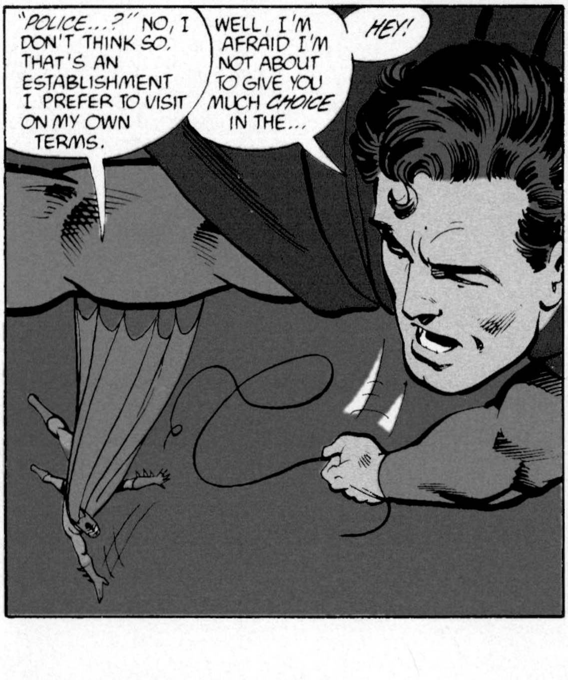
"POLICE...?" NO, I DON'T THINK SO. THAT'S AN ESTABLISHMENT I PREFER TO VISIT ON MY OWN TERMS.
WELL, I'M AFRAID I'M NOT ABOUT TO GIVE YOU MUCH CHOICE IN THE...
HEY!

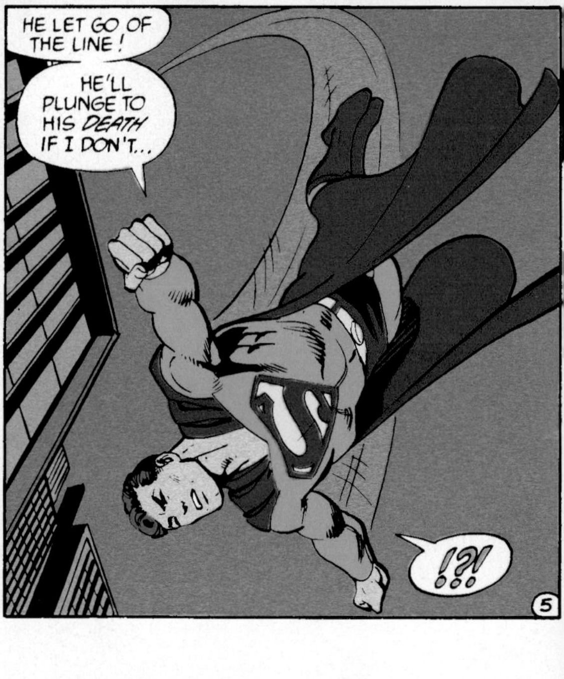
HE LET GO OF THE LINE!
HE'LL PLUNGE TO HIS DEATH IF I DON'T...
!?!

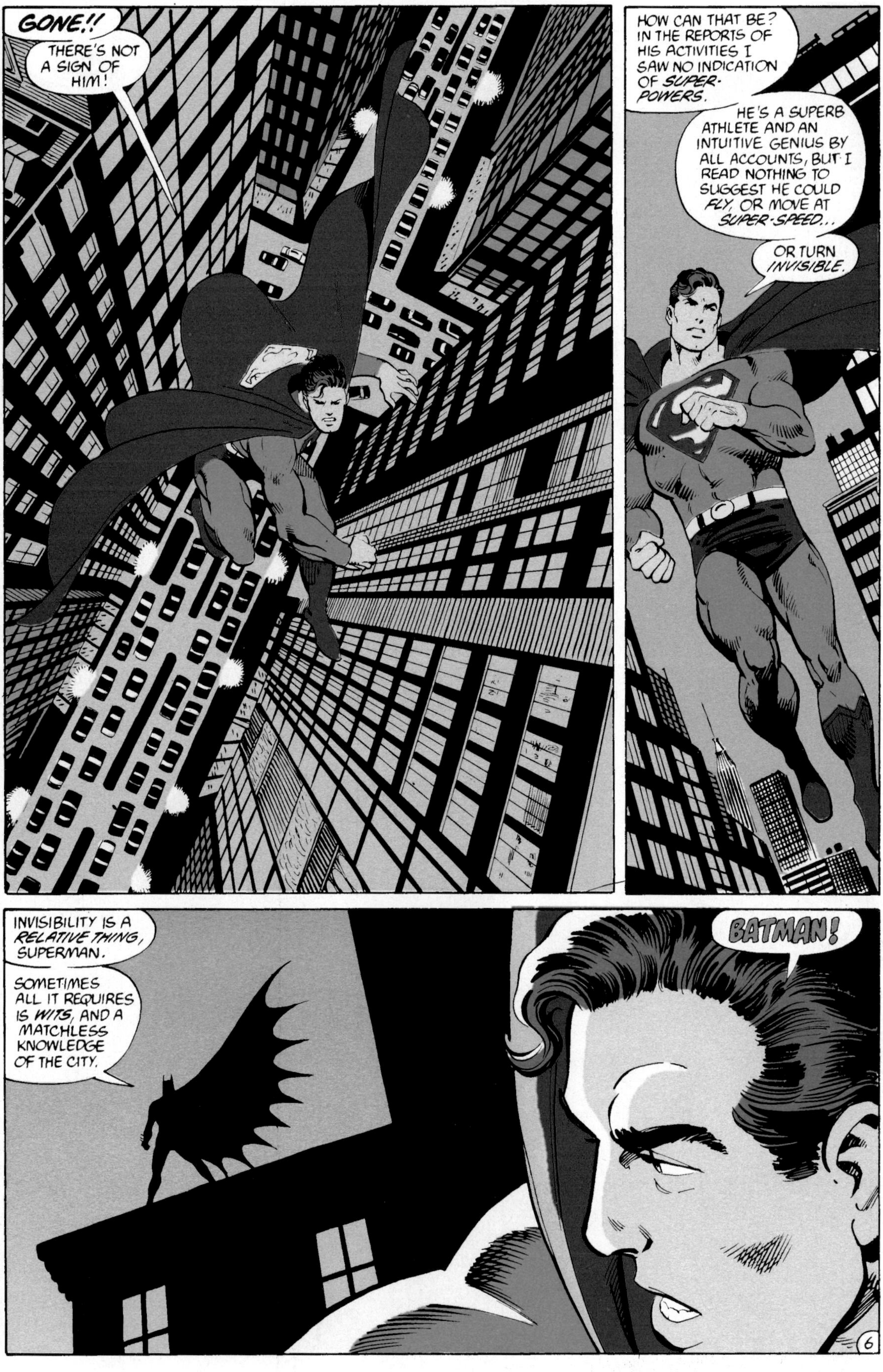
GONE!!
THERE'S NOT A SIGN OF HIM!
HOW CAN THAT BE? IN THE REPORTS OF HIS ACTIVITIES I SAW NO INDICATION OF SUPER-POWERS.
HE'S A SUPERB ATHLETE AND AN INTUITIVE GENIUS BY ALL ACCOUNTS, BUT I READ NOTHING TO SUGGEST HE COULD FLY, OR MOVE AT SUPER-SPEED...
OR TURN INVISIBLE.
INVISIBILITY IS A RELATIVE THING, SUPERMAN.
SOMETIMES ALL IT REQUIRES IS WITS, AND A MATCHLESS KNOWLEDGE OF THE CITY.
BATMAN!
6

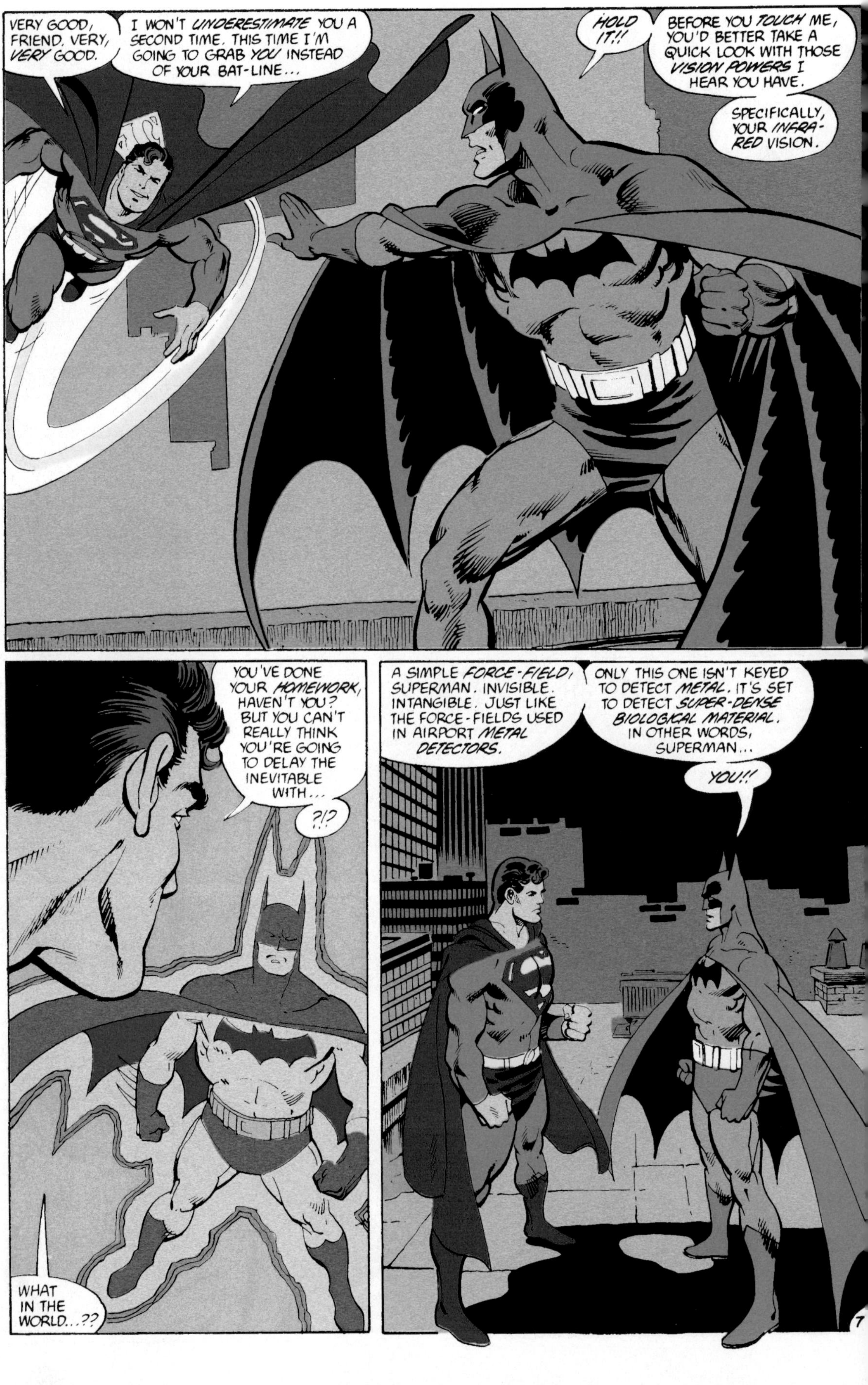
VERY GOOD, FRIEND. VERY, VERY GOOD.
I WON'T UNDERESTIMATE YOU A SECOND TIME. THIS TIME I'M GOING TO GRAB YOU INSTEAD OF YOUR BAT-LINE...
HOLD IT!!
BEFORE YOU TOUCH ME, YOU'D BETTER TAKE A QUICK LOOK WITH THOSE VISION POWERS I HEAR YOU HAVE.
SPECIFICALLY, YOUR INFRA-RED VISION.
YOU'VE DONE YOUR HOMEWORK, HAVEN'T YOU? BUT YOU CAN'T REALLY THINK YOU'RE GOING TO DELAY THE INEVITABLE WITH...
?!?
WHAT IN THE WORLD...??
A SIMPLE FORCE-FIELD, SUPERMAN. INVISIBLE. INTANGIBLE. JUST LIKE THE FORCE-FIELDS USED IN AIRPORT METAL DETECTORS.
ONLY THIS ONE ISN'T KEYED TO DETECT METAL. IT'S SET TO DETECT SUPER-DENSE BIOLOGICAL MATERIAL. IN OTHER WORDS, SUPERMAN...
YOU!!

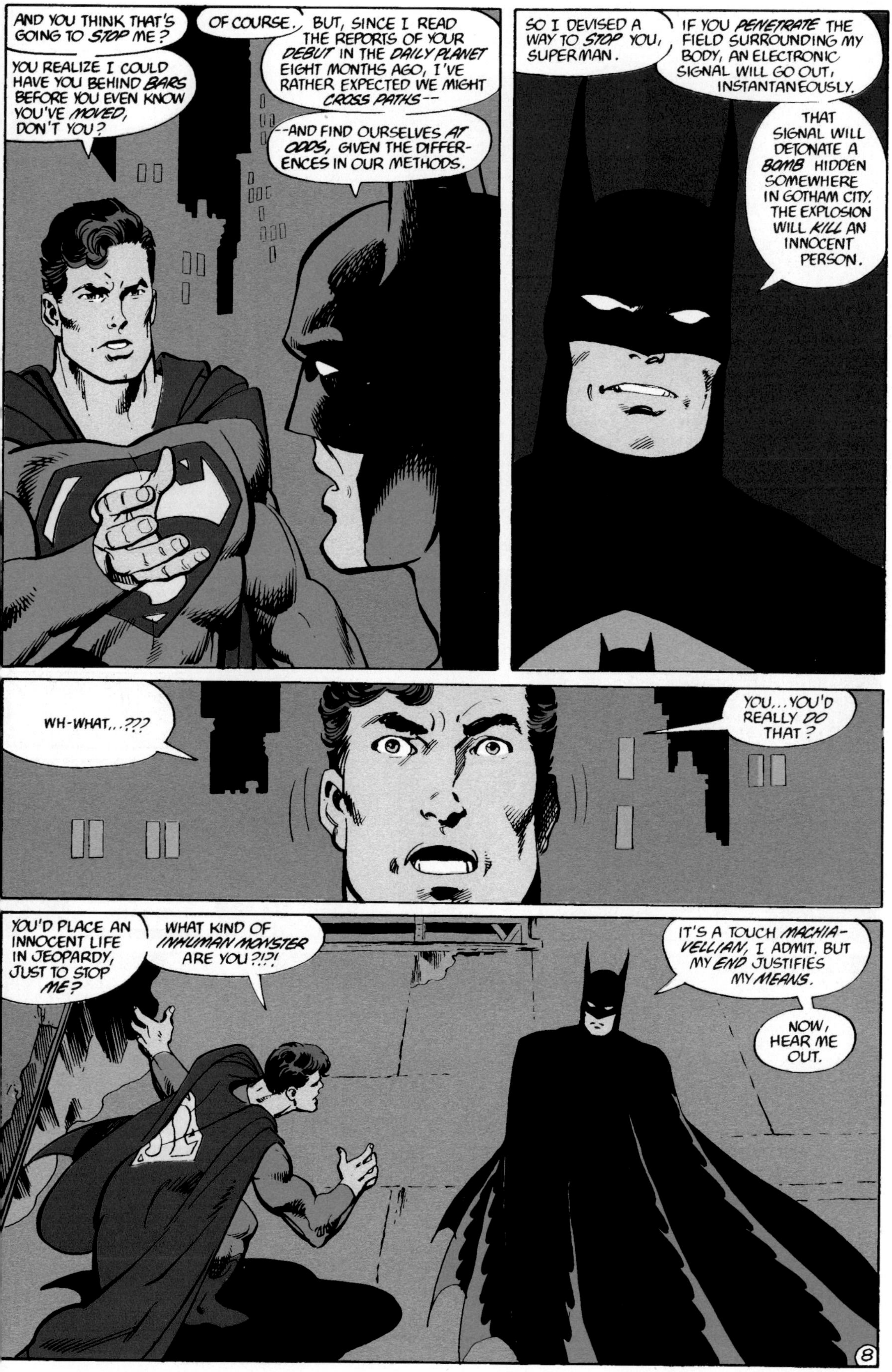
AND YOU THINK THAT'S GOING TO STOP ME?
YOU REALIZE I COULD HAVE YOU BEHIND BARS BEFORE YOU EVEN KNOW YOU'VE MOVED, DON'T YOU?
OF COURSE.
BUT, SINCE I READ THE REPORTS OF YOUR DEBUT IN THE DAILY PLANET EIGHT MONTHS AGO, I'VE RATHER EXPECTED WE MIGHT CROSS PATHS--
--AND FIND OURSELVES AT ODDS, GIVEN THE DIFFERENCES IN OUR METHODS.
SO I DEVISED A WAY TO STOP YOU, SUPERMAN.
IF YOU PENETRATE THE FIELD SURROUNDING MY BODY, AN ELECTRONIC SIGNAL WILL GO OUT, INSTANTANEOUSLY.
THAT SIGNAL WILL DETONATE A BOMB HIDDEN SOMEWHERE IN GOTHAM CITY. THE EXPLOSION WILL KILL AN INNOCENT PERSON.
WH-WHAT...???
YOU... YOU'D REALLY DO THAT?
YOU'D PLACE AN INNOCENT LIFE IN JEOPARDY, JUST TO STOP ME?
WHAT KIND OF INHUMAN MONSTER ARE YOU?!?!
IT'S A TOUCH MACHIAVELLIAN, I ADMIT. BUT MY END JUSTIFIES MY MEANS.
NOW, HEAR ME OUT.
8

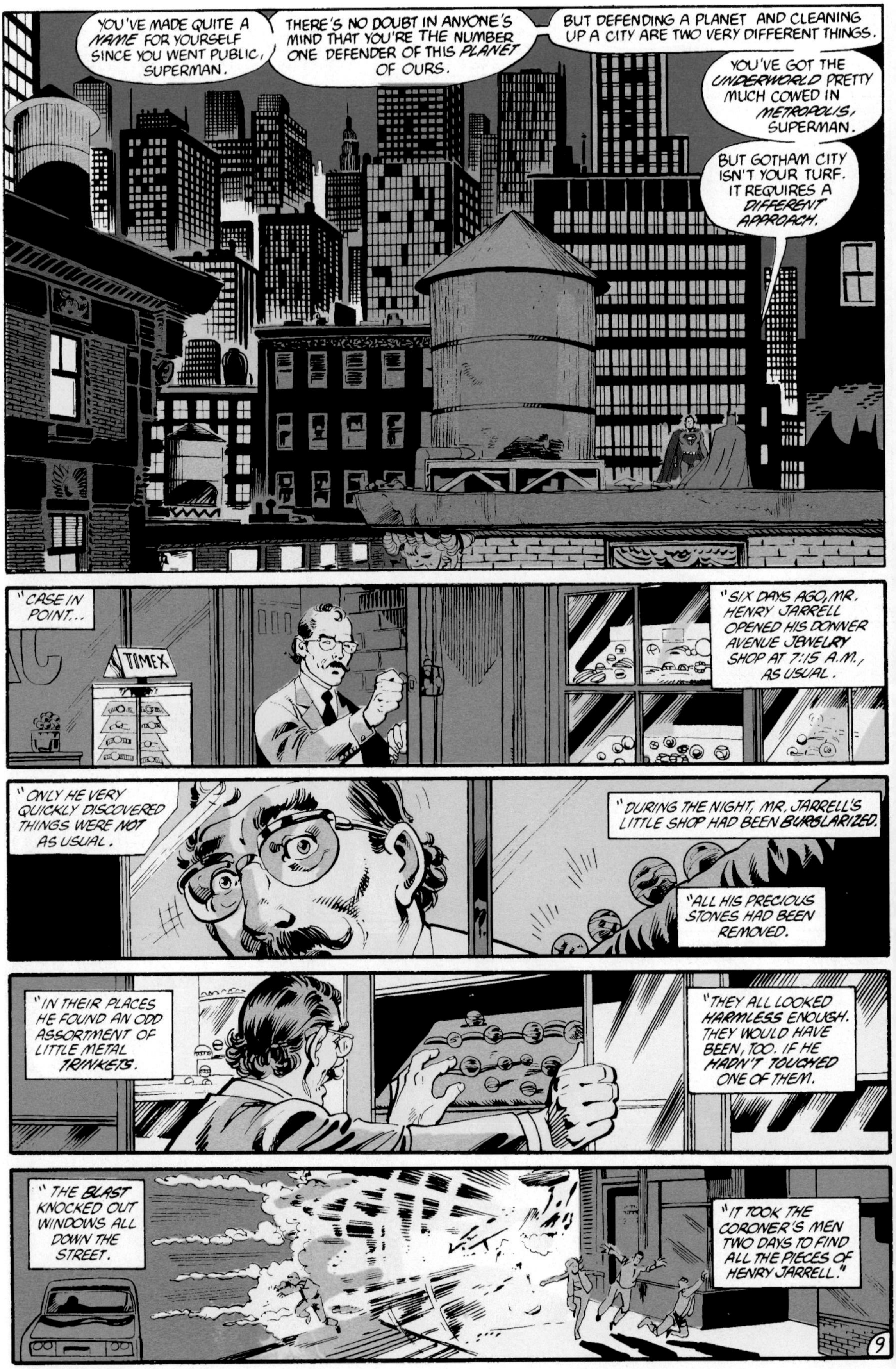
YOU'VE MADE QUITE A NAME FOR YOURSELF SINCE YOU WENT PUBLIC, SUPERMAN.
THERE'S NO DOUBT IN ANYONE'S MIND THAT YOU'RE THE NUMBER ONE DEFENDER OF THIS PLANET OF OURS.
BUT DEFENDING A PLANET AND CLEANING UP A CITY ARE TWO VERY DIFFERENT THINGS.
YOU'VE GOT THE UNDERWORLD PRETTY MUCH COWED IN METROPOLIS, SUPERMAN.
BUT GOTHAM CITY ISN'T YOUR TURF. IT REQUIRES A DIFFERENT APPROACH.
"CASE IN POINT...
TIMEX
"SIX DAYS AGO, MR. HENRY JARRELL OPENED HIS DONNER AVENUE JEWELRY SHOP AT 7:15 A.M., AS USUAL.
"ONLY HE VERY QUICKLY DISCOVERED THINGS WERE NOT AS USUAL.
"DURING THE NIGHT, MR. JARRELL'S LITTLE SHOP HAD BEEN BURGLARIZED.
"ALL HIS PRECIOUS STONES HAD BEEN REMOVED.
"IN THEIR PLACES HE FOUND AN ODD ASSORTMENT OF LITTLE METAL TRINKETS.
"THEY ALL LOOKED HARMLESS ENOUGH. THEY WOULD HAVE BEEN, TOO, IF HE HADN'T TOUCHED ONE OF THEM.
"THE BLAST KNOCKED OUT WINDOWS ALL DOWN THE STREET.
"IT TOOK THE CORONER'S MEN TWO DAYS TO FIND ALL THE PIECES OF HENRY JARRELL."
9

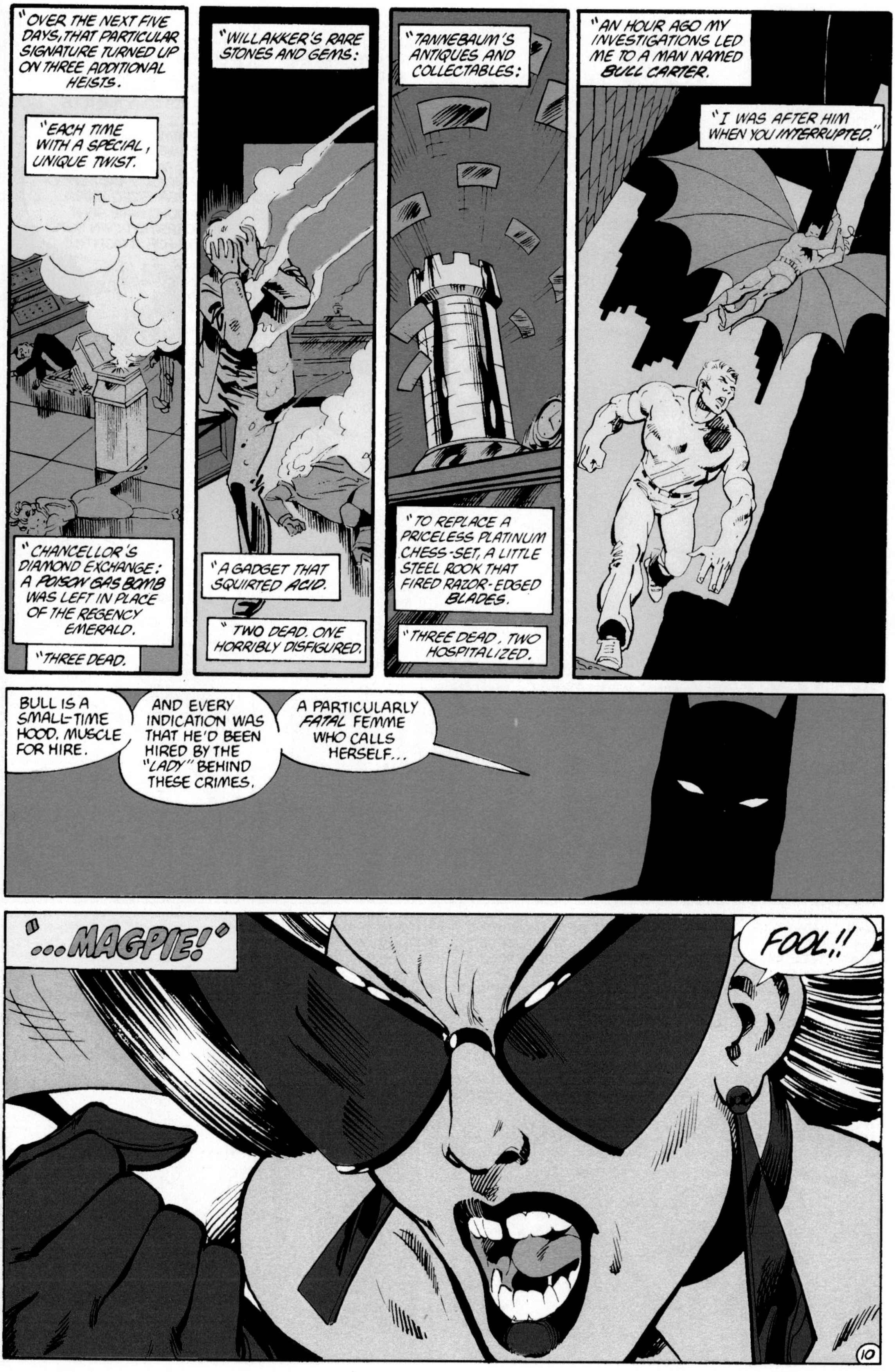
"OVER THE NEXT FIVE DAYS, THAT PARTICULAR SIGNATURE TURNED UP ON THREE ADDITIONAL HEISTS.
"EACH TIME WITH A SPECIAL, UNIQUE TWIST.
"CHANCELLOR'S DIAMOND EXCHANGE: A POISON GAS BOMB WAS LEFT IN PLACE OF THE REGENCY EMERALD.
"THREE DEAD.
"WILLAKKER'S RARE STONES AND GEMS:
"A GADGET THAT SQUIRTED ACID.
"TWO DEAD. ONE HORRIBLY DISFIGURED.
"TANNEBAUM'S ANTIQUES AND COLLECTABLES:
"TO REPLACE A PRICELESS PLATINUM CHESS-SET, A LITTLE STEEL ROOK THAT FIRED RAZOR-EDGED BLADES.
"THREE DEAD. TWO HOSPITALIZED.
"AN HOUR AGO MY INVESTIGATIONS LED ME TO A MAN NAMED BULL CARTER.
"I WAS AFTER HIM WHEN YOU INTERRUPTED."
BULL IS A SMALL-TIME HOOD. MUSCLE FOR HIRE.
AND EVERY INDICATION WAS THAT HE'D BEEN HIRED BY THE "LADY" BEHIND THESE CRIMES.
A PARTICULARLY FATAL FEMME WHO CALLS HERSELF...
"...MAGPIE!"
FOOL!!
10

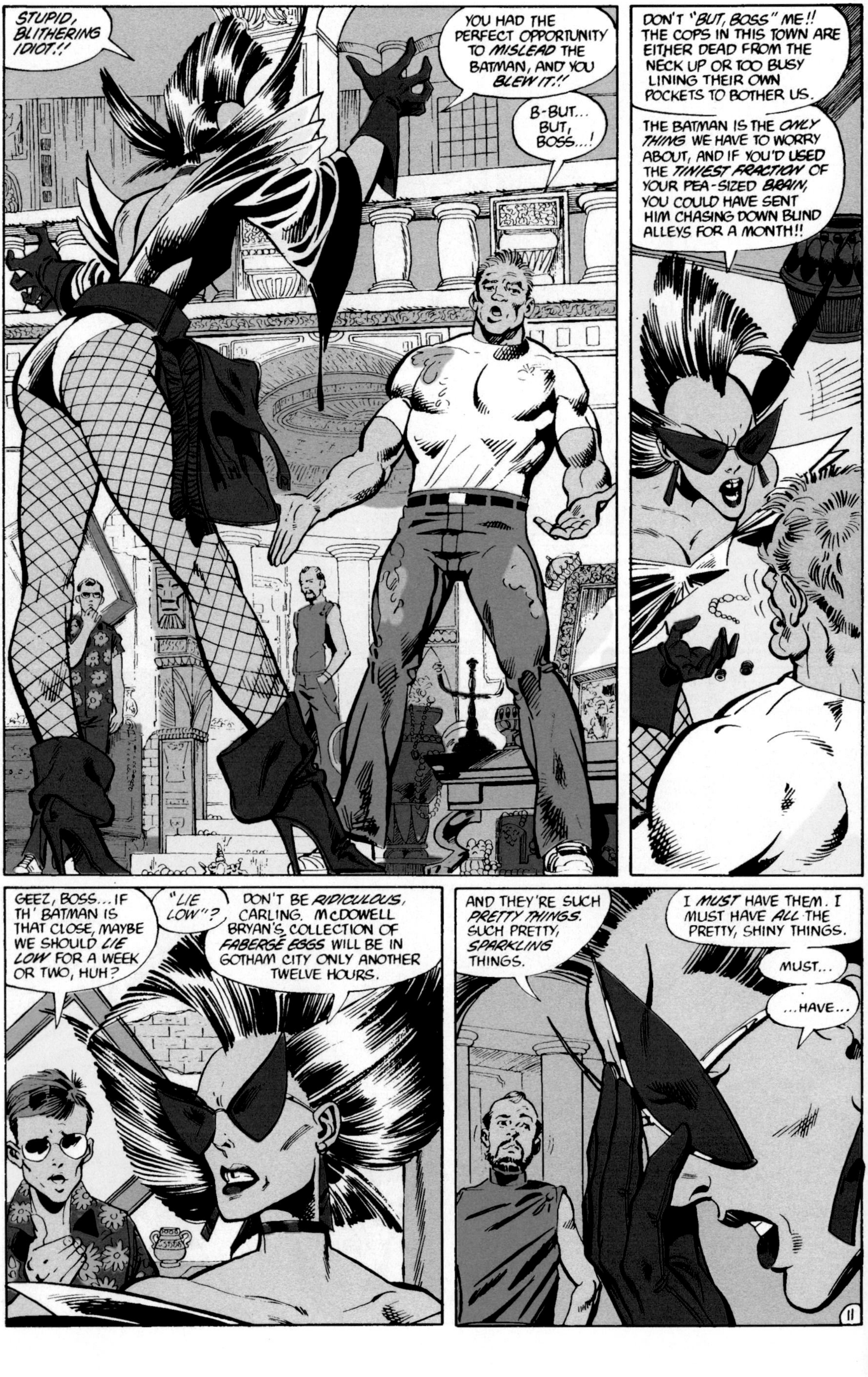
STUPID, BLITHERING IDIOT!!
YOU HAD THE PERFECT OPPORTUNITY TO MISLEAD THE BATMAN, AND YOU BLEW IT!!
B-BUT... BUT, BOSS...!
DON'T "BUT, BOSS" ME!! THE COPS IN THIS TOWN ARE EITHER DEAD FROM THE NECK UP OR TOO BUSY LINING THEIR OWN POCKETS TO BOTHER US.
THE BATMAN IS THE ONLY THING WE HAVE TO WORRY ABOUT, AND IF YOU'D USED THE TINIEST FRACTION OF YOUR PEA-SIZED BRAIN, YOU COULD HAVE SENT HIM CHASING DOWN BLIND ALLEYS FOR A MONTH!!
GEEZ, BOSS... IF TH' BATMAN IS THAT CLOSE, MAYBE WE SHOULD LIE LOW FOR A WEEK OR TWO, HUH?
"LIE LOW"?
DON'T BE RIDICULOUS, CARLING. MCDOWELL BRYAN'S COLLECTION OF FABERGÉ EGGS WILL BE IN GOTHAM CITY ONLY ANOTHER TWELVE HOURS.
AND THEY'RE SUCH PRETTY THINGS. SUCH PRETTY, SPARKLING THINGS.
I MUST HAVE THEM. I MUST HAVE ALL THE PRETTY, SHINY THINGS.
MUST...
...HAVE...

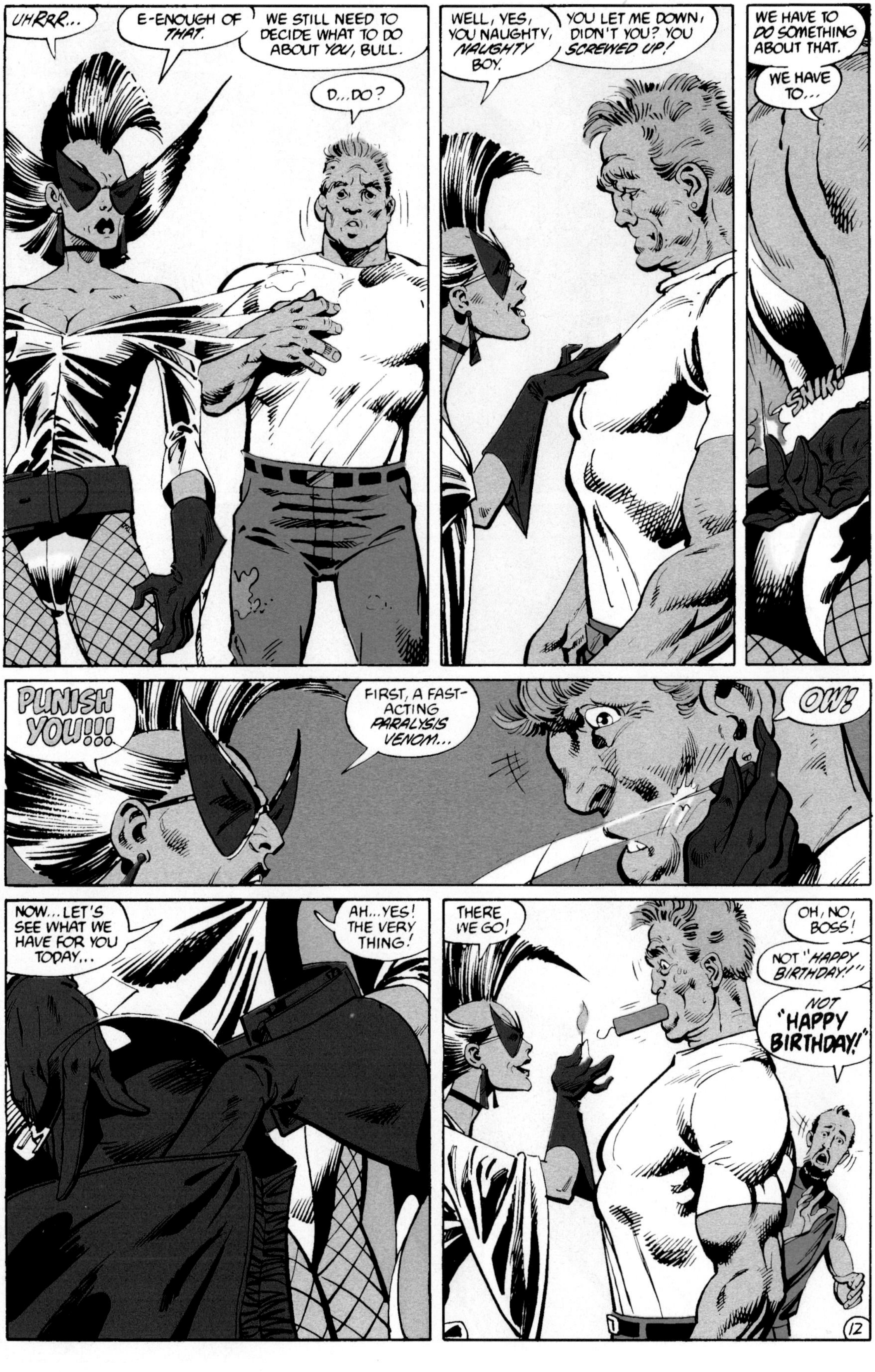
UHRRR...
E-ENOUGH OF THAT.
WE STILL NEED TO DECIDE WHAT TO DO ABOUT YOU, BULL.
D...DO?
WELL, YES, YOU NAUGHTY, NAUGHTY BOY.
YOU LET ME DOWN, DIDN'T YOU? YOU SCREWED UP!
WE HAVE TO DO SOMETHING ABOUT THAT.
WE HAVE TO...
SNIK!
PUNISH YOU!!!
FIRST, A FAST-ACTING PARALYSIS VENOM...
OW!
NOW... LET'S SEE WHAT WE HAVE FOR YOU TODAY...
AH... YES! THE VERY THING!
THERE WE GO!
OH, NO, BOSS!
NOT "HAPPY BIRTHDAY!"
NOT "HAPPY BIRTHDAY!"
12

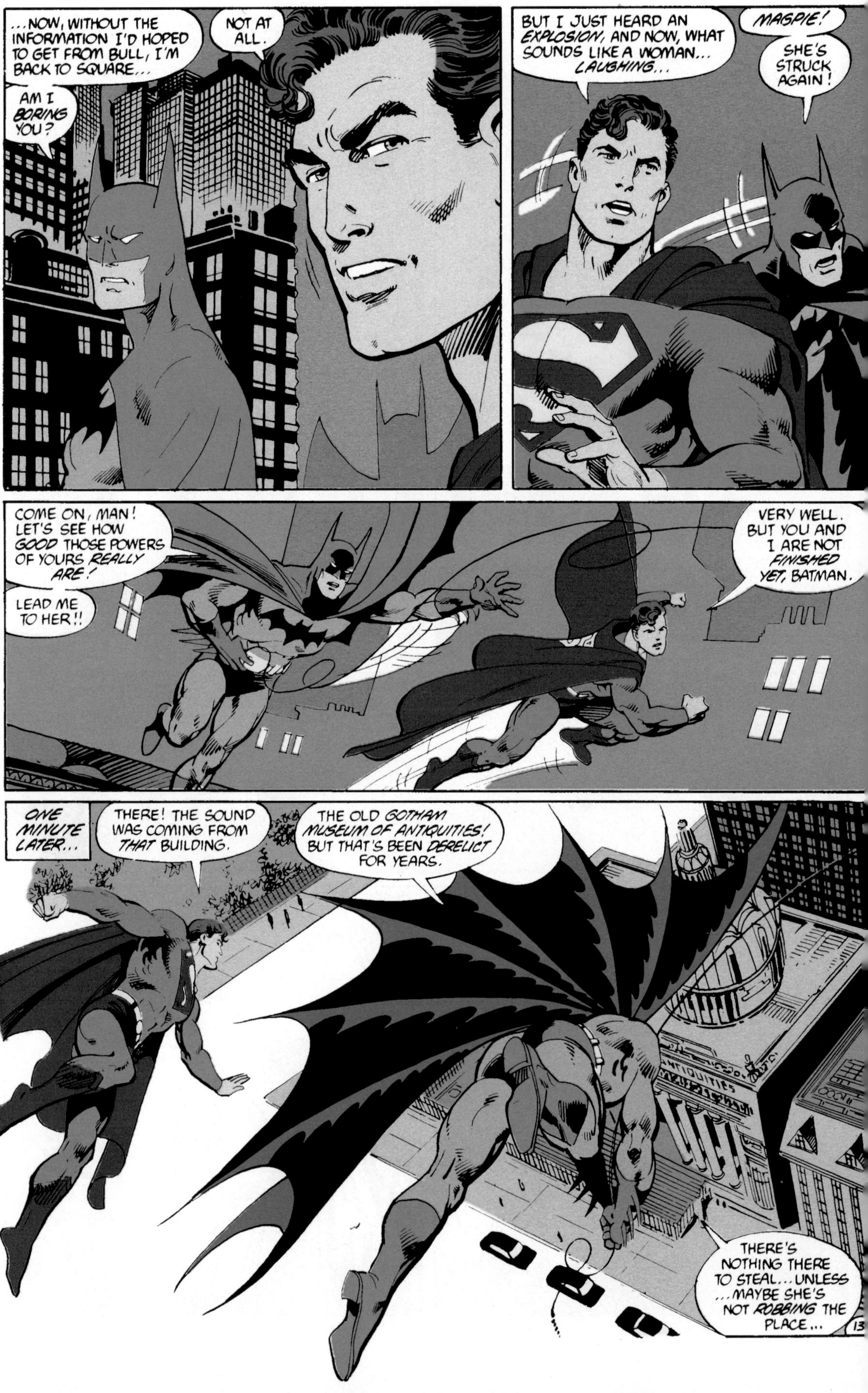
...NOW, WITHOUT THE INFORMATION I'D HOPED TO GET FROM BULL, I'M BACK TO SQUARE...
AM I BORING YOU?
NOT AT ALL.
BUT I JUST HEARD AN EXPLOSION, AND NOW, WHAT SOUNDS LIKE A WOMAN... LAUGHING...
MAGPIE!
SHE'S STRUCK AGAIN!
COME ON, MAN! LET'S SEE HOW GOOD THOSE POWERS OF YOURS REALLY ARE!
LEAD ME TO HER!!
VERY WELL. BUT YOU AND I ARE NOT FINISHED YET, BATMAN.
ONE MINUTE LATER...
THERE! THE SOUND WAS COMING FROM THAT BUILDING.
THE OLD GOTHAM MUSEUM OF ANTIQUITIES! BUT THAT'S BEEN DERELICT FOR YEARS.
ANTIQUITIES
THERE'S NOTHING THERE TO STEAL...UNLESS ...MAYBE SHE'S NOT ROBBING THE PLACE...
13

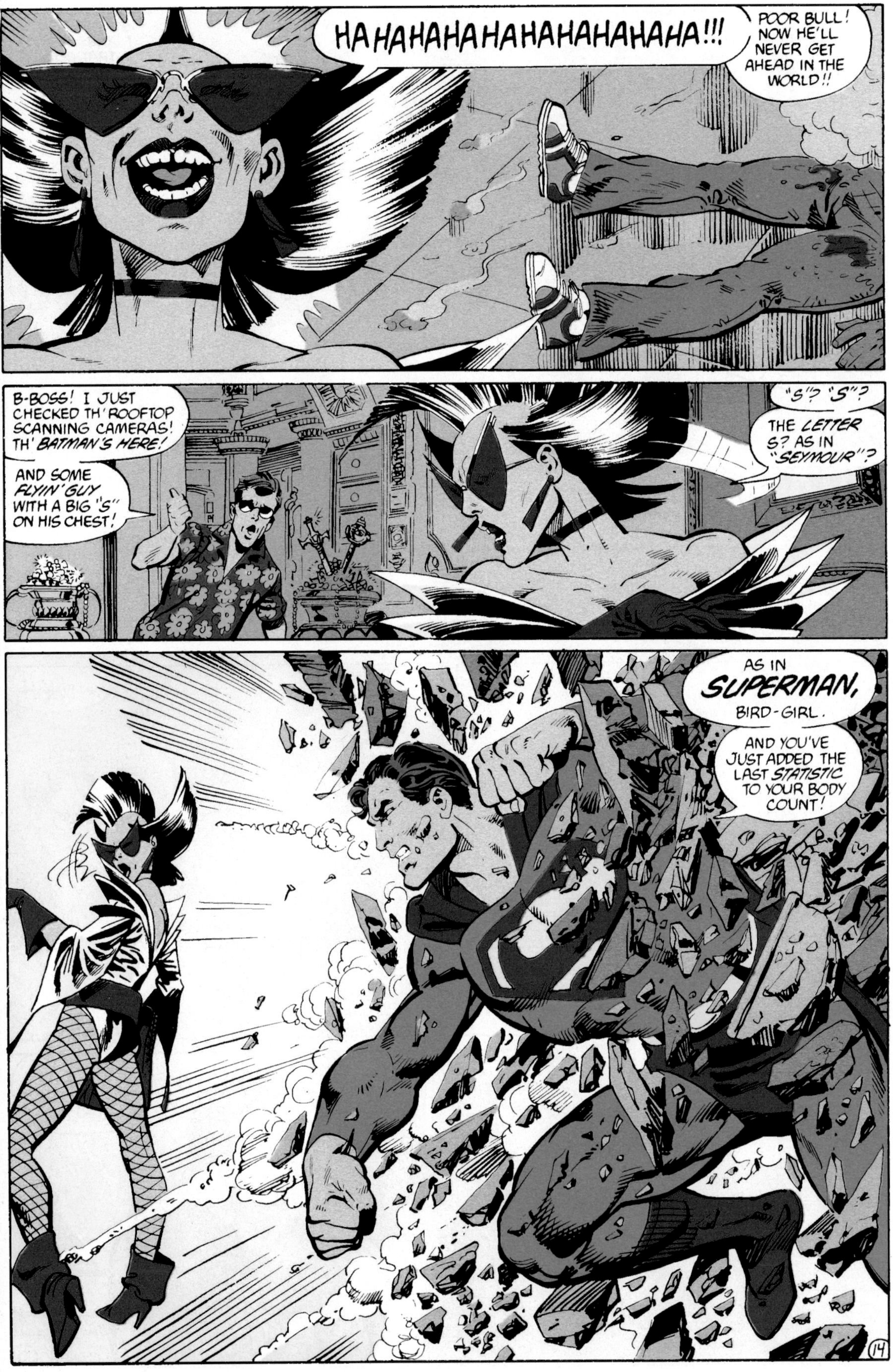
HAHAHAHAHAHAHAHAHAHAHA!!!
POOR BULL! NOW HE'LL NEVER GET AHEAD IN THE WORLD!!
B-BOSS! I JUST CHECKED TH' ROOFTOP SCANNING CAMERAS! TH' BATMAN'S HERE!
AND SOME FLYIN' GUY WITH A BIG "S" ON HIS CHEST!
"S"? "S"?
THE LETTER S? AS IN "SEYMOUR"?
AS IN SUPERMAN, BIRD-GIRL.
AND YOU'VE JUST ADDED THE LAST STATISTIC TO YOUR BODY COUNT!
14

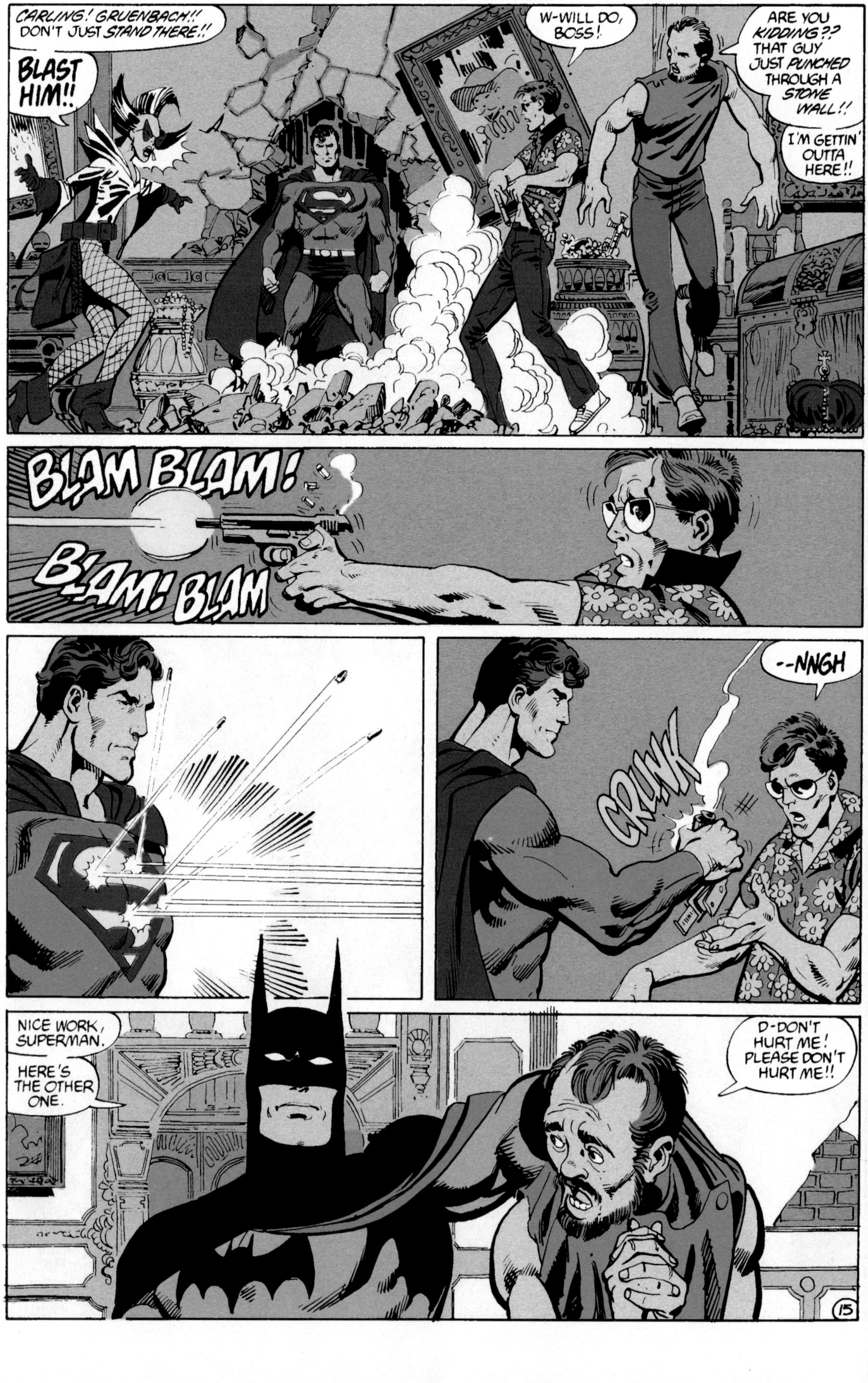
CARLING! GRUENBACH!! DON'T JUST STAND THERE!!
BLAST HIM!!
W-WILL DO, BOSS!
ARE YOU KIDDING?? THAT GUY JUST PUNCHED THROUGH A STONE WALL!!
I'M GETTIN' OUTTA HERE!!
BLAM BLAM!
BLAM! BLAM
--NNGH
CRUNK
NICE WORK, SUPERMAN.
HERE'S THE OTHER ONE.
D-DON'T HURT ME! PLEASE DON'T HURT ME!!
15

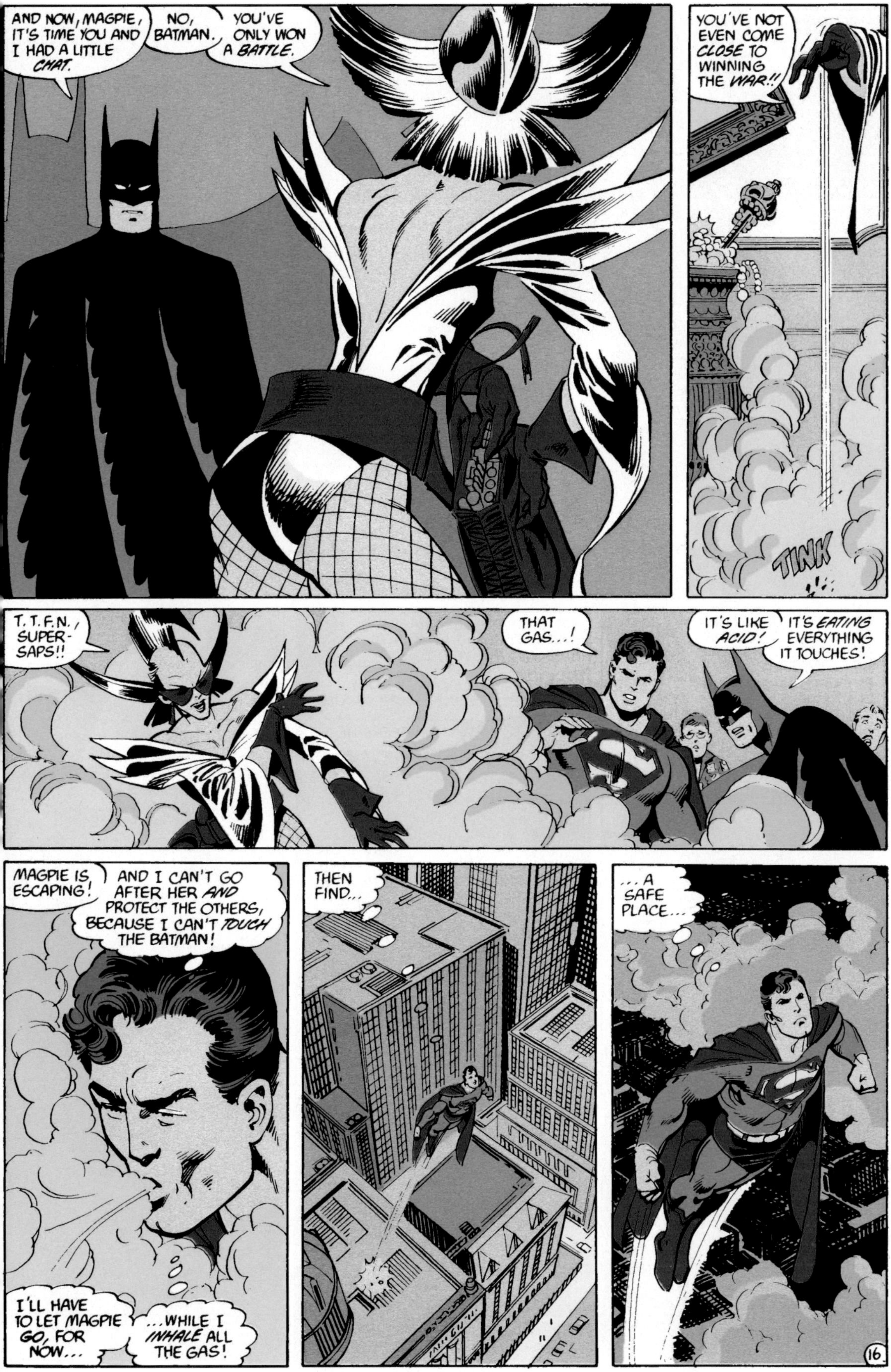
AND NOW, MAGPIE, IT'S TIME YOU AND I HAD A LITTLE CHAT.
NO, BATMAN.
YOU'VE ONLY WON A BATTLE.
YOU'VE NOT EVEN COME CLOSE TO WINNING THE WAR!!
TINK
T.T.F.N., SUPER-SAPS!!
THAT GAS...!
IT'S LIKE ACID!
IT'S EATING EVERYTHING IT TOUCHES!
MAGPIE IS ESCAPING!
AND I CAN'T GO AFTER HER AND PROTECT THE OTHERS, BECAUSE I CAN'T TOUCH THE BATMAN!
I'LL HAVE TO LET MAGPIE GO, FOR NOW...
...WHILE I INHALE ALL THE GAS!
THEN FIND...
...A SAFE PLACE...
16

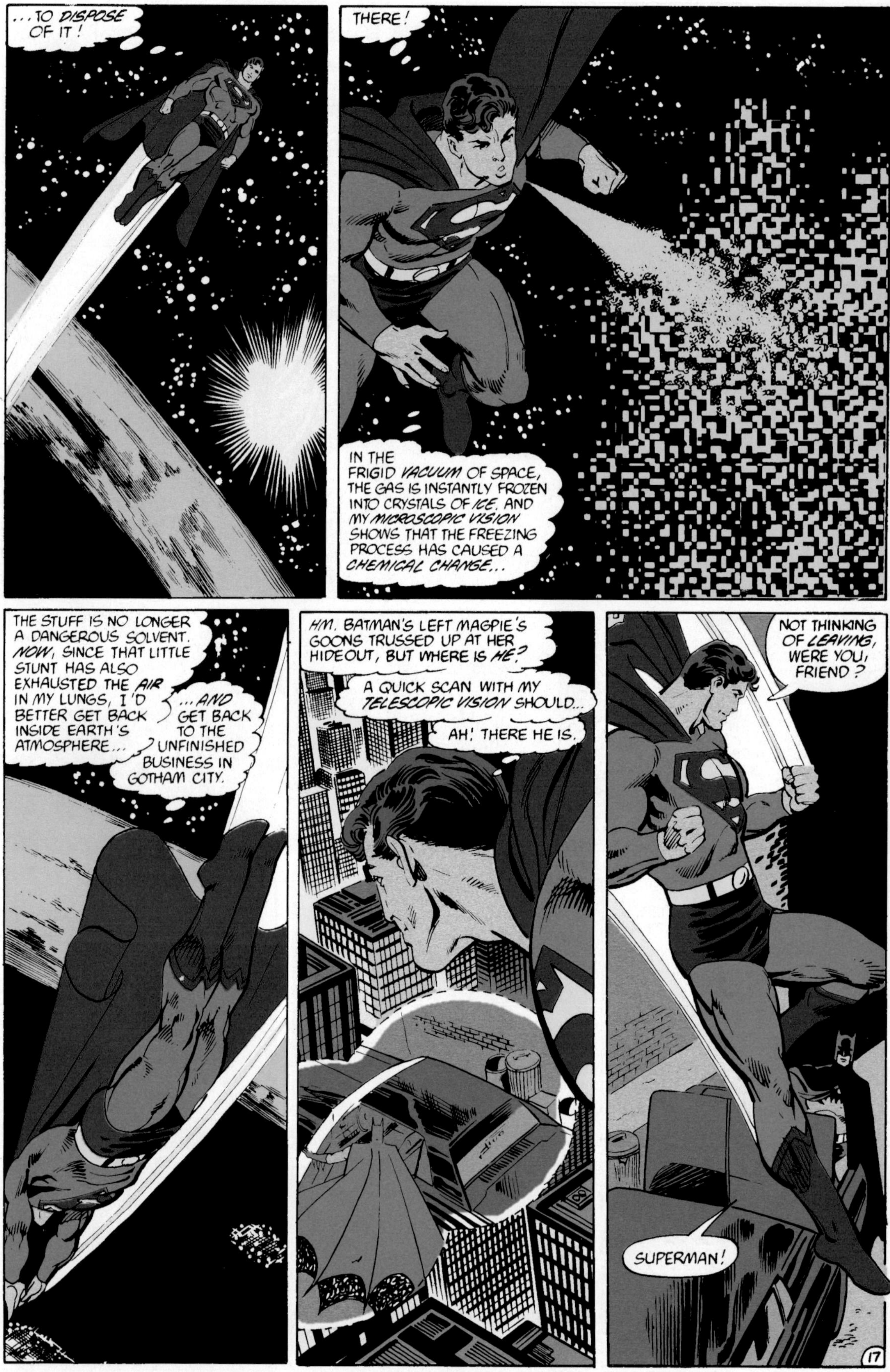

...TO DISPOSE OF IT!
THERE!
IN THE FRIGID VACUUM OF SPACE, THE GAS IS INSTANTLY FROZEN INTO CRYSTALS OF ICE, AND MY MICROSCOPIC VISION SHOWS THAT THE FREEZING PROCESS HAS CAUSED A CHEMICAL CHANGE...
THE STUFF IS NO LONGER A DANGEROUS SOLVENT. NOW, SINCE THAT LITTLE STUNT HAS ALSO EXHAUSTED THE AIR IN MY LUNGS, I'D BETTER GET BACK INSIDE EARTH'S ATMOSPHERE...
...AND GET BACK TO THE UNFINISHED BUSINESS IN GOTHAM CITY.
HM. BATMAN'S LEFT MAGPIE'S GOONS TRUSSED UP AT HER HIDEOUT, BUT WHERE IS HE?
A QUICK SCAN WITH MY TELESCOPIC VISION SHOULD...
AH! THERE HE IS.
NOT THINKING OF LEAVING, WERE YOU, FRIEND?
SUPERMAN!

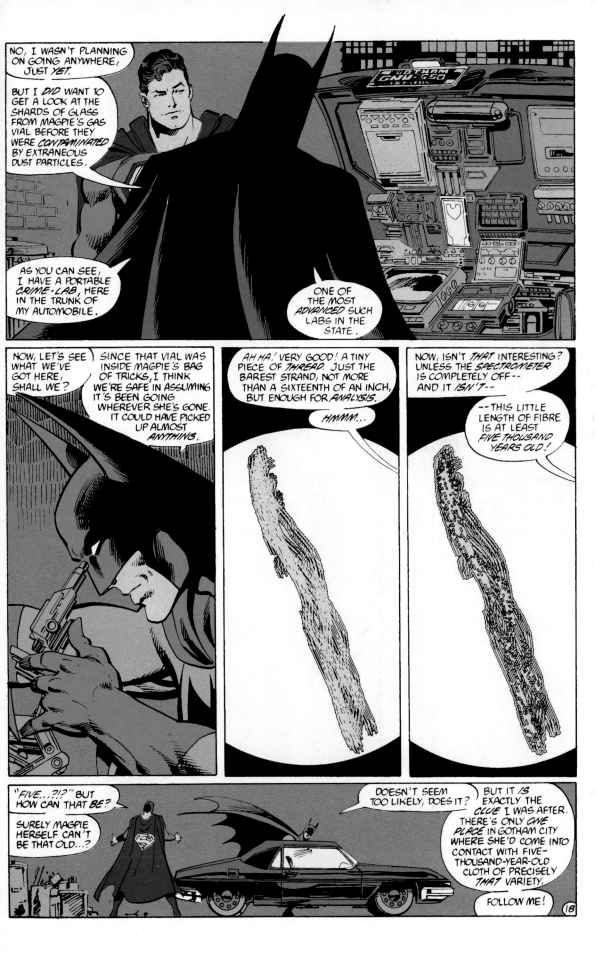

NO, I WASN'T PLANNING ON GOING ANYWHERE, JUST *YET.*

BUT I *DID* WANT TO GET A LOOK AT THE SHARDS OF GLASS FROM MAGPIE'S GAS VIAL BEFORE THEY WERE *CONTAMINATED* BY EXTRANEOUS DUST PARTICLES.

AS YOU CAN SEE, I HAVE A PORTABLE *CRIME-LAB,* HERE IN THE TRUNK OF MY AUTOMOBILE.

ONE OF THE *MOST ADVANCED* SUCH LABS IN THE STATE.

NOW, LET'S SEE WHAT WE'VE GOT HERE, SHALL WE?

SINCE THAT VIAL WAS INSIDE MAGPIE'S *BAG OF TRICKS,* I THINK WE'RE SAFE IN ASSUMING IT'S BEEN GOING WHEREVER SHE'S GONE. IT COULD HAVE PICKED UP ALMOST *ANYTHING.*

AH HA! VERY GOOD! A TINY PIECE OF *THREAD.* JUST THE BAREST STRAND, NOT MORE THAN A SIXTEENTH OF AN INCH, BUT ENOUGH FOR *ANALYSIS.*

HMMM...

NOW, ISN'T *THAT* INTERESTING? UNLESS THE *SPECTROMETER* IS COMPLETELY OFF-- AND IT *ISN'T* --

--THIS LITTLE LENGTH OF FIBRE IS AT LEAST *FIVE THOUSAND YEARS OLD!*

"FIVE...?!?" BUT HOW CAN THAT *BE?*

SURELY MAGPIE HERSELF CAN'T BE THAT OLD...?

DOESN'T SEEM TOO LIKELY, DOES IT?

BUT IT *IS* EXACTLY THE *CLUE* I WAS AFTER. THERE'S ONLY *ONE PLACE* IN GOTHAM CITY WHERE SHE'D COME INTO CONTACT WITH FIVE-THOUSAND-YEAR-OLD CLOTH OF PRECISELY *THAT* VARIETY.

FOLLOW ME!

18

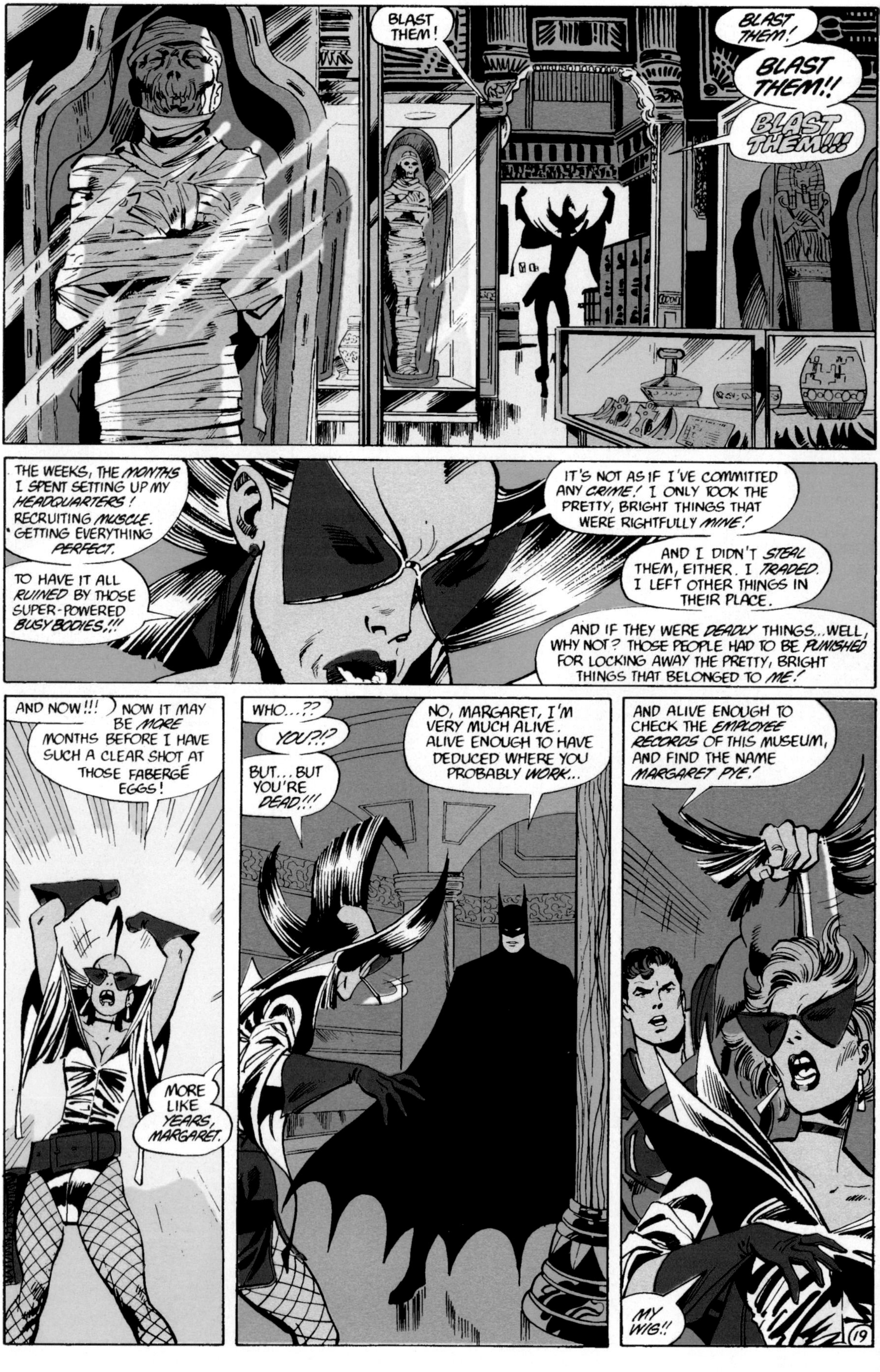
BLAST THEM!
BLAST THEM!
BLAST THEM!!
BLAST THEM!!!
THE WEEKS, THE MONTHS I SPENT SETTING UP MY HEADQUARTERS! RECRUITING MUSCLE. GETTING EVERYTHING PERFECT.
TO HAVE IT ALL RUINED BY THOSE SUPER-POWERED BUSYBODIES!!!
IT'S NOT AS IF I'VE COMMITTED ANY CRIME! I ONLY TOOK THE PRETTY, BRIGHT THINGS THAT WERE RIGHTFULLY MINE!
AND I DIDN'T STEAL THEM, EITHER. I TRADED. I LEFT OTHER THINGS IN THEIR PLACE.
AND IF THEY WERE DEADLY THINGS...WELL, WHY NOT? THOSE PEOPLE HAD TO BE PUNISHED FOR LOCKING AWAY THE PRETTY, BRIGHT THINGS THAT BELONGED TO ME!
AND NOW!!!
NOW IT MAY BE MORE MONTHS BEFORE I HAVE SUCH A CLEAR SHOT AT THOSE FABERGÉ EGGS!
MORE LIKE YEARS, MARGARET.
WHO...??
YOU?!?
BUT... BUT YOU'RE DEAD!!!
NO, MARGARET, I'M VERY MUCH ALIVE. ALIVE ENOUGH TO HAVE DEDUCED WHERE YOU PROBABLY WORK...
AND ALIVE ENOUGH TO CHECK THE EMPLOYEE RECORDS OF THIS MUSEUM, AND FIND THE NAME MARGARET PYE!
MY WIG!!

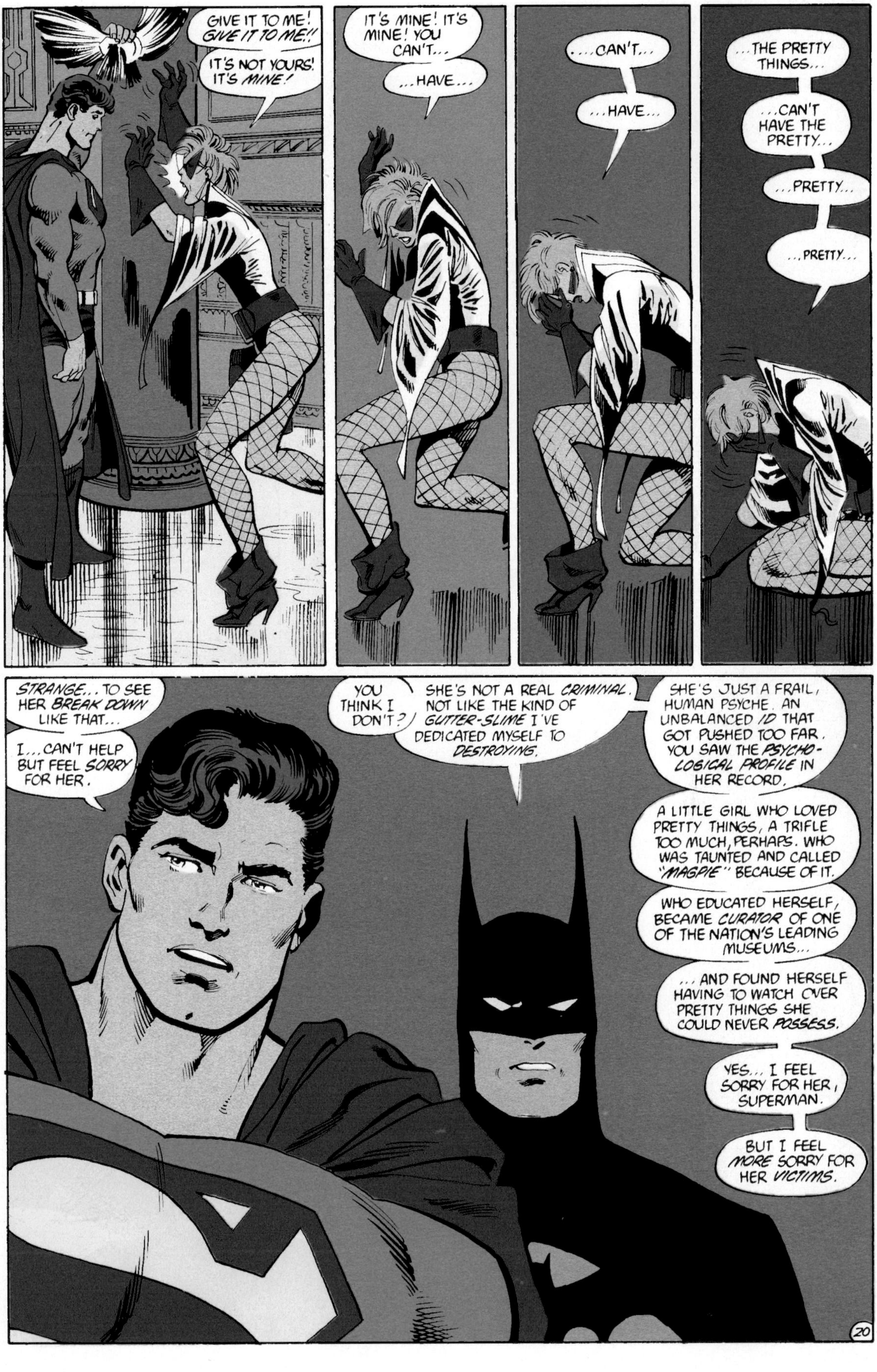
GIVE IT TO ME! GIVE IT TO ME!!
IT'S NOT YOURS! IT'S MINE!
IT'S MINE! IT'S MINE! YOU CAN'T...
...HAVE...
....CAN'T...
...HAVE...
...THE PRETTY THINGS...
...CAN'T HAVE THE PRETTY...
...PRETTY...
...PRETTY...
STRANGE... TO SEE HER BREAK DOWN LIKE THAT...
I... CAN'T HELP BUT FEEL SORRY FOR HER.
YOU THINK I DON'T?
SHE'S NOT A REAL CRIMINAL. NOT LIKE THE KIND OF GUTTER-SLIME I'VE DEDICATED MYSELF TO DESTROYING.
SHE'S JUST A FRAIL, HUMAN PSYCHE. AN UNBALANCED ID THAT GOT PUSHED TOO FAR. YOU SAW THE PSYCHOLOGICAL PROFILE IN HER RECORD.
A LITTLE GIRL WHO LOVED PRETTY THINGS, A TRIFLE TOO MUCH, PERHAPS. WHO WAS TAUNTED AND CALLED "MAGPIE" BECAUSE OF IT.
WHO EDUCATED HERSELF, BECAME CURATOR OF ONE OF THE NATION'S LEADING MUSEUMS...
...AND FOUND HERSELF HAVING TO WATCH OVER PRETTY THINGS SHE COULD NEVER POSSESS.
YES... I FEEL SORRY FOR HER, SUPERMAN.
BUT I FEEL MORE SORRY FOR HER VICTIMS.
20

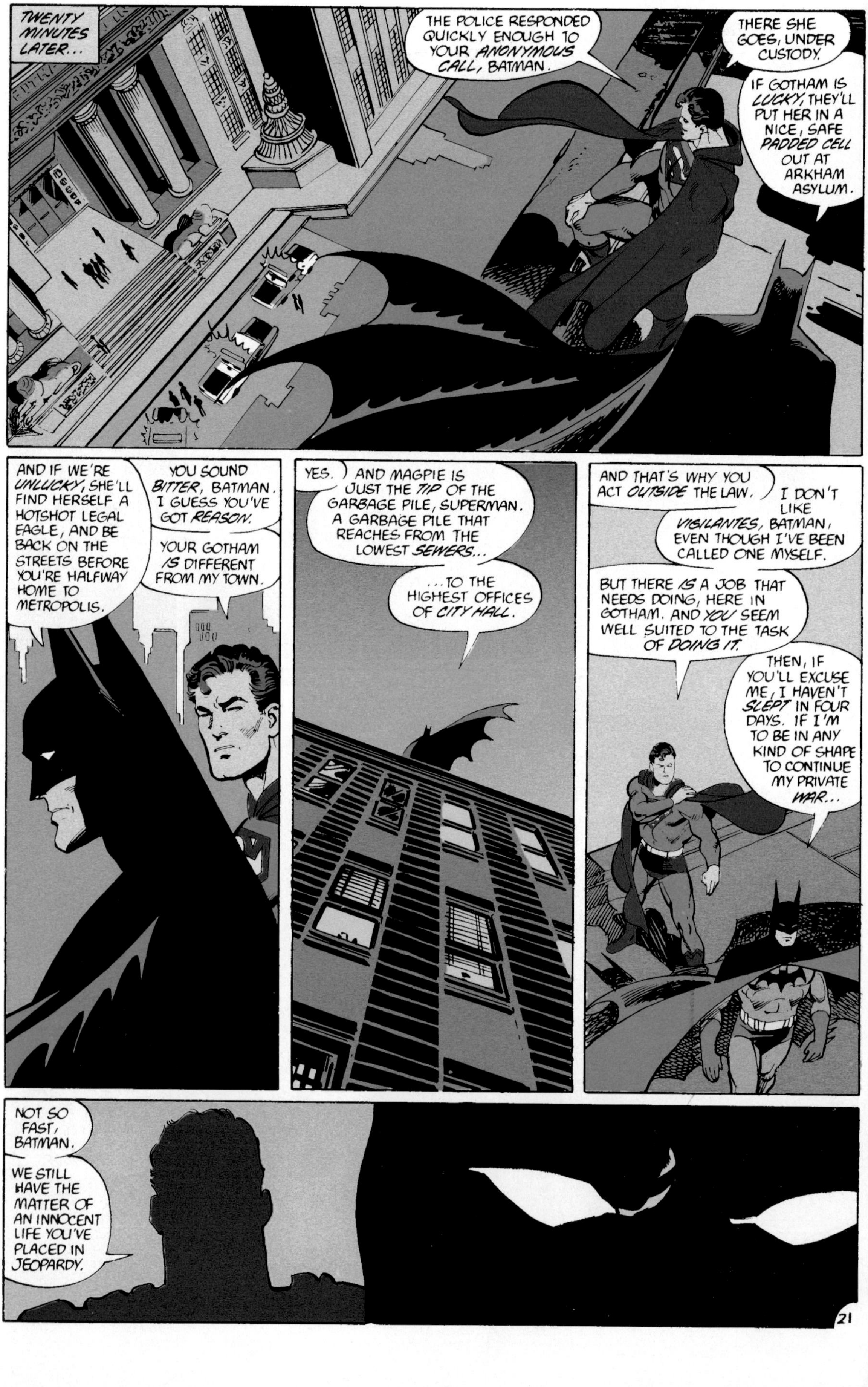
TWENTY MINUTES LATER...
THE POLICE RESPONDED QUICKLY ENOUGH TO YOUR ANONYMOUS CALL, BATMAN.
THERE SHE GOES, UNDER CUSTODY.
IF GOTHAM IS LUCKY, THEY'LL PUT HER IN A NICE, SAFE PADDED CELL OUT AT ARKHAM ASYLUM.
AND IF WE'RE UNLUCKY, SHE'LL FIND HERSELF A HOTSHOT LEGAL EAGLE, AND BE BACK ON THE STREETS BEFORE YOU'RE HALFWAY HOME TO METROPOLIS.
YOU SOUND BITTER, BATMAN. I GUESS YOU'VE GOT REASON.
YOUR GOTHAM IS DIFFERENT FROM MY TOWN.
YES.
AND MAGPIE IS JUST THE TIP OF THE GARBAGE PILE, SUPERMAN. A GARBAGE PILE THAT REACHES FROM THE LOWEST SEWERS...
...TO THE HIGHEST OFFICES OF CITY HALL.
AND THAT'S WHY YOU ACT OUTSIDE THE LAW.
I DON'T LIKE VIGILANTES, BATMAN, EVEN THOUGH I'VE BEEN CALLED ONE MYSELF.
BUT THERE IS A JOB THAT NEEDS DOING, HERE IN GOTHAM. AND YOU SEEM WELL SUITED TO THE TASK OF DOING IT.
THEN, IF YOU'LL EXCUSE ME, I HAVEN'T SLEPT IN FOUR DAYS. IF I'M TO BE IN ANY KIND OF SHAPE TO CONTINUE MY PRIVATE WAR...
NOT SO FAST, BATMAN.
WE STILL HAVE THE MATTER OF AN INNOCENT LIFE YOU'VE PLACED IN JEOPARDY.

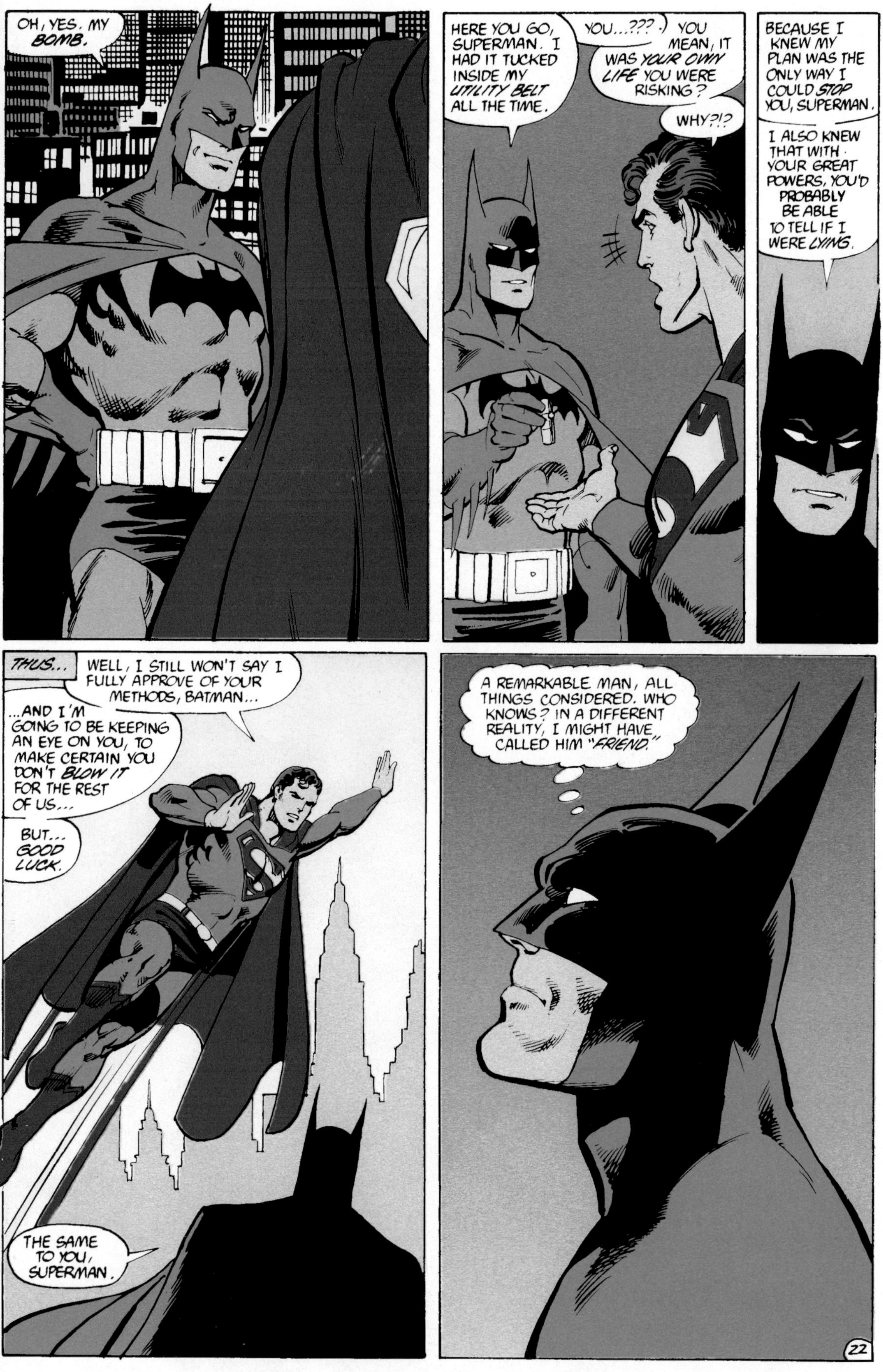
OH, YES. MY *BOMB*.
HERE YOU GO, SUPERMAN. I HAD IT TUCKED INSIDE MY *UTILITY BELT* ALL THE TIME.
YOU...???
YOU MEAN, IT WAS *YOUR OWN LIFE* YOU WERE RISKING?
WHY?!?
BECAUSE I KNEW MY PLAN WAS THE ONLY WAY I COULD *STOP* YOU, SUPERMAN.
I ALSO KNEW THAT WITH YOUR GREAT POWERS, YOU'D PROBABLY BE ABLE TO TELL IF I WERE *LYING*.
THUS...
WELL, I STILL WON'T SAY I FULLY APPROVE OF YOUR METHODS, BATMAN...
...AND I'M GOING TO BE KEEPING AN EYE ON YOU, TO MAKE CERTAIN YOU DON'T *BLOW IT* FOR THE REST OF US...
BUT... *GOOD LUCK*.
THE SAME TO YOU, SUPERMAN.
A REMARKABLE MAN, ALL THINGS CONSIDERED. WHO KNOWS? IN A DIFFERENT REALITY, I MIGHT HAVE CALLED HIM *"FRIEND."*

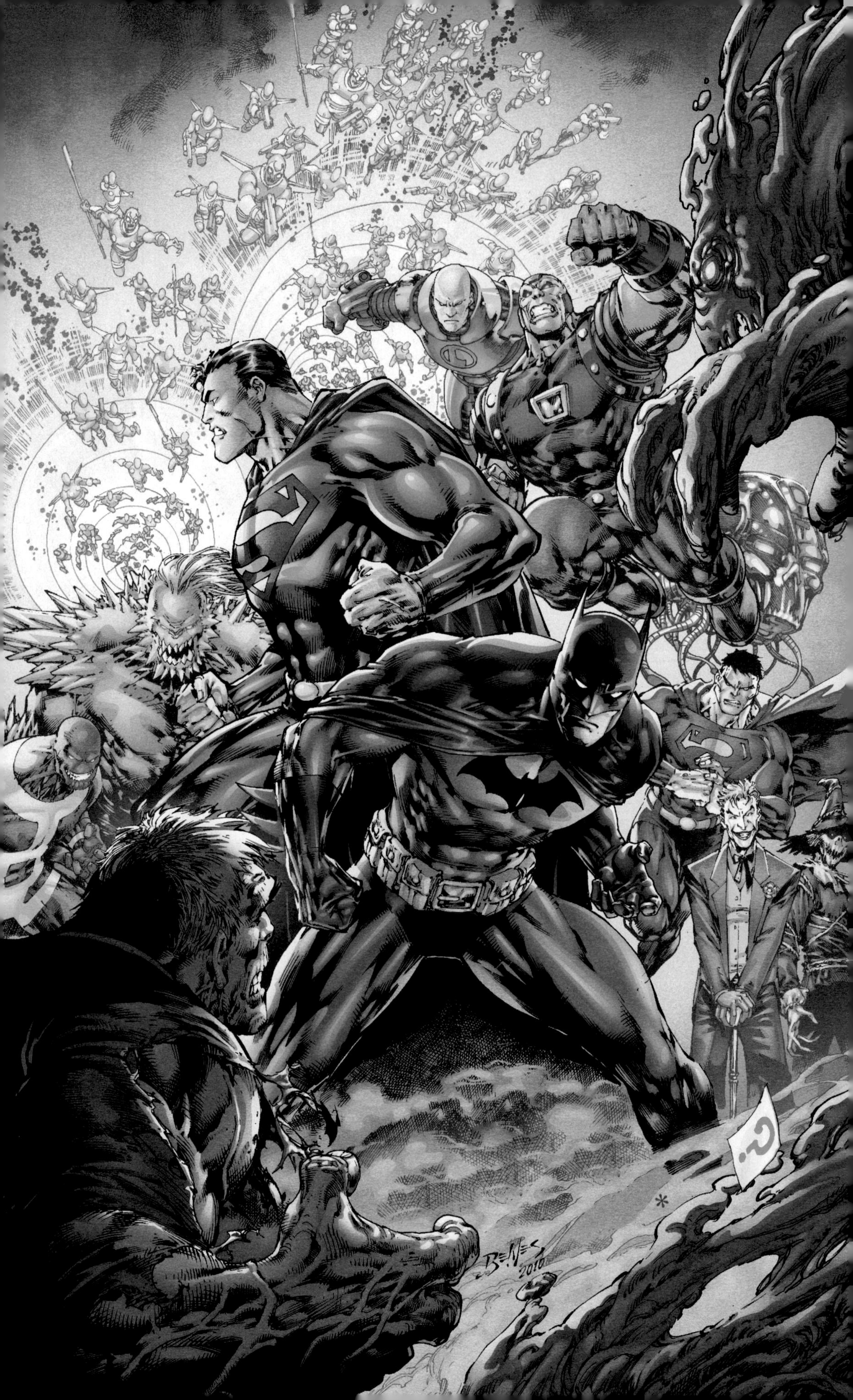
BENES
2010

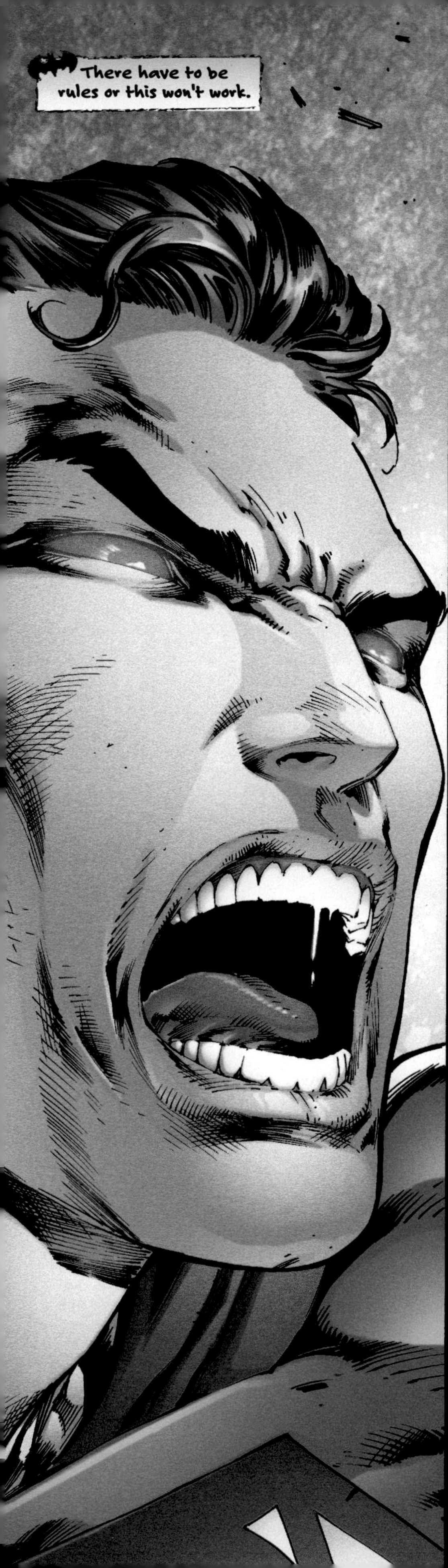
There have to be rules or this won't work.

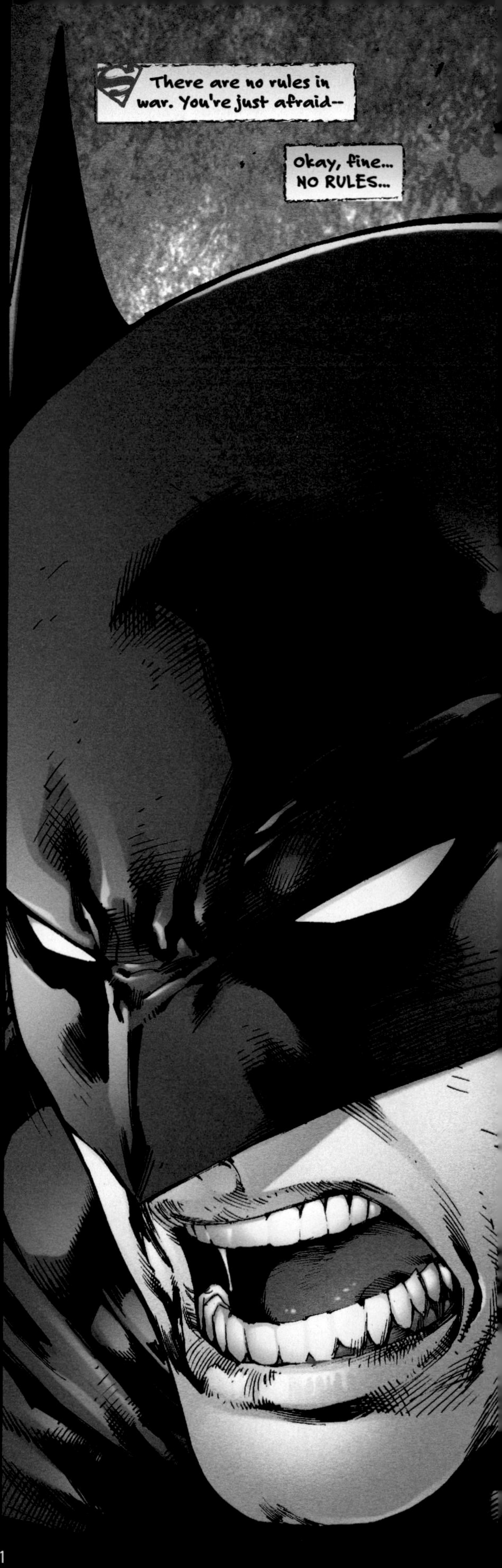
There are no rules in war. You're just afraid--
Okay, fine... NO RULES...

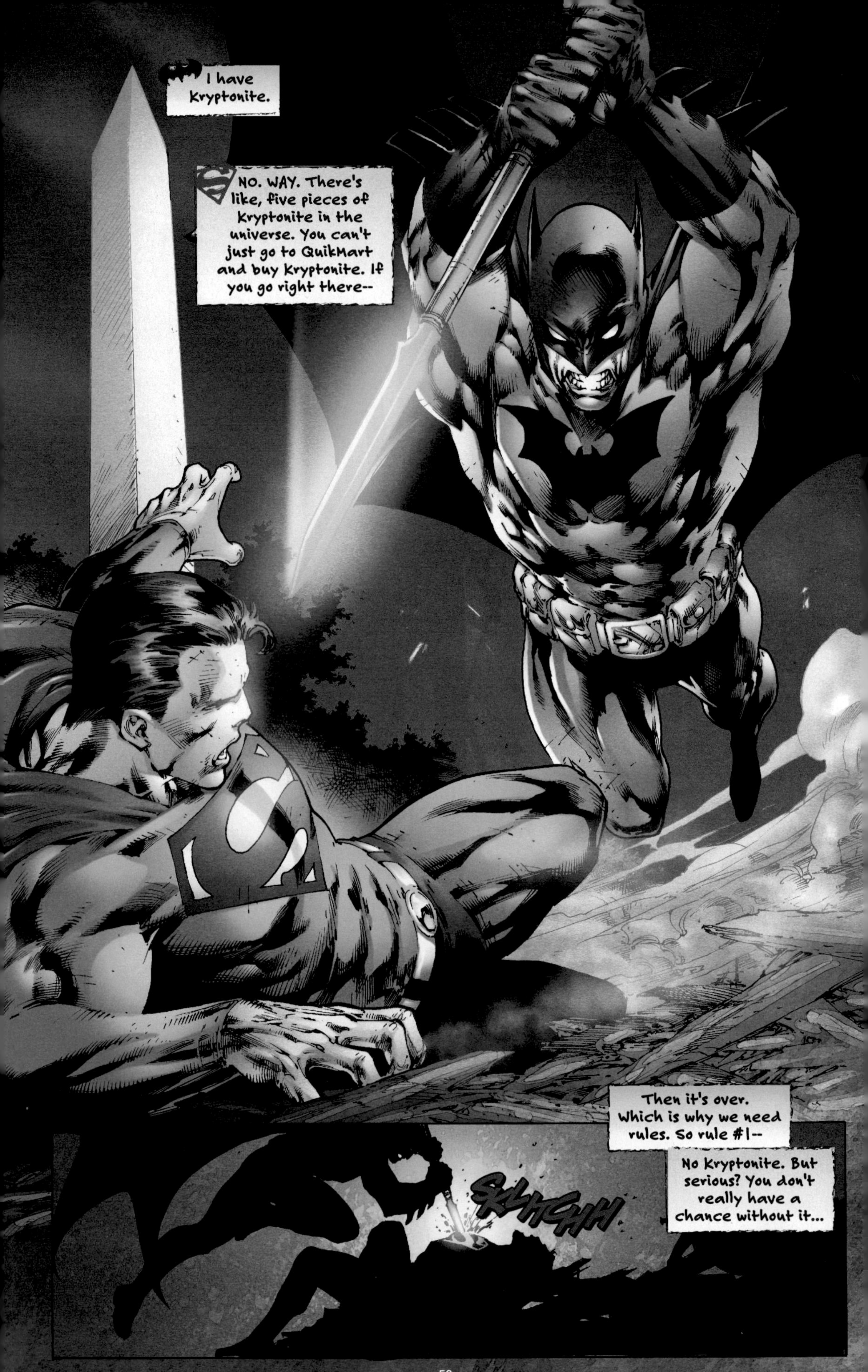

I have Kryptonite.
NO. WAY. There's like, five pieces of Kryptonite in the universe. You can't just go to QuikMart and buy Kryptonite. If you go right there--
Then it's over. Which is why we need rules. So rule #1--
SKLITCHH
No Kryptonite. But serious? You don't really have a chance without it...

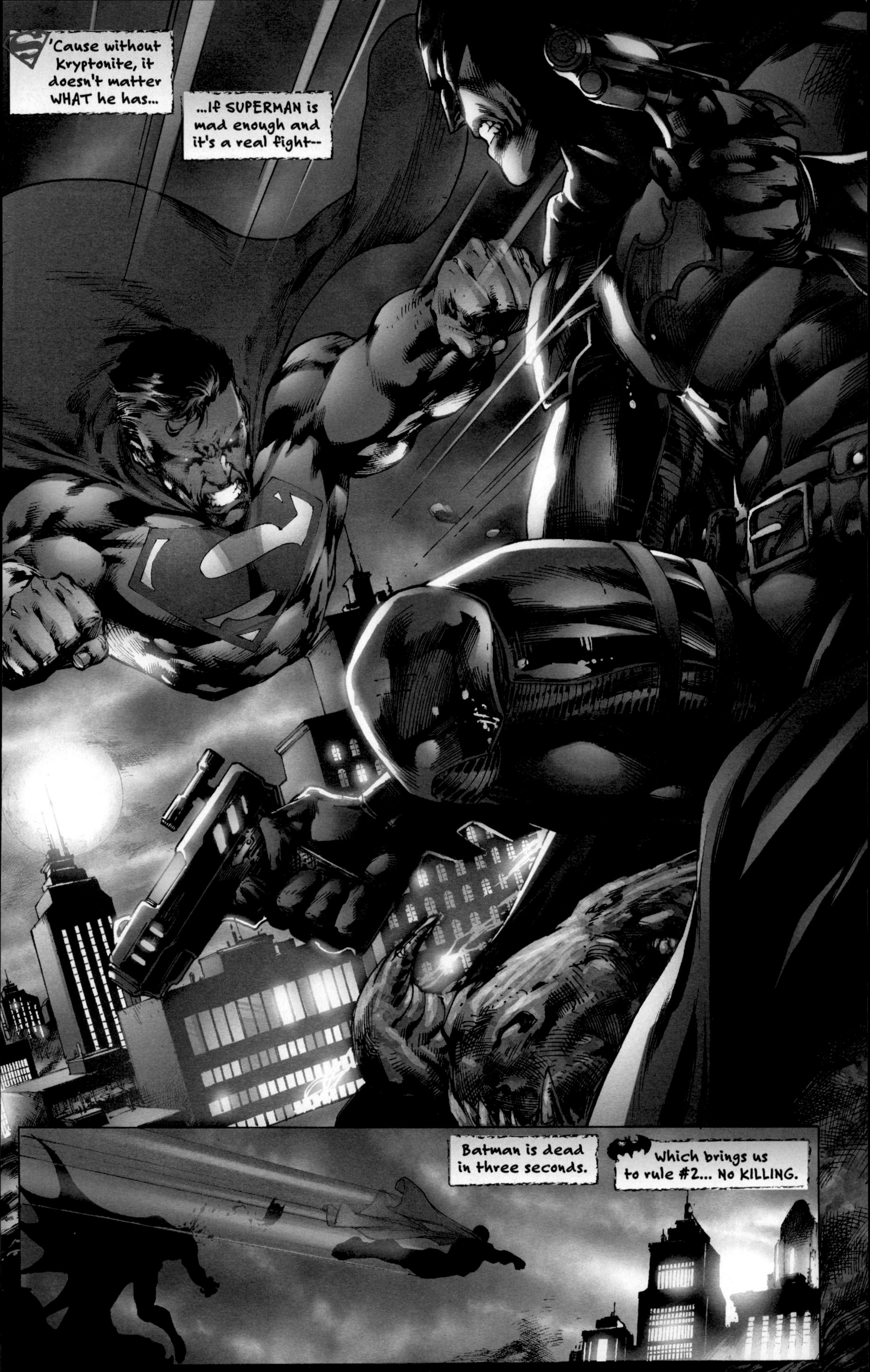
'Cause without Kryptonite, it doesn't matter WHAT he has...
...If SUPERMAN is mad enough and it's a real fight--
Batman is dead in three seconds.
Which brings us to rule #2... No KILLING.

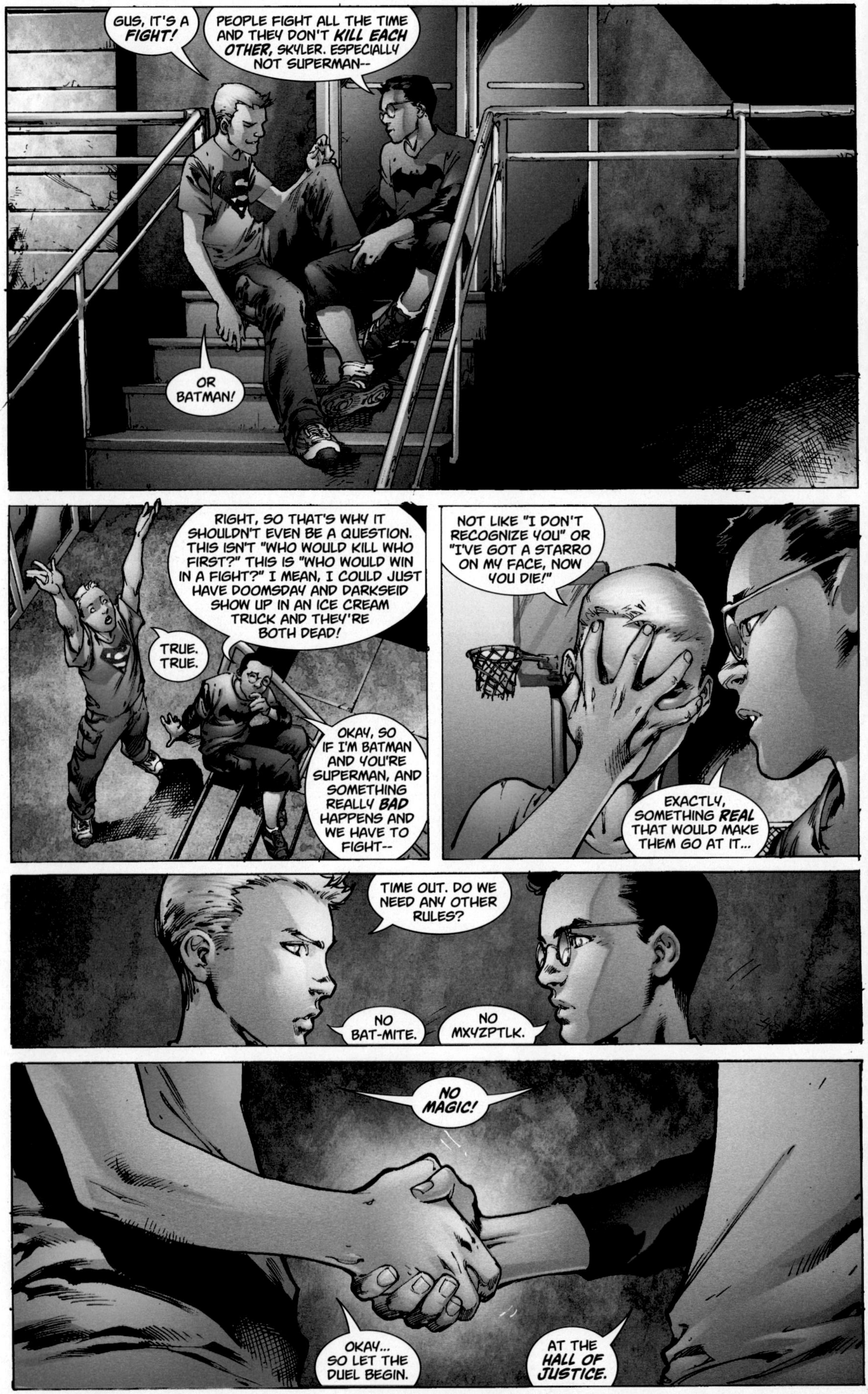
GUS, IT'S A FIGHT!
PEOPLE FIGHT ALL THE TIME AND THEY DON'T KILL EACH OTHER, SKYLER. ESPECIALLY NOT SUPERMAN--
OR BATMAN!
RIGHT, SO THAT'S WHY IT SHOULDN'T EVEN BE A QUESTION. THIS ISN'T "WHO WOULD KILL WHO FIRST?" THIS IS "WHO WOULD WIN IN A FIGHT?" I MEAN, I COULD JUST HAVE DOOMSDAY AND DARKSEID SHOW UP IN AN ICE CREAM TRUCK AND THEY'RE BOTH DEAD!
TRUE. TRUE.
OKAY, SO IF I'M BATMAN AND YOU'RE SUPERMAN, AND SOMETHING REALLY BAD HAPPENS AND WE HAVE TO FIGHT--
NOT LIKE "I DON'T RECOGNIZE YOU" OR "I'VE GOT A STARRO ON MY FACE, NOW YOU DIE!"
EXACTLY, SOMETHING REAL THAT WOULD MAKE THEM GO AT IT...
TIME OUT. DO WE NEED ANY OTHER RULES?
NO BAT-MITE.
NO MXYZPTLK.
NO MAGIC!
OKAY... SO LET THE DUEL BEGIN.
AT THE HALL OF JUSTICE.

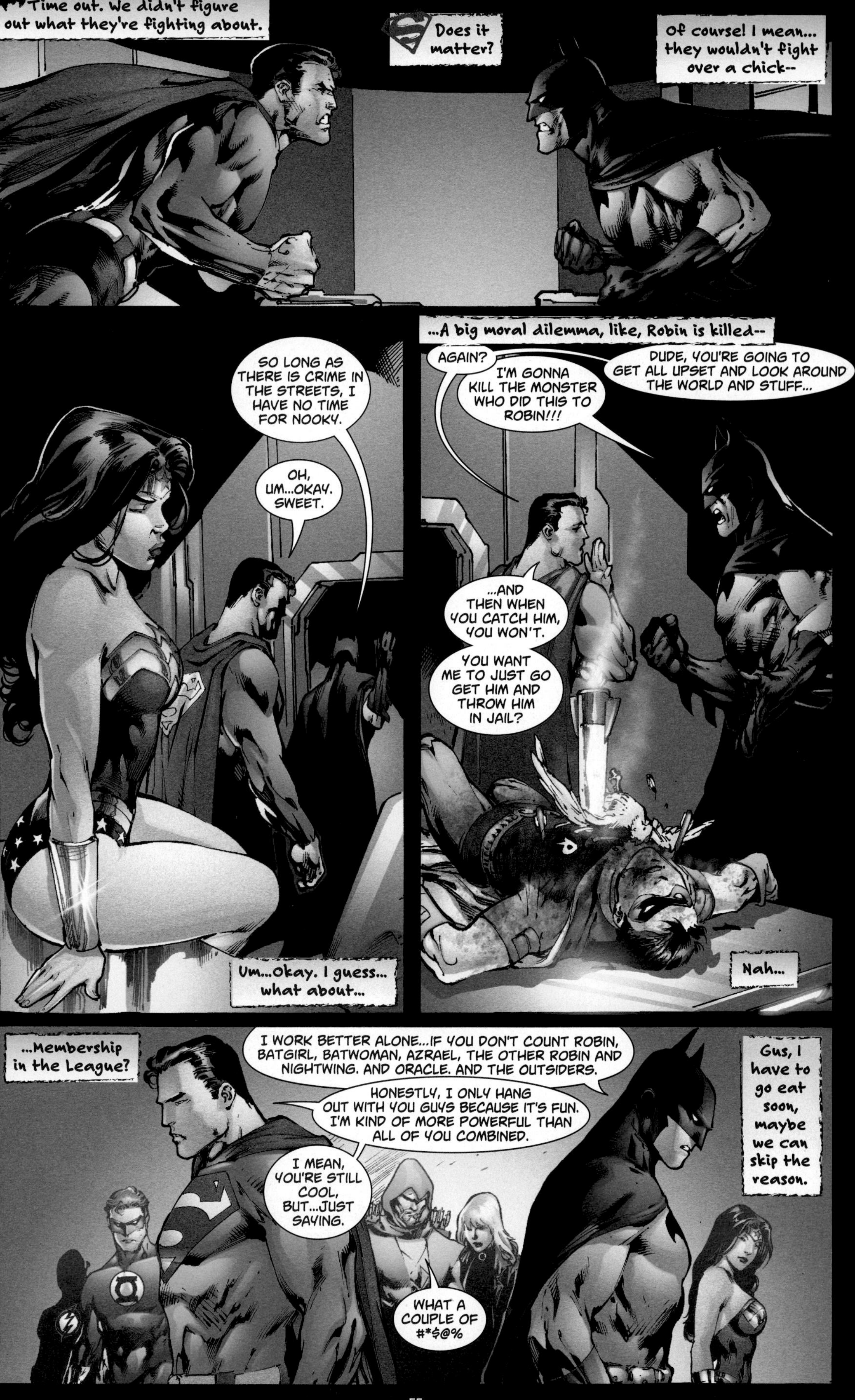
Time out. We didn't figure out what they're fighting about.
Does it matter?
Of course! I mean... they wouldn't fight over a chick--
SO LONG AS THERE IS CRIME IN THE STREETS, I HAVE NO TIME FOR NOOKY.
OH, UM...OKAY. SWEET.
Um...Okay. I guess... what about...
...A big moral dilemma, like, Robin is killed--
AGAIN?
I'M GONNA KILL THE MONSTER WHO DID THIS TO ROBIN!!!
DUDE, YOU'RE GOING TO GET ALL UPSET AND LOOK AROUND THE WORLD AND STUFF...
...AND THEN WHEN YOU CATCH HIM, YOU WON'T.
YOU WANT ME TO JUST GO GET HIM AND THROW HIM IN JAIL?
Nah...
...Membership in the League?
I WORK BETTER ALONE...IF YOU DON'T COUNT ROBIN, BATGIRL, BATWOMAN, AZRAEL, THE OTHER ROBIN AND NIGHTWING. AND ORACLE. AND THE OUTSIDERS.
HONESTLY, I ONLY HANG OUT WITH YOU GUYS BECAUSE IT'S FUN. I'M KIND OF MORE POWERFUL THAN ALL OF YOU COMBINED.
I MEAN, YOU'RE STILL COOL, BUT...JUST SAYING.
WHAT A COUPLE OF #*$@%
Gus, I have to go eat soon, maybe we can skip the reason.

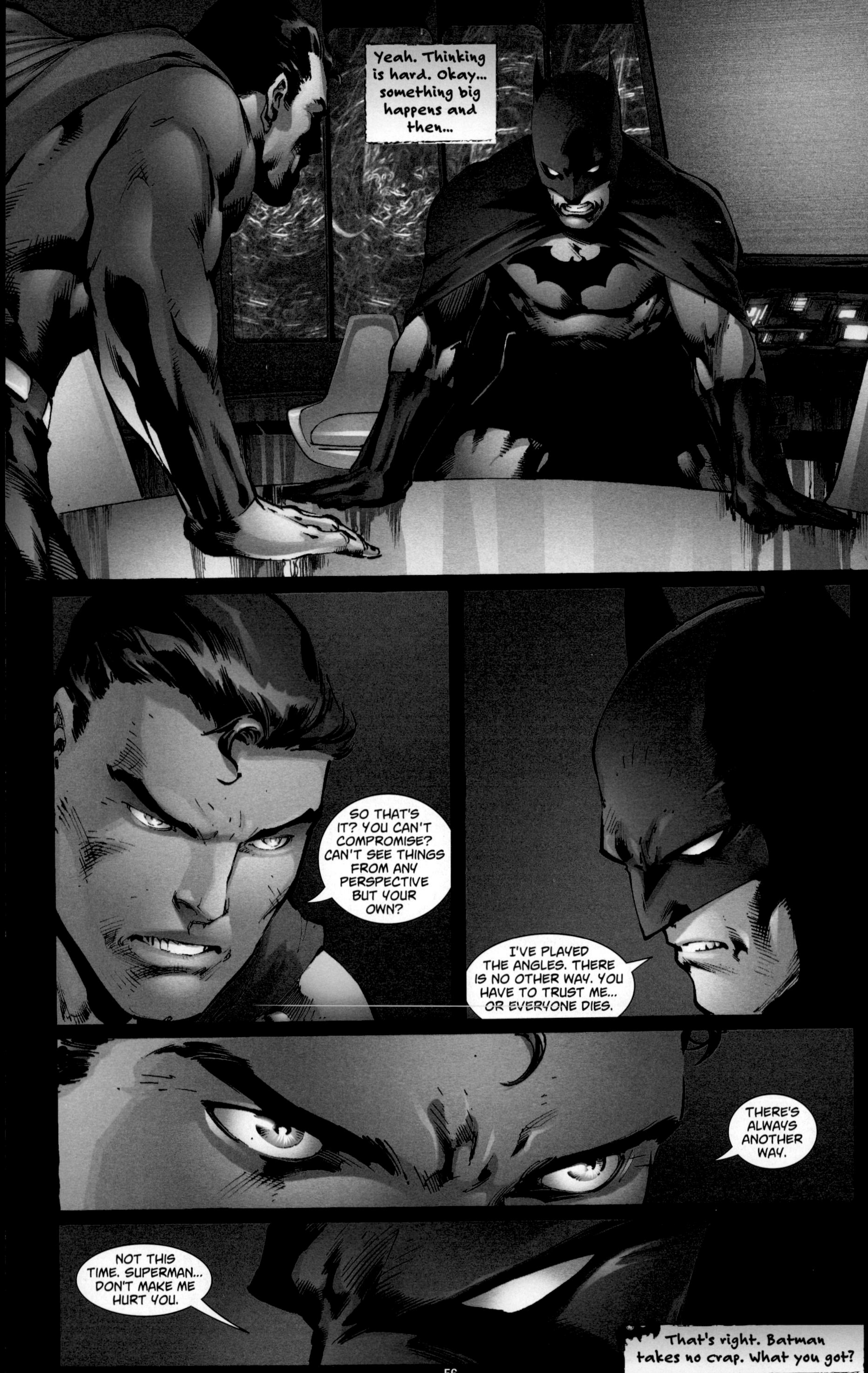

Yeah. Thinking is hard. Okay... something big happens and then...
SO THAT'S IT? YOU CAN'T COMPROMISE? CAN'T SEE THINGS FROM ANY PERSPECTIVE BUT YOUR OWN?
I'VE PLAYED THE ANGLES. THERE IS NO OTHER WAY. YOU HAVE TO TRUST ME... OR EVERYONE DIES.
THERE'S ALWAYS ANOTHER WAY.
NOT THIS TIME. SUPERMAN... DON'T MAKE ME HURT YOU.
That's right. Batman takes no crap. What you got?

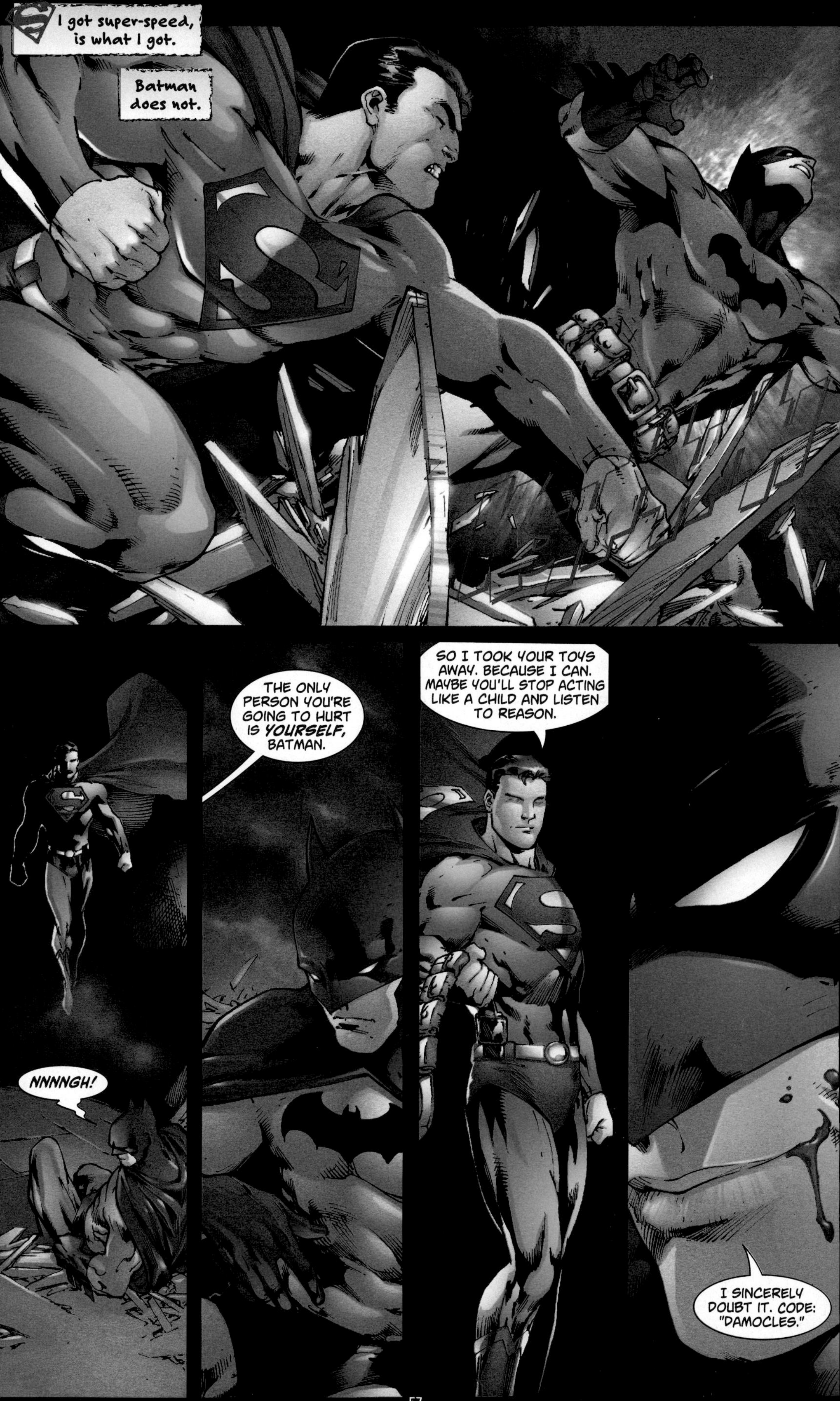
I got super-speed, is what I got.
Batman does not.
THE ONLY PERSON YOU'RE GOING TO HURT IS *YOURSELF*, BATMAN.
NNNNGH!
SO I TOOK YOUR TOYS AWAY. BECAUSE I CAN. MAYBE YOU'LL STOP ACTING LIKE A CHILD AND LISTEN TO REASON.
I SINCERELY DOUBT IT. CODE: "DAMOCLES."

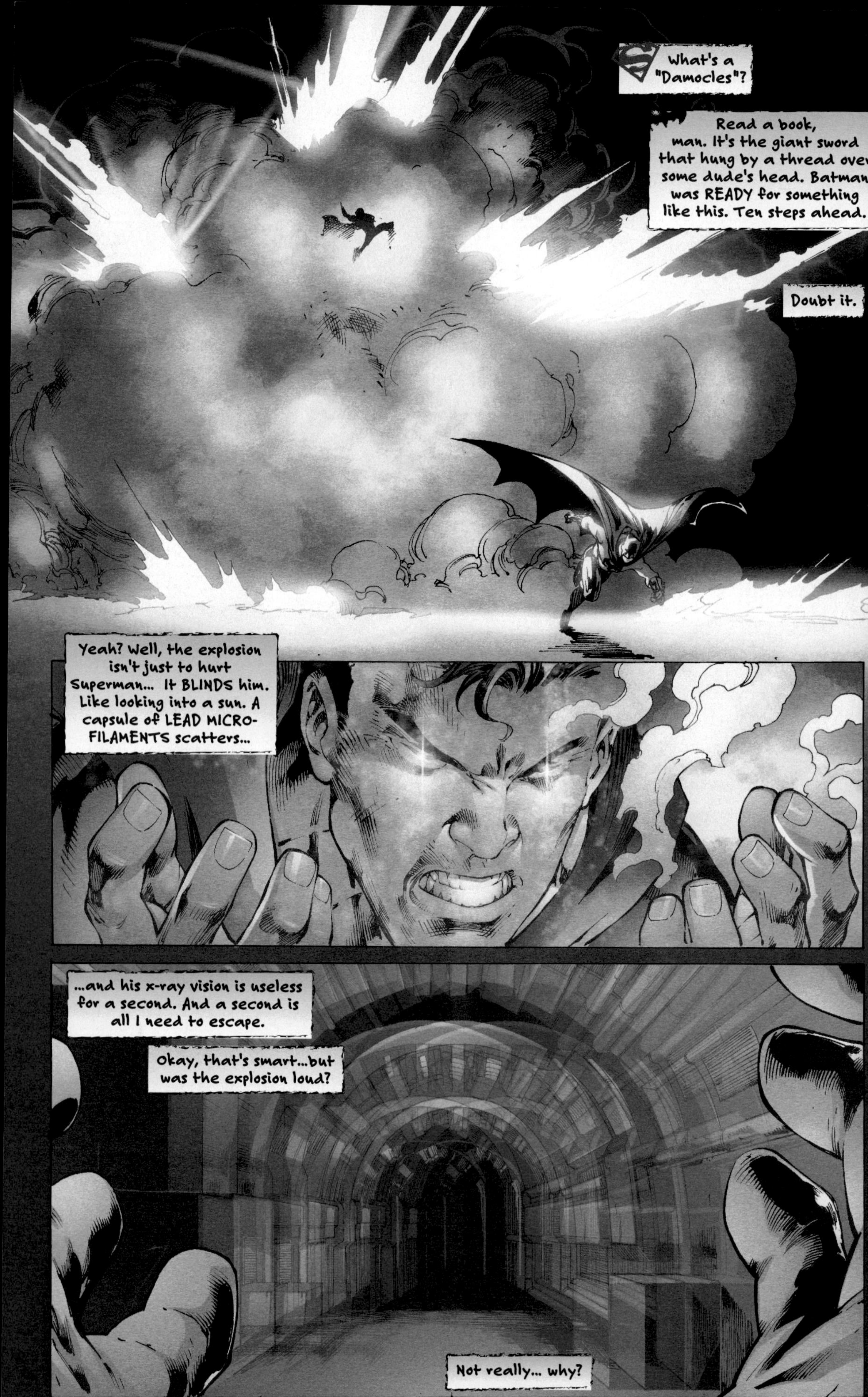
What's a "Damocles"?
Read a book, man. It's the giant sword that hung by a thread over some dude's head. Batman was READY for something like this. Ten steps ahead.
Doubt it.
Yeah? Well, the explosion isn't just to hurt Superman... It BLINDS him. Like looking into a sun. A capsule of LEAD MICRO-FILAMENTS scatters...
...and his x-ray vision is useless for a second. And a second is all I need to escape.
Okay, that's smart...but was the explosion loud?
Not really... why?

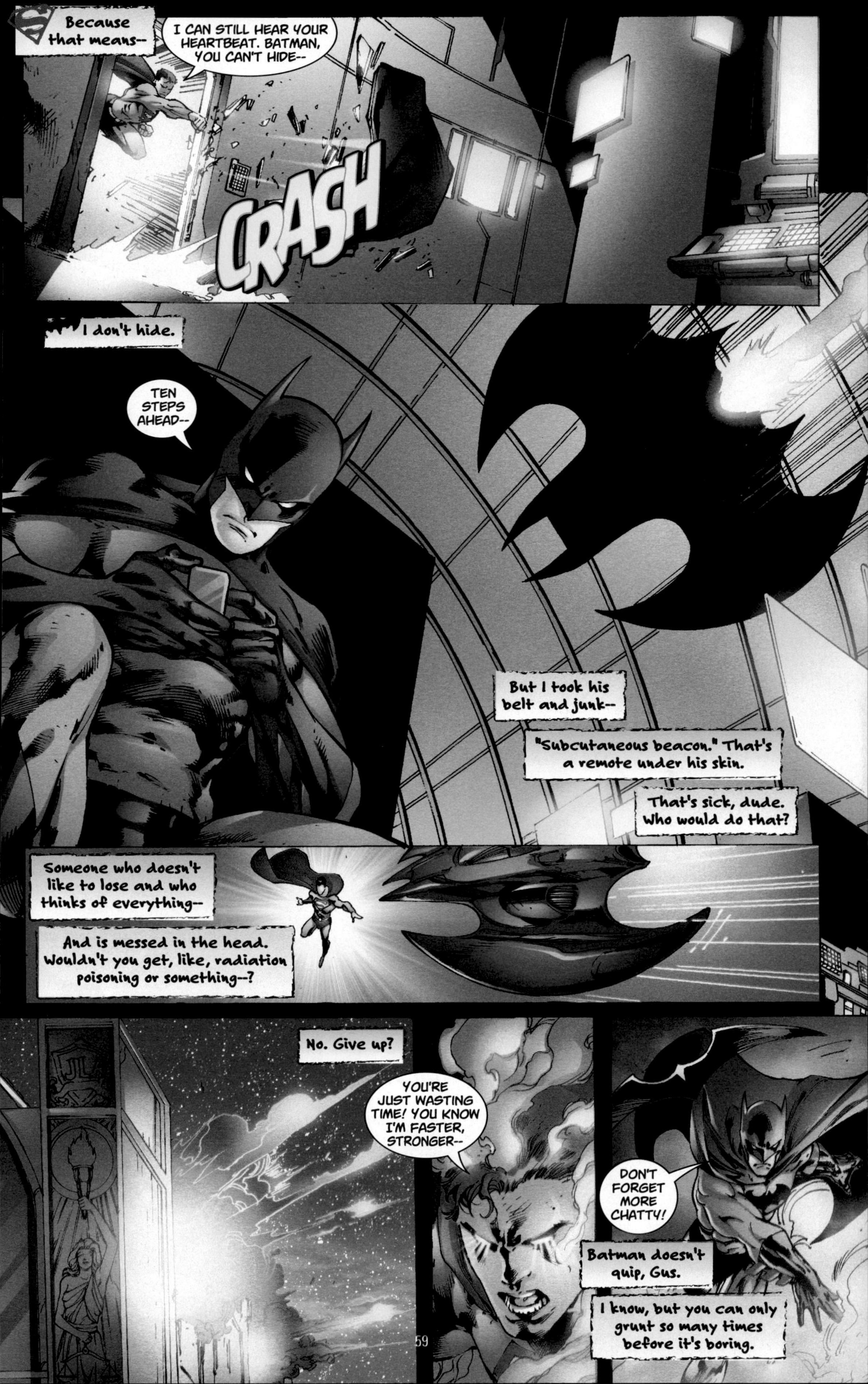
Because that means--
I CAN STILL HEAR YOUR HEARTBEAT. BATMAN, YOU CAN'T HIDE--
CRASH
I don't hide.
TEN STEPS AHEAD--
But I took his belt and junk--
"Subcutaneous beacon." That's a remote under his skin.
That's sick, dude. Who would do that?
Someone who doesn't like to lose and who thinks of everything--
And is messed in the head. Wouldn't you get, like, radiation poisoning or something--?
No. Give up?
YOU'RE JUST WASTING TIME! YOU KNOW I'M FASTER, STRONGER--
DON'T FORGET MORE CHATTY!
Batman doesn't quip, Gus.
I know, but you can only grunt so many times before it's boring.

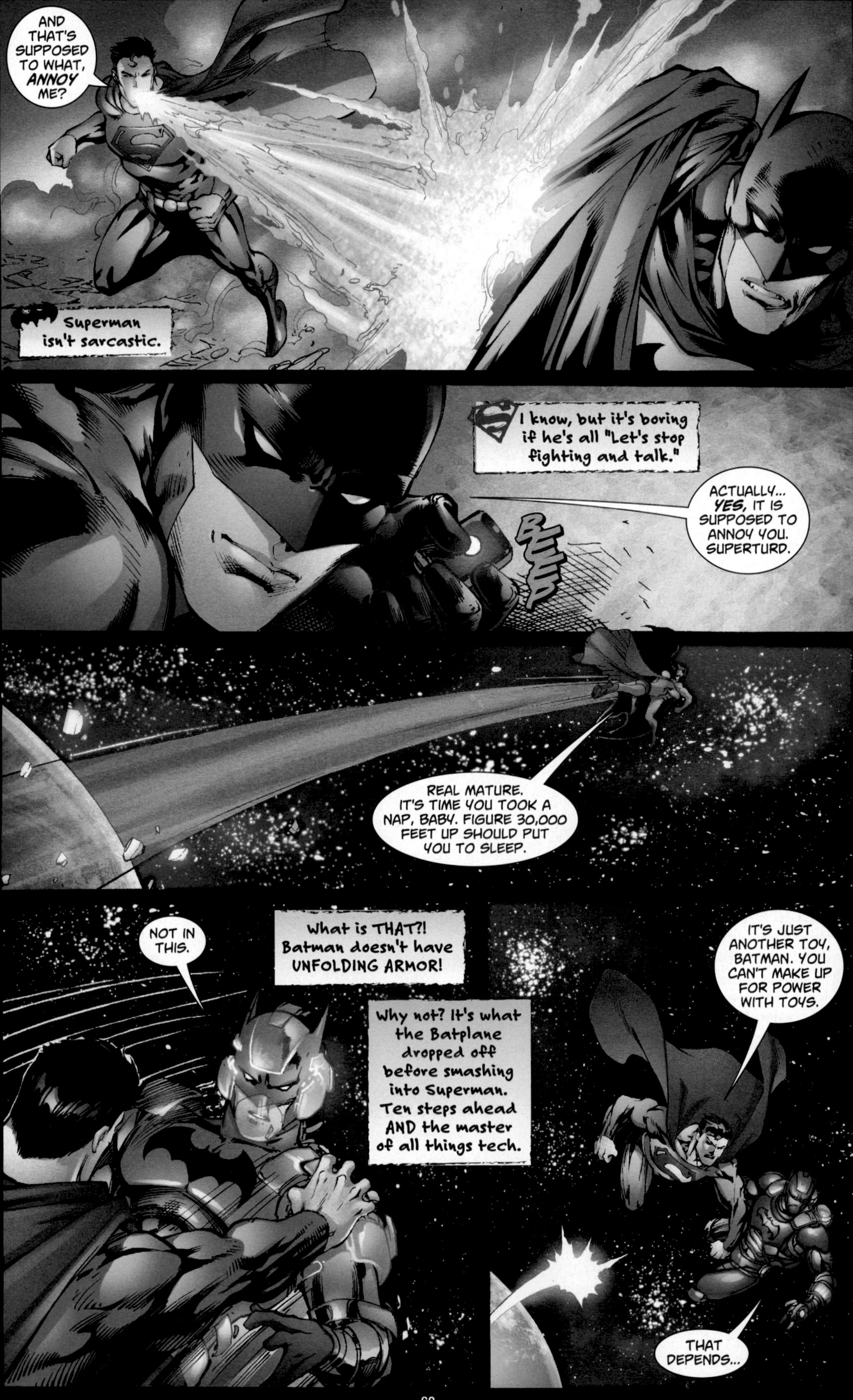
AND THAT'S SUPPOSED TO WHAT, ANNOY ME?
Superman isn't sarcastic.
I know, but it's boring if he's all "Let's stop fighting and talk."
ACTUALLY... YES, IT IS SUPPOSED TO ANNOY YOU. SUPERTURD.
BEEP
REAL MATURE. IT'S TIME YOU TOOK A NAP, BABY. FIGURE 30,000 FEET UP SHOULD PUT YOU TO SLEEP.
NOT IN THIS.
What is THAT?! Batman doesn't have UNFOLDING ARMOR!
Why not? It's what the Batplane dropped off before smashing into Superman. Ten steps ahead AND the master of all things tech.
IT'S JUST ANOTHER TOY, BATMAN. YOU CAN'T MAKE UP FOR POWER WITH TOYS.
THAT DEPENDS...

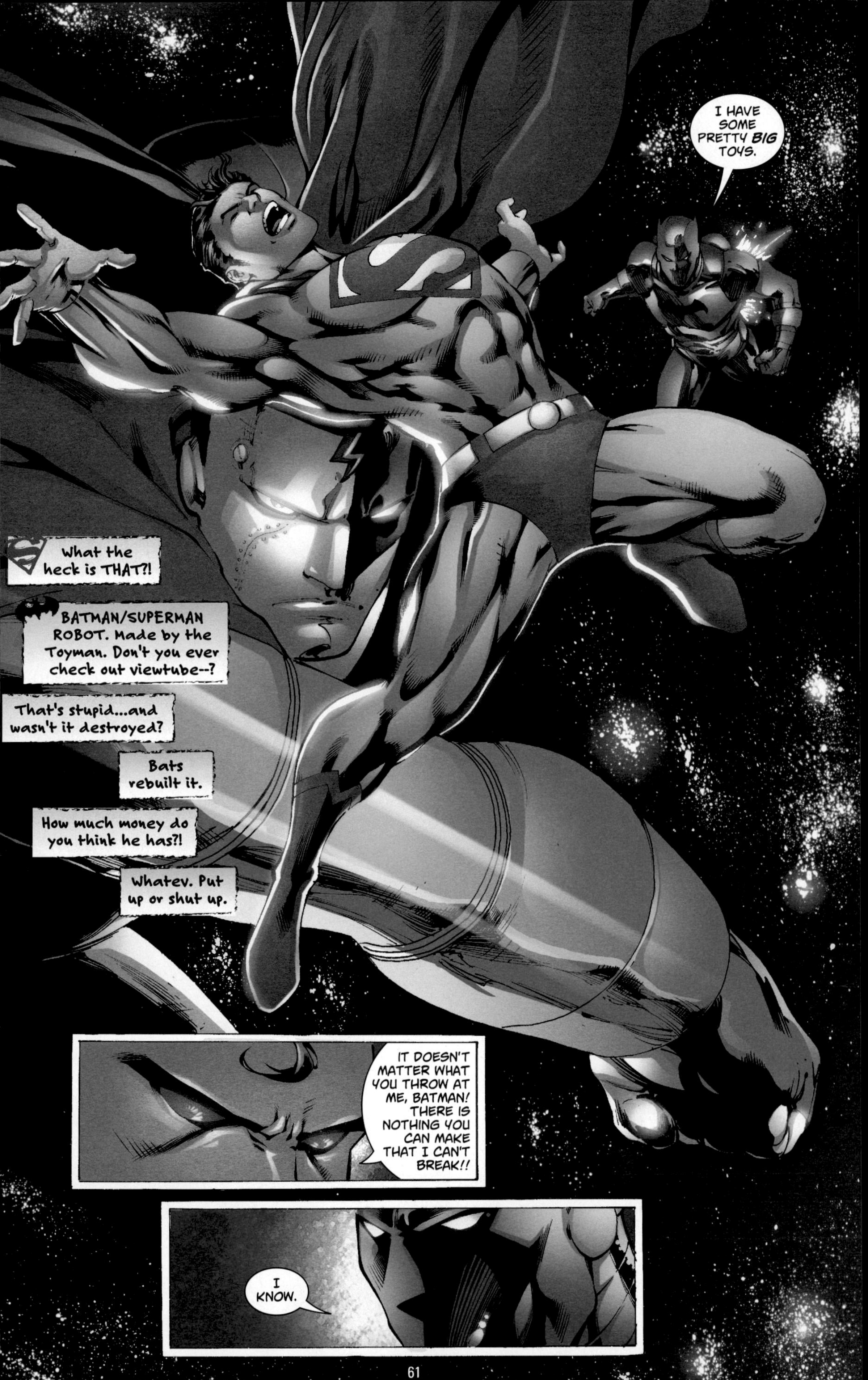

I HAVE SOME PRETTY BIG TOYS.
What the heck is THAT?!
BATMAN/SUPERMAN ROBOT. Made by the Toyman. Don't you ever check out viewtube--?
That's stupid...and wasn't it destroyed?
Bats rebuilt it.
How much money do you think he has?!
Whatev. Put up or shut up.
IT DOESN'T MATTER WHAT YOU THROW AT ME, BATMAN! THERE IS NOTHING YOU CAN MAKE THAT I CAN'T BREAK!!
I KNOW.

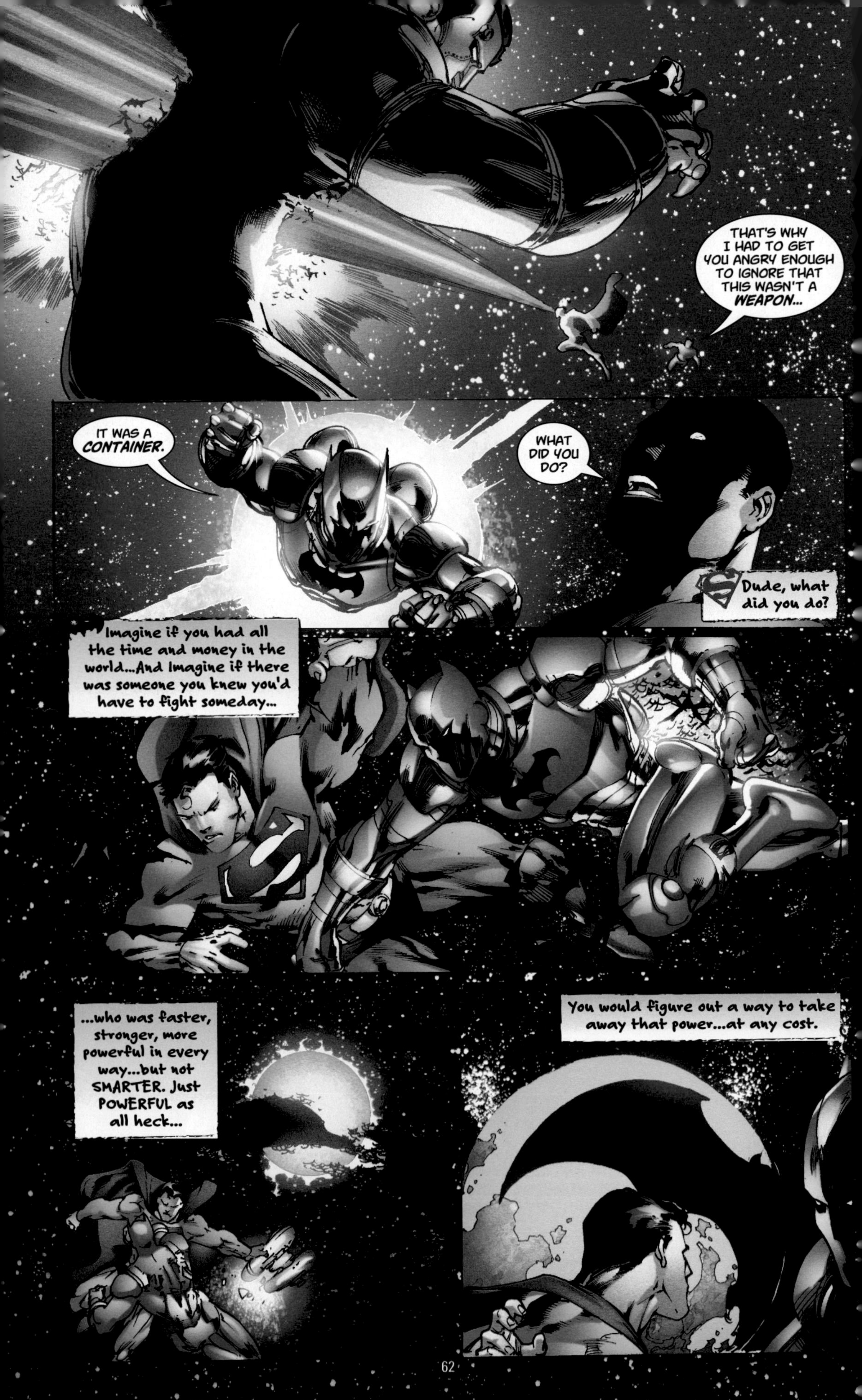

THAT'S WHY I HAD TO GET YOU ANGRY ENOUGH TO IGNORE THAT THIS WASN'T A WEAPON...
IT WAS A CONTAINER.
WHAT DID YOU DO?
Dude, what did you do?
Imagine if you had all the time and money in the world...And Imagine if there was someone you knew you'd have to fight someday...
...who was faster, stronger, more powerful in every way...but not SMARTER. Just POWERFUL as all heck...
You would figure out a way to take away that power...at any cost.

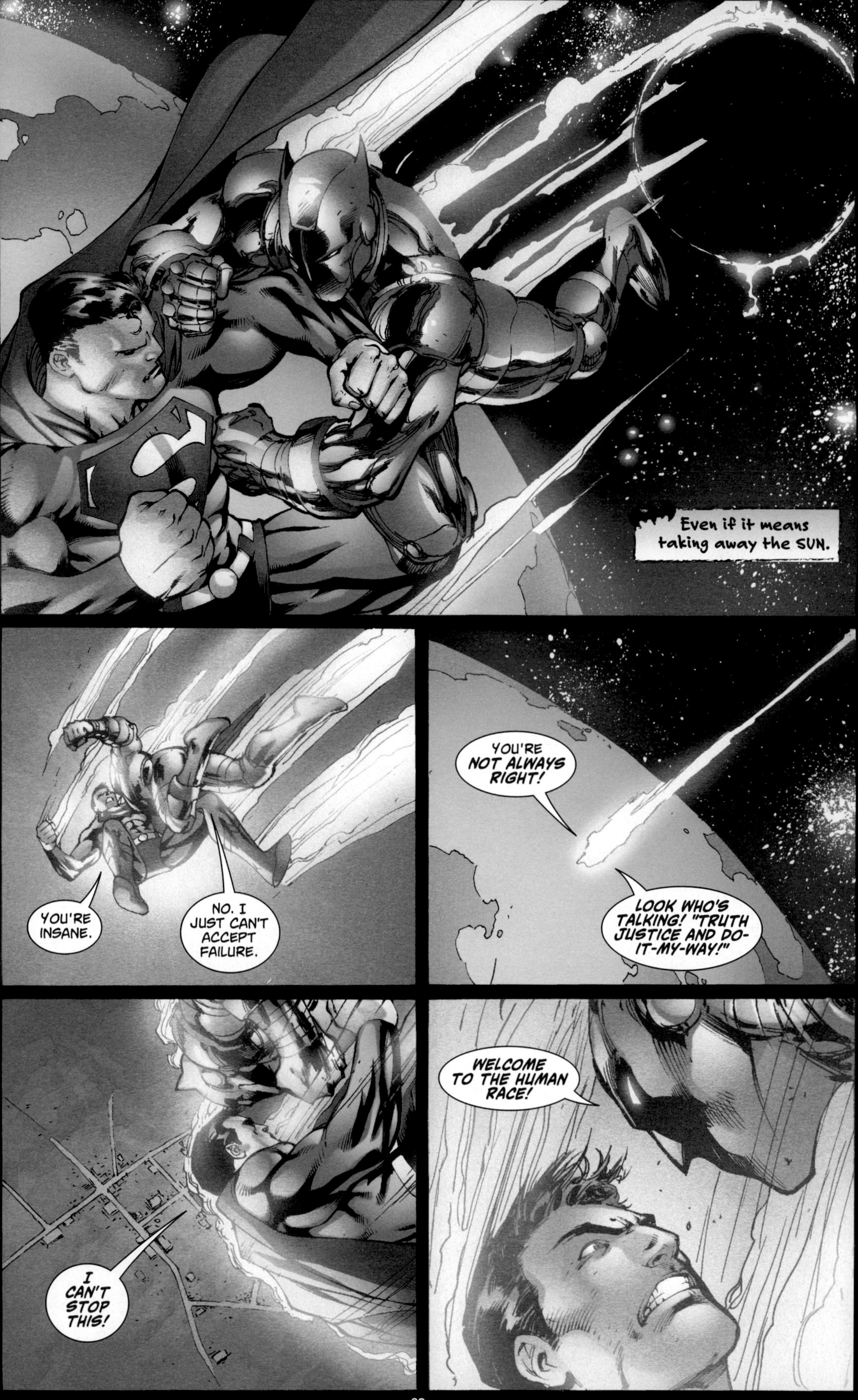
Even if it means taking away the SUN.
YOU'RE INSANE.
NO. I JUST CAN'T ACCEPT FAILURE.
YOU'RE NOT ALWAYS RIGHT!
LOOK WHO'S TALKING! "TRUTH JUSTICE AND DO-IT-MY-WAY!"
I CAN'T STOP THIS!
WELCOME TO THE HUMAN RACE!

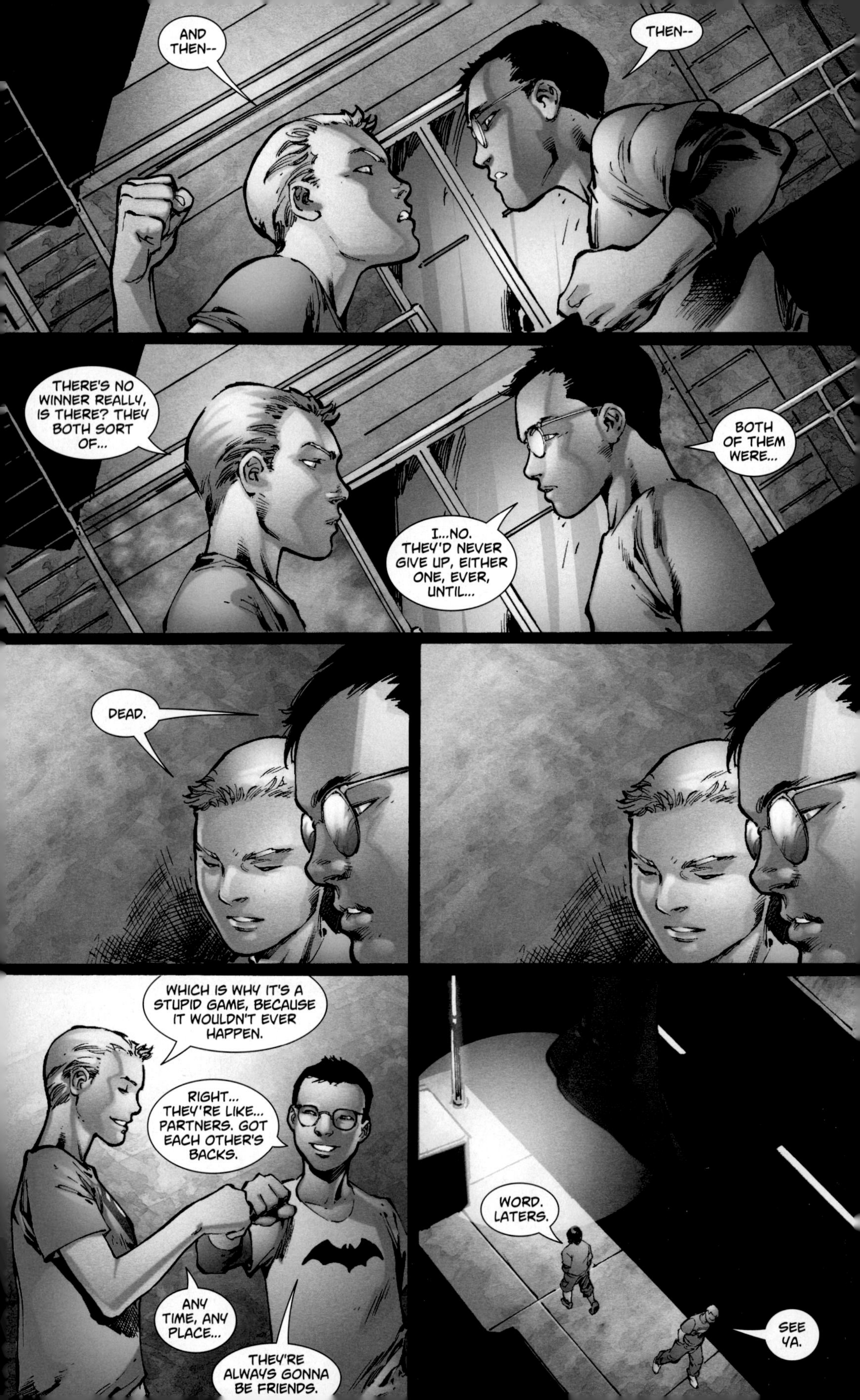
AND THEN--
THEN--
THERE'S NO WINNER REALLY, IS THERE? THEY BOTH SORT OF...
BOTH OF THEM WERE...
I...NO. THEY'D NEVER GIVE UP, EITHER ONE, EVER, UNTIL...
DEAD.
WHICH IS WHY IT'S A STUPID GAME, BECAUSE IT WOULDN'T EVER HAPPEN.
RIGHT... THEY'RE LIKE... PARTNERS. GOT EACH OTHER'S BACKS.
ANY TIME, ANY PLACE...
THEY'RE ALWAYS GONNA BE FRIENDS.
WORD. LATERS.
SEE YA.

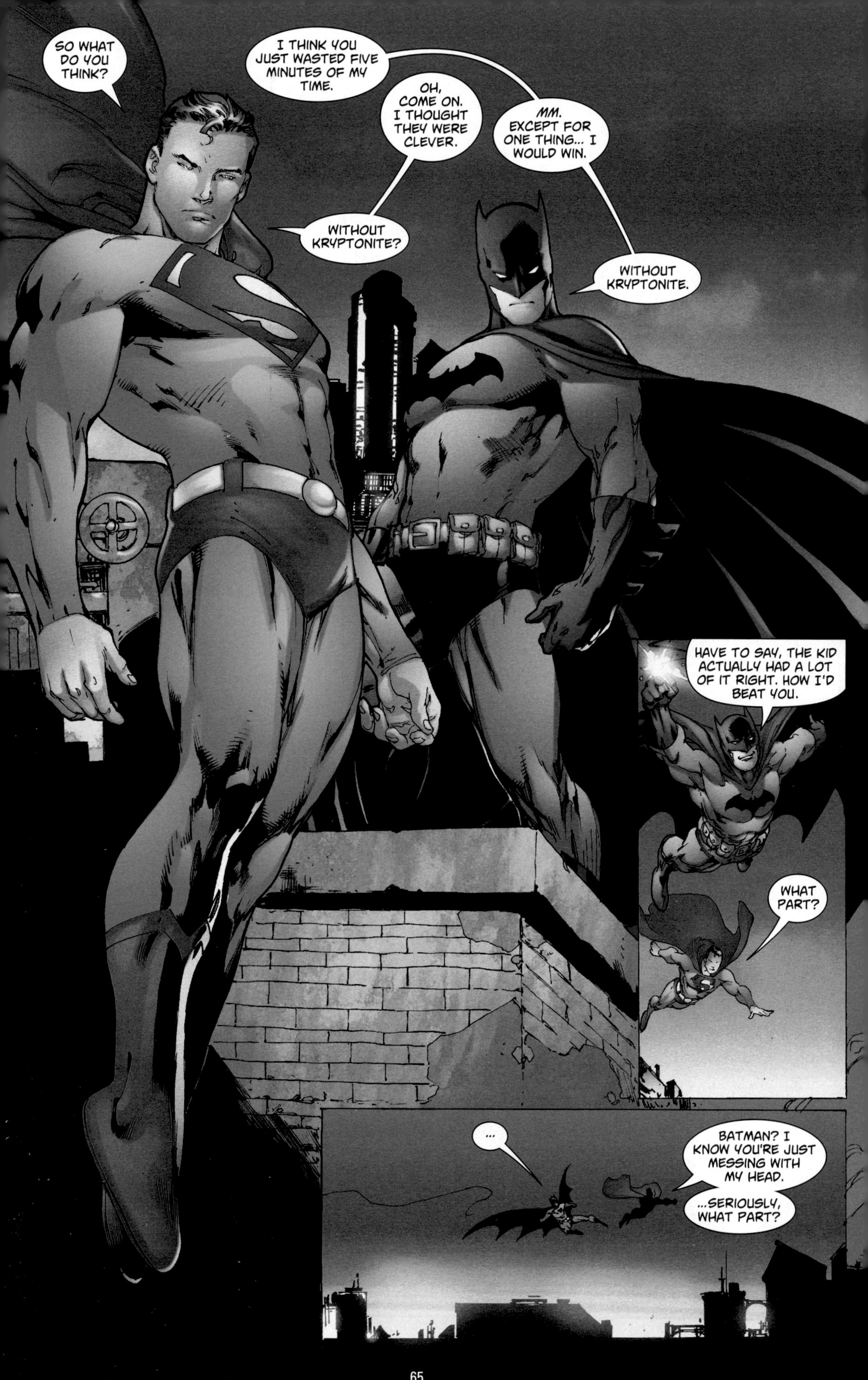
SO WHAT DO YOU THINK?
I THINK YOU JUST WASTED FIVE MINUTES OF MY TIME.
OH, COME ON. I THOUGHT THEY WERE CLEVER.
MM. EXCEPT FOR ONE THING... I WOULD WIN.
WITHOUT KRYPTONITE?
WITHOUT KRYPTONITE.
HAVE TO SAY, THE KID ACTUALLY HAD A LOT OF IT RIGHT. HOW I'D BEAT YOU.
WHAT PART?
...
BATMAN? I KNOW YOU'RE JUST MESSING WITH MY HEAD.
...SERIOUSLY, WHAT PART?

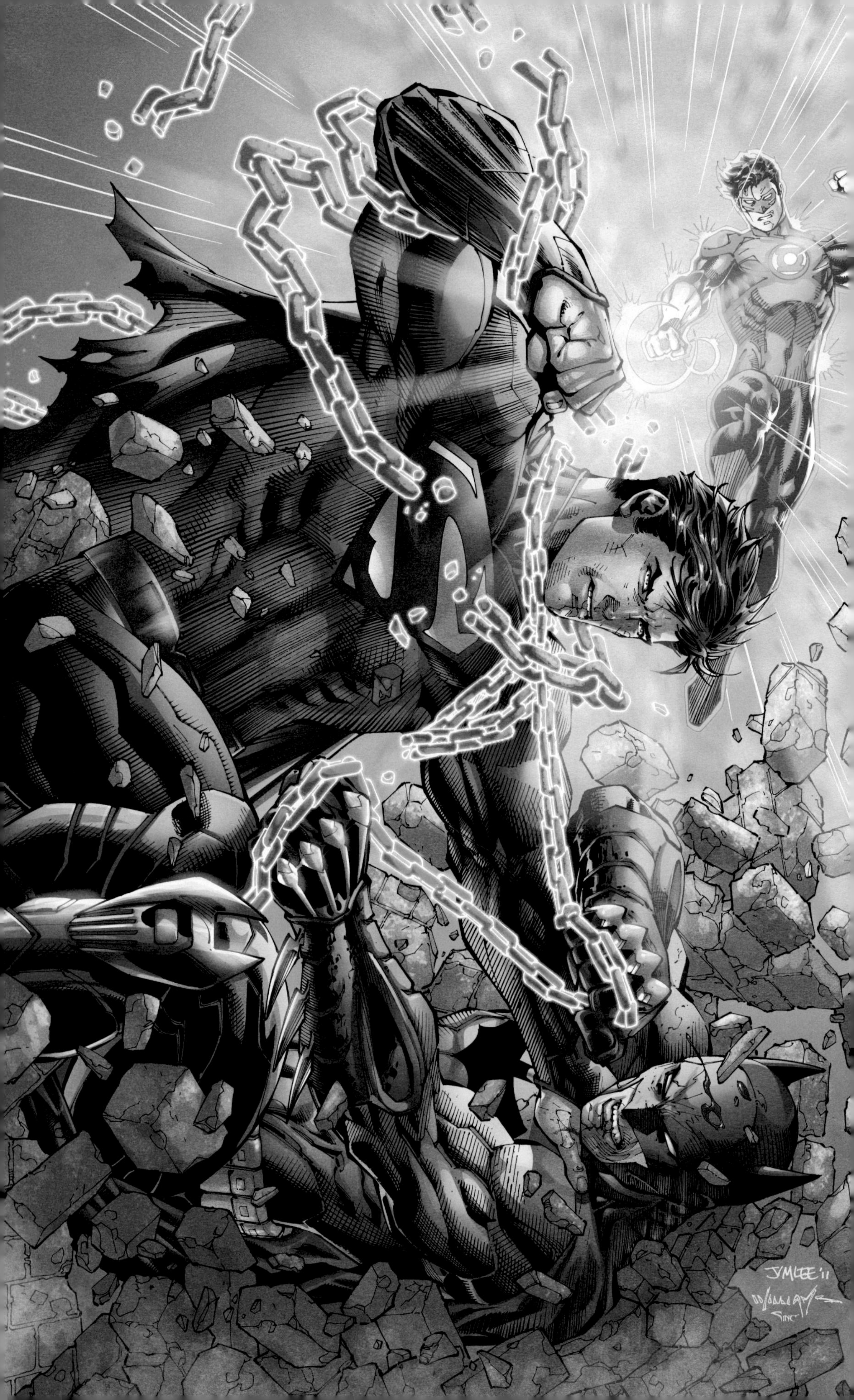
JMLEE '11

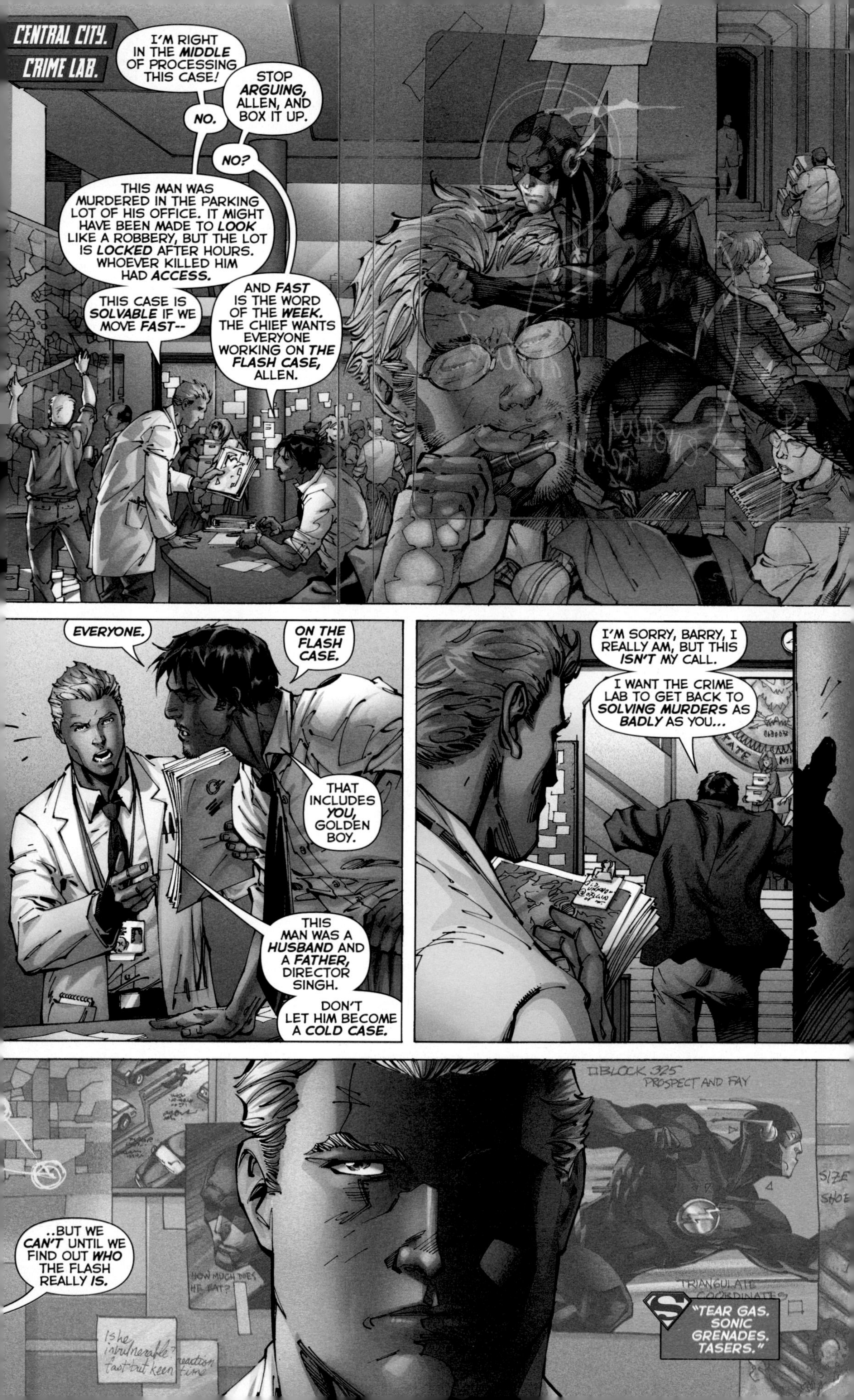
CENTRAL CITY.
CRIME LAB.
I'M RIGHT IN THE MIDDLE OF PROCESSING THIS CASE!
STOP ARGUING, ALLEN, AND BOX IT UP.
NO.
NO?
THIS MAN WAS MURDERED IN THE PARKING LOT OF HIS OFFICE. IT MIGHT HAVE BEEN MADE TO LOOK LIKE A ROBBERY, BUT THE LOT IS LOCKED AFTER HOURS. WHOEVER KILLED HIM HAD ACCESS.
THIS CASE IS SOLVABLE IF WE MOVE FAST--
AND FAST IS THE WORD OF THE WEEK. THE CHIEF WANTS EVERYONE WORKING ON THE FLASH CASE, ALLEN.
EVERYONE.
ON THE FLASH CASE.
THAT INCLUDES YOU, GOLDEN BOY.
THIS MAN WAS A HUSBAND AND A FATHER, DIRECTOR SINGH.
DON'T LET HIM BECOME A COLD CASE.
I'M SORRY, BARRY, I REALLY AM, BUT THIS ISN'T MY CALL.
I WANT THE CRIME LAB TO GET BACK TO SOLVING MURDERS AS BADLY AS YOU...
..BUT WE CAN'T UNTIL WE FIND OUT WHO THE FLASH REALLY IS.
BLOCK 325
PROSPECT AND FAY
SIZE
SHOE
HOW MUCH DOES HE EAT?
TRIANGULATE COORDINATES
"TEAR GAS. SONIC GRENADES. TASERS."

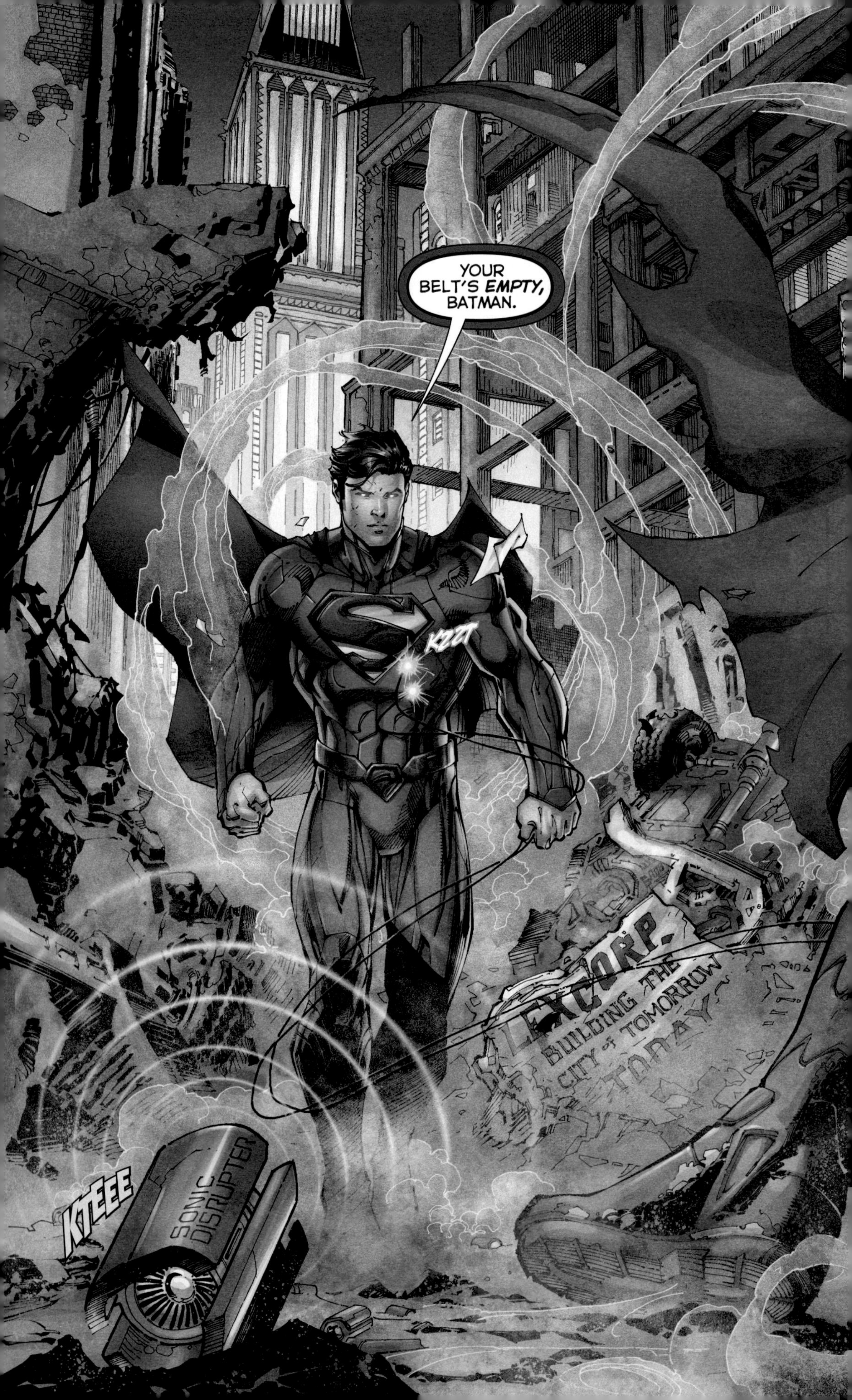
YOUR BELT'S EMPTY, BATMAN.
KZZT
LEXCORP.
BUILDING THE CITY of TOMORROW TODAY
SONIC DISRUPTER
KTEEE

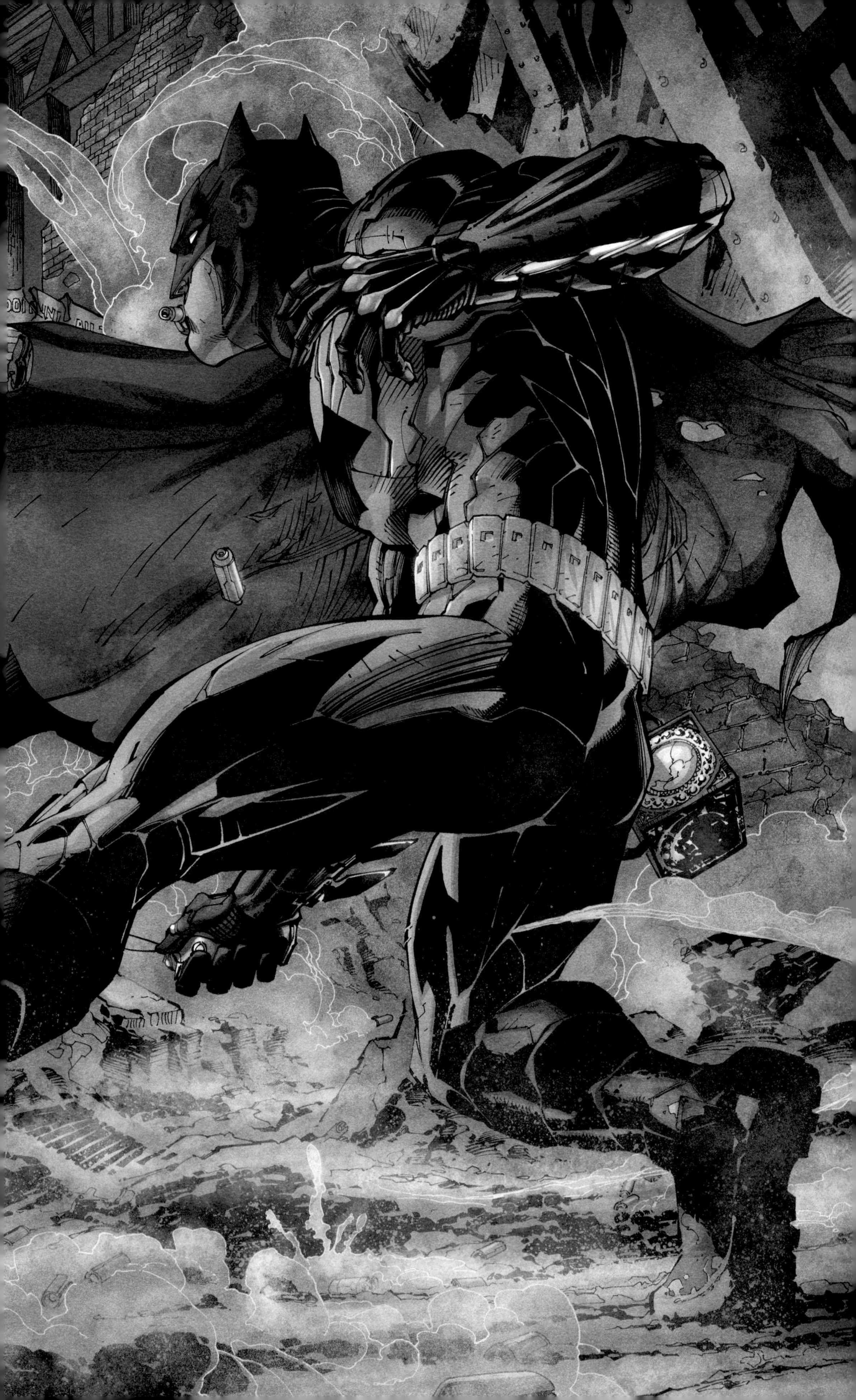

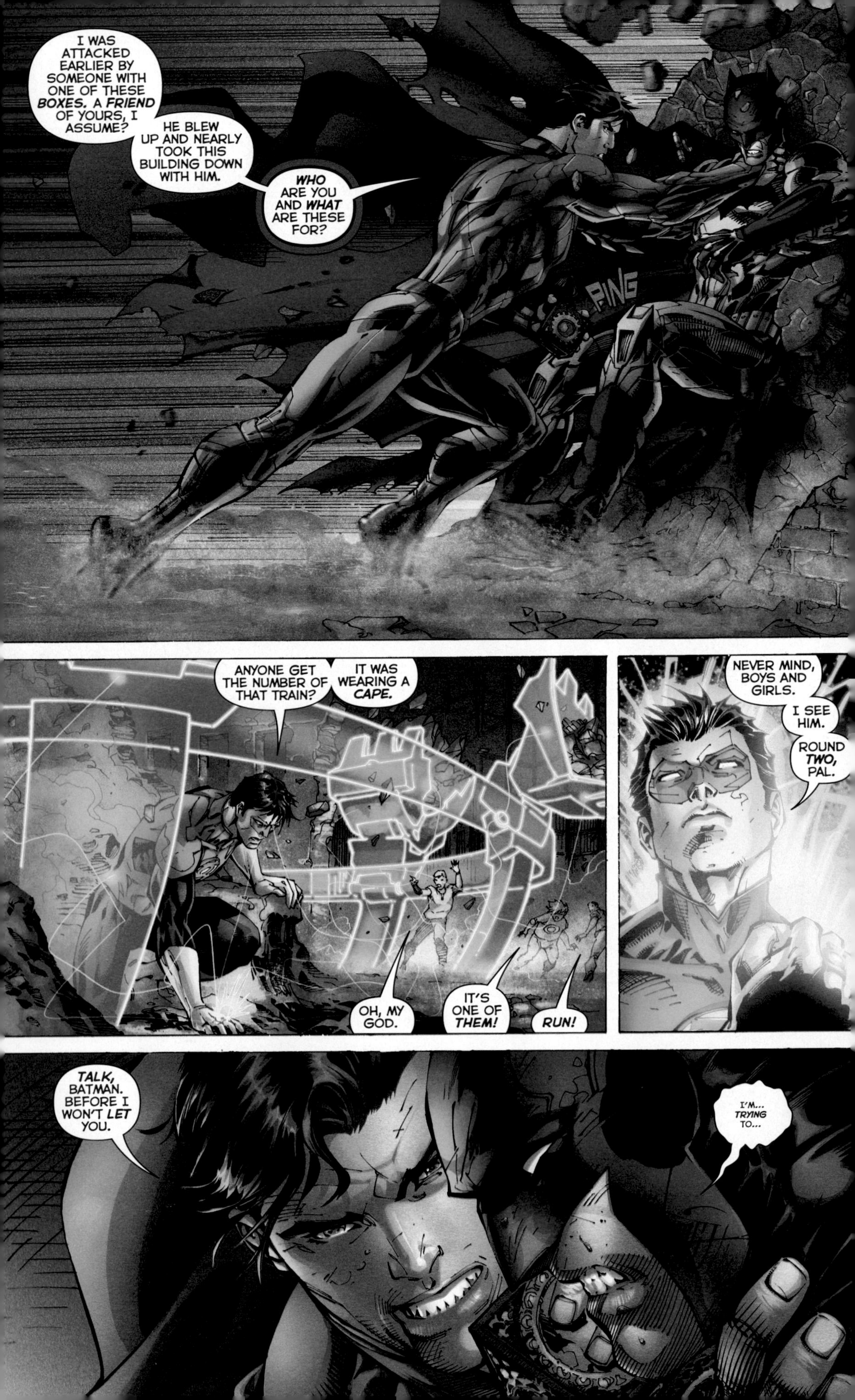
I WAS ATTACKED EARLIER BY SOMEONE WITH ONE OF THESE BOXES. A FRIEND OF YOURS, I ASSUME?
HE BLEW UP AND NEARLY TOOK THIS BUILDING DOWN WITH HIM.
WHO ARE YOU AND WHAT ARE THESE FOR?
PING
ANYONE GET THE NUMBER OF THAT TRAIN?
IT WAS WEARING A CAPE.
OH, MY GOD.
IT'S ONE OF THEM!
RUN!
NEVER MIND, BOYS AND GIRLS.
I SEE HIM.
ROUND TWO, PAL.
TALK, BATMAN. BEFORE I WON'T LET YOU.
I'M... TRYING TO...

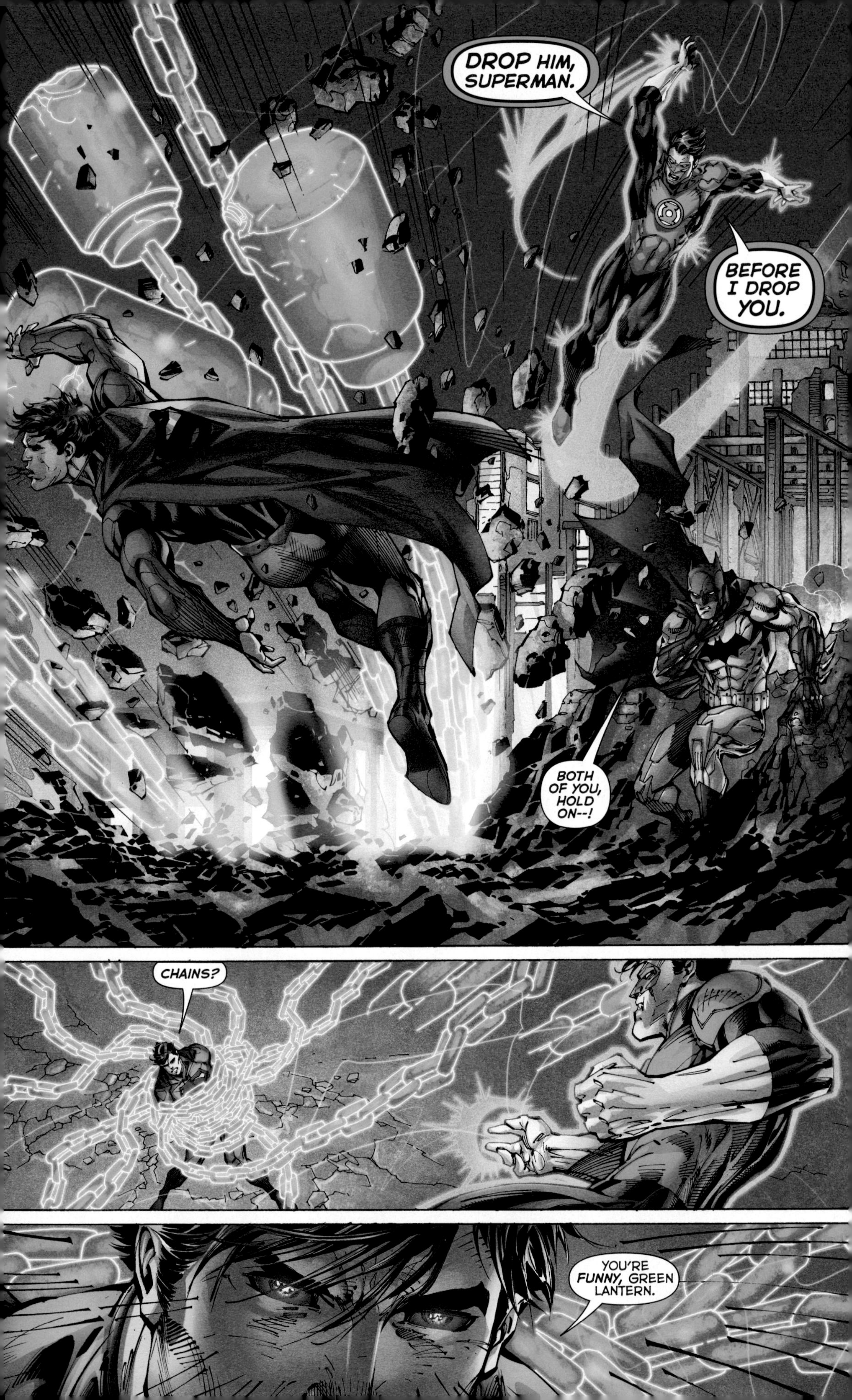
DROP HIM, SUPERMAN.
BEFORE I DROP YOU.
BOTH OF YOU, HOLD ON--!
CHAINS?
YOU'RE FUNNY, GREEN LANTERN.

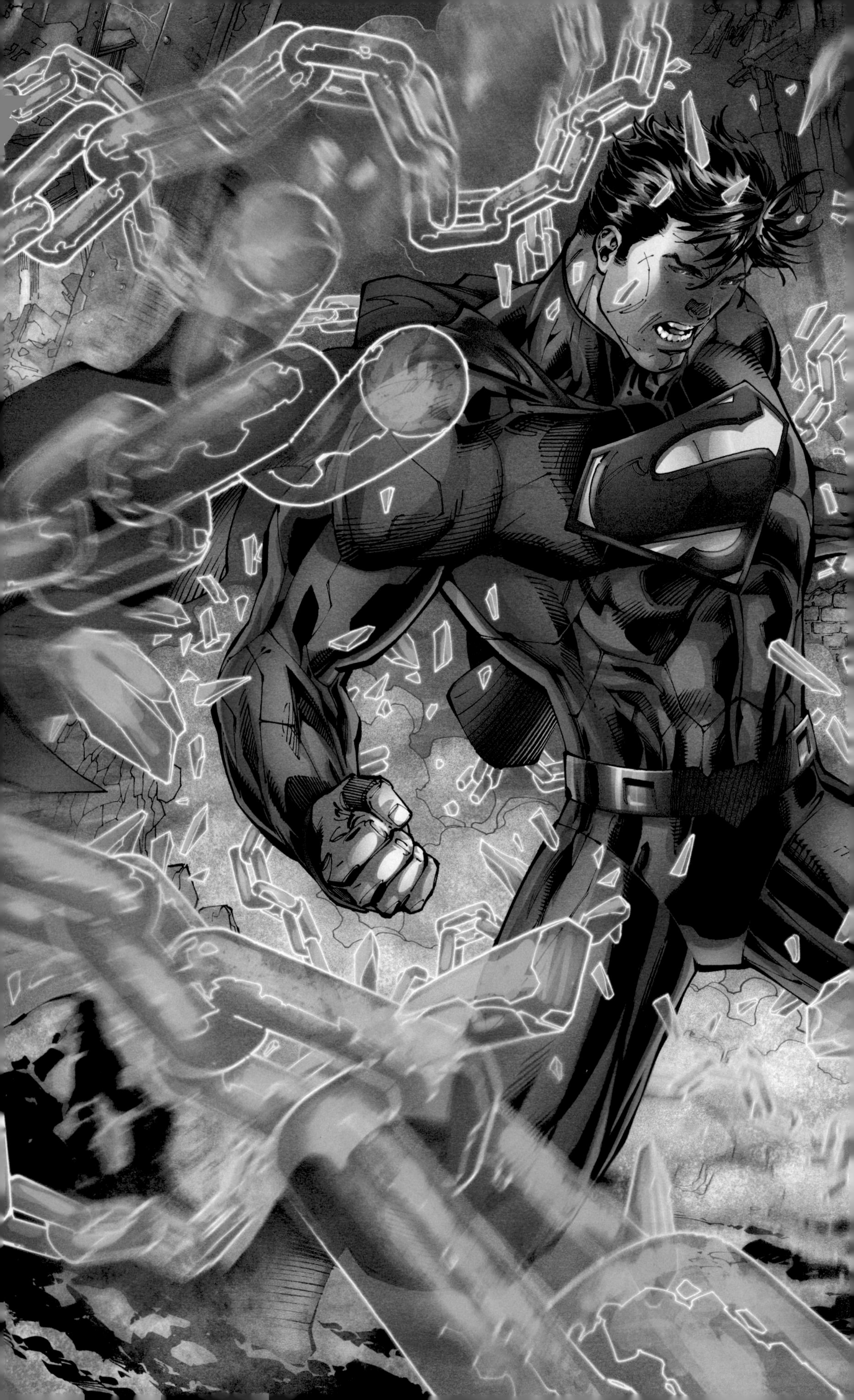

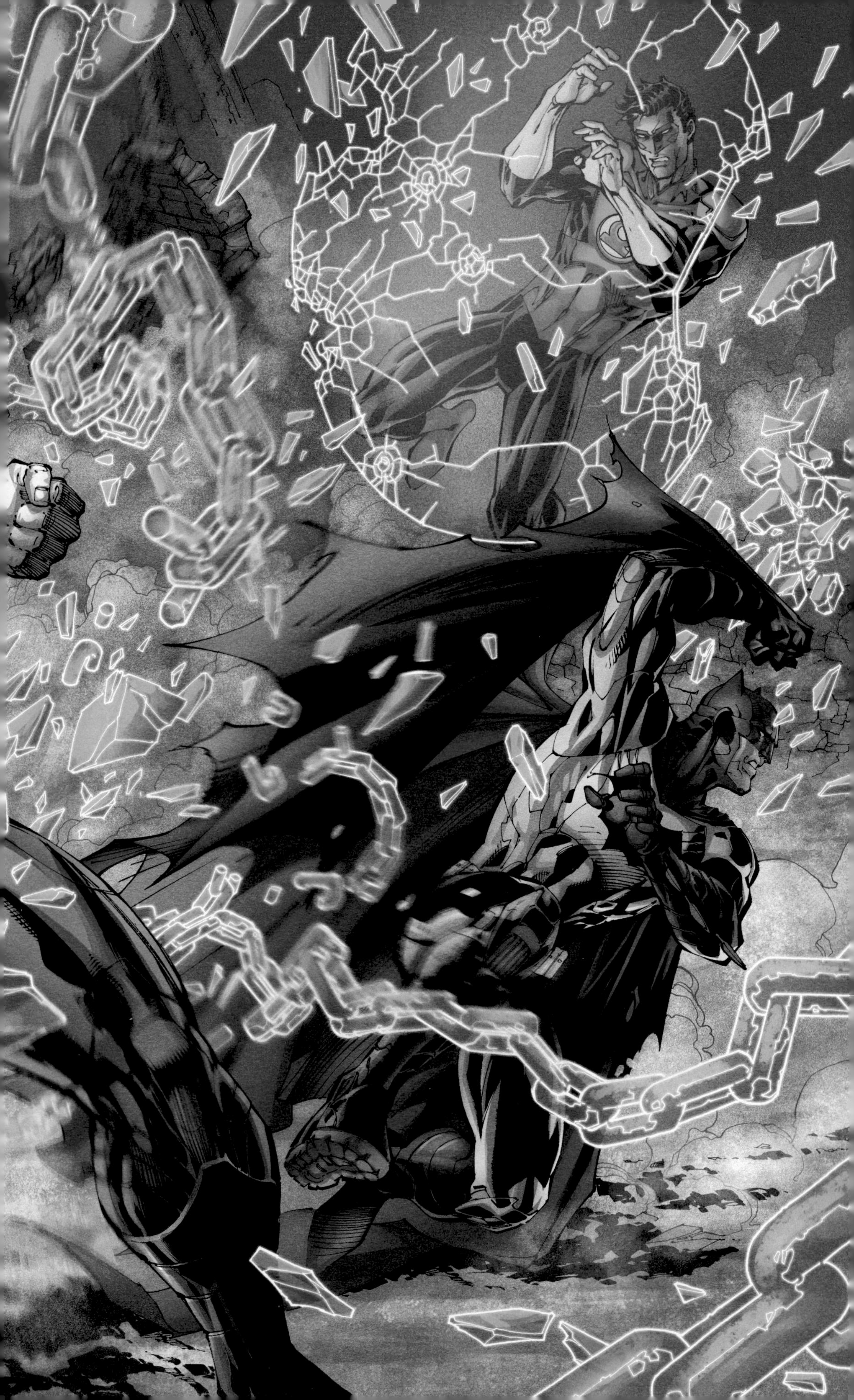

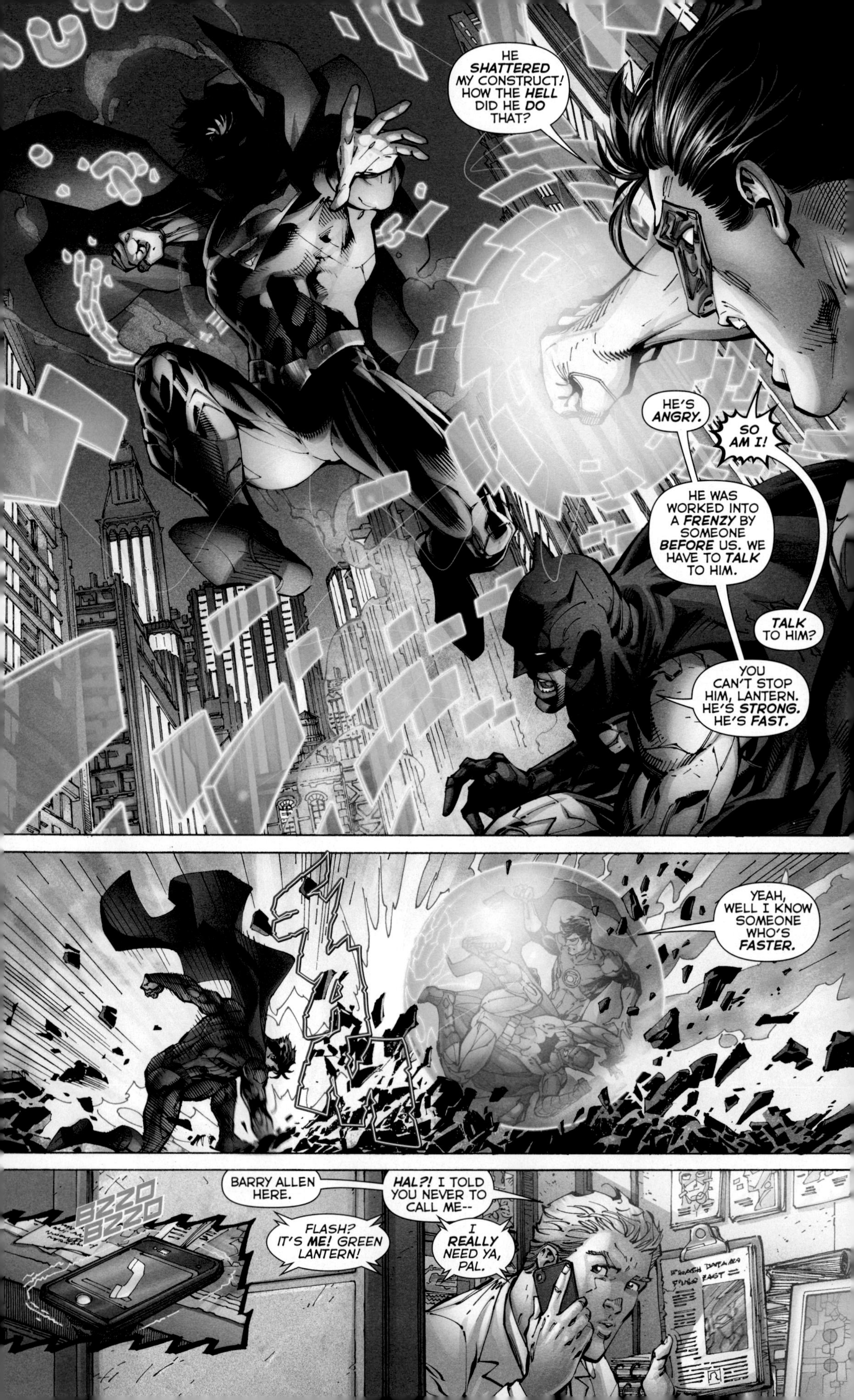
HE SHATTERED MY CONSTRUCT! HOW THE HELL DID HE DO THAT?
HE'S ANGRY.
SO AM I!
HE WAS WORKED INTO A FRENZY BY SOMEONE BEFORE US. WE HAVE TO TALK TO HIM.
TALK TO HIM?
YOU CAN'T STOP HIM, LANTERN. HE'S STRONG. HE'S FAST.
YEAH, WELL I KNOW SOMEONE WHO'S FASTER.
BZZO BZZO
BARRY ALLEN HERE.
FLASH? IT'S ME! GREEN LANTERN!
HAL?! I TOLD YOU NEVER TO CALL ME--
I REALLY NEED YA, PAL.

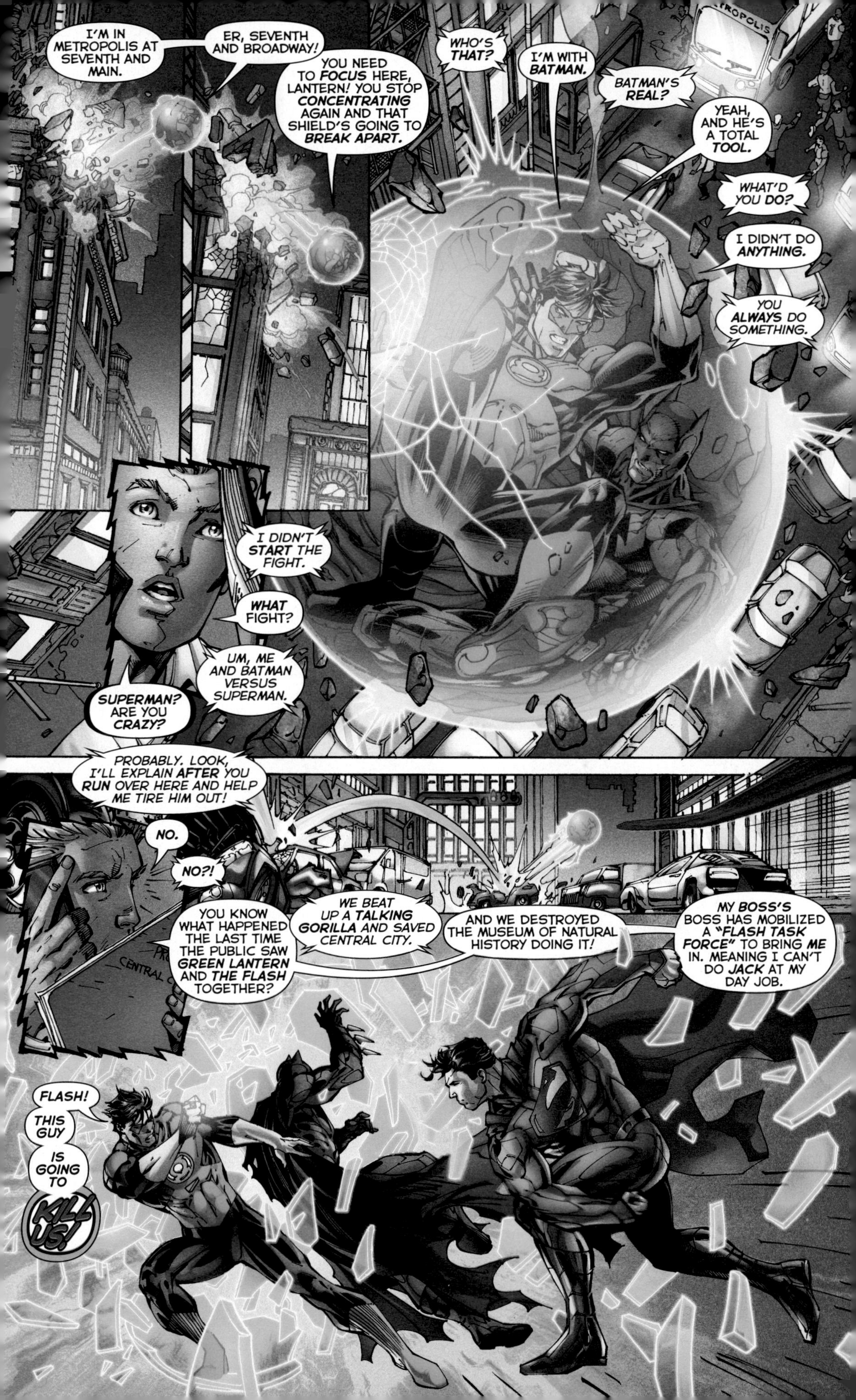
I'M IN METROPOLIS AT SEVENTH AND MAIN.
ER, SEVENTH AND BROADWAY!
YOU NEED TO FOCUS HERE, LANTERN! YOU STOP CONCENTRATING AGAIN AND THAT SHIELD'S GOING TO BREAK APART.
WHO'S THAT?
I'M WITH BATMAN.
BATMAN'S REAL?
YEAH, AND HE'S A TOTAL TOOL.
WHAT'D YOU DO?
I DIDN'T DO ANYTHING.
YOU ALWAYS DO SOMETHING.
I DIDN'T START THE FIGHT.
WHAT FIGHT?
UM, ME AND BATMAN VERSUS SUPERMAN.
SUPERMAN? ARE YOU CRAZY?
PROBABLY. LOOK, I'LL EXPLAIN AFTER YOU RUN OVER HERE AND HELP ME TIRE HIM OUT!
NO.
NO?!
YOU KNOW WHAT HAPPENED THE LAST TIME THE PUBLIC SAW GREEN LANTERN AND THE FLASH TOGETHER?
WE BEAT UP A TALKING GORILLA AND SAVED CENTRAL CITY.
AND WE DESTROYED THE MUSEUM OF NATURAL HISTORY DOING IT!
MY BOSS'S BOSS HAS MOBILIZED A "FLASH TASK FORCE" TO BRING ME IN. MEANING I CAN'T DO JACK AT MY DAY JOB.
FLASH!
THIS GUY
IS GOING TO
KILL US!

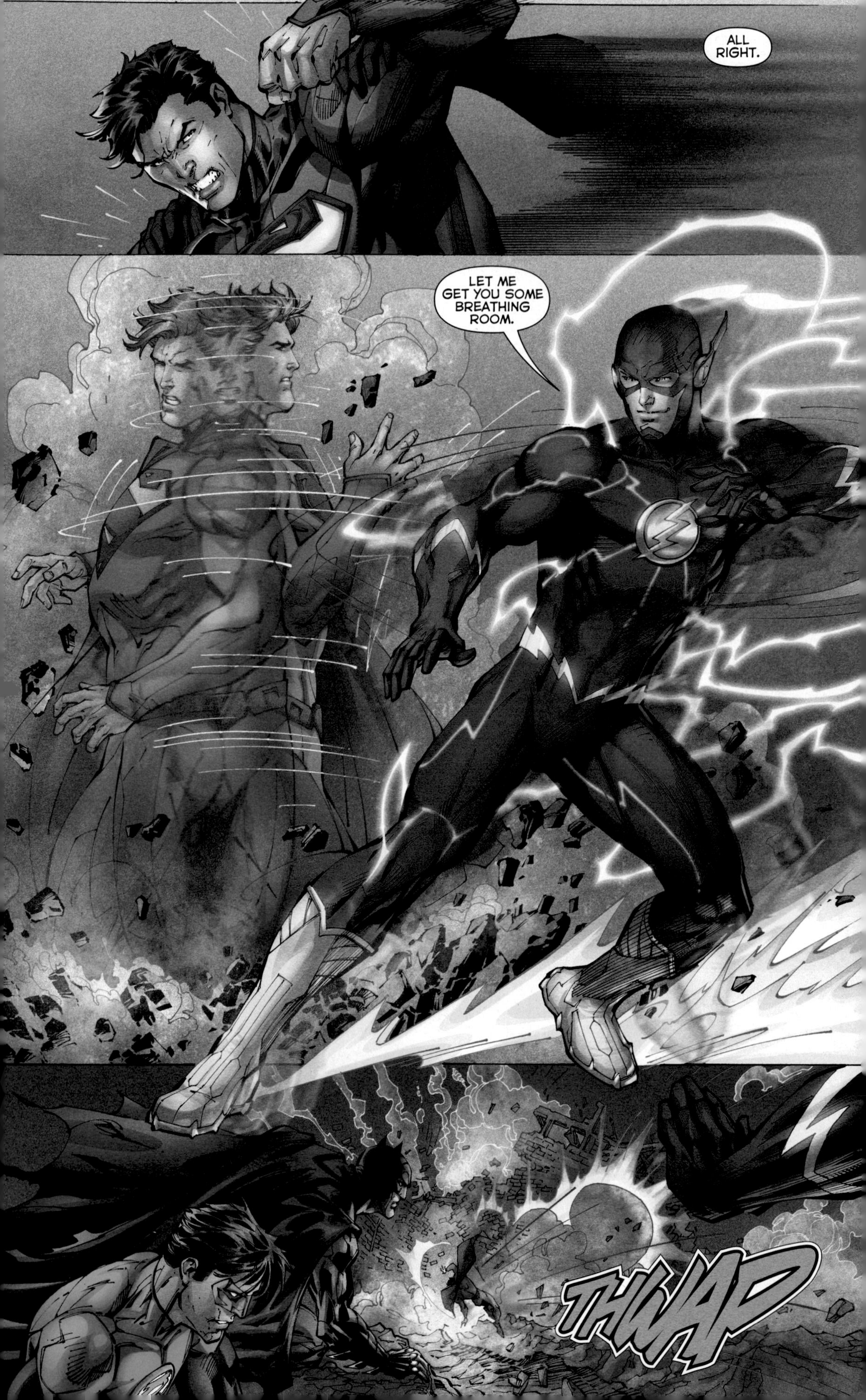
ALL RIGHT.
LET ME GET YOU SOME BREATHING ROOM.
THWAP

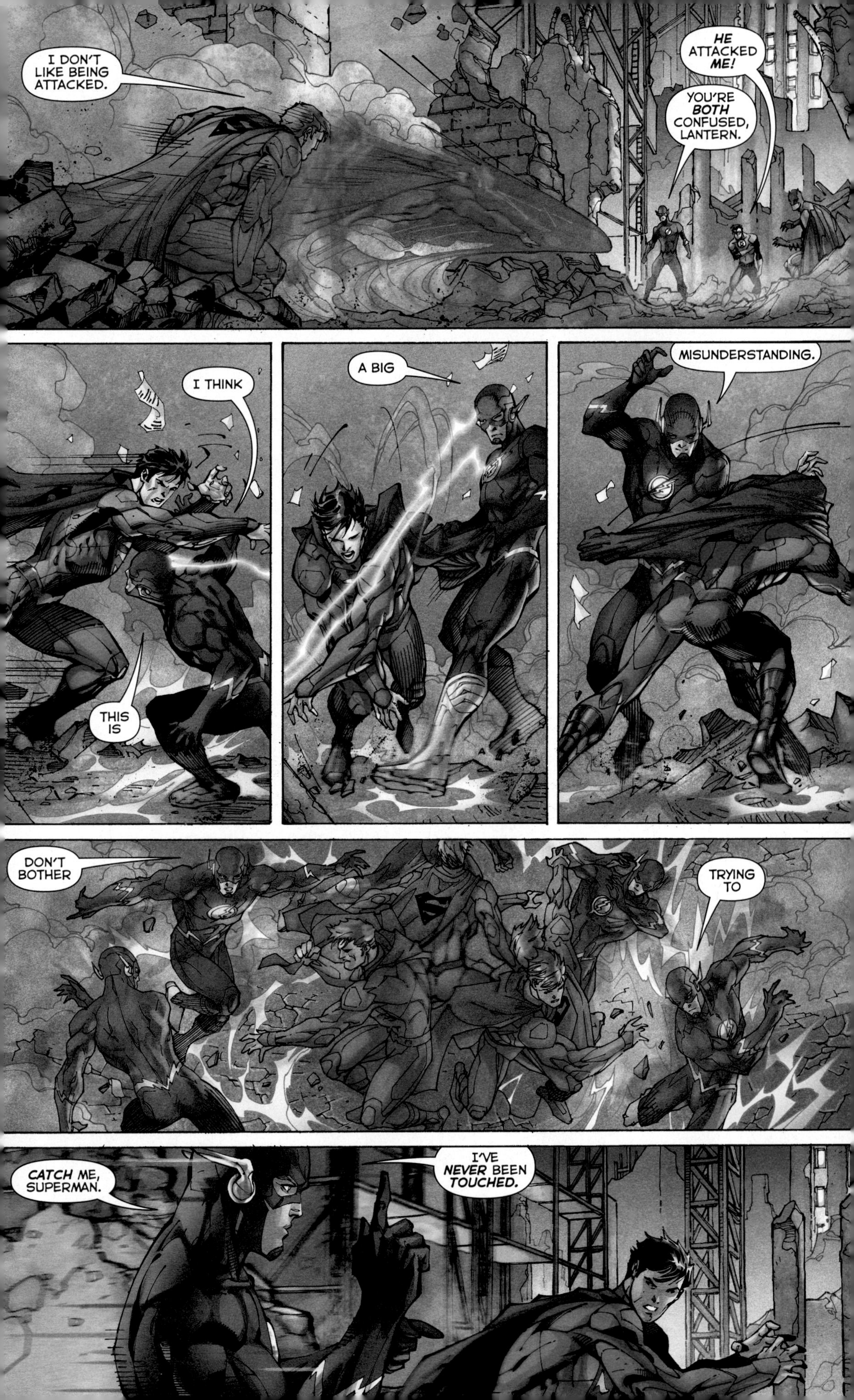
I DON'T LIKE BEING ATTACKED.
HE ATTACKED ME!
YOU'RE BOTH CONFUSED, LANTERN.
I THINK
THIS IS
A BIG
MISUNDERSTANDING.
DON'T BOTHER
TRYING TO
CATCH ME, SUPERMAN.
I'VE NEVER BEEN TOUCHED.

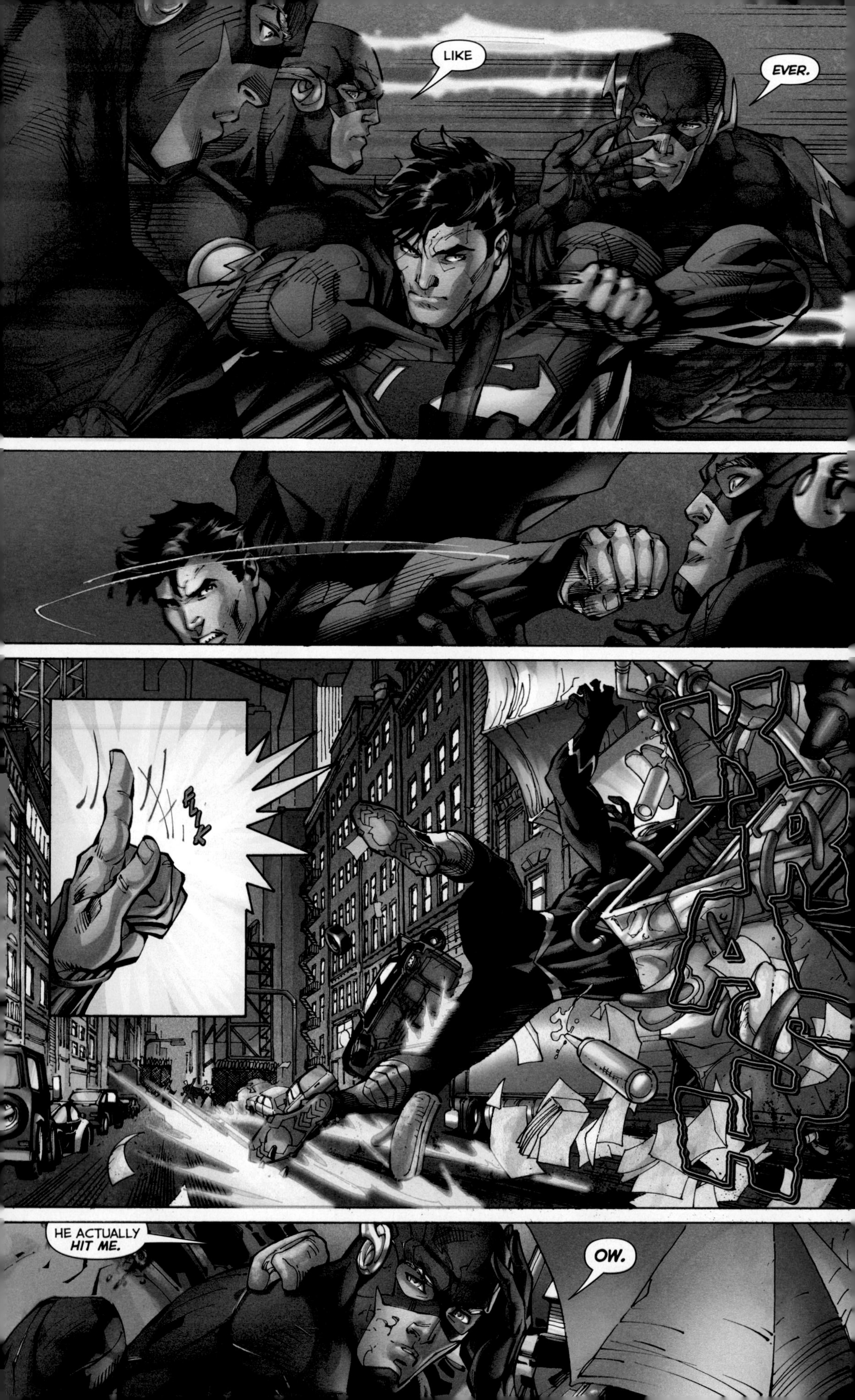
LIKE
EVER.
FWK
HE ACTUALLY HIT ME.
OW.

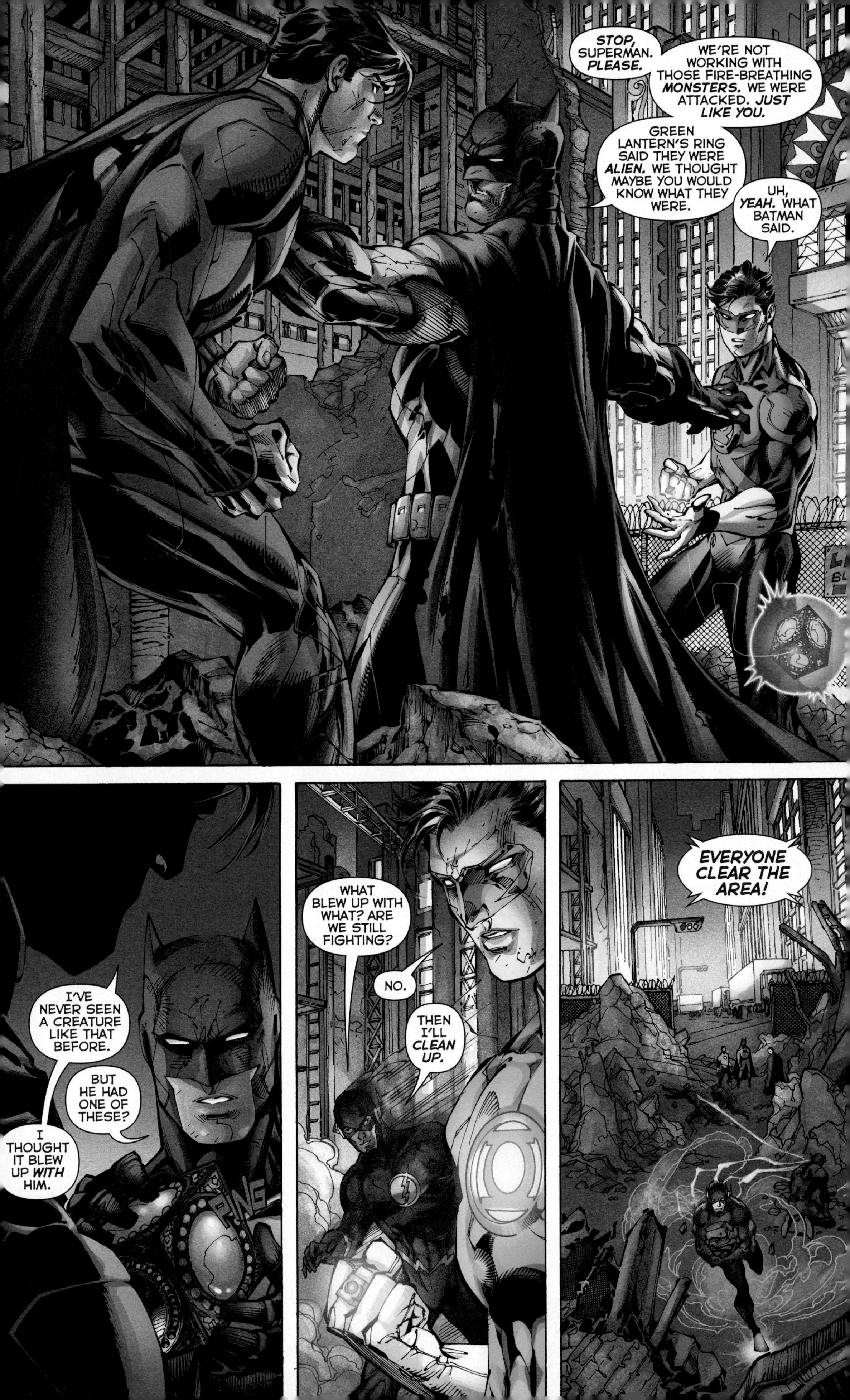
STOP, SUPERMAN. PLEASE.
WE'RE NOT WORKING WITH THOSE FIRE-BREATHING MONSTERS. WE WERE ATTACKED. JUST LIKE YOU.
GREEN LANTERN'S RING SAID THEY WERE ALIEN. WE THOUGHT MAYBE YOU WOULD KNOW WHAT THEY WERE.
UH, YEAH. WHAT BATMAN SAID.
I'VE NEVER SEEN A CREATURE LIKE THAT BEFORE.
BUT HE HAD ONE OF THESE?
I THOUGHT IT BLEW UP WITH HIM.
WHAT BLEW UP WITH WHAT? ARE WE STILL FIGHTING?
NO.
THEN I'LL CLEAN UP.
EVERYONE CLEAR THE AREA!

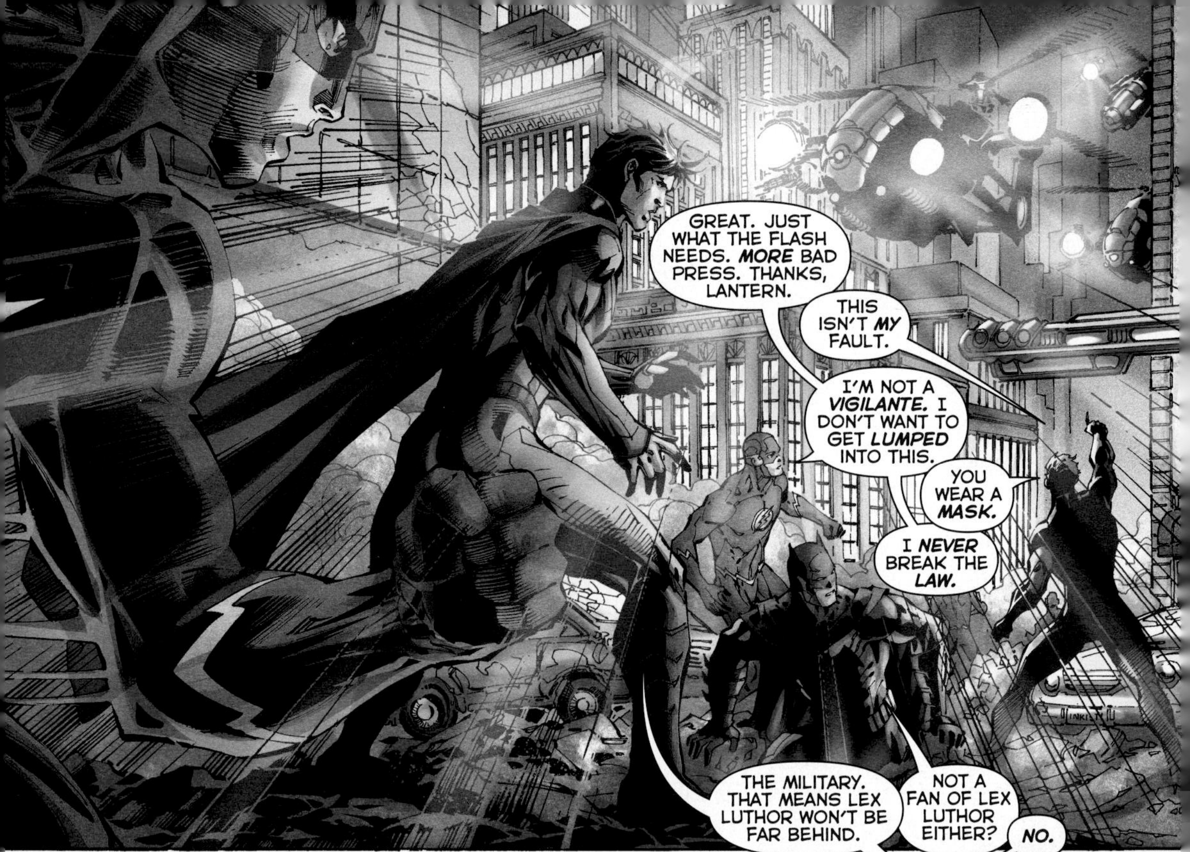
GREAT. JUST WHAT THE FLASH NEEDS. *MORE* BAD PRESS. THANKS, LANTERN.
THIS ISN'T *MY* FAULT.
I'M NOT A *VIGILANTE.* I DON'T WANT TO GET *LUMPED* INTO THIS.
YOU WEAR A *MASK.*
I *NEVER* BREAK THE *LAW.*
THE MILITARY. THAT MEANS LEX LUTHOR WON'T BE FAR BEHIND.
NOT A FAN OF LEX LUTHOR EITHER?
NO.

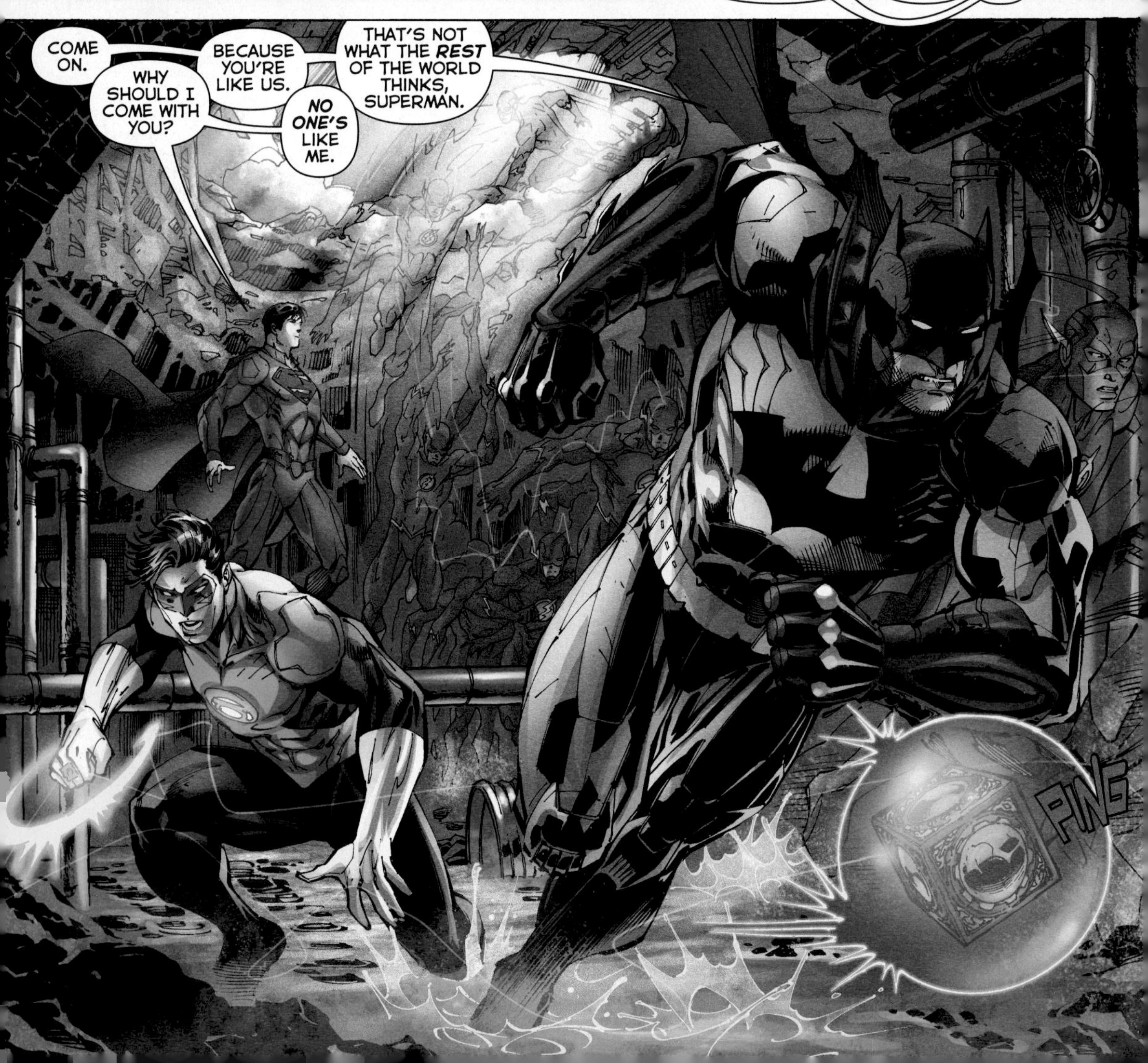
COME ON.
WHY SHOULD I COME WITH YOU?
BECAUSE YOU'RE LIKE US.
NO ONE'S LIKE ME.
THAT'S NOT WHAT THE *REST* OF THE WORLD THINKS, SUPERMAN.
PING

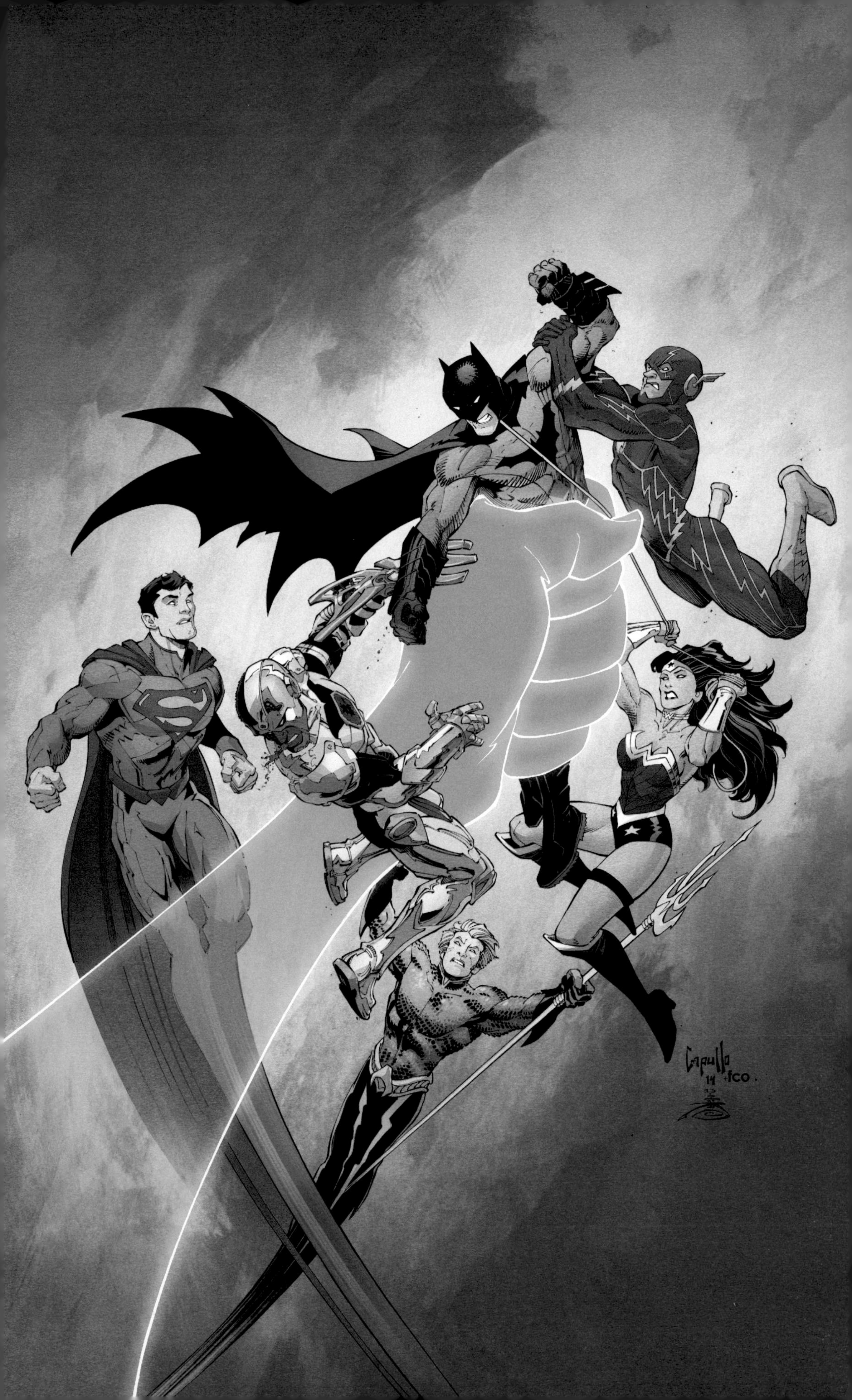

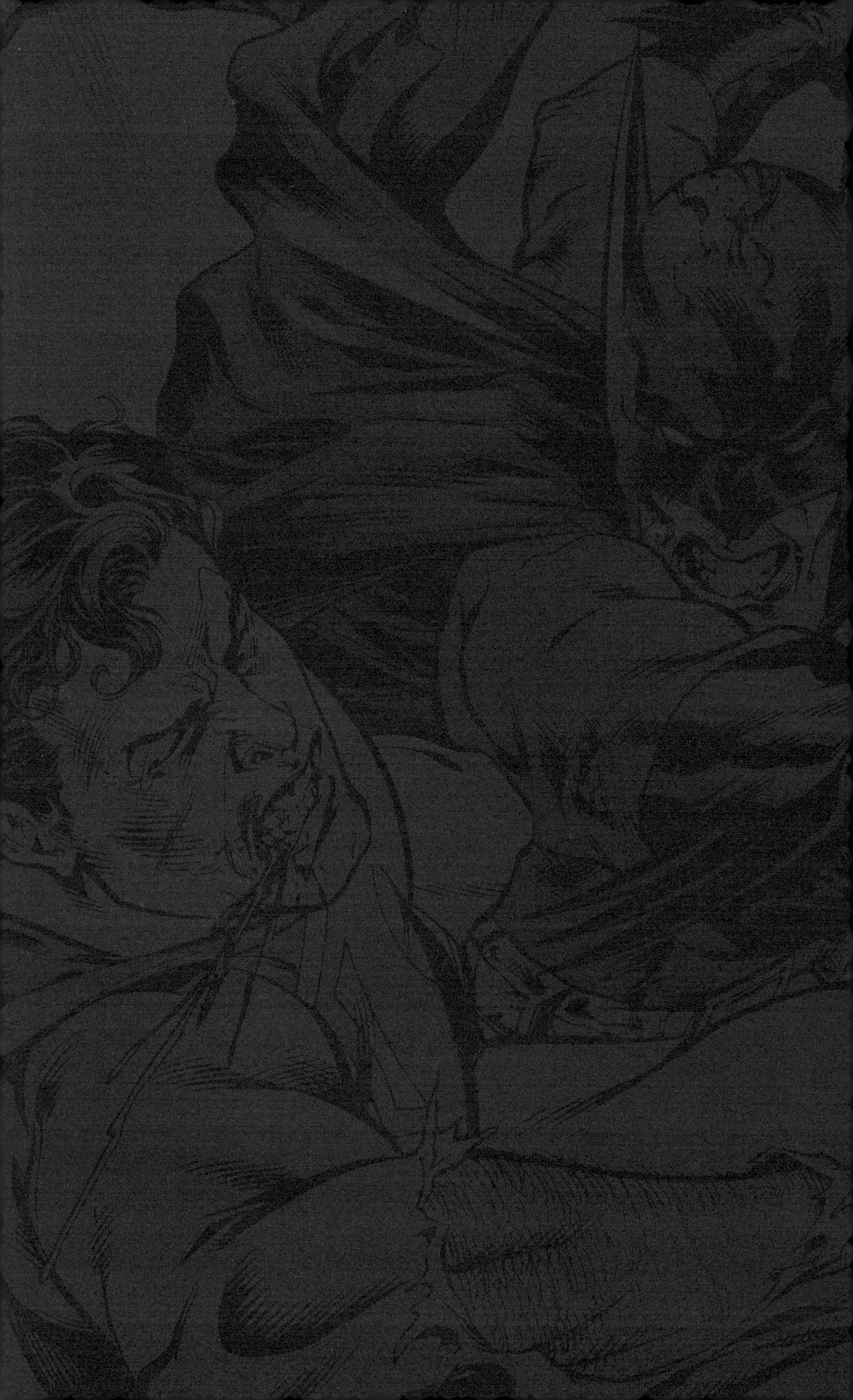

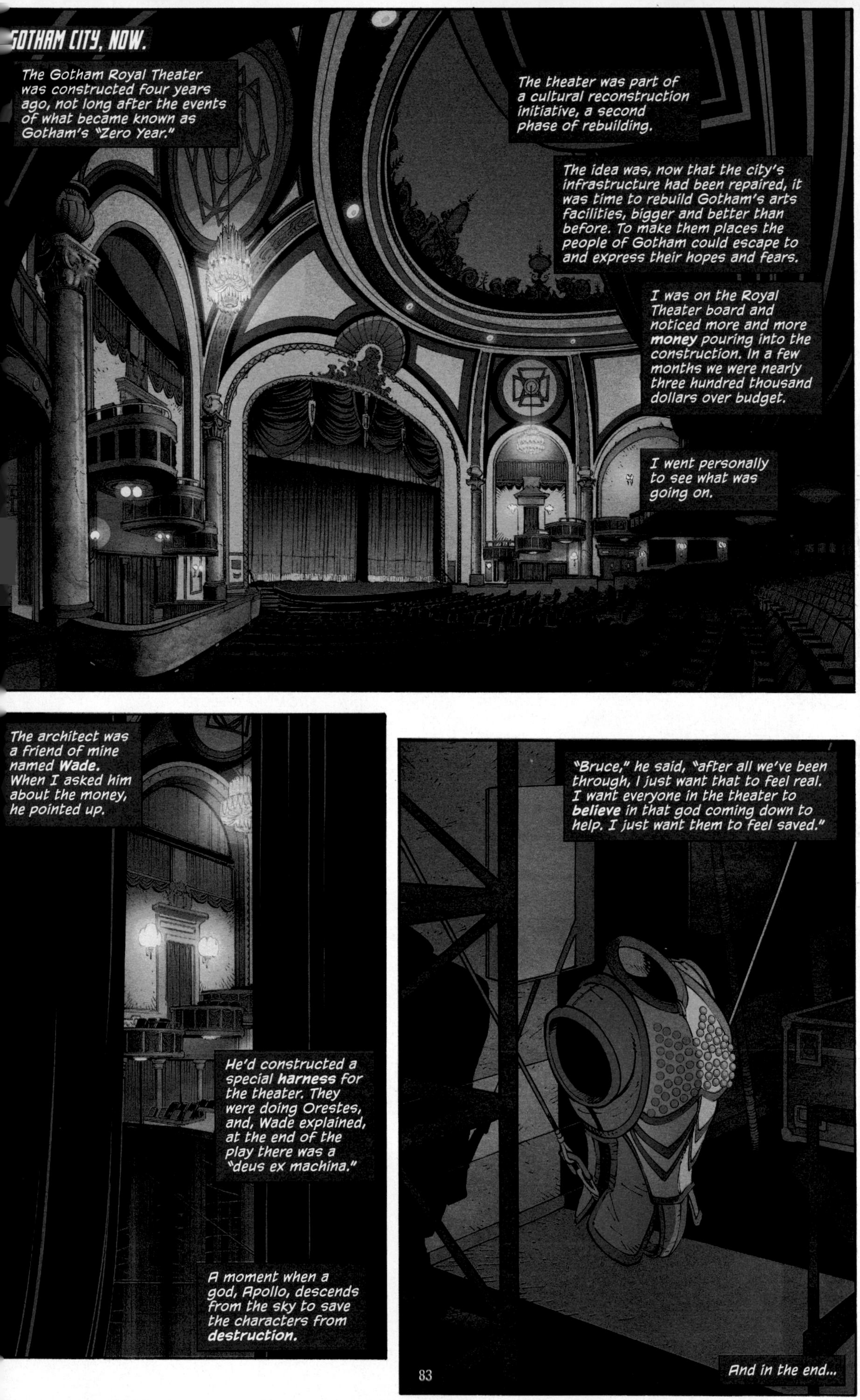
GOTHAM CITY, NOW.
The Gotham Royal Theater was constructed four years ago, not long after the events of what became known as Gotham's "Zero Year."
The theater was part of a cultural reconstruction initiative, a second phase of rebuilding.
The idea was, now that the city's infrastructure had been repaired, it was time to rebuild Gotham's arts facilities, bigger and better than before. To make them places the people of Gotham could escape to and express their hopes and fears.
I was on the Royal Theater board and noticed more and more **money** pouring into the construction. In a few months we were nearly three hundred thousand dollars over budget.
I went personally to see what was going on.
The architect was a friend of mine named **Wade.** When I asked him about the money, he pointed up.
He'd constructed a special **harness** for the theater. They were doing Orestes, and, Wade explained, at the end of the play there was a "deus ex machina."
A moment when a god, Apollo, descends from the sky to save the characters from **destruction.**
"Bruce," he said, "after all we've been through, I just want that to feel real. I want everyone in the theater to **believe** in that god coming down to help. I just want them to feel saved."
And in the end...

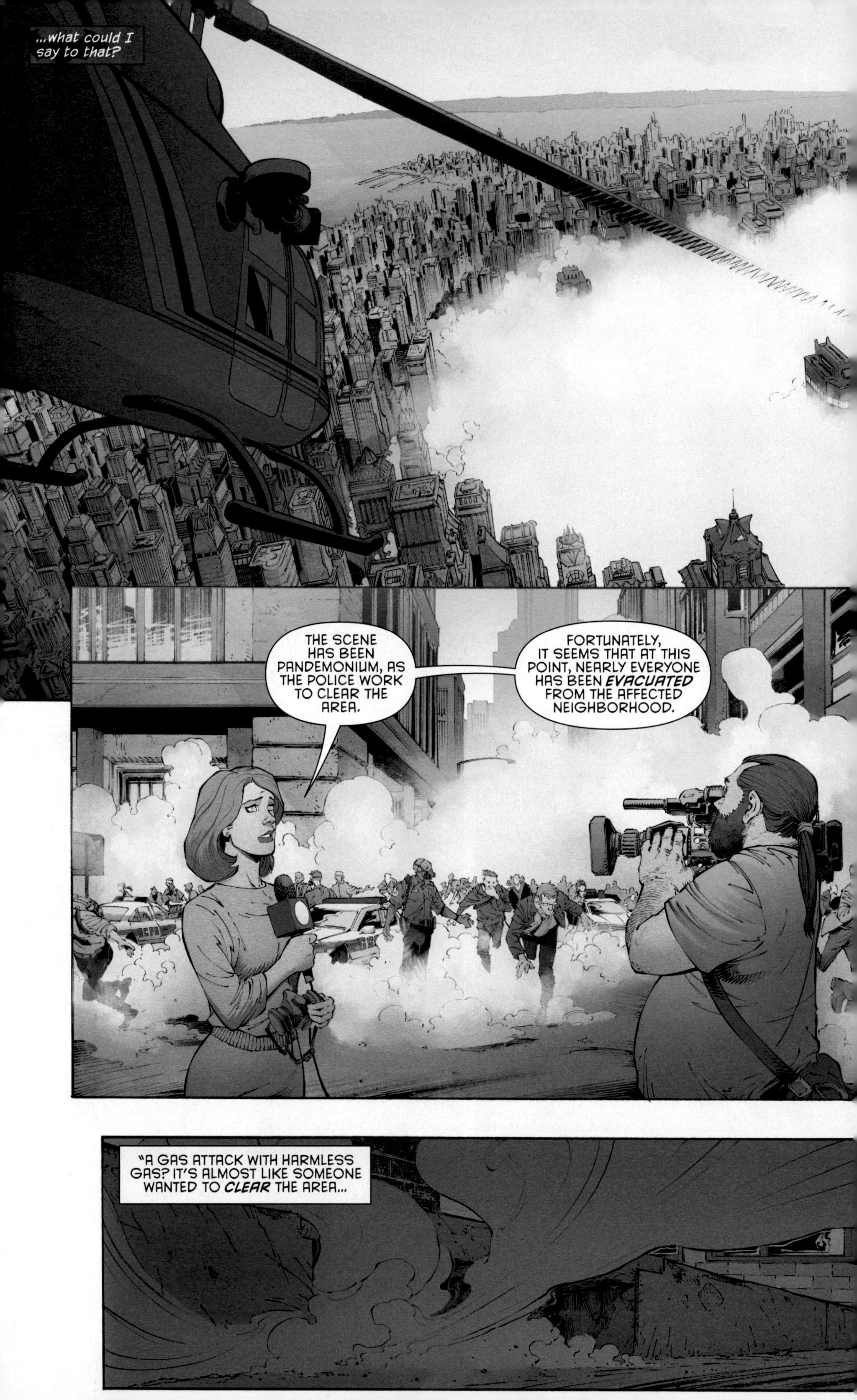
...what could I say to that?
THE SCENE HAS BEEN PANDEMONIUM, AS THE POLICE WORK TO CLEAR THE AREA.
FORTUNATELY, IT SEEMS THAT AT THIS POINT, NEARLY EVERYONE HAS BEEN *EVACUATED* FROM THE AFFECTED NEIGHBORHOOD.
"A GAS ATTACK WITH HARMLESS GAS? IT'S ALMOST LIKE SOMEONE WANTED TO *CLEAR* THE AREA...

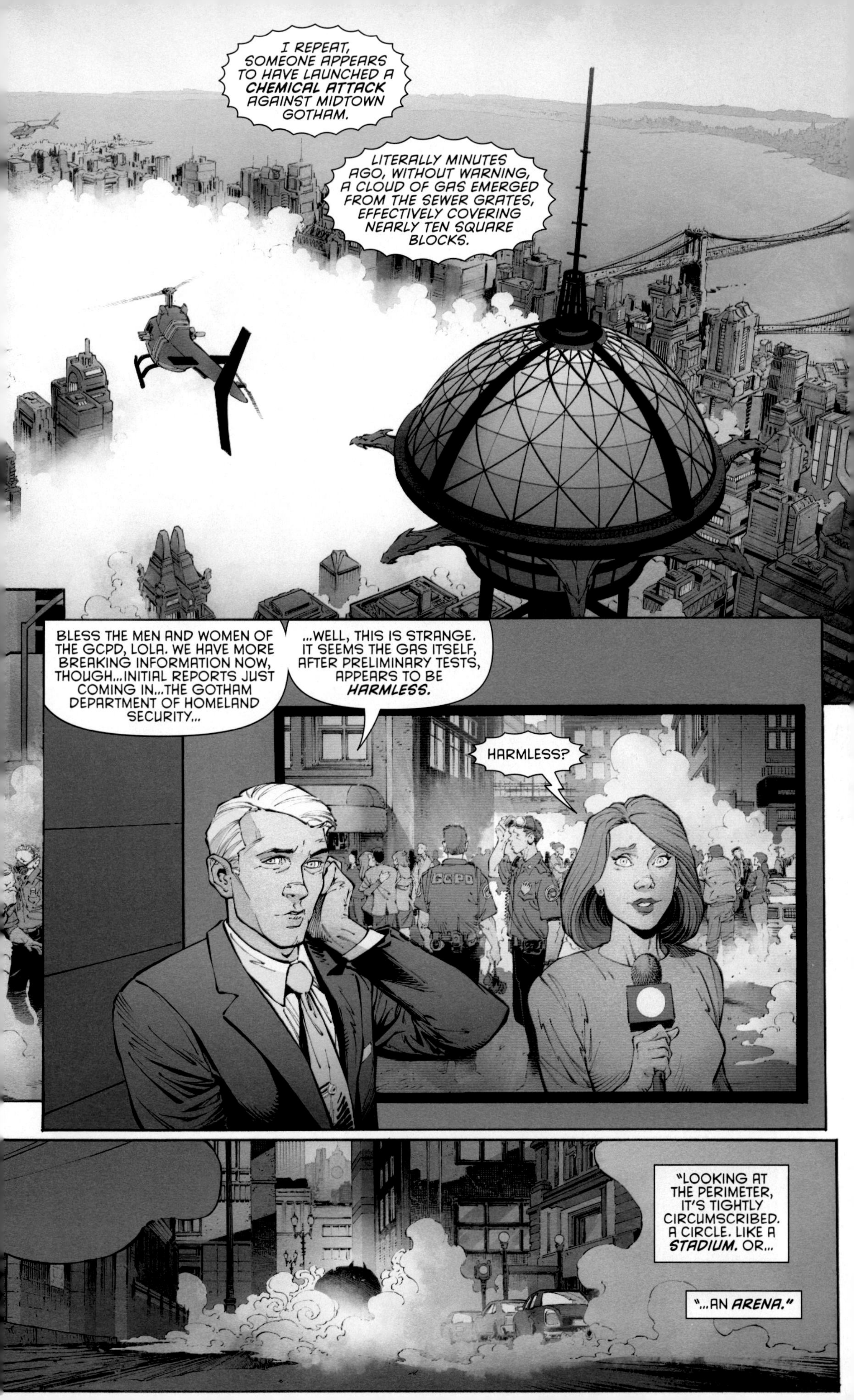
I REPEAT, SOMEONE APPEARS TO HAVE LAUNCHED A CHEMICAL ATTACK AGAINST MIDTOWN GOTHAM.
LITERALLY MINUTES AGO, WITHOUT WARNING, A CLOUD OF GAS EMERGED FROM THE SEWER GRATES, EFFECTIVELY COVERING NEARLY TEN SQUARE BLOCKS.
BLESS THE MEN AND WOMEN OF THE GCPD, LOLA. WE HAVE MORE BREAKING INFORMATION NOW, THOUGH...INITIAL REPORTS JUST COMING IN...THE GOTHAM DEPARTMENT OF HOMELAND SECURITY...
...WELL, THIS IS STRANGE. IT SEEMS THE GAS ITSELF, AFTER PRELIMINARY TESTS, APPEARS TO BE HARMLESS.
HARMLESS?
GCPD
"LOOKING AT THE PERIMETER, IT'S TIGHTLY CIRCUMSCRIBED. A CIRCLE. LIKE A STADIUM. OR...
"...AN ARENA."

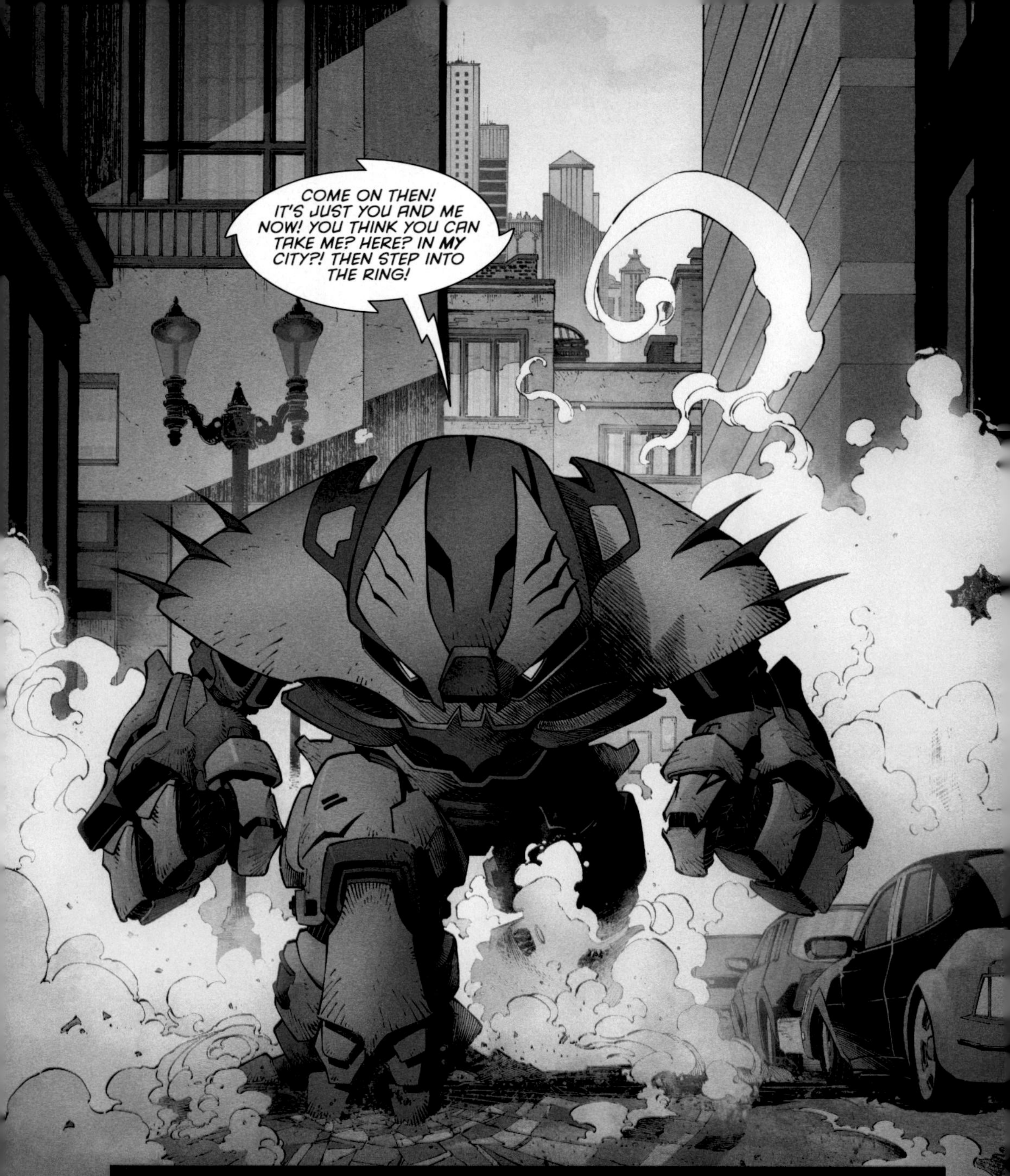
COME ON THEN! IT'S JUST YOU AND ME NOW! YOU THINK YOU CAN TAKE ME? HERE? IN MY CITY?! THEN STEP INTO THE RING!

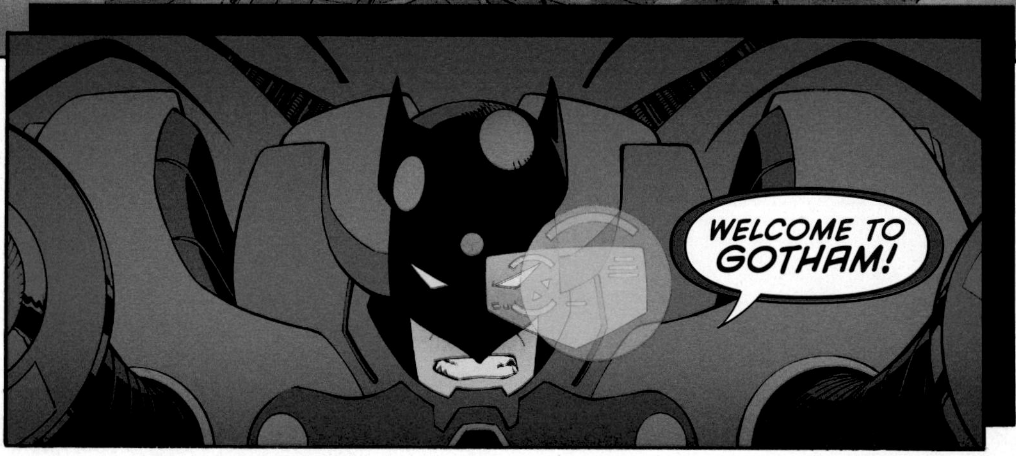
WELCOME TO GOTHAM!

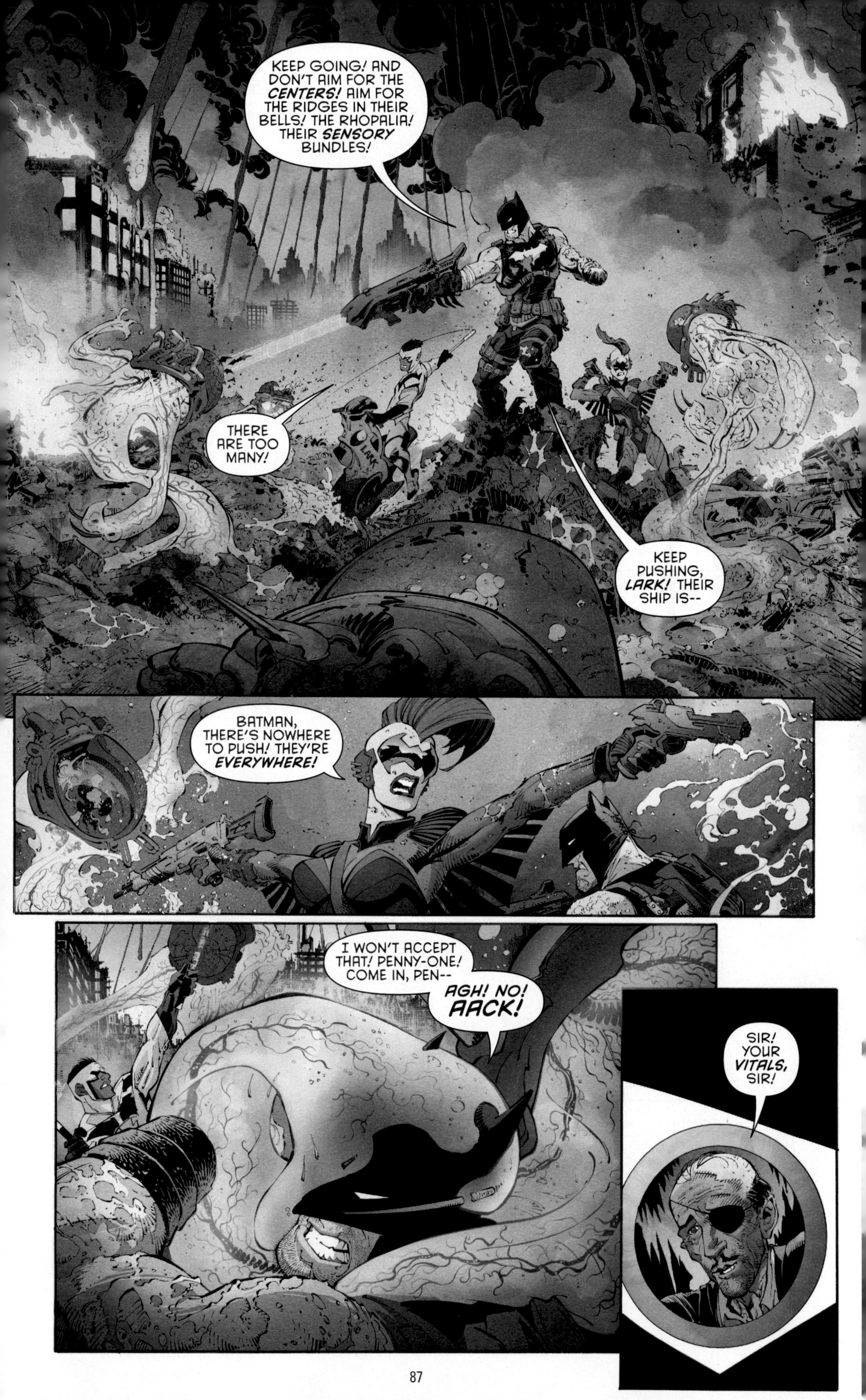
KEEP GOING! AND DON'T AIM FOR THE CENTERS! AIM FOR THE RIDGES IN THEIR BELLS! THE RHOPALIA! THEIR SENSORY BUNDLES!
THERE ARE TOO MANY!
KEEP PUSHING, LARK! THEIR SHIP IS--
BATMAN, THERE'S NOWHERE TO PUSH! THEY'RE EVERYWHERE!
I WON'T ACCEPT THAT! PENNY-ONE! COME IN, PEN--
AGH! NO! AACK!
SIR! YOUR VITALS, SIR!

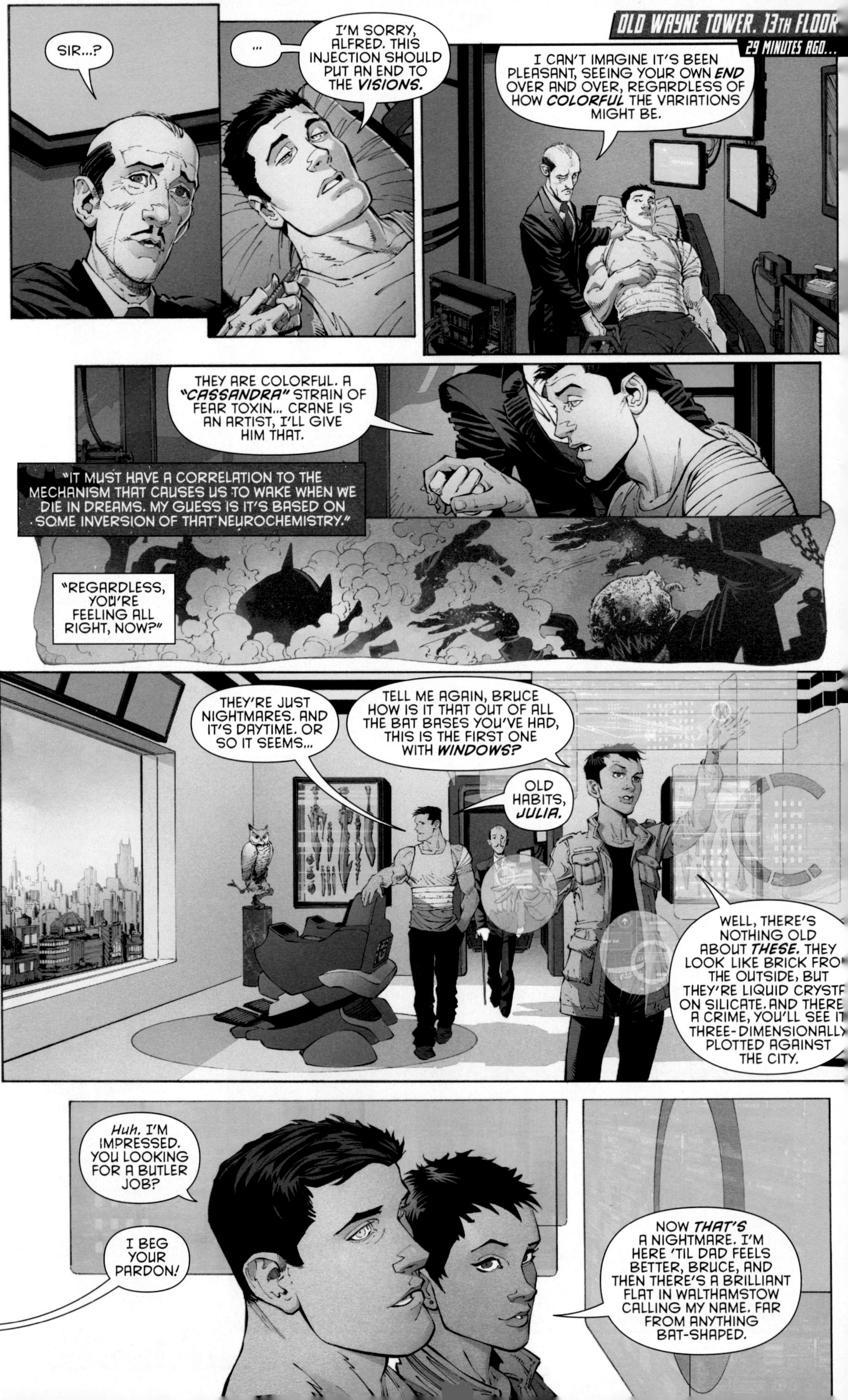
OLD WAYNE TOWER, 13TH FLOOR
29 MINUTES AGO...
SIR...?
...
I'M SORRY, ALFRED. THIS INJECTION SHOULD PUT AN END TO THE VISIONS.
I CAN'T IMAGINE IT'S BEEN PLEASANT, SEEING YOUR OWN END OVER AND OVER, REGARDLESS OF HOW COLORFUL THE VARIATIONS MIGHT BE.
THEY ARE COLORFUL. A "CASSANDRA" STRAIN OF FEAR TOXIN... CRANE IS AN ARTIST, I'LL GIVE HIM THAT.
"IT MUST HAVE A CORRELATION TO THE MECHANISM THAT CAUSES US TO WAKE WHEN WE DIE IN DREAMS. MY GUESS IS IT'S BASED ON SOME INVERSION OF THAT NEUROCHEMISTRY."
"REGARDLESS, YOU'RE FEELING ALL RIGHT, NOW?"
THEY'RE JUST NIGHTMARES. AND IT'S DAYTIME. OR SO IT SEEMS...
TELL ME AGAIN, BRUCE HOW IS IT THAT OUT OF ALL THE BAT BASES YOU'VE HAD, THIS IS THE FIRST ONE WITH WINDOWS?
OLD HABITS, JULIA.
WELL, THERE'S NOTHING OLD ABOUT THESE. THEY LOOK LIKE BRICK FRO THE OUTSIDE, BUT THEY'RE LIQUID CRYSTA ON SILICATE. AND THERE A CRIME, YOU'LL SEE IT THREE-DIMENSIONALLY PLOTTED AGAINST THE CITY.
Huh. I'M IMPRESSED. YOU LOOKING FOR A BUTLER JOB?
I BEG YOUR PARDON!
NOW THAT'S A NIGHTMARE. I'M HERE 'TIL DAD FEELS BETTER, BRUCE, AND THEN THERE'S A BRILLIANT FLAT IN WALTHAMSTOW CALLING MY NAME. FAR FROM ANYTHING BAT-SHAPED.

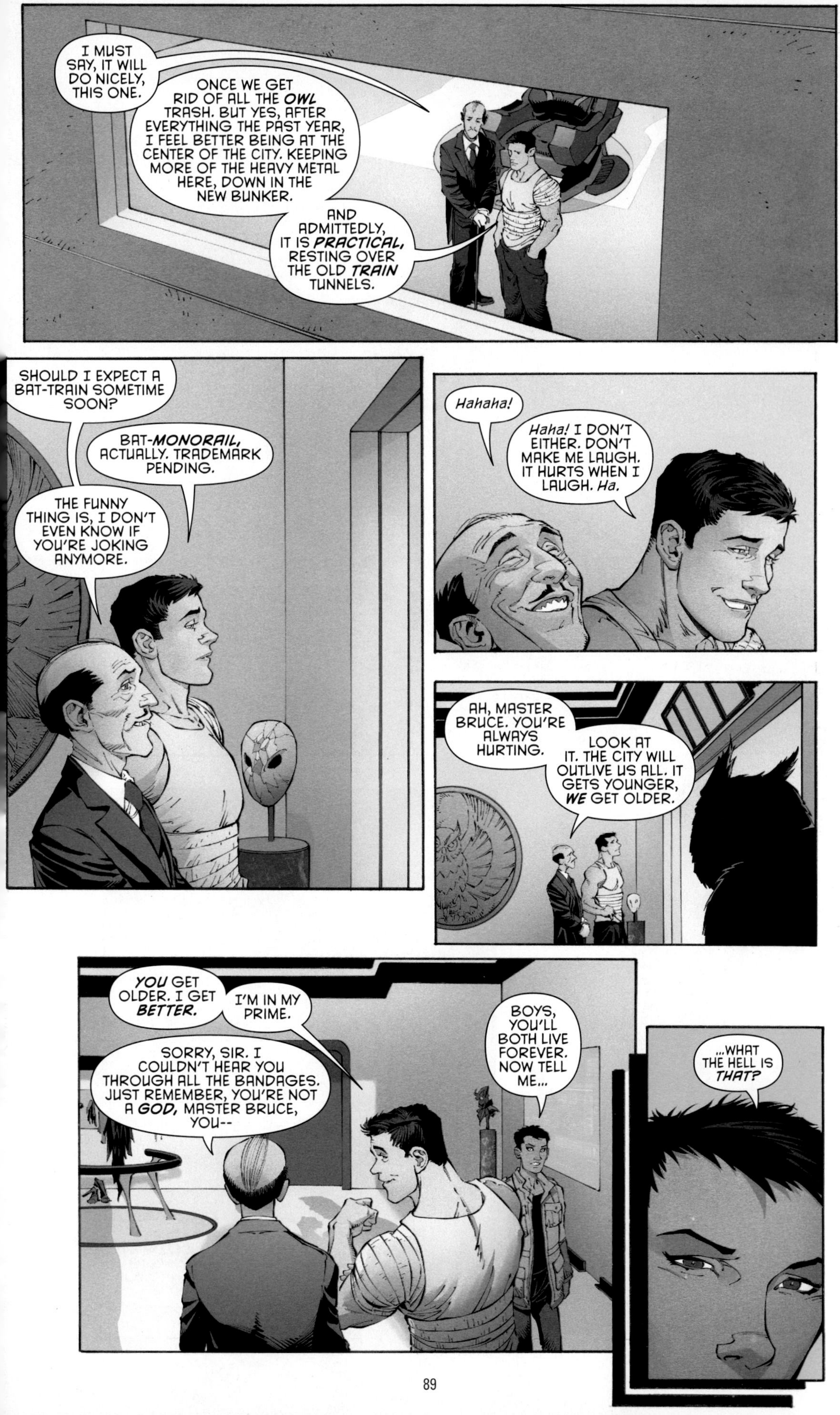
I MUST SAY, IT WILL DO NICELY, THIS ONE.
ONCE WE GET RID OF ALL THE OWL TRASH. BUT YES, AFTER EVERYTHING THE PAST YEAR, I FEEL BETTER BEING AT THE CENTER OF THE CITY. KEEPING MORE OF THE HEAVY METAL HERE, DOWN IN THE NEW BUNKER.
AND ADMITTEDLY, IT IS PRACTICAL, RESTING OVER THE OLD TRAIN TUNNELS.
SHOULD I EXPECT A BAT-TRAIN SOMETIME SOON?
BAT-MONORAIL, ACTUALLY. TRADEMARK PENDING.
THE FUNNY THING IS, I DON'T EVEN KNOW IF YOU'RE JOKING ANYMORE.
Hahaha!
Haha! I DON'T EITHER. DON'T MAKE ME LAUGH. IT HURTS WHEN I LAUGH. Ha.
AH, MASTER BRUCE. YOU'RE ALWAYS HURTING.
LOOK AT IT. THE CITY WILL OUTLIVE US ALL. IT GETS YOUNGER, WE GET OLDER.
YOU GET OLDER. I GET BETTER.
I'M IN MY PRIME.
SORRY, SIR. I COULDN'T HEAR YOU THROUGH ALL THE BANDAGES. JUST REMEMBER, YOU'RE NOT A GOD, MASTER BRUCE, YOU--
BOYS, YOU'LL BOTH LIVE FOREVER. NOW TELL ME...
...WHAT THE HELL IS THAT?

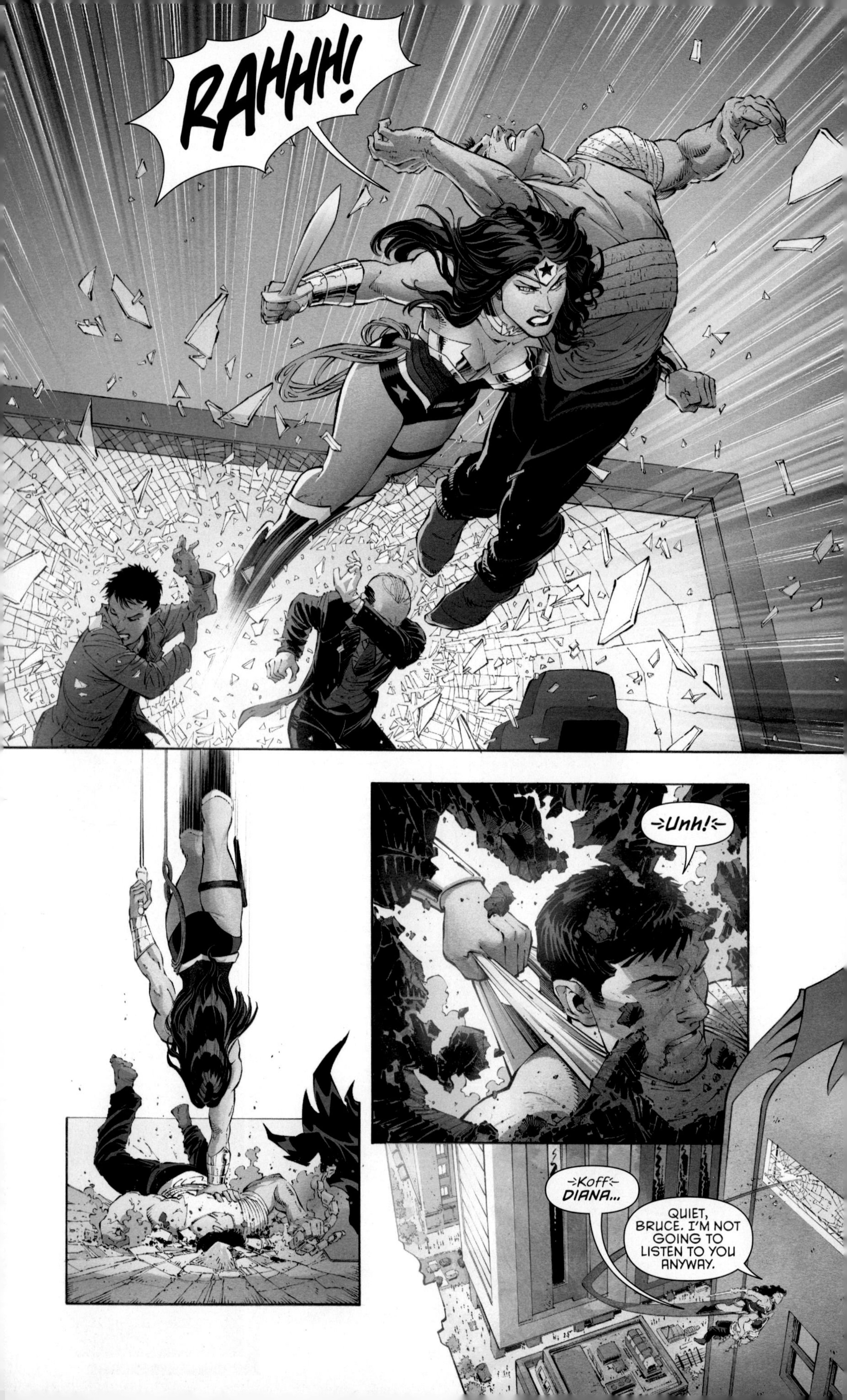
RAHHH!
Unh!
Koff
DIANA...
QUIET, BRUCE. I'M NOT GOING TO LISTEN TO YOU ANYWAY.

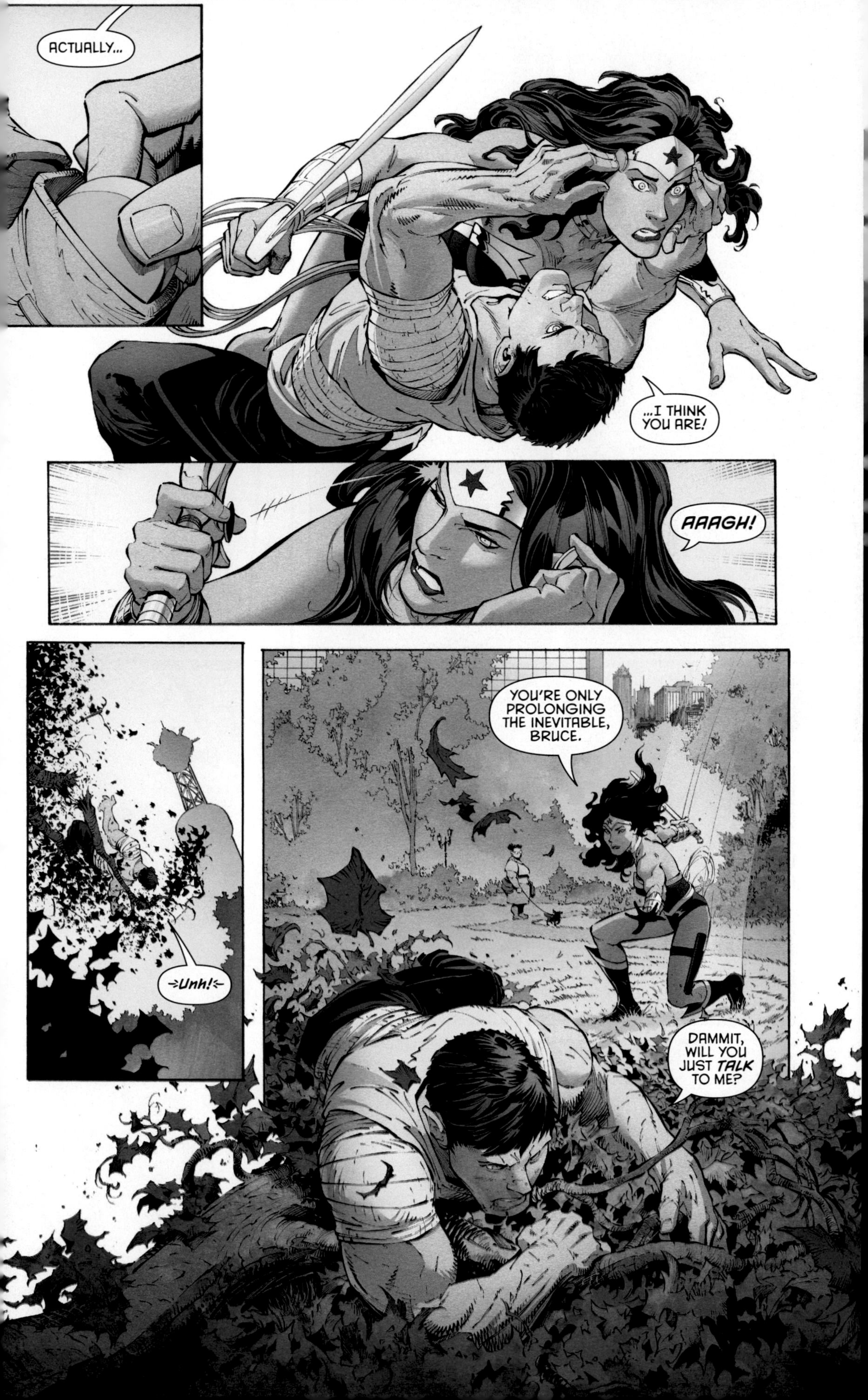
ACTUALLY...
...I THINK YOU ARE!
AAAGH!
~Unh!~
YOU'RE ONLY PROLONGING THE INEVITABLE, BRUCE.
DAMMIT, WILL YOU JUST TALK TO ME?

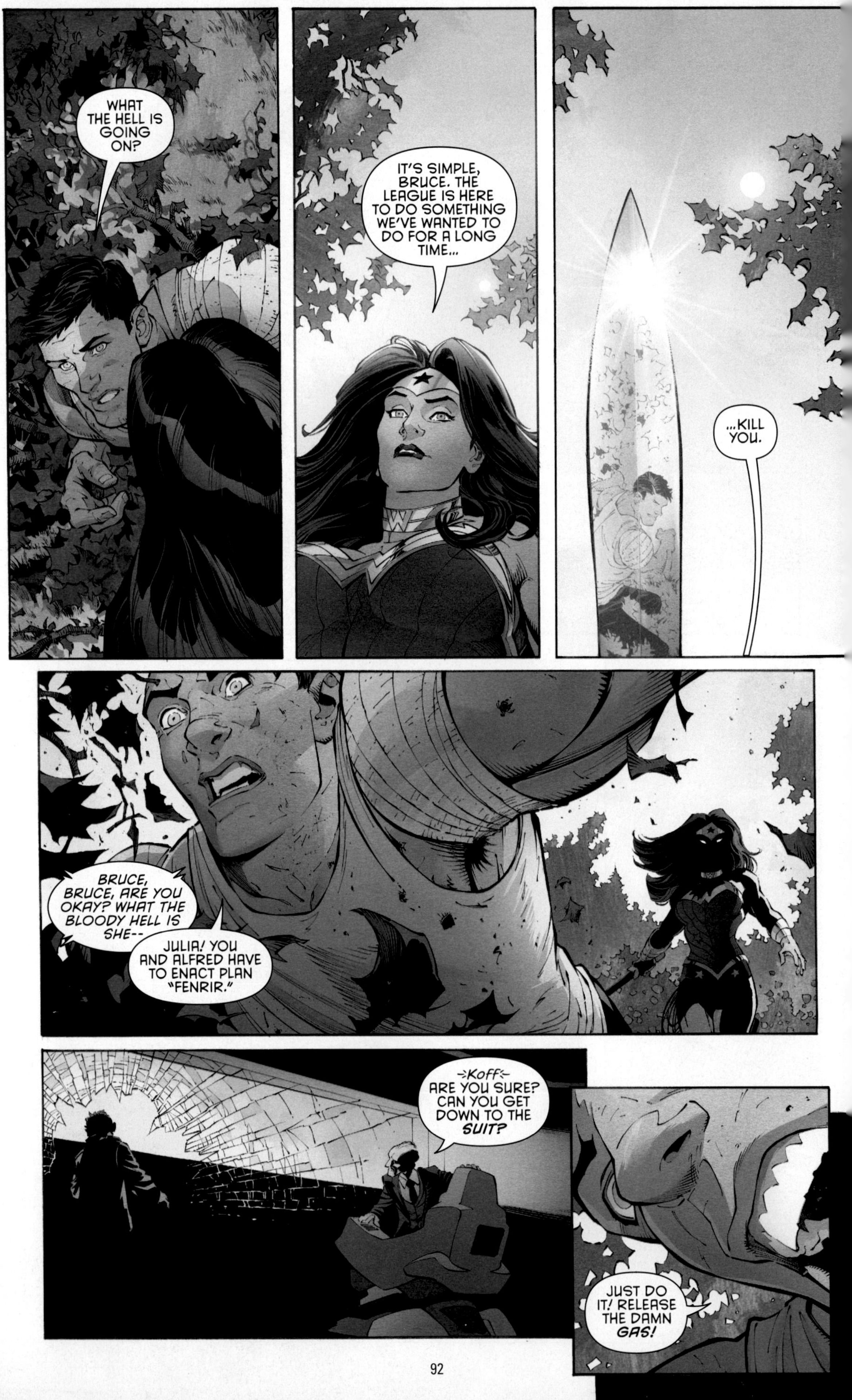
WHAT THE HELL IS GOING ON?
IT'S SIMPLE, BRUCE. THE LEAGUE IS HERE TO DO SOMETHING WE'VE WANTED TO DO FOR A LONG TIME...
...KILL YOU.
BRUCE, BRUCE, ARE YOU OKAY? WHAT THE BLOODY HELL IS SHE--
JULIA! YOU AND ALFRED HAVE TO ENACT PLAN "FENRIR."
-KOFF- ARE YOU SURE? CAN YOU GET DOWN TO THE SUIT?
JUST DO IT! RELEASE THE DAMN GAS!

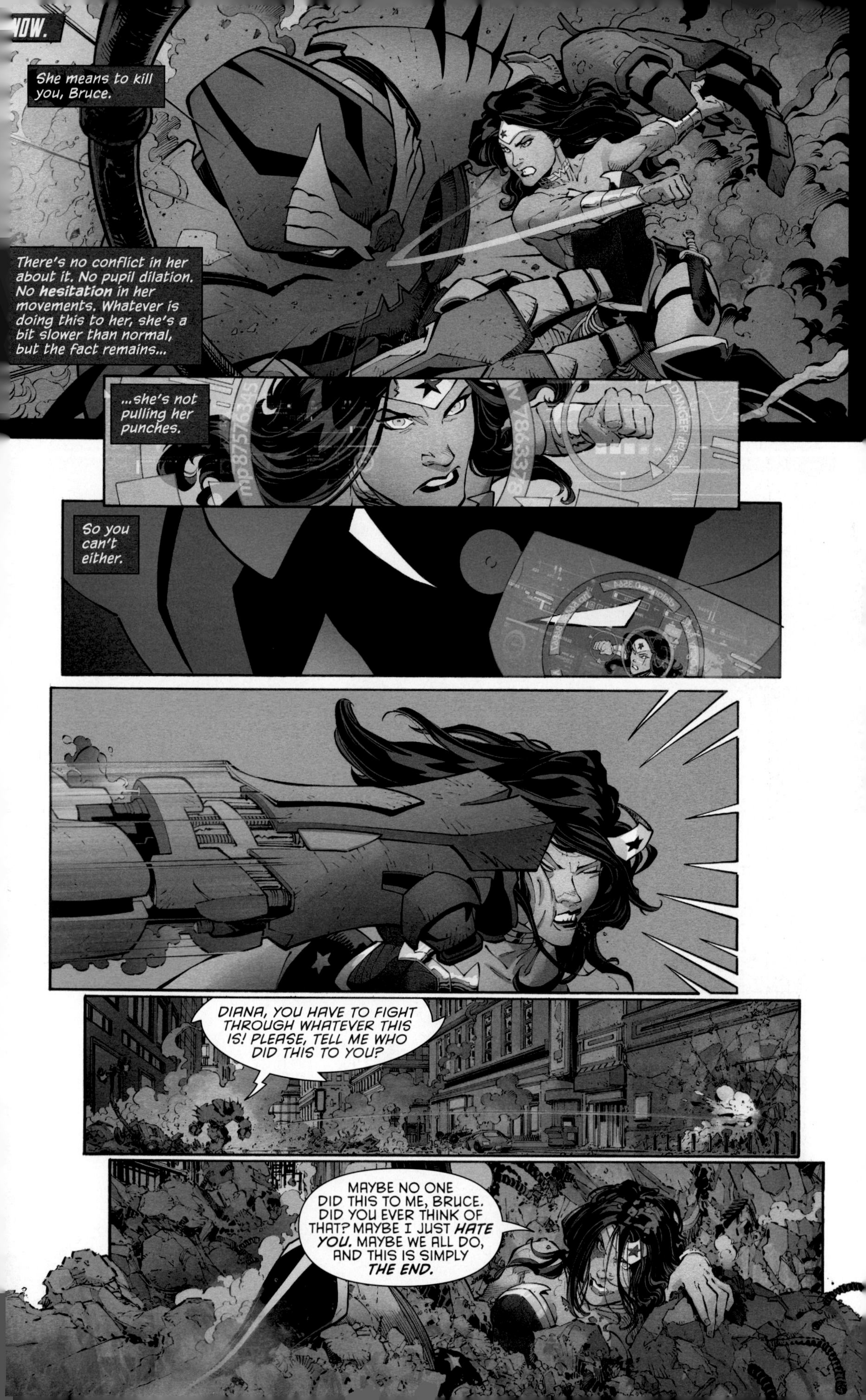
NOW.
She means to kill you, Bruce.
There's no conflict in her about it. No pupil dilation. No hesitation in her movements. Whatever is doing this to her, she's a bit slower than normal, but the fact remains...
...she's not pulling her punches.
So you can't either.
DIANA, YOU HAVE TO FIGHT THROUGH WHATEVER THIS IS! PLEASE, TELL ME WHO DID THIS TO YOU?
MAYBE NO ONE DID THIS TO ME, BRUCE. DID YOU EVER THINK OF THAT? MAYBE I JUST HATE YOU. MAYBE WE ALL DO, AND THIS IS SIMPLY THE END.

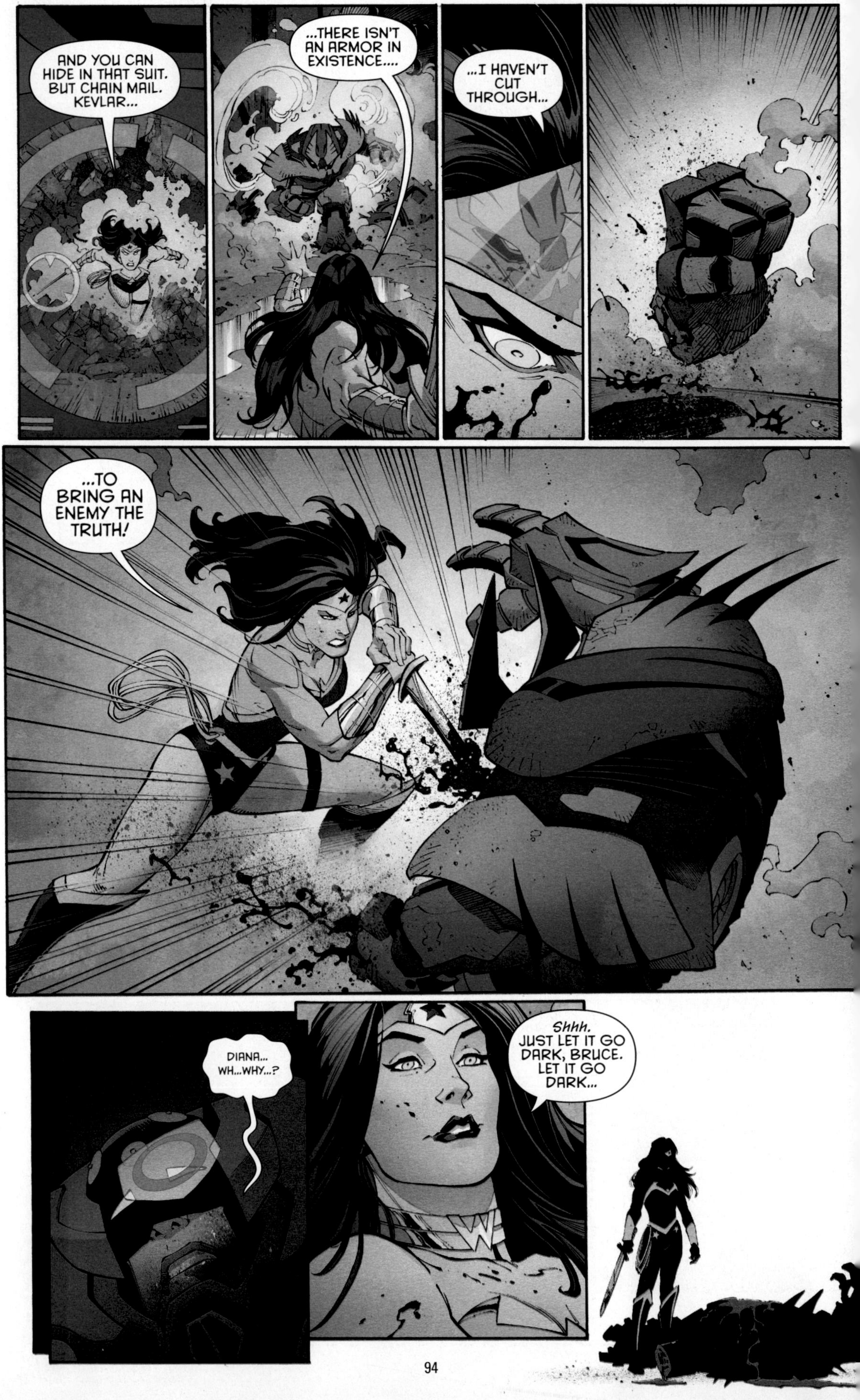
AND YOU CAN HIDE IN THAT SUIT. BUT CHAIN MAIL. KEVLAR...
...THERE ISN'T AN ARMOR IN EXISTENCE....
...I HAVEN'T CUT THROUGH...
...TO BRING AN ENEMY THE TRUTH!
DIANA... WH...WHY...?
Shhh. JUST LET IT GO DARK, BRUCE. LET IT GO DARK...

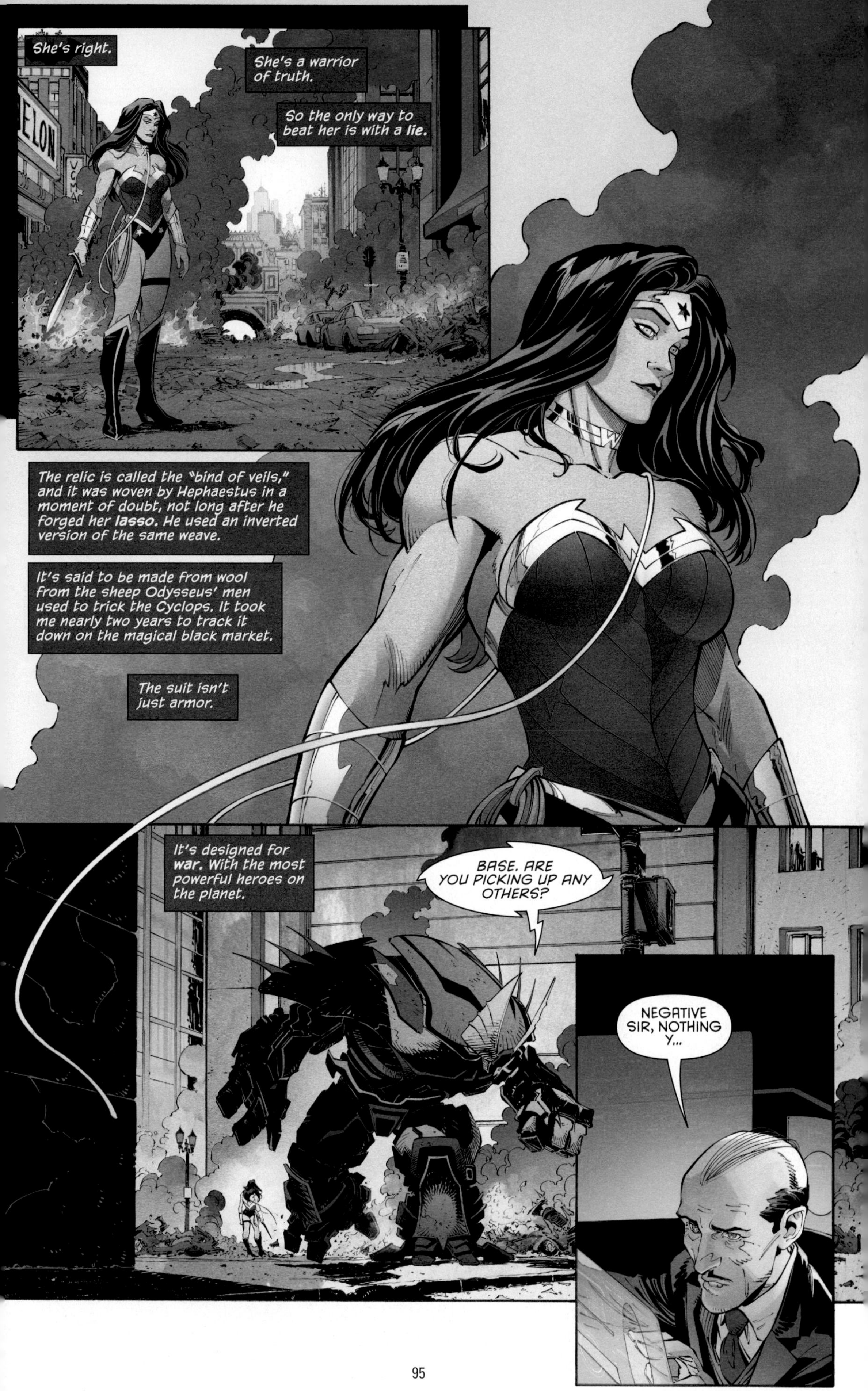
She's right.
She's a warrior of truth.
So the only way to beat her is with a **lie.**
The relic is called the "bind of veils," and it was woven by Hephaestus in a moment of doubt, not long after he forged her **lasso.** He used an inverted version of the same weave.
It's said to be made from wool from the sheep Odysseus' men used to trick the Cyclops. It took me nearly two years to track it down on the magical black market.
The suit isn't just armor.
It's designed for **war.** With the most powerful heroes on the planet.
BASE. ARE YOU PICKING UP ANY OTHERS?
NEGATIVE SIR, NOTHING Y...

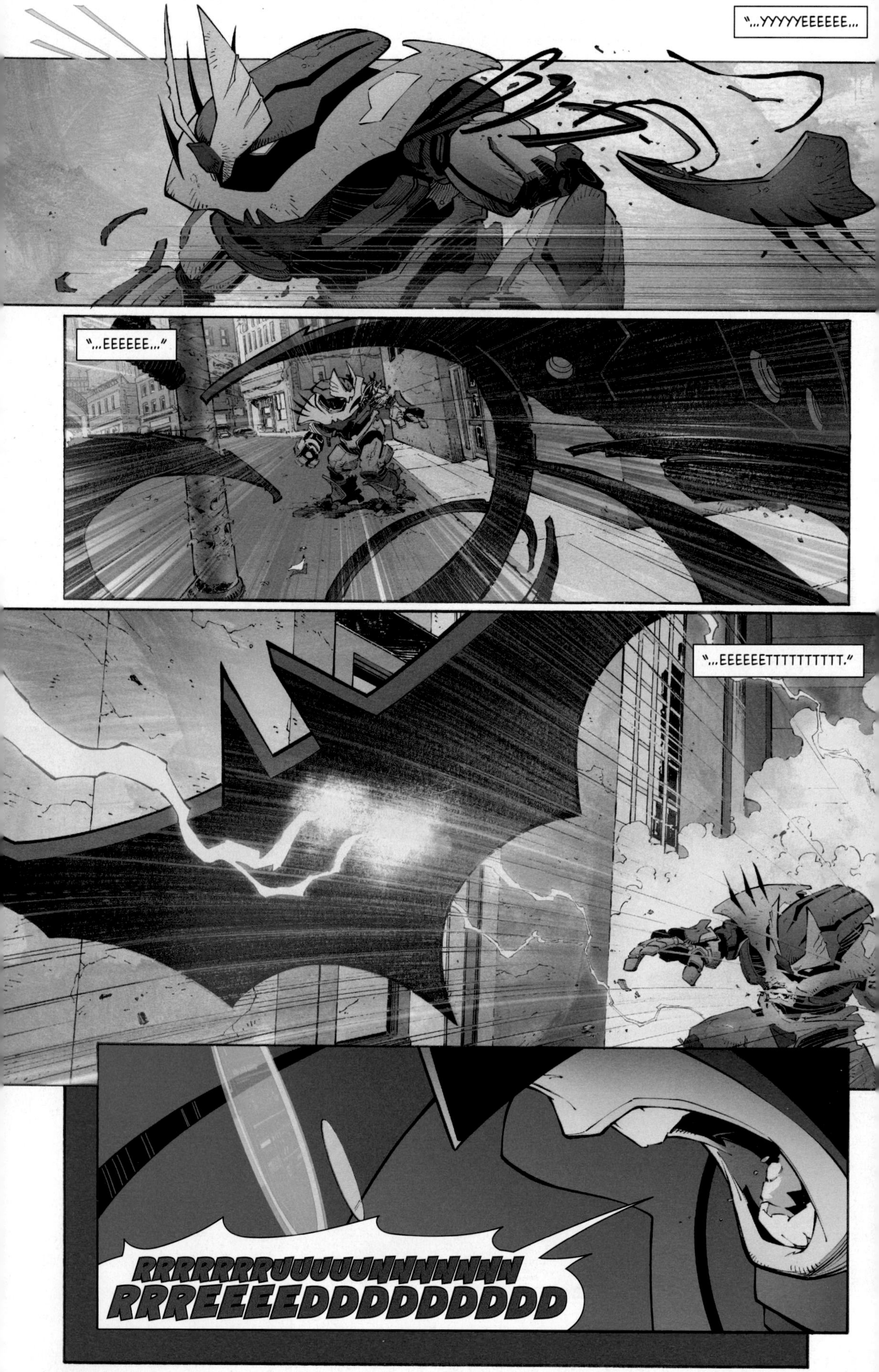
"...YYYYYEEEEEE...
"...EEEEEE..."
"...EEEEEETTTTTTTTTT."
RRRRRRRUUUUUUNNNNNNN
RRREEEEEDDDDDDDDDD

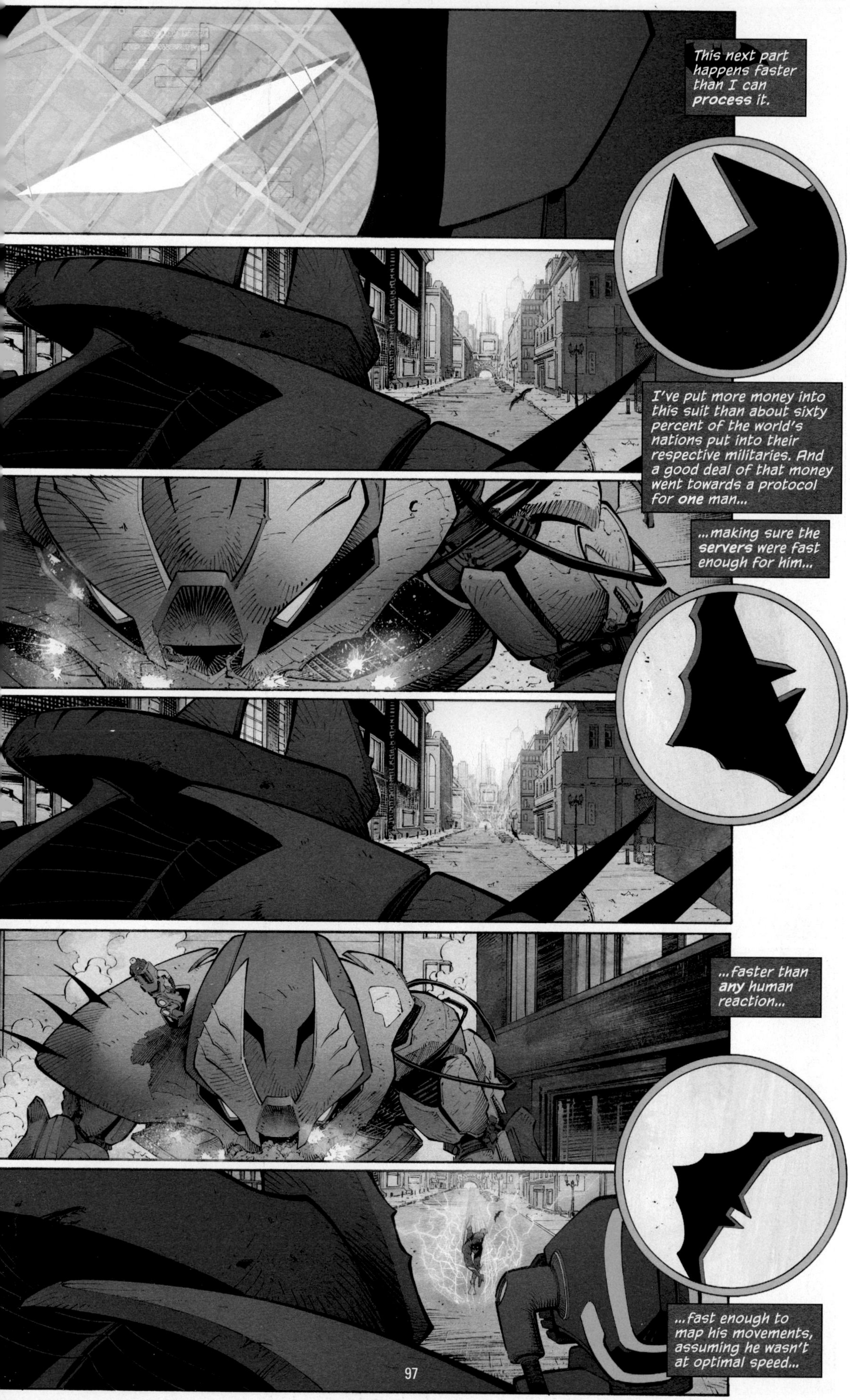
This next part happens faster than I can process it.
I've put more money into this suit than about sixty percent of the world's nations put into their respective militaries. And a good deal of that money went towards a protocol for one man...
...making sure the servers were fast enough for him...
...faster than any human reaction...
...fast enough to map his movements, assuming he wasn't at optimal speed...

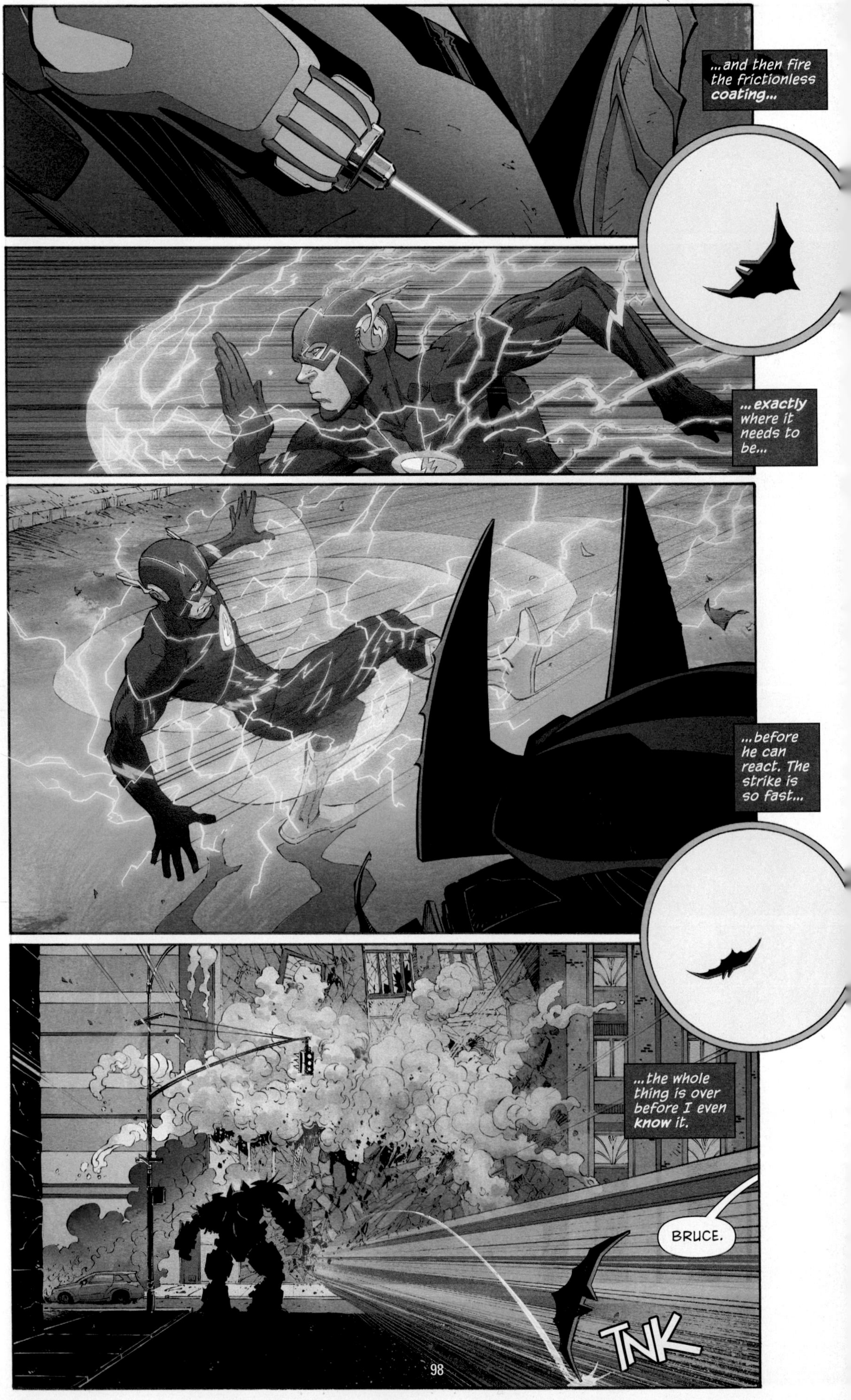
...and then fire the frictionless coating...
...exactly where it needs to be...
...before he can react. The strike is so fast...
...the whole thing is over before I even know it.
BRUCE.
TNK

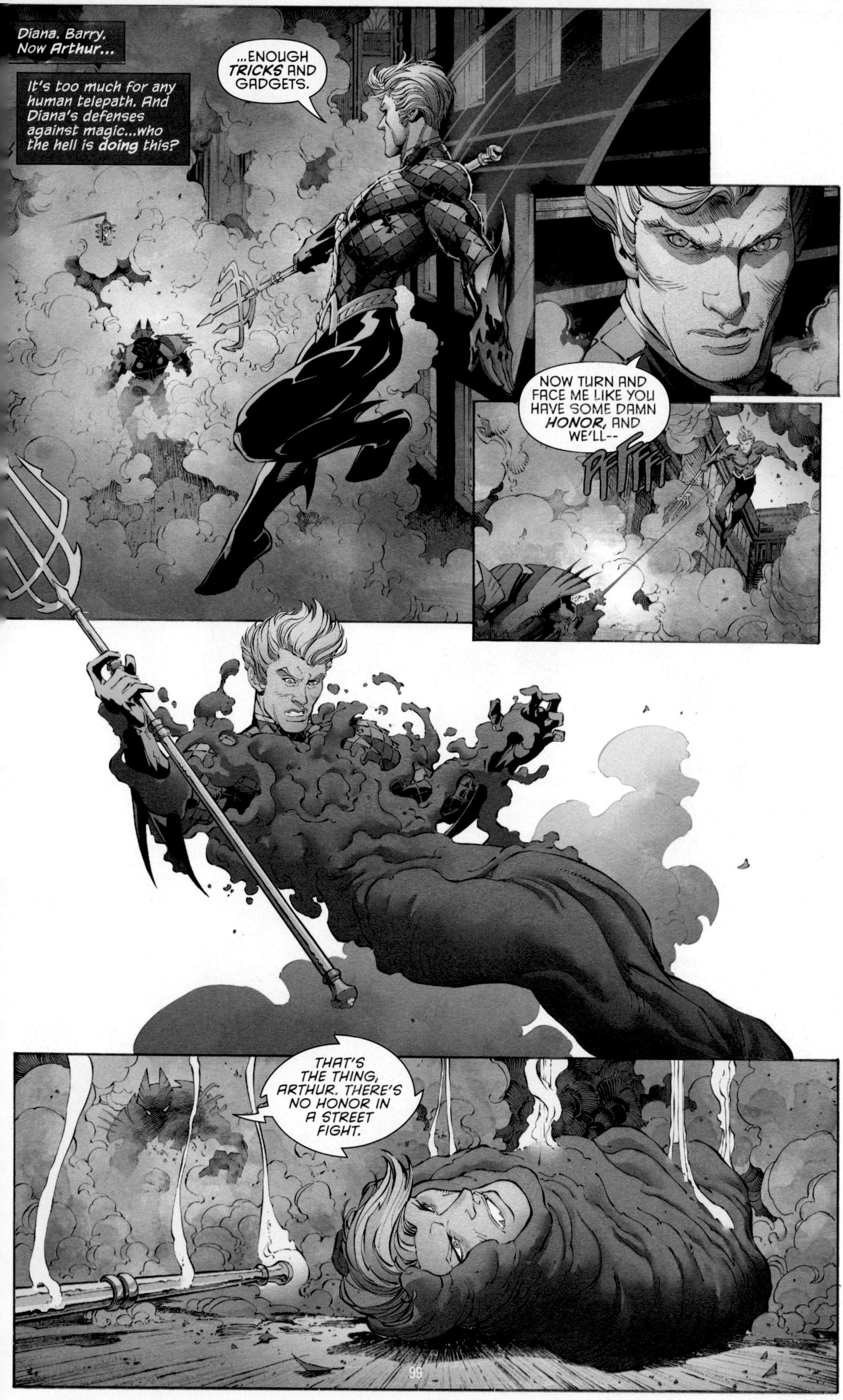
Diana. Barry. Now Arthur...
It's too much for any human telepath. And Diana's defenses against magic...who the hell is doing this?
...ENOUGH TRICKS AND GADGETS.
NOW TURN AND FACE ME LIKE YOU HAVE SOME DAMN HONOR, AND WE'LL--
PFFFT
THAT'S THE THING, ARTHUR. THERE'S NO HONOR IN A STREET FIGHT.

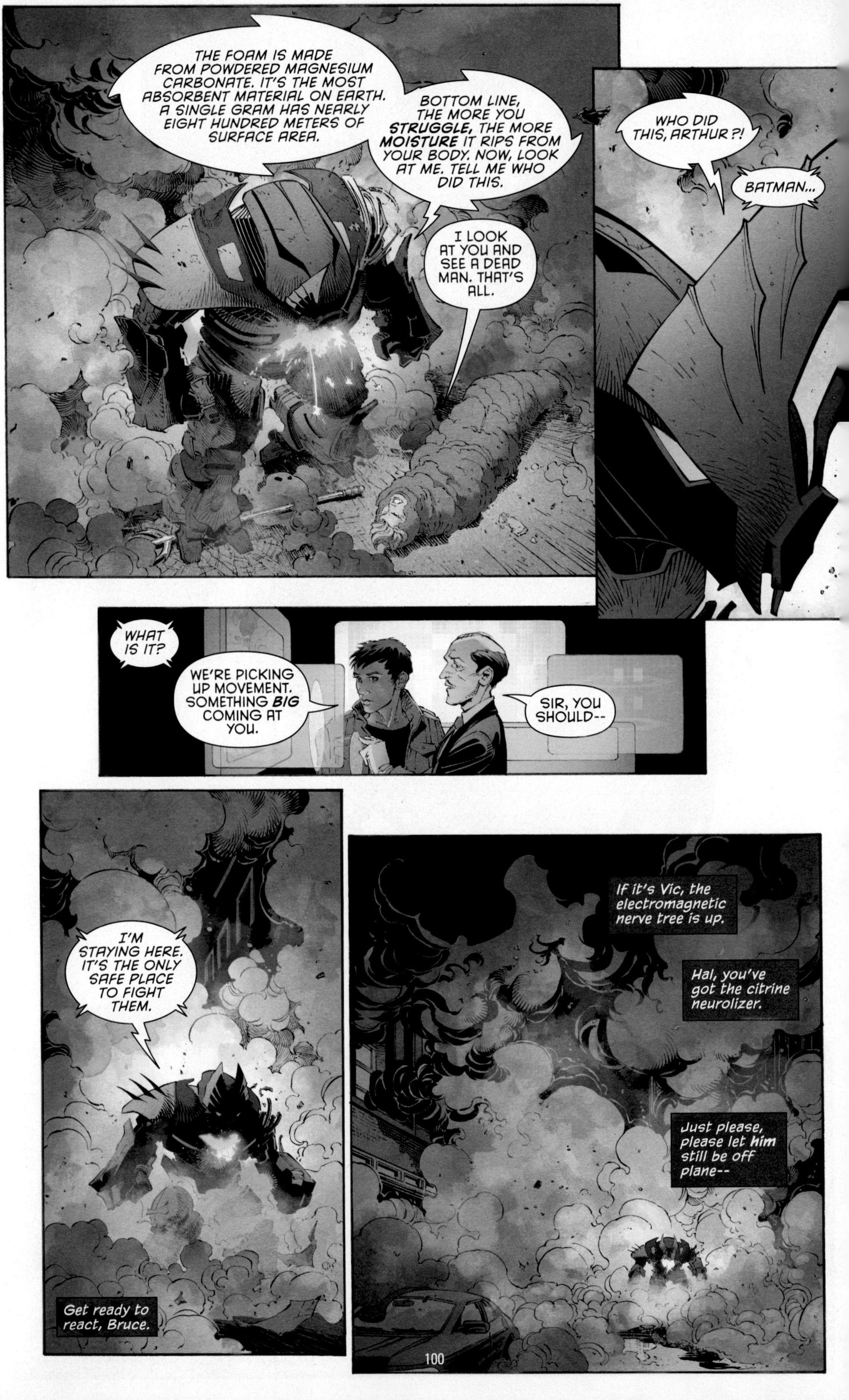
THE FOAM IS MADE FROM POWDERED MAGNESIUM CARBONATE. IT'S THE MOST ABSORBENT MATERIAL ON EARTH. A SINGLE GRAM HAS NEARLY EIGHT HUNDRED METERS OF SURFACE AREA.
BOTTOM LINE, THE MORE YOU STRUGGLE, THE MORE MOISTURE IT RIPS FROM YOUR BODY. NOW, LOOK AT ME. TELL ME WHO DID THIS.
I LOOK AT YOU AND SEE A DEAD MAN. THAT'S ALL.
WHO DID THIS, ARTHUR?!
BATMAN...
WHAT IS IT?
WE'RE PICKING UP MOVEMENT. SOMETHING BIG COMING AT YOU.
SIR, YOU SHOULD--
I'M STAYING HERE. IT'S THE ONLY SAFE PLACE TO FIGHT THEM.
Get ready to react, Bruce.
If it's Vic, the electromagnetic nerve tree is up.
Hal, you've got the citrine neurolizer.
Just please, please let him still be off plane--

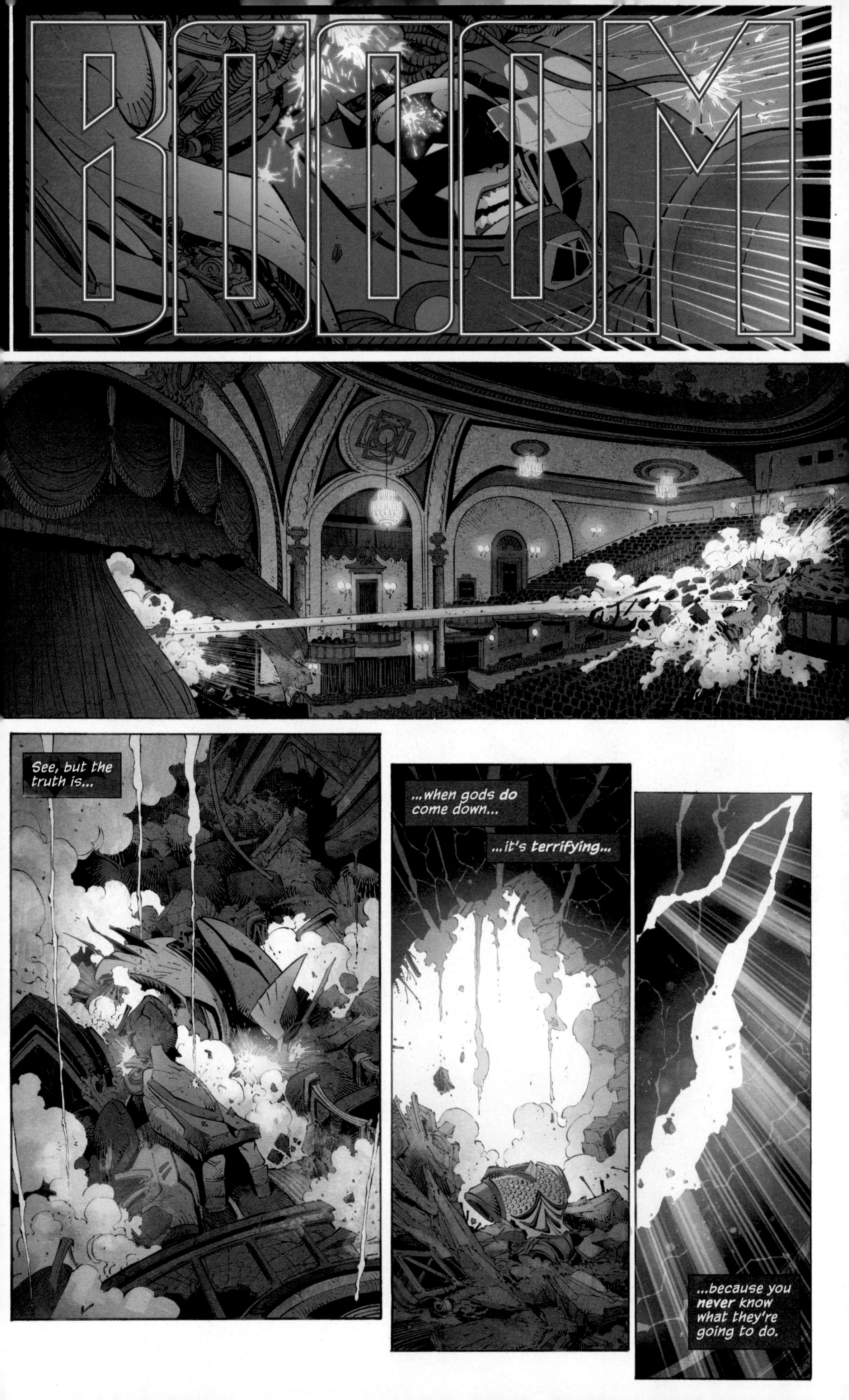
BOOOM
See, but the truth is...
...when gods do come down...
...it's terrifying...
...because you never know what they're going to do.

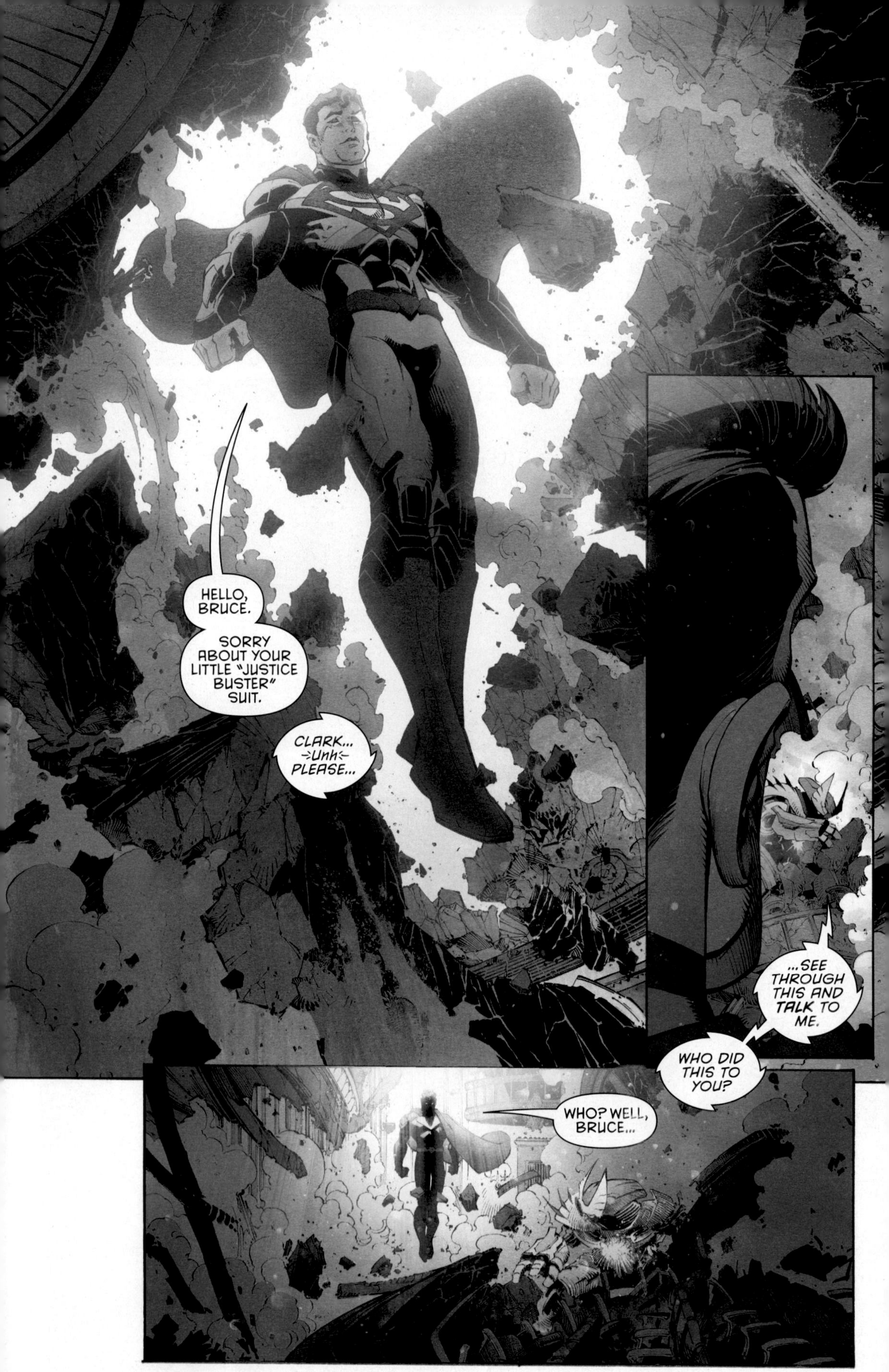
HELLO, BRUCE.
SORRY ABOUT YOUR LITTLE "JUSTICE BUSTER" SUIT.
CLARK... -Unh- PLEASE...
...SEE THROUGH THIS AND TALK TO ME.
WHO DID THIS TO YOU?
WHO? WELL, BRUCE...

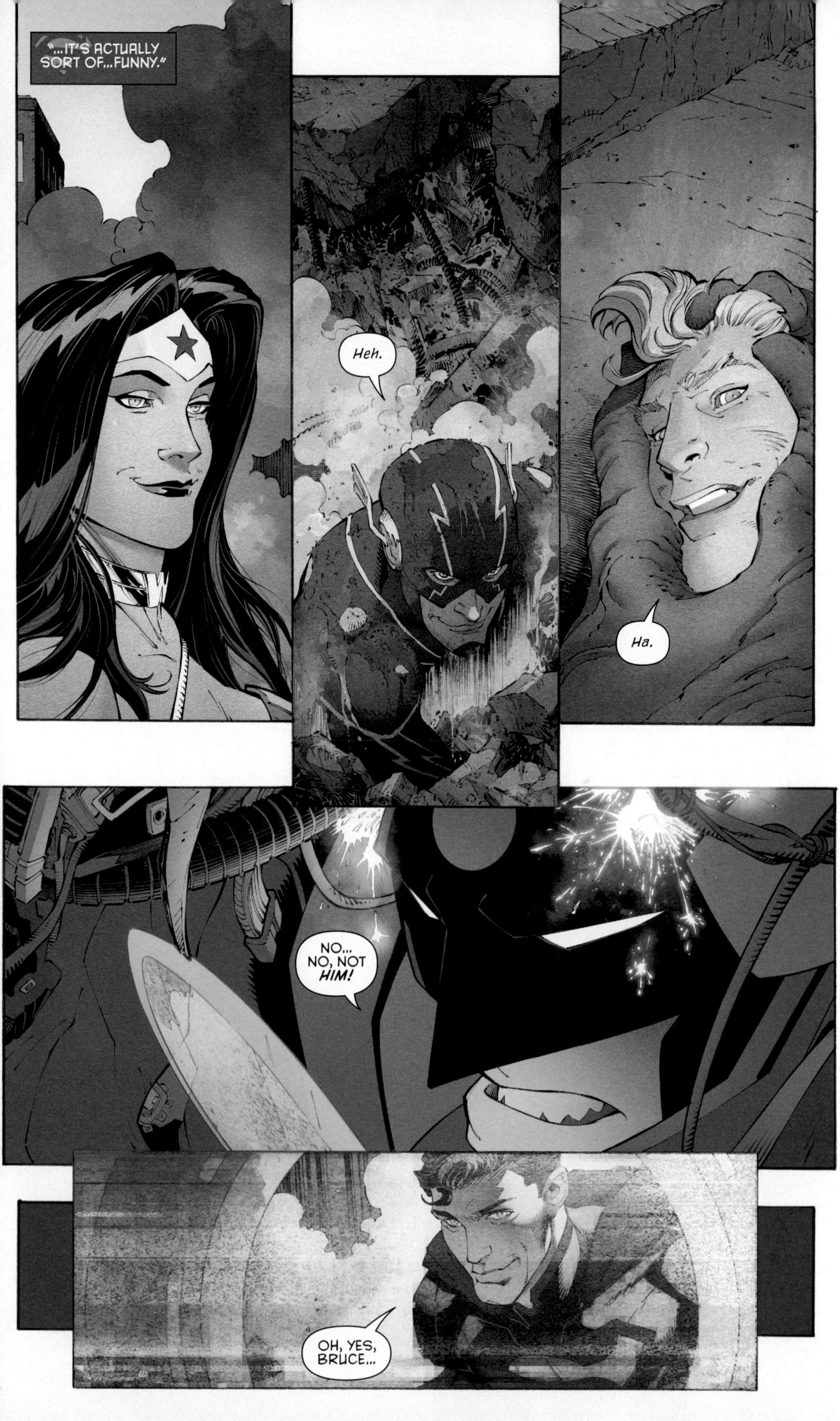
"...IT'S ACTUALLY SORT OF...FUNNY."
Heh.
Ha.
NO... NO, NOT HIM!
OH, YES, BRUCE...

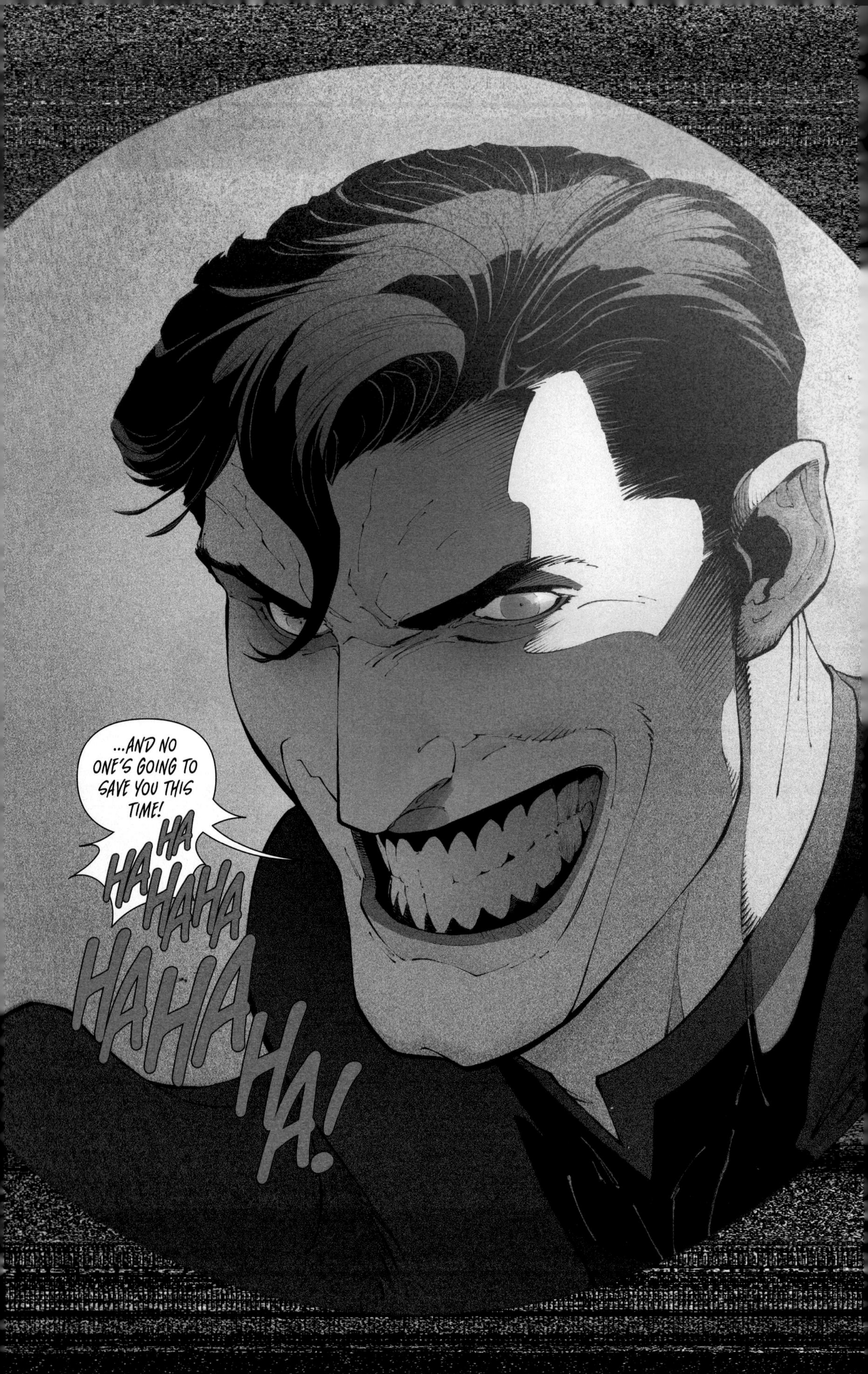
...AND NO ONE'S GOING TO SAVE YOU THIS TIME!
HA HAHAHA HAHAHA HA!

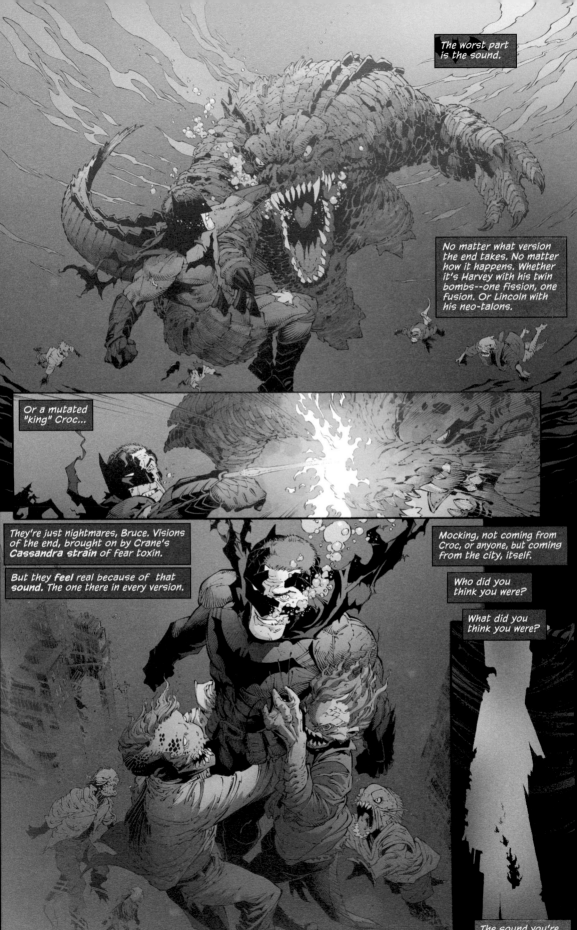

The worst part is the sound.

No matter what version the end takes. No matter how it happens. Whether it's Harvey with his twin bombs--one fission, one fusion. Or Lincoln with his neo-talons.

Or a mutated "king" Croc...

They're just nightmares, Bruce. Visions of the end, brought on by Crane's *Cassandra* strain of fear toxin.

But they *feel* real because of that *sound.* The one there in every version.

Mocking, not coming from Croc, or anyone, but coming from the city, itself.

Who did you think you were?

What did you think you were?

The sound you're afraid will be there in the real end...

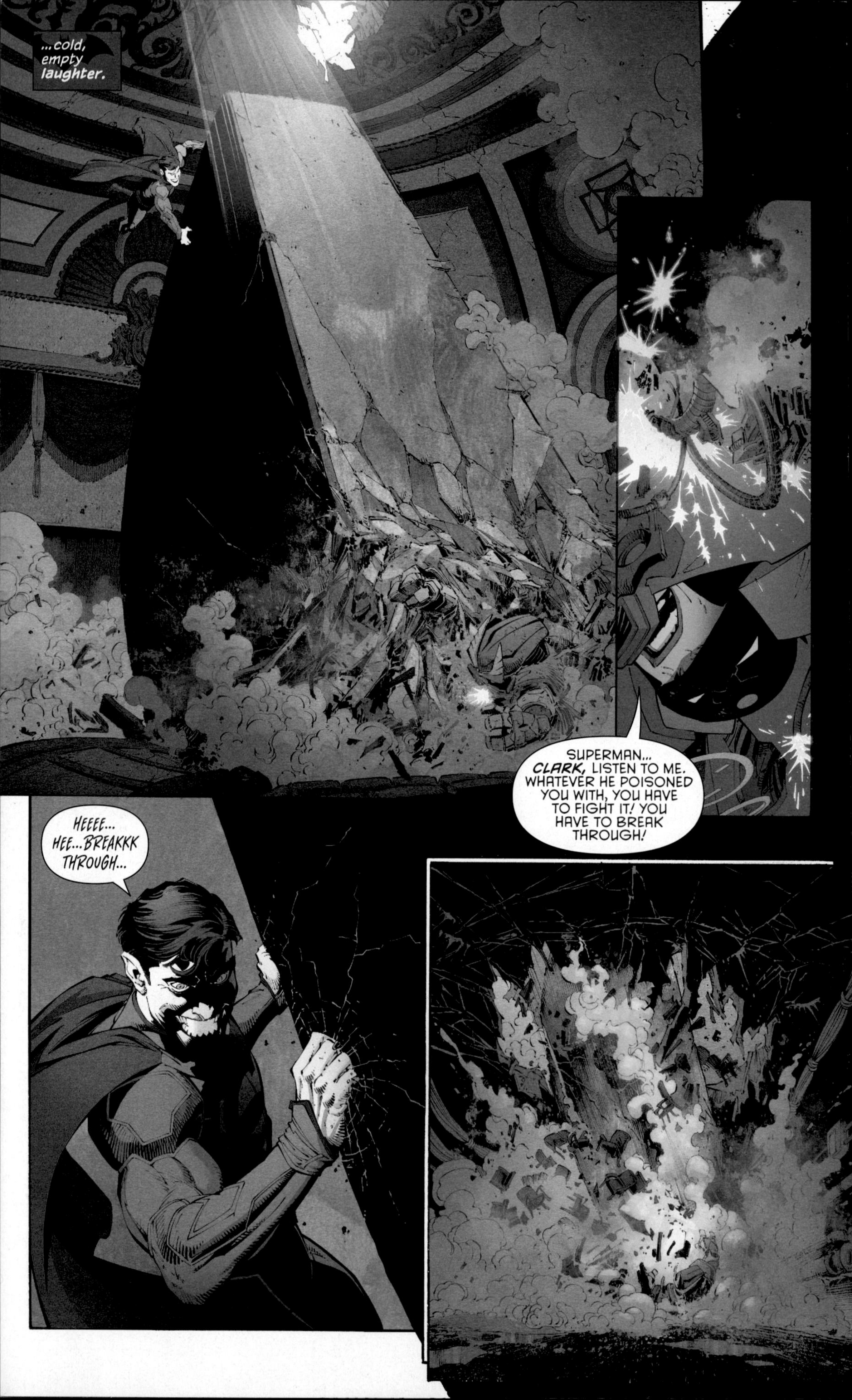
...cold, empty laughter.
SUPERMAN... CLARK, LISTEN TO ME. WHATEVER HE POISONED YOU WITH, YOU HAVE TO FIGHT IT! YOU HAVE TO BREAK THROUGH!
HEEEE... HEE...BREAKKK THROUGH...

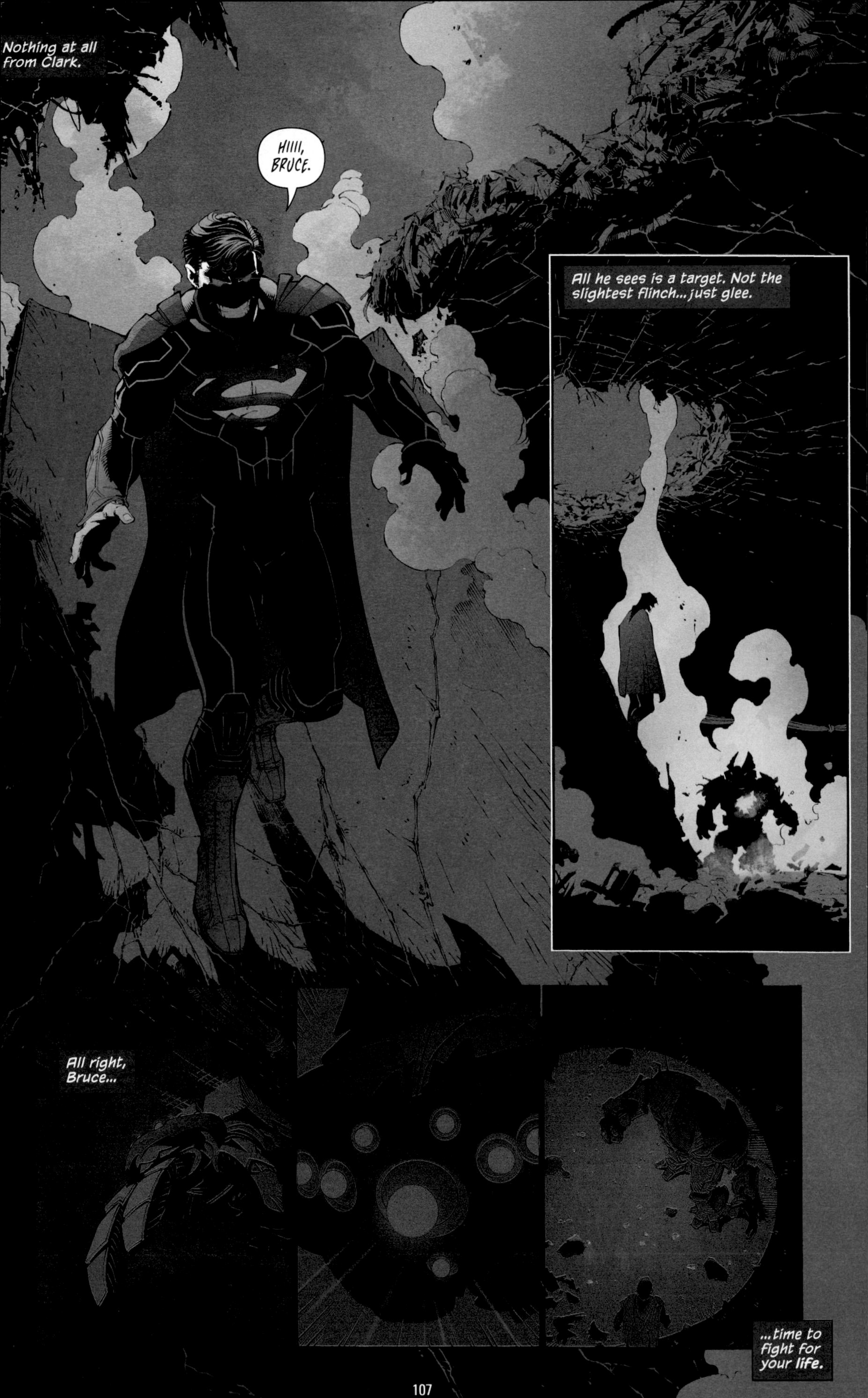
Nothing at all from Clark.
HIIII, BRUCE.
All he sees is a target. Not the slightest flinch... just glee.
All right, Bruce...
...time to fight for your life.

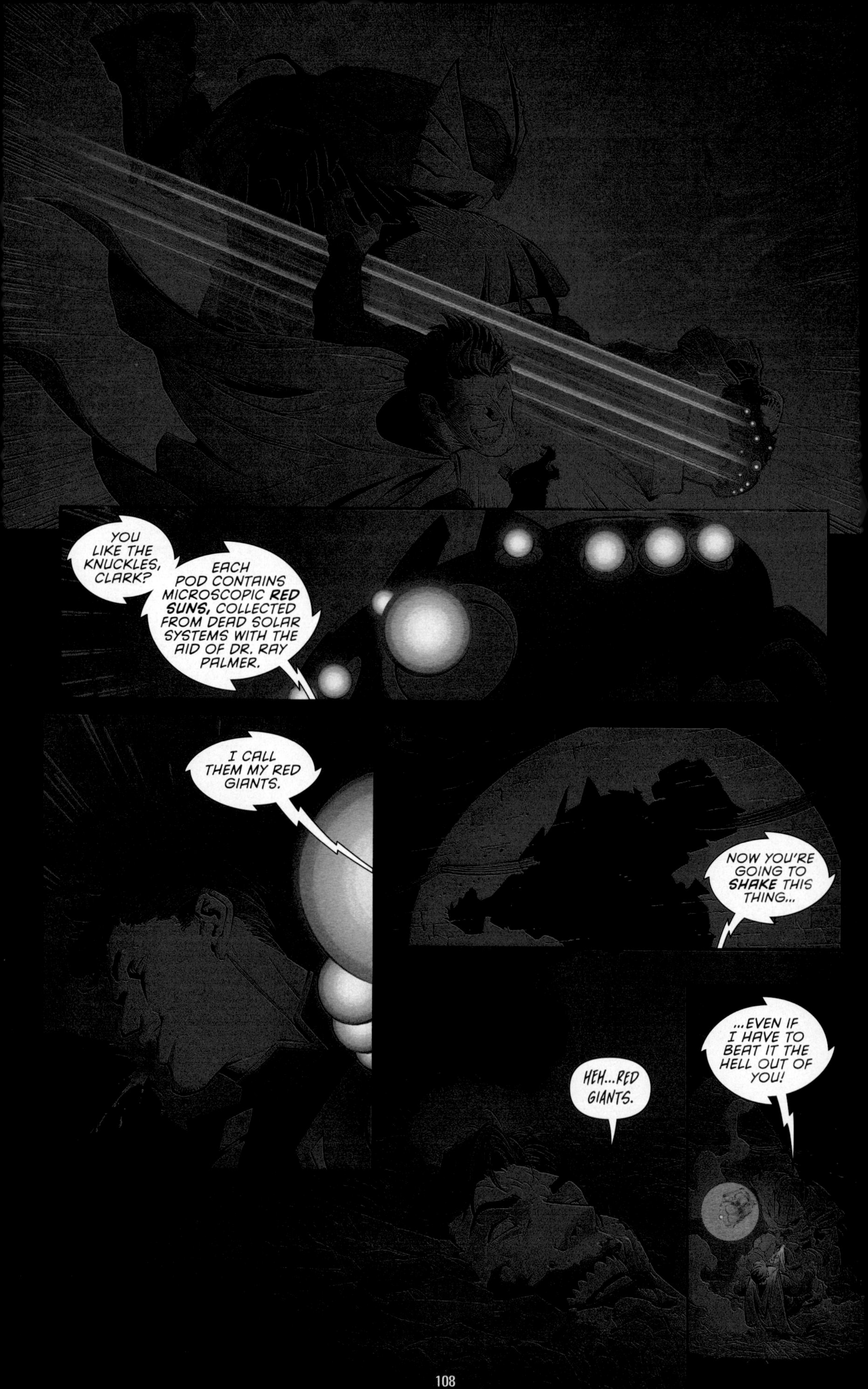
YOU LIKE THE KNUCKLES, CLARK?
EACH POD CONTAINS MICROSCOPIC RED SUNS, COLLECTED FROM DEAD SOLAR SYSTEMS WITH THE AID OF DR. RAY PALMER.
I CALL THEM MY RED GIANTS.
NOW YOU'RE GOING TO SHAKE THIS THING...
HEH...RED GIANTS.
...EVEN IF I HAVE TO BEAT IT THE HELL OUT OF YOU!

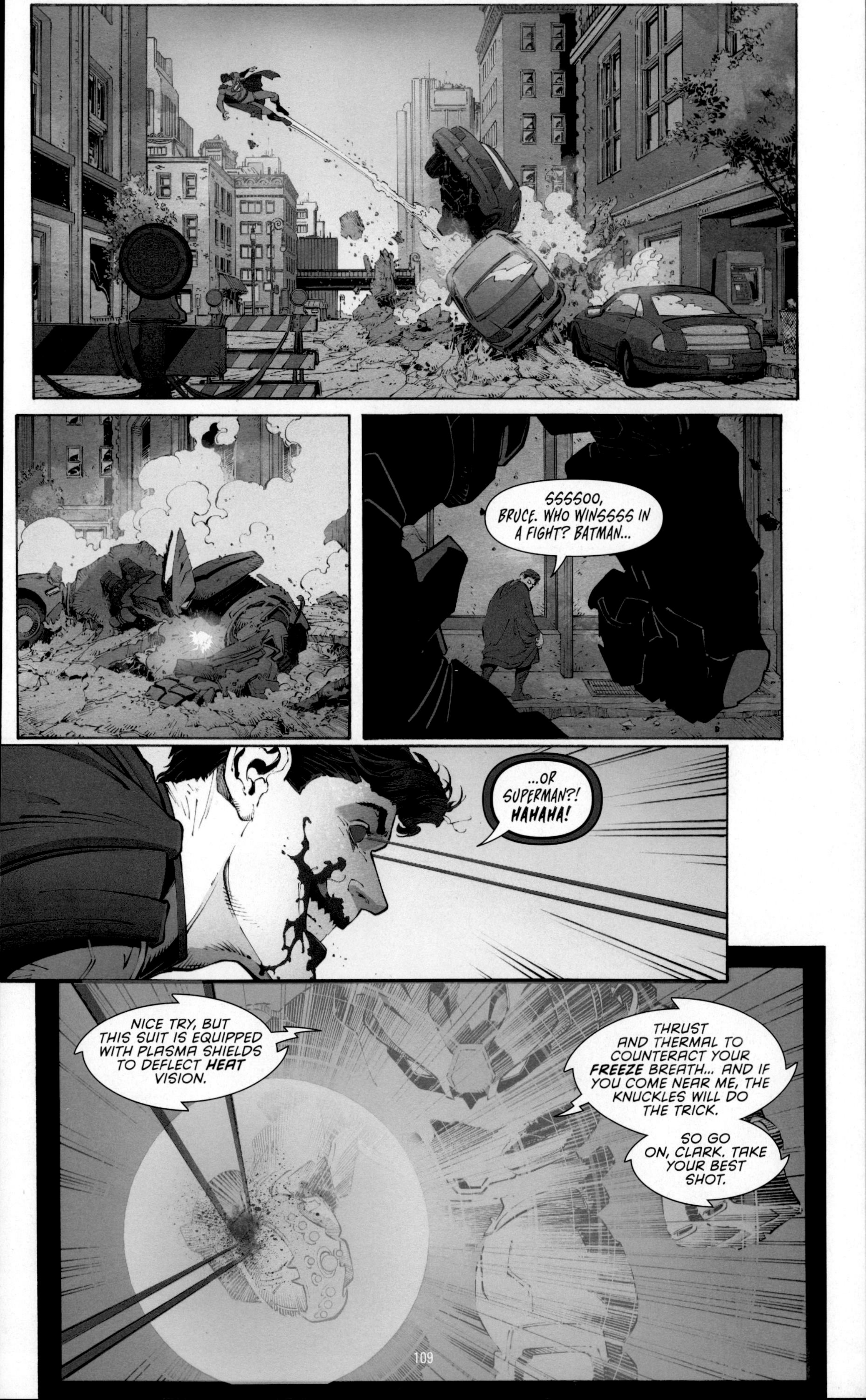
SSSSOO, BRUCE. WHO WINSSSS IN A FIGHT? BATMAN...
...OR SUPERMAN?! HAHAHA!
NICE TRY, BUT THIS SUIT IS EQUIPPED WITH PLASMA SHIELDS TO DEFLECT HEAT VISION.
THRUST AND THERMAL TO COUNTERACT YOUR FREEZE BREATH... AND IF YOU COME NEAR ME, THE KNUCKLES WILL DO THE TRICK.
SO GO ON, CLARK. TAKE YOUR BEST SHOT.

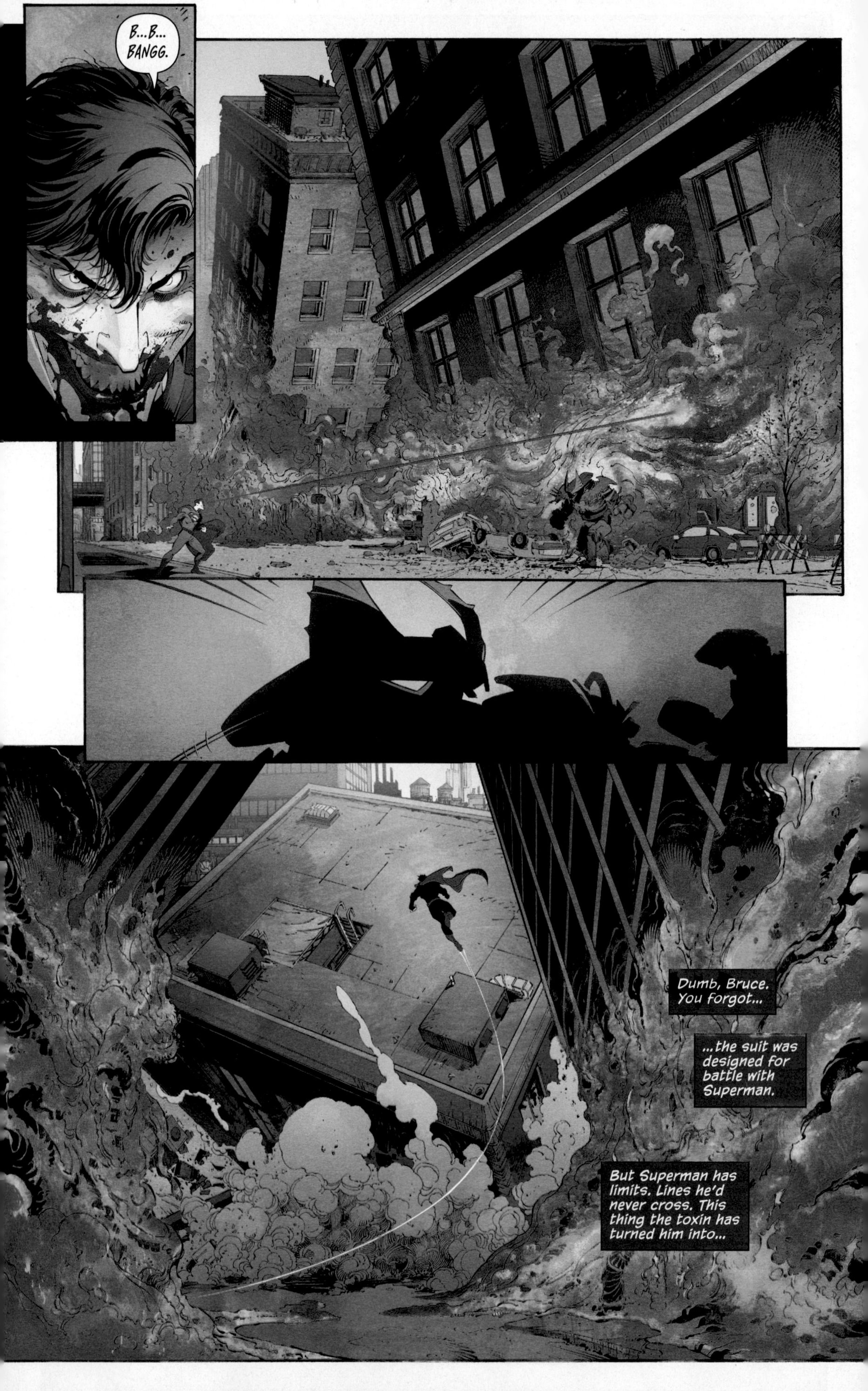
B...B... BANGG.
Dumb, Bruce. You forgot...
...the suit was designed for battle with Superman.
But Superman has limits. Lines he'd never cross. This thing the toxin has turned him into...

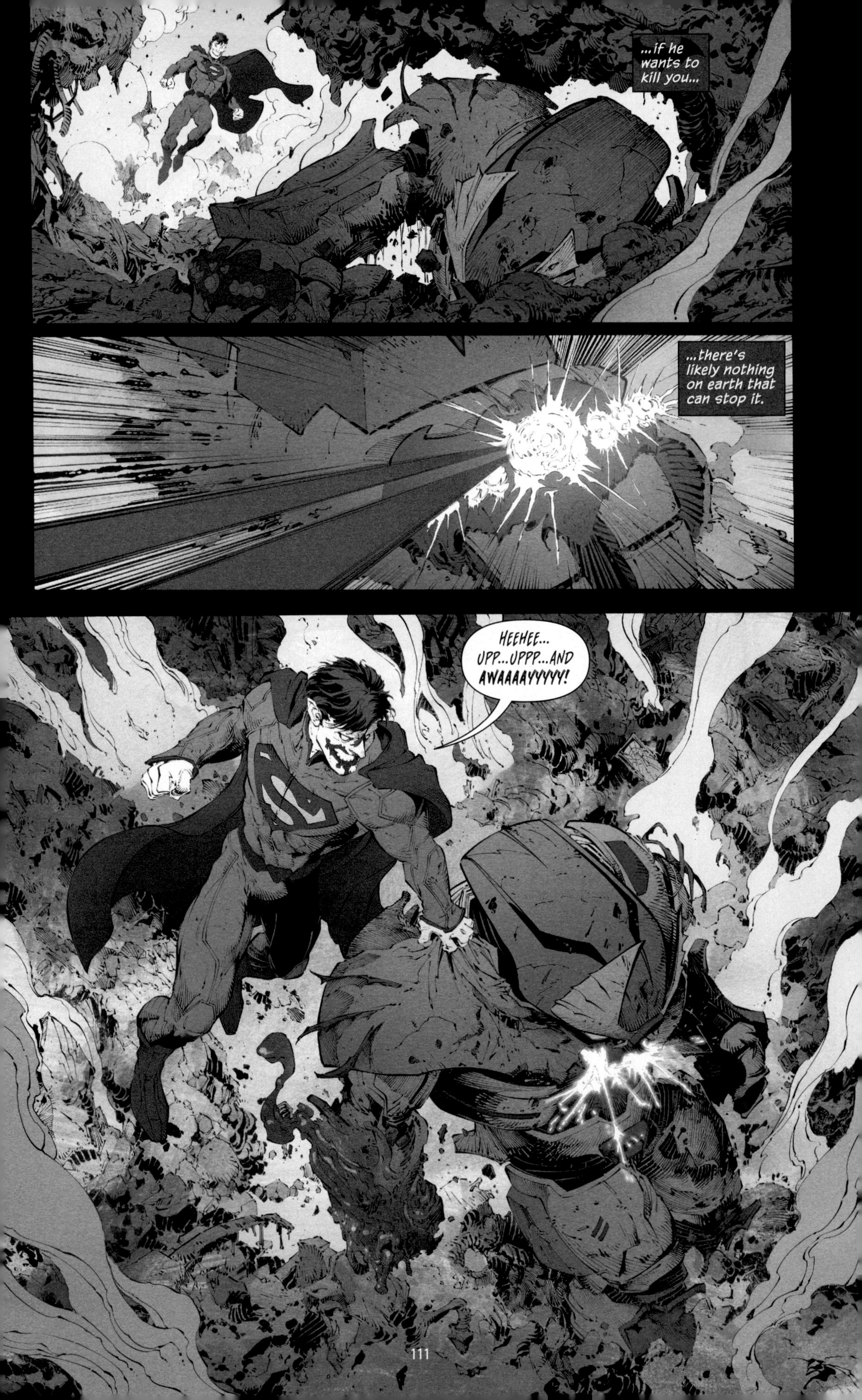
...if he wants to kill you...
...there's likely nothing on earth that can stop it.
HEEHEE... UPP...UPPP...AND AWAAAAYYYYY!

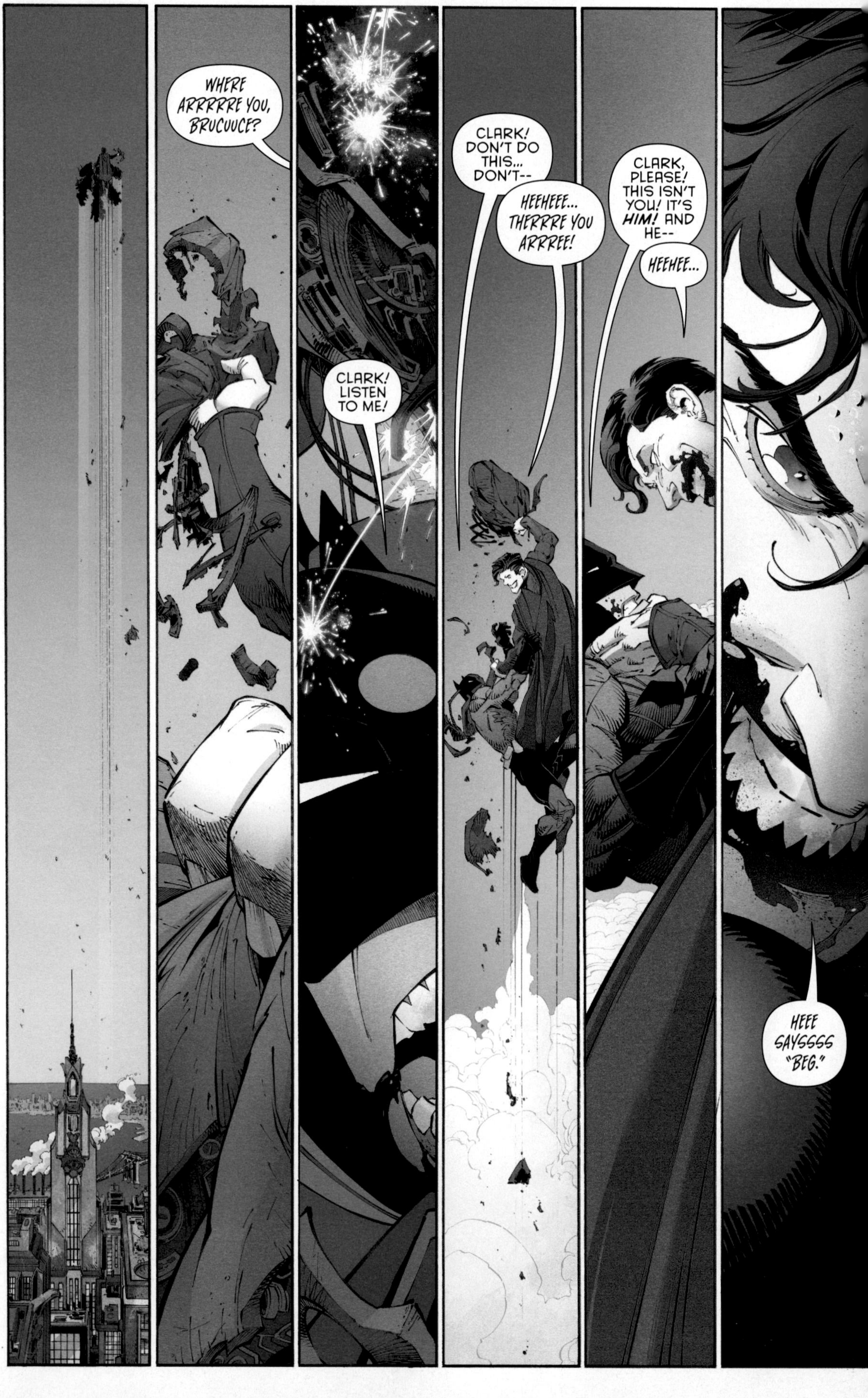
WHERE ARRRRRE YOU, BRUCUUCE?
CLARK! LISTEN TO ME!
CLARK! DON'T DO THIS... DON'T--
HEEHEEE... THERRRE YOU ARRREE!
CLARK, PLEASE! THIS ISN'T YOU! IT'S HIM! AND HE--
HEEHEE...
HEEE SAYSSSS "BEG."

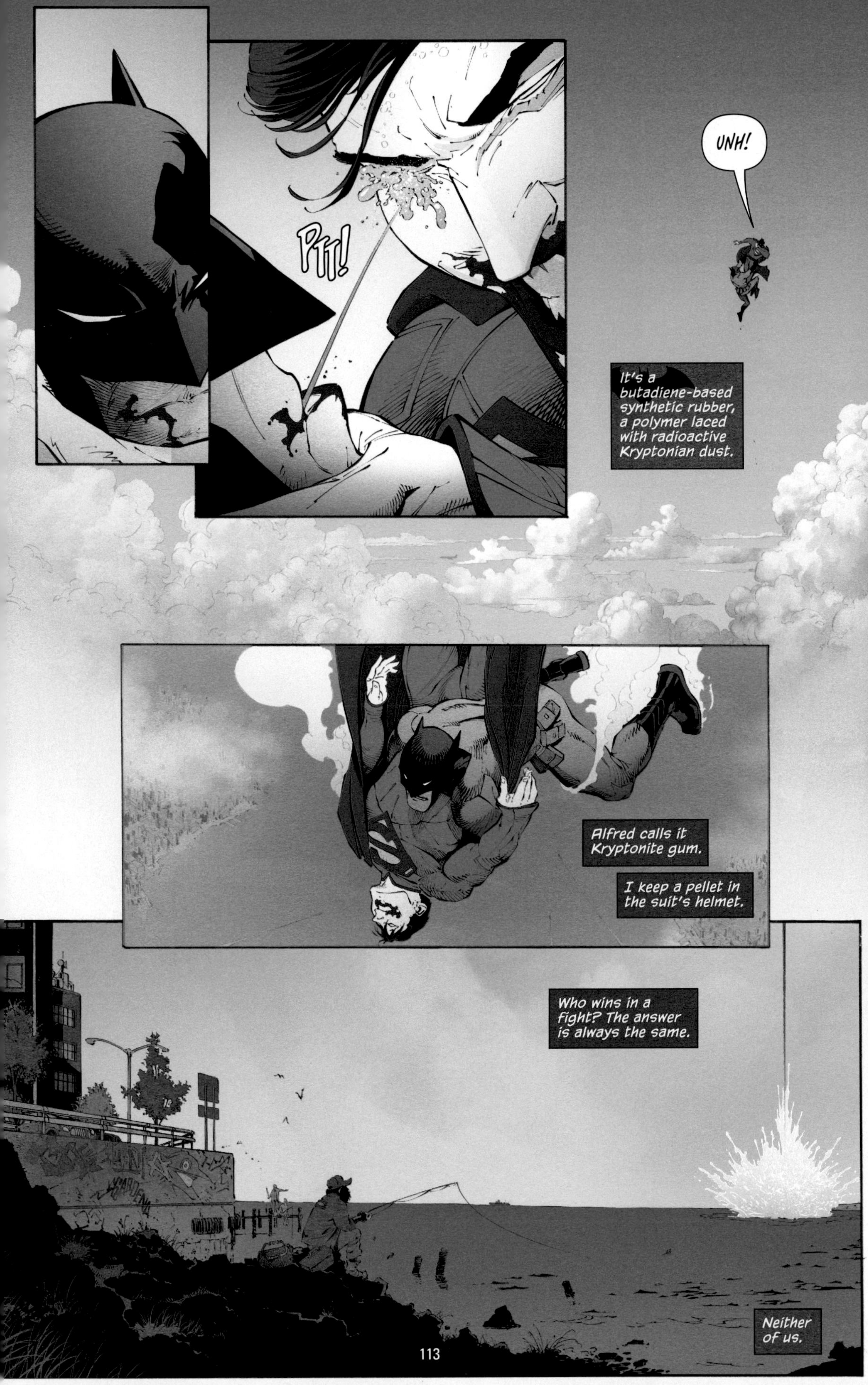
PTT!
UNH!
It's a butadiene-based synthetic rubber, a polymer laced with radioactive Kryptonian dust.
Alfred calls it Kryptonite gum.
I keep a pellet in the suit's helmet.
Who wins in a fight? The answer is always the same.
Neither of us.

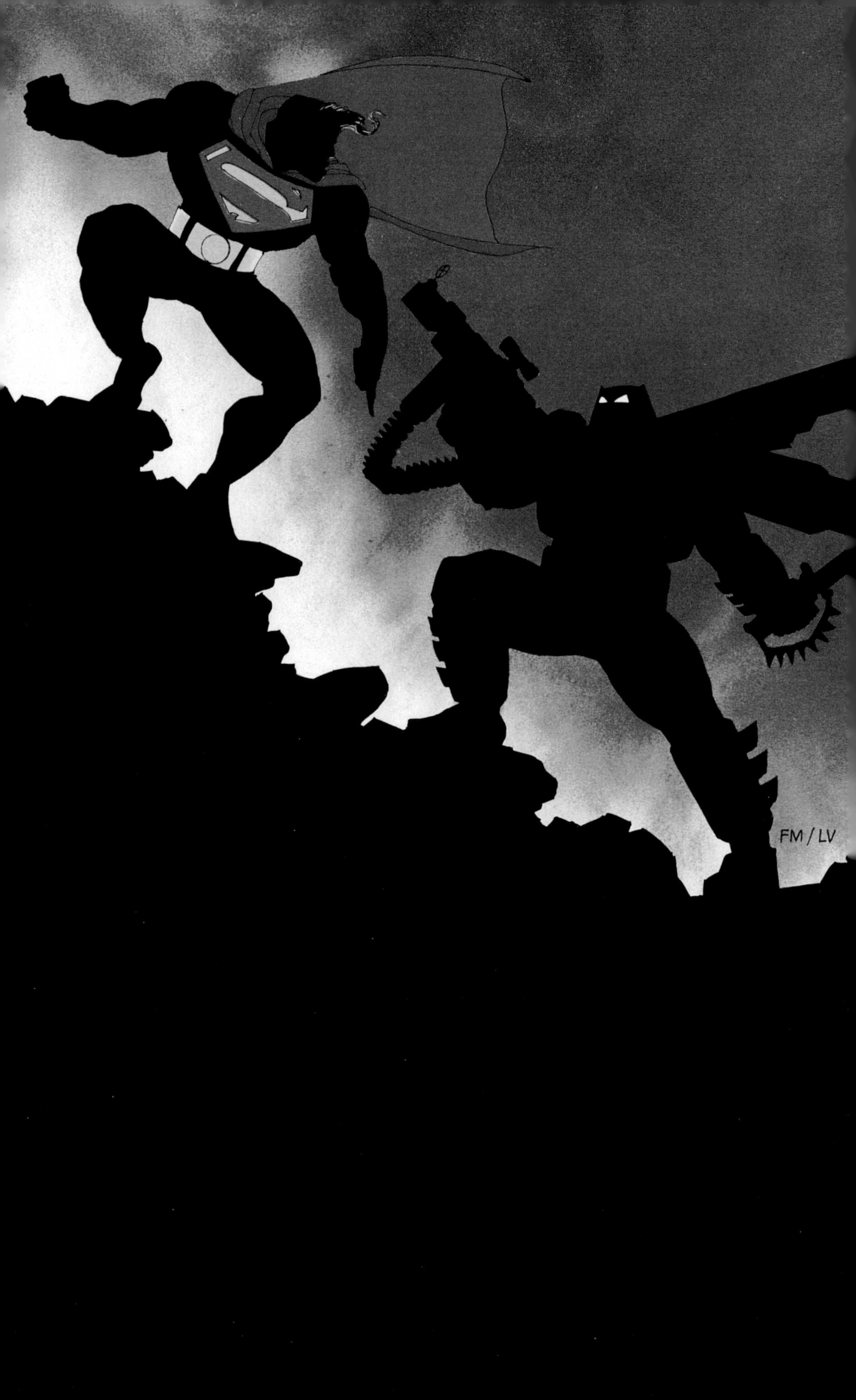
FM / LV

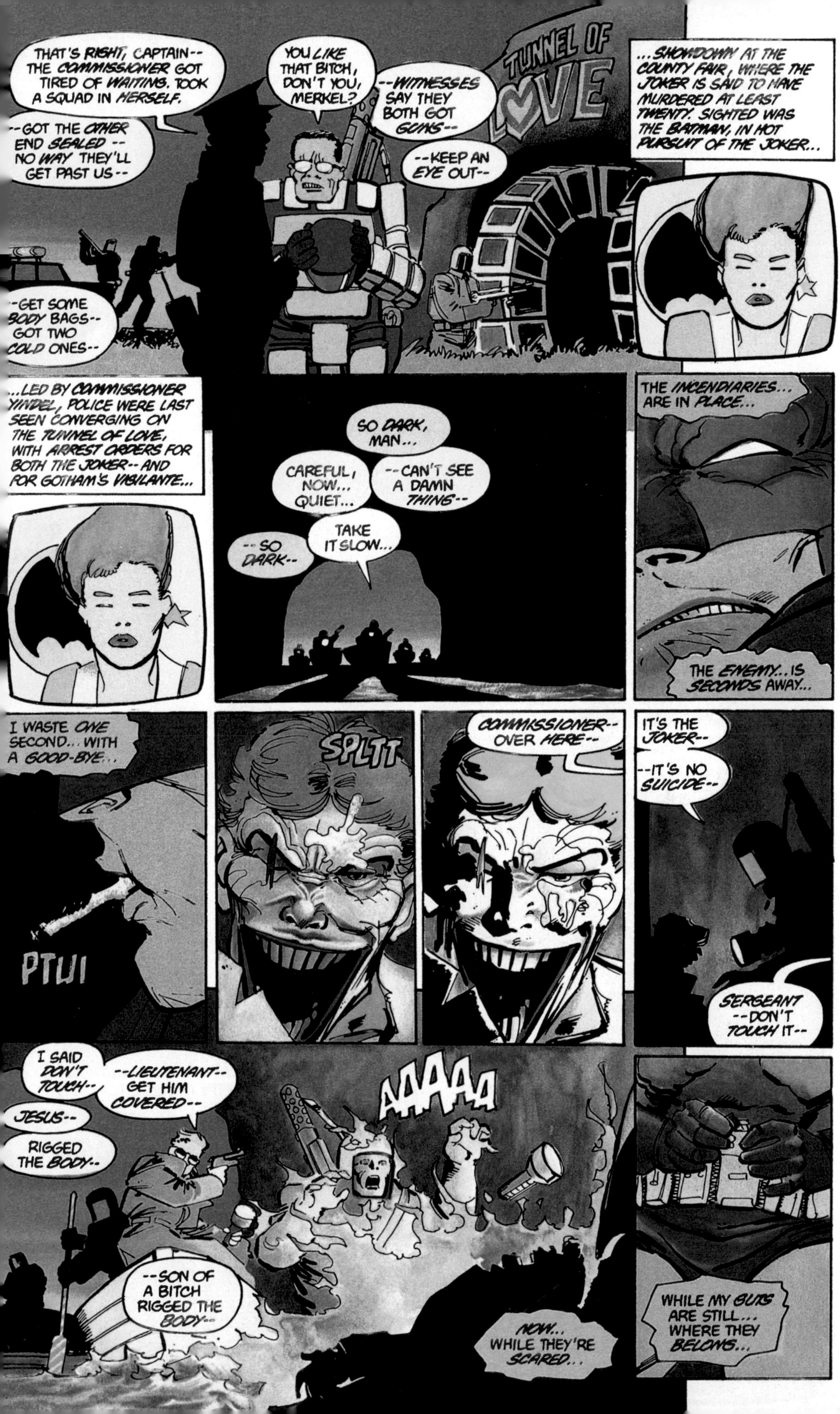
THAT'S RIGHT, CAPTAIN-- THE COMMISSIONER GOT TIRED OF WAITING. TOOK A SQUAD IN HERSELF.
--GOT THE OTHER END SEALED-- NO WAY THEY'LL GET PAST US--
YOU LIKE THAT BITCH, DON'T YOU, MERKEL?
--WITNESSES SAY THEY BOTH GOT GUNS--
--KEEP AN EYE OUT--
TUNNEL OF LOVE
--GET SOME BODY BAGS-- GOT TWO COLD ONES--
...SHOWDOWN AT THE COUNTY FAIR, WHERE THE JOKER IS SAID TO HAVE MURDERED AT LEAST TWENTY. SIGHTED WAS THE BATMAN, IN HOT PURSUIT OF THE JOKER...
...LED BY COMMISSIONER YINDEL, POLICE WERE LAST SEEN CONVERGING ON THE TUNNEL OF LOVE, WITH ARREST ORDERS FOR BOTH THE JOKER-- AND FOR GOTHAM'S VIGILANTE...
SO DARK, MAN...
CAREFUL, NOW... QUIET...
--CAN'T SEE A DAMN THING--
TAKE IT SLOW...
--SO DARK--
THE INCENDIARIES... ARE IN PLACE...
THE ENEMY... IS SECONDS AWAY...
I WASTE ONE SECOND... WITH A GOOD-BYE...
PTUI
SPLTT
COMMISSIONER-- OVER HERE--
IT'S THE JOKER--
--IT'S NO SUICIDE--
SERGEANT --DON'T TOUCH IT--
I SAID DON'T TOUCH--
--LIEUTENANT-- GET HIM COVERED--
JESUS--
RIGGED THE BODY--
AAAAA
--SON OF A BITCH RIGGED THE BODY--
NOW... WHILE THEY'RE SCARED...
WHILE MY GUTS ARE STILL... WHERE THEY BELONG...

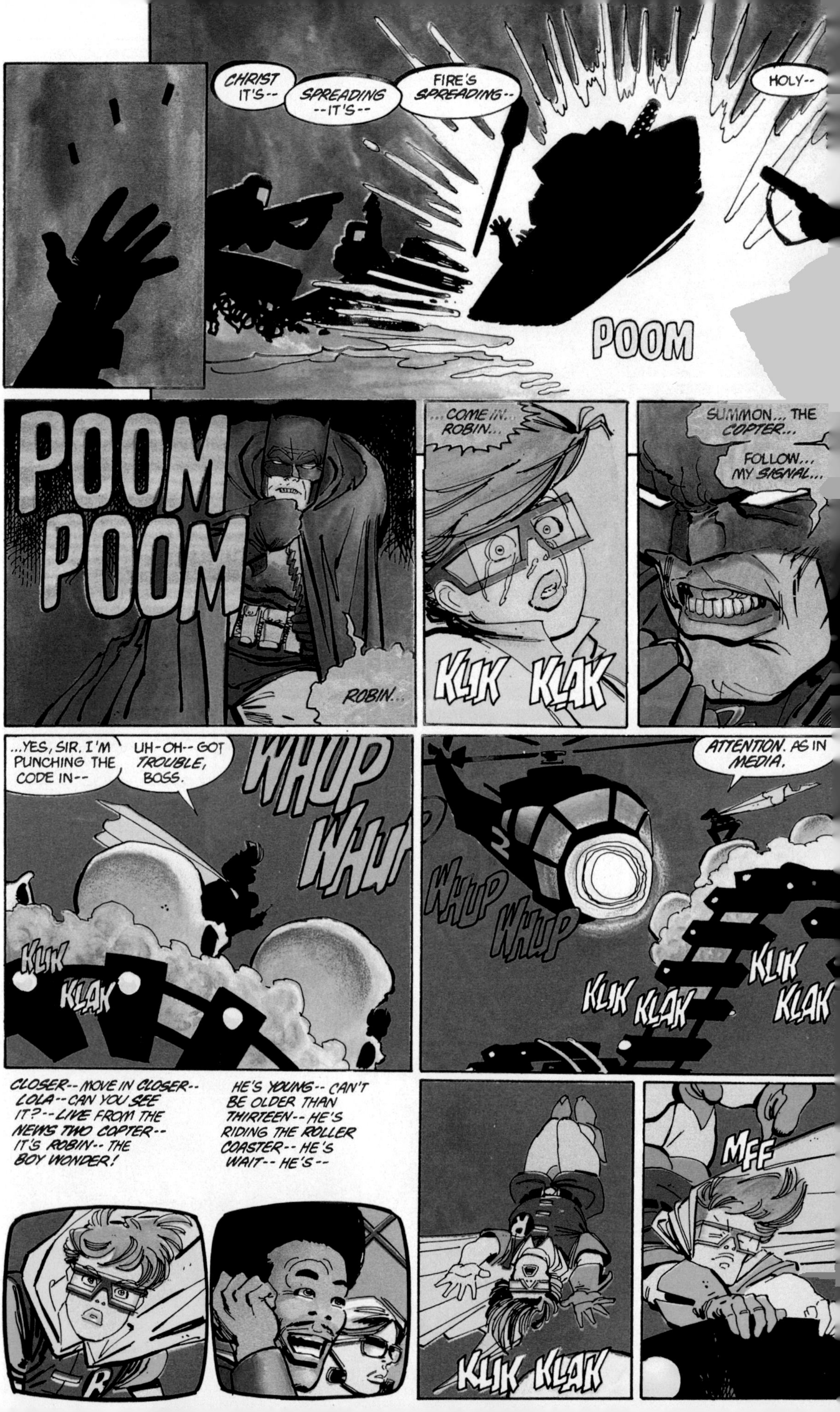
CHRIST IT'S--
SPREADING --IT'S--
FIRE'S SPREADING--
HOLY--
POOM
POOM POOM
ROBIN...
...COME IN, ROBIN...
KLIK KLAK
SUMMON... THE COPTER...
FOLLOW... MY SIGNAL...
...YES, SIR. I'M PUNCHING THE CODE IN--
UH-OH-- GOT TROUBLE, BOSS.
WHUP
KLIK
KLAK
ATTENTION. AS IN MEDIA.
WHUP WHUP
KLIK KLAK
KLIK KLAK
CLOSER-- MOVE IN CLOSER-- LOLA-- CAN YOU SEE IT?-- LIVE FROM THE NEWS TWO COPTER-- IT'S ROBIN-- THE BOY WONDER!
HE'S YOUNG-- CAN'T BE OLDER THAN THIRTEEN-- HE'S RIDING THE ROLLER COASTER-- HE'S WAIT-- HE'S--
MFF
KLIK KLAK

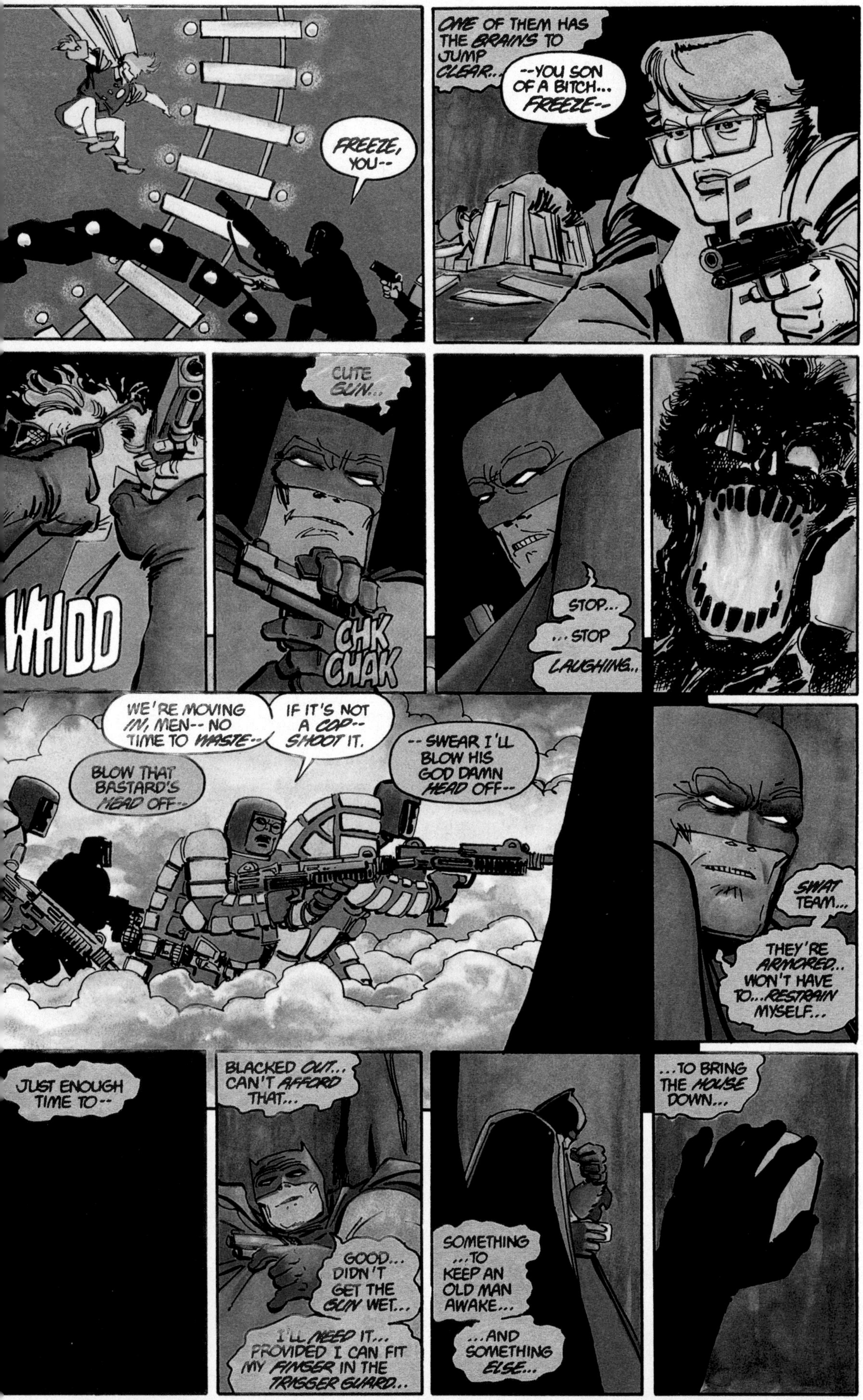
FREEZE, YOU--
ONE OF THEM HAS THE BRAINS TO JUMP CLEAR...
--YOU SON OF A BITCH... FREEZE--
WHDD
CUTE GUN...
CHK CHAK
STOP...
...STOP
LAUGHING...
WE'RE MOVING IN, MEN-- NO TIME TO WASTE--
IF IT'S NOT A COP-- SHOOT IT.
BLOW THAT BASTARD'S HEAD OFF--
-- SWEAR I'LL BLOW HIS GOD DAMN HEAD OFF--
SWAT TEAM...
THEY'RE ARMORED... WON'T HAVE TO...RESTRAIN MYSELF...
JUST ENOUGH TIME TO--
BLACKED OUT... CAN'T AFFORD THAT...
GOOD... DIDN'T GET THE GUN WET...
I'LL NEED IT... PROVIDED I CAN FIT MY FINGER IN THE TRIGGER GUARD...
SOMETHING ...TO KEEP AN OLD MAN AWAKE...
...AND SOMETHING ELSE...
...TO BRING THE HOUSE DOWN...

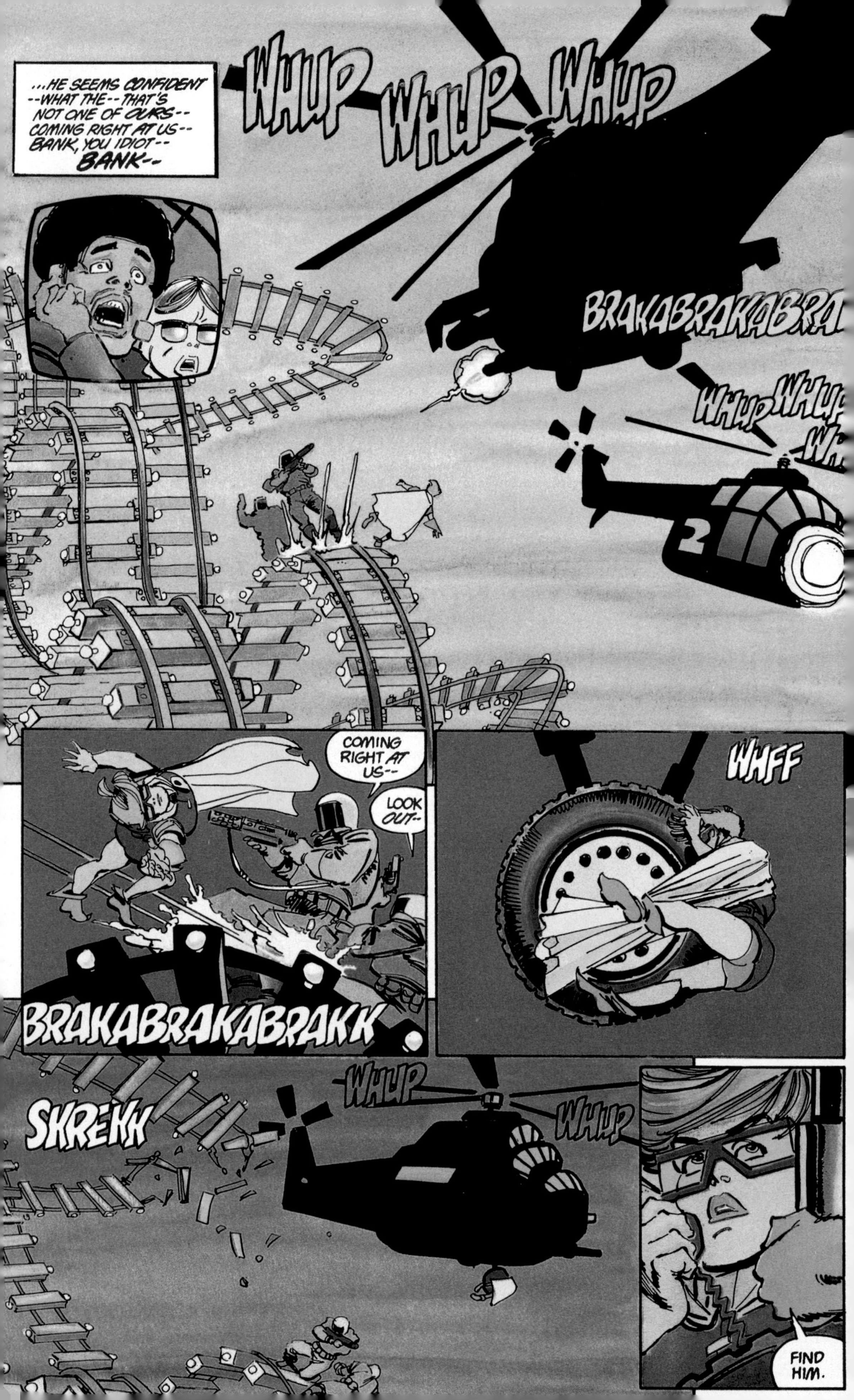
...HE SEEMS CONFIDENT --WHAT THE-- THAT'S NOT ONE OF OURS-- COMING RIGHT AT US-- BANK, YOU IDIOT-- BANK--
WHUP WHUP WHUP
BRAKABRAKABRA
WHUP WHUP
COMING RIGHT AT US--
LOOK OUT--
BRAKABRAKABRAKK
WHFF
SKREKK
WHUP
WHUP
FIND HIM.

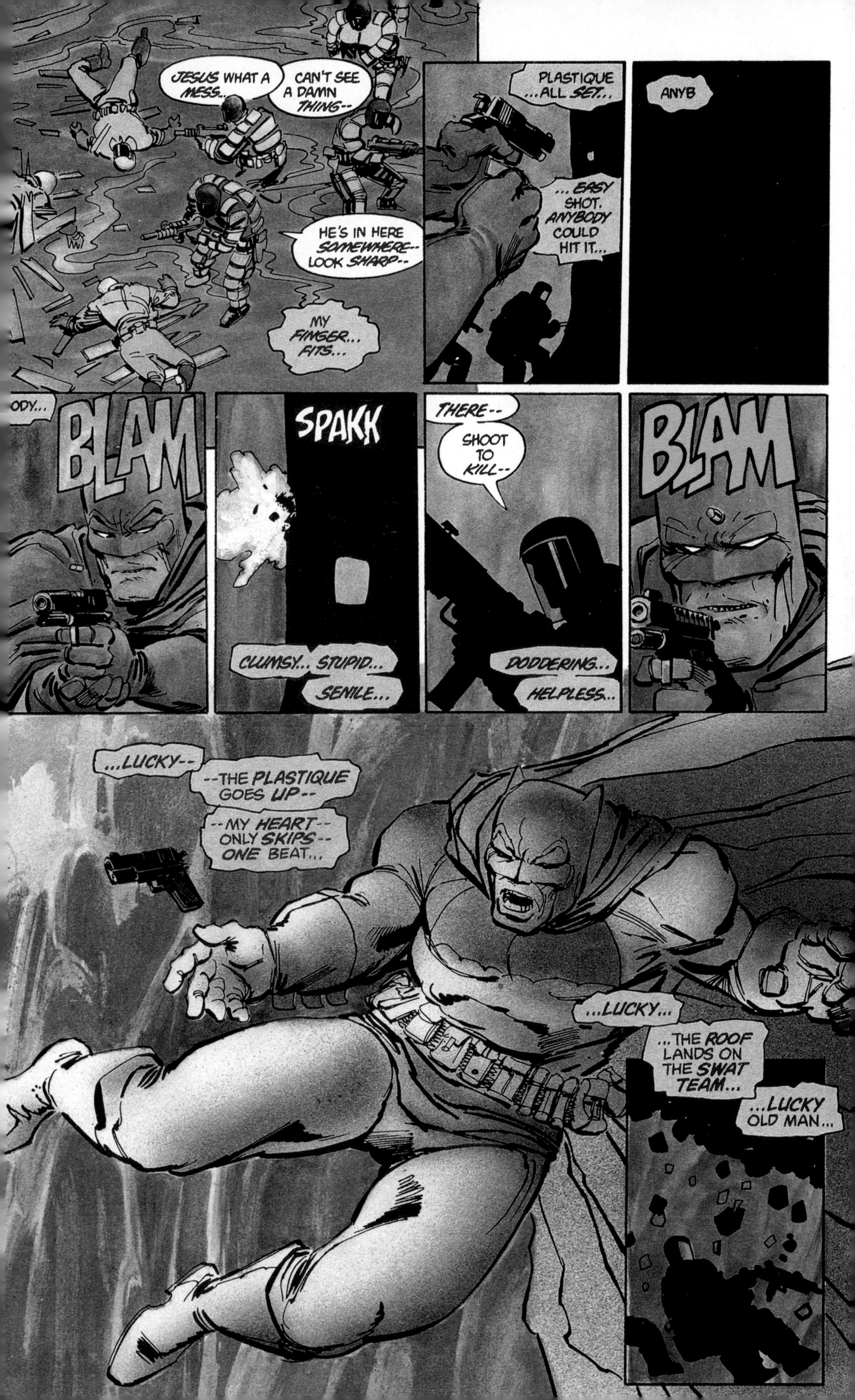
JESUS WHAT A MESS..
CAN'T SEE A DAMN THING--
HE'S IN HERE SOMEWHERE-- LOOK SHARP--
MY FINGER... FITS...
PLASTIQUE ...ALL SET...
...EASY SHOT. ANYBODY COULD HIT IT...
ANYB
ODY...
BLAM
SPAKK
CLUMSY... STUPID...
SENILE...
THERE--
SHOOT TO KILL--
DODDERING...
HELPLESS...
BLAM
...LUCKY--
--THE PLASTIQUE GOES UP--
--MY HEART-- ONLY SKIPS-- ONE BEAT...
...LUCKY...
...THE ROOF LANDS ON THE SWAT TEAM...
...LUCKY OLD MAN...

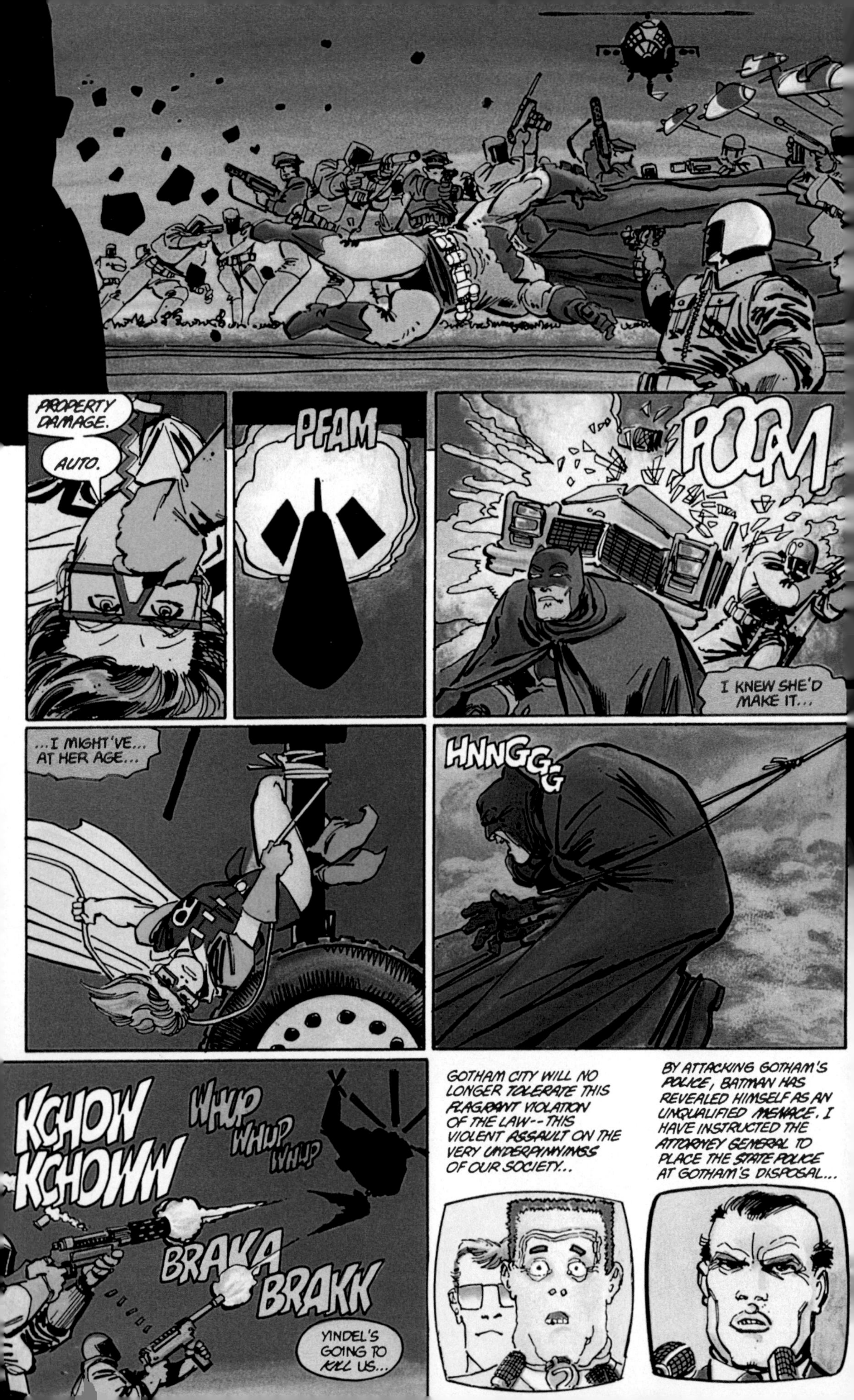

PROPERTY DAMAGE.
AUTO.
PFAM
POOM
I KNEW SHE'D MAKE IT...
...I MIGHT'VE... AT HER AGE...
HNNGGG
KCHOW KCHOWW
WHUP WHUP WHUP
BRAKA BRAKK
YINDEL'S GOING TO KILL US...
GOTHAM CITY WILL NO LONGER TOLERATE THIS FLAGRANT VIOLATION OF THE LAW--THIS VIOLENT ASSAULT ON THE VERY UNDERPINNINGS OF OUR SOCIETY...
BY ATTACKING GOTHAM'S POLICE, BATMAN HAS REVEALED HIMSELF AS AN UNQUALIFIED MENACE. I HAVE INSTRUCTED THE ATTORNEY GENERAL TO PLACE THE STATE POLICE AT GOTHAM'S DISPOSAL...

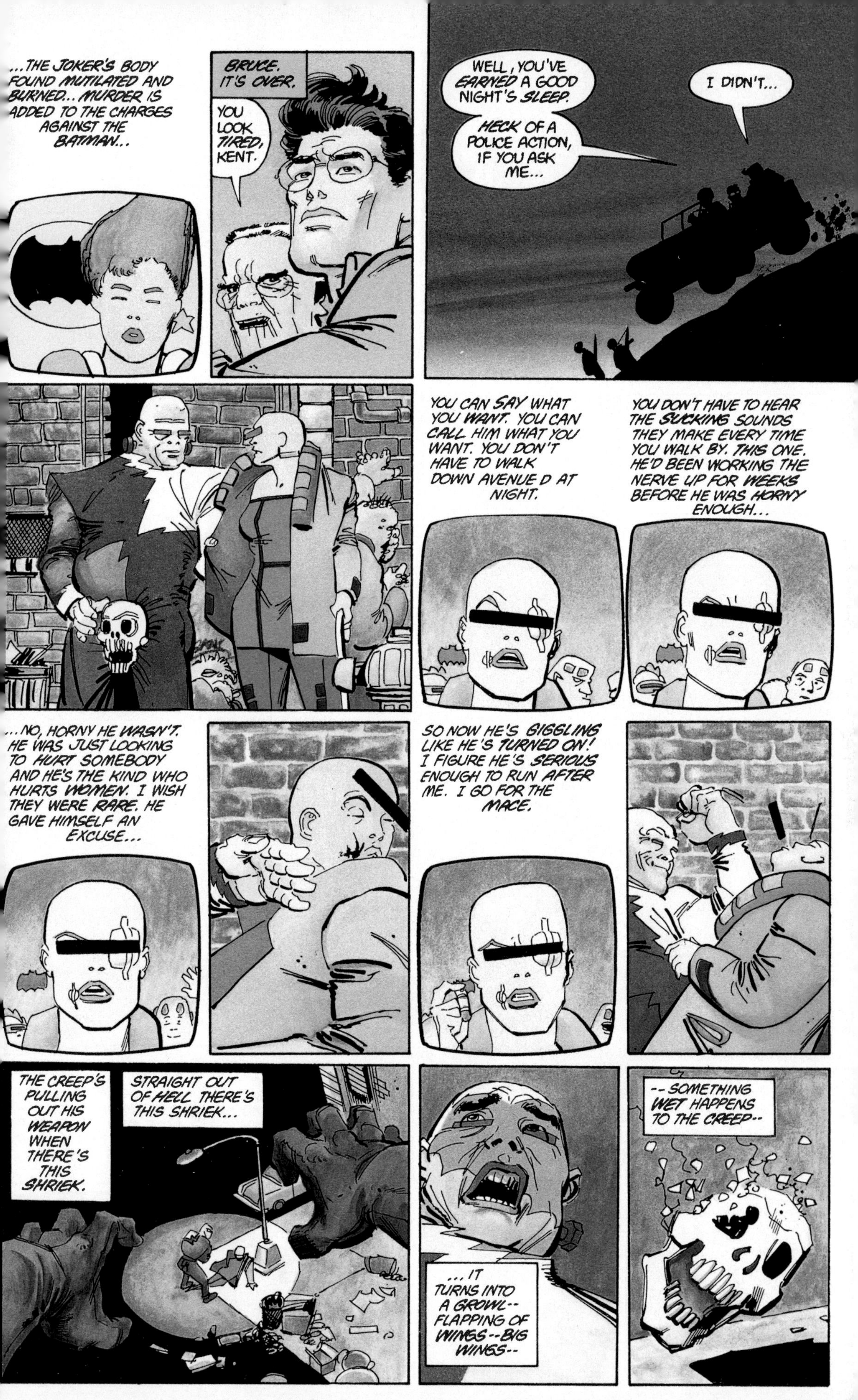
...THE JOKER'S BODY FOUND MUTILATED AND BURNED... MURDER IS ADDED TO THE CHARGES AGAINST THE BATMAN...
BRUCE. IT'S OVER.
YOU LOOK TIRED, KENT.
WELL, YOU'VE EARNED A GOOD NIGHT'S SLEEP.
HECK OF A POLICE ACTION, IF YOU ASK ME...
I DIDN'T...
YOU CAN SAY WHAT YOU WANT. YOU CAN CALL HIM WHAT YOU WANT. YOU DON'T HAVE TO WALK DOWN AVENUE D AT NIGHT.
YOU DON'T HAVE TO HEAR THE SUCKING SOUNDS THEY MAKE EVERY TIME YOU WALK BY. THIS ONE. HE'D BEEN WORKING THE NERVE UP FOR WEEKS BEFORE HE WAS HORNY ENOUGH...
...NO, HORNY HE WASN'T. HE WAS JUST LOOKING TO HURT SOMEBODY AND HE'S THE KIND WHO HURTS WOMEN. I WISH THEY WERE RARE. HE GAVE HIMSELF AN EXCUSE...
SO NOW HE'S GIGGLING LIKE HE'S TURNED ON! I FIGURE HE'S SERIOUS ENOUGH TO RUN AFTER ME. I GO FOR THE MACE.
THE CREEP'S PULLING OUT HIS WEAPON WHEN THERE'S THIS SHRIEK.
STRAIGHT OUT OF HELL THERE'S THIS SHRIEK...
...IT TURNS INTO A GROWL-- FLAPPING OF WINGS--BIG WINGS--
--SOMETHING WET HAPPENS TO THE CREEP--

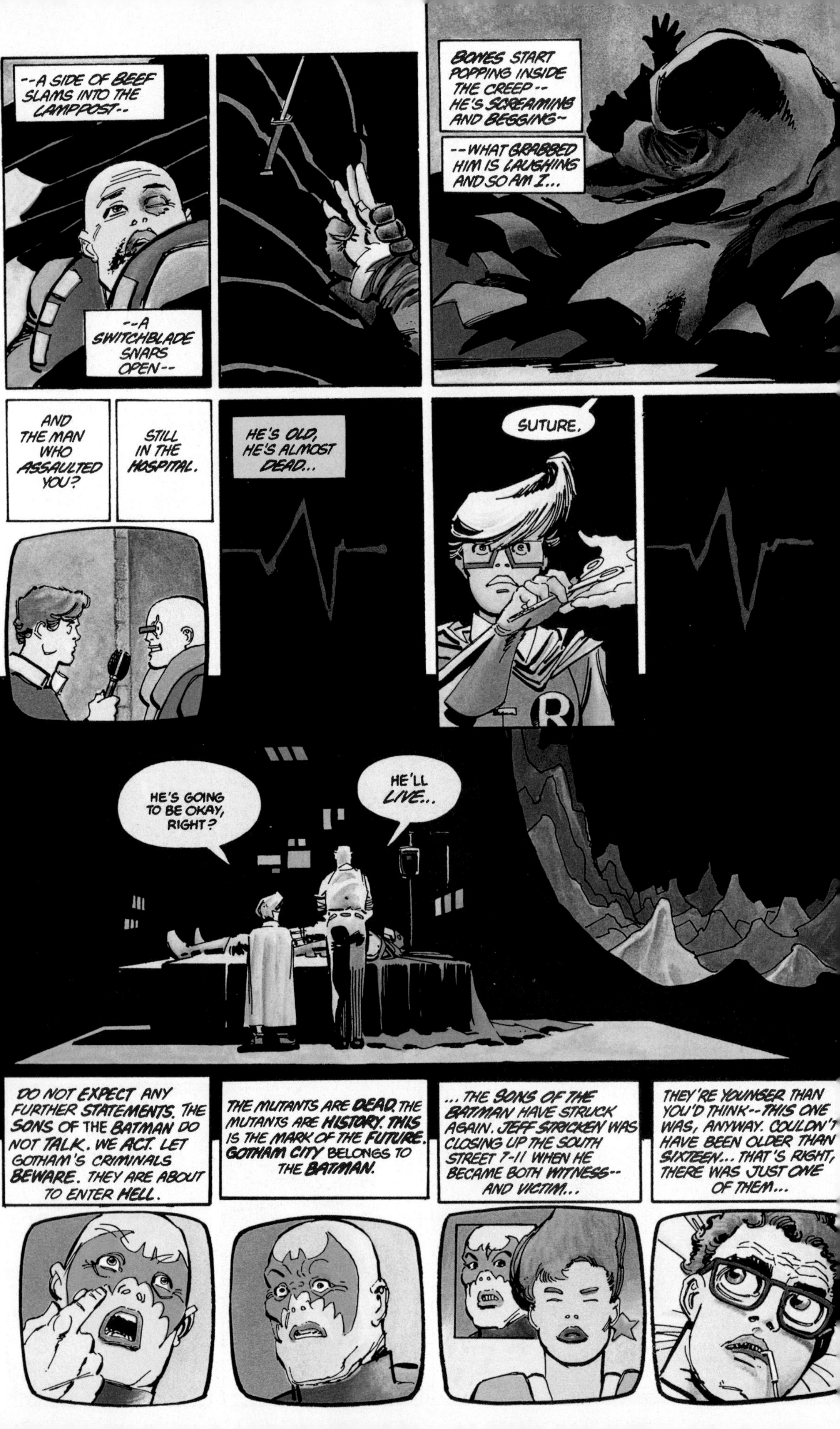
--A SIDE OF BEEF SLAMS INTO THE LAMPPOST--
--A SWITCHBLADE SNAPS OPEN--
BONES START POPPING INSIDE THE CREEP-- HE'S SCREAMING AND BEGGING--
--WHAT GRABBED HIM IS LAUGHING AND SO AM I...
AND THE MAN WHO ASSAULTED YOU?
STILL IN THE HOSPITAL.
HE'S OLD, HE'S ALMOST DEAD...
SUTURE.
HE'S GOING TO BE OKAY, RIGHT?
HE'LL LIVE...
DO NOT EXPECT ANY FURTHER STATEMENTS. THE SONS OF THE BATMAN DO NOT TALK. WE ACT. LET GOTHAM'S CRIMINALS BEWARE. THEY ARE ABOUT TO ENTER HELL.
THE MUTANTS ARE DEAD. THE MUTANTS ARE HISTORY. THIS IS THE MARK OF THE FUTURE. GOTHAM CITY BELONGS TO THE BATMAN.
...THE SONS OF THE BATMAN HAVE STRUCK AGAIN. JEFF STRICKEN WAS CLOSING UP THE SOUTH STREET 7-11 WHEN HE BECAME BOTH WITNESS-- AND VICTIM...
THEY'RE YOUNGER THAN YOU'D THINK--THIS ONE WAS, ANYWAY. COULDN'T HAVE BEEN OLDER THAN SIXTEEN... THAT'S RIGHT, THERE WAS JUST ONE OF THEM...

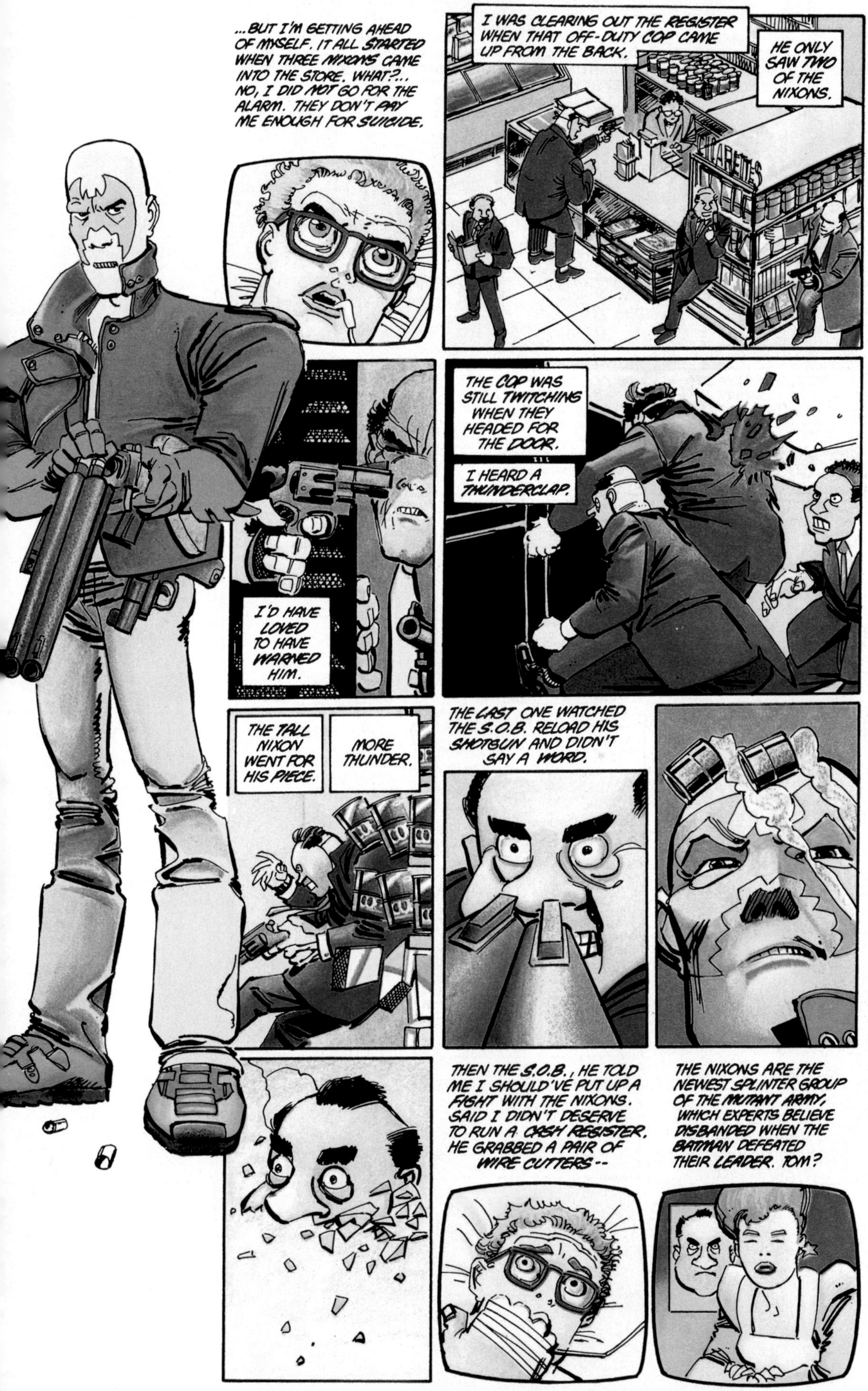
...BUT I'M GETTING AHEAD OF MYSELF. IT ALL STARTED WHEN THREE NIXONS CAME INTO THE STORE. WHAT?... NO, I DID NOT GO FOR THE ALARM. THEY DON'T PAY ME ENOUGH FOR SUICIDE.
I WAS CLEARING OUT THE REGISTER WHEN THAT OFF-DUTY COP CAME UP FROM THE BACK.
HE ONLY SAW TWO OF THE NIXONS.
CIGARETTES
I'D HAVE LOVED TO HAVE WARNED HIM.
THE COP WAS STILL TWITCHING WHEN THEY HEADED FOR THE DOOR.
I HEARD A THUNDERCLAP.
THE TALL NIXON WENT FOR HIS PIECE.
MORE THUNDER.
THE LAST ONE WATCHED THE S.O.B. RELOAD HIS SHOTGUN AND DIDN'T SAY A WORD.
THEN THE S.O.B., HE TOLD ME I SHOULD'VE PUT UP A FIGHT WITH THE NIXONS. SAID I DIDN'T DESERVE TO RUN A CASH REGISTER. HE GRABBED A PAIR OF WIRE CUTTERS--
THE NIXONS ARE THE NEWEST SPLINTER GROUP OF THE MUTANT ARMY, WHICH EXPERTS BELIEVE DISBANDED WHEN THE BATMAN DEFEATED THEIR LEADER. TOM?

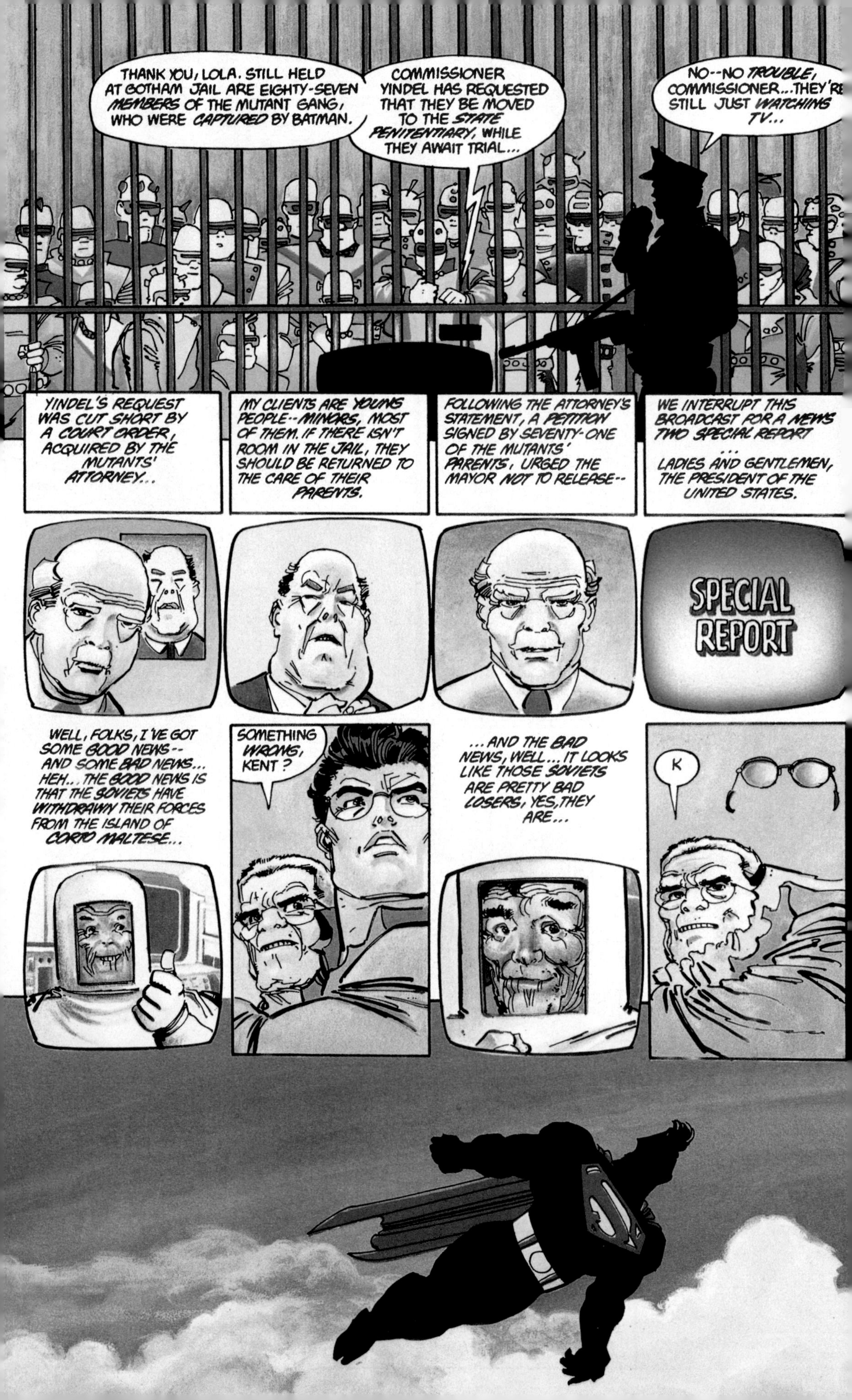
THANK YOU, LOLA. STILL HELD AT GOTHAM JAIL ARE EIGHTY-SEVEN MEMBERS OF THE MUTANT GANG, WHO WERE CAPTURED BY BATMAN.
COMMISSIONER YINDEL HAS REQUESTED THAT THEY BE MOVED TO THE STATE PENITENTIARY, WHILE THEY AWAIT TRIAL...
NO--NO TROUBLE, COMMISSIONER...THEY'RE STILL JUST WATCHING TV...
YINDEL'S REQUEST WAS CUT SHORT BY A COURT ORDER, ACQUIRED BY THE MUTANTS' ATTORNEY...
MY CLIENTS ARE YOUNG PEOPLE--MINORS, MOST OF THEM. IF THERE ISN'T ROOM IN THE JAIL, THEY SHOULD BE RETURNED TO THE CARE OF THEIR PARENTS.
FOLLOWING THE ATTORNEY'S STATEMENT, A PETITION SIGNED BY SEVENTY-ONE OF THE MUTANTS' PARENTS, URGED THE MAYOR NOT TO RELEASE--
WE INTERRUPT THIS BROADCAST FOR A NEWS TWO SPECIAL REPORT ... LADIES AND GENTLEMEN, THE PRESIDENT OF THE UNITED STATES.
SPECIAL REPORT
WELL, FOLKS, I'VE GOT SOME GOOD NEWS--AND SOME BAD NEWS... HEH... THE GOOD NEWS IS THAT THE SOVIETS HAVE WITHDRAWN THEIR FORCES FROM THE ISLAND OF CORTO MALTESE...
SOMETHING WRONG, KENT?
...AND THE BAD NEWS, WELL... IT LOOKS LIKE THOSE SOVIETS ARE PRETTY BAD LOSERS, YES, THEY ARE...
K

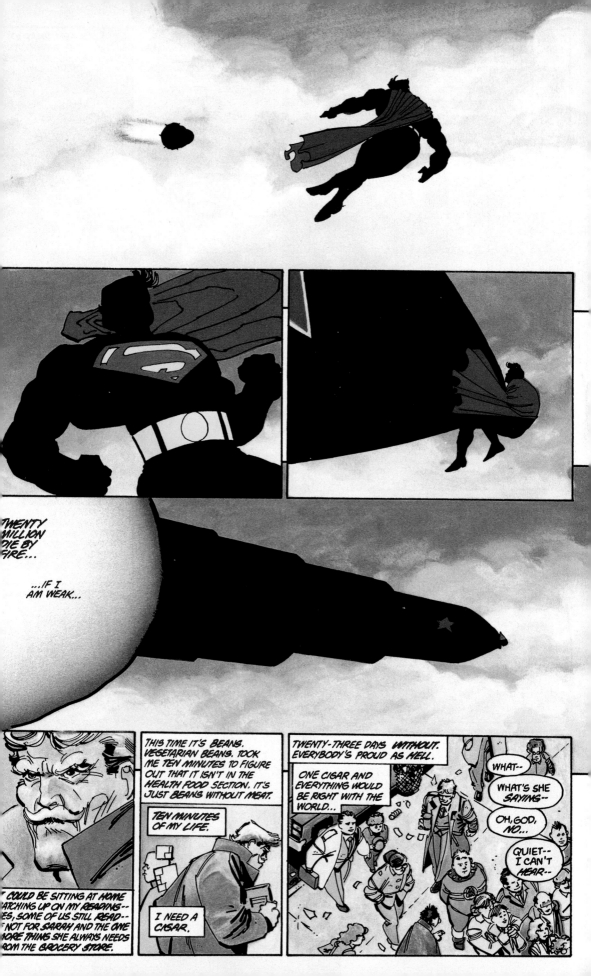

TWENTY
MILLION
DIE BY
FIRE...

...IF I
AM WEAK...

THIS TIME IT'S BEANS.
VEGETARIAN BEANS. TOOK
ME TEN MINUTES TO FIGURE
OUT THAT IT ISN'T IN THE
HEALTH FOOD SECTION. IT'S
JUST BEANS WITHOUT MEAT.

TEN MINUTES
OF MY LIFE.

COULD BE SITTING AT HOME
ATCHING UP ON MY READING--
ES, SOME OF US STILL READ--
NOT FOR SARAH AND THE ONE
ORE THING SHE ALWAYS NEEDS
ROM THE GROCERY STORE.

I NEED A
CIGAR.

TWENTY-THREE DAYS WITHOUT.
EVERYBODY'S PROUD AS HELL.

ONE CIGAR AND
EVERYTHING WOULD
BE RIGHT WITH THE
WORLD...

WHAT--

WHAT'S SHE
SAYING--

OH, GOD,
NO...

QUIET--
I CAN'T
HEAR--

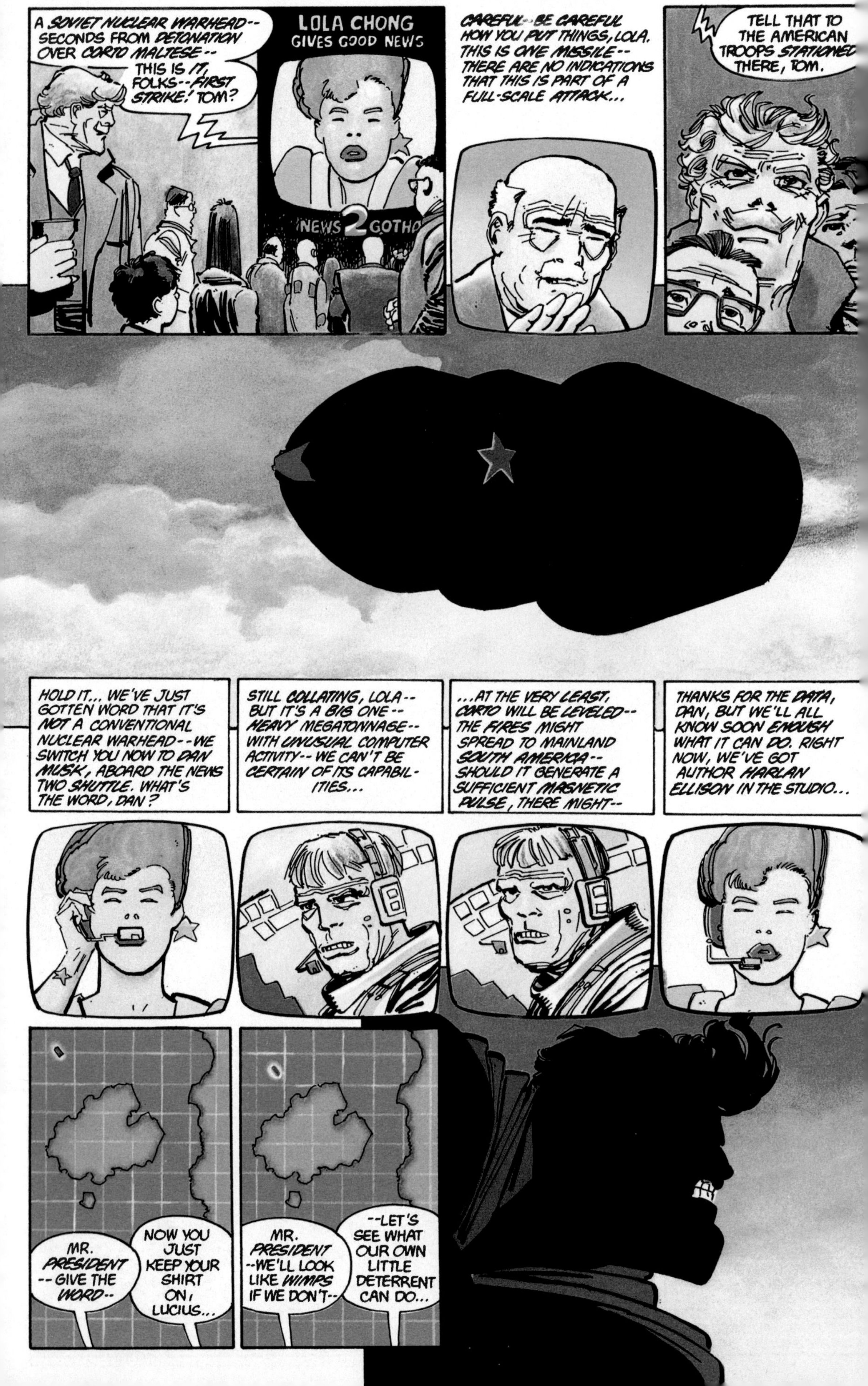
A SOVIET NUCLEAR WARHEAD-- SECONDS FROM DETONATION OVER CORTO MALTESE--
THIS IS IT, FOLKS--FIRST STRIKE! TOM?
LOLA CHONG GIVES GOOD NEWS
NEWS 2 GOTHA
CAREFUL--BE CAREFUL HOW YOU PUT THINGS, LOLA. THIS IS ONE MISSILE-- THERE ARE NO INDICATIONS THAT THIS IS PART OF A FULL-SCALE ATTACK...
TELL THAT TO THE AMERICAN TROOPS STATIONED THERE, TOM.
HOLD IT... WE'VE JUST GOTTEN WORD THAT IT'S NOT A CONVENTIONAL NUCLEAR WARHEAD--WE SWITCH YOU NOW TO DAN MUSK, ABOARD THE NEWS TWO SHUTTLE. WHAT'S THE WORD, DAN?
STILL COLLATING, LOLA-- BUT IT'S A BIG ONE-- HEAVY MEGATONNAGE-- WITH UNUSUAL COMPUTER ACTIVITY--WE CAN'T BE CERTAIN OF ITS CAPABIL-ITIES...
...AT THE VERY LEAST, CORTO WILL BE LEVELED-- THE FIRES MIGHT SPREAD TO MAINLAND SOUTH AMERICA-- SHOULD IT GENERATE A SUFFICIENT MAGNETIC PULSE, THERE MIGHT--
THANKS FOR THE DATA, DAN, BUT WE'LL ALL KNOW SOON ENOUGH WHAT IT CAN DO. RIGHT NOW, WE'VE GOT AUTHOR HARLAN ELLISON IN THE STUDIO...
MR. PRESIDENT --GIVE THE WORD--
NOW YOU JUST KEEP YOUR SHIRT ON, LUCIUS...
MR. PRESIDENT --WE'LL LOOK LIKE WIMPS IF WE DON'T--
--LET'S SEE WHAT OUR OWN LITTLE DETERRENT CAN DO...

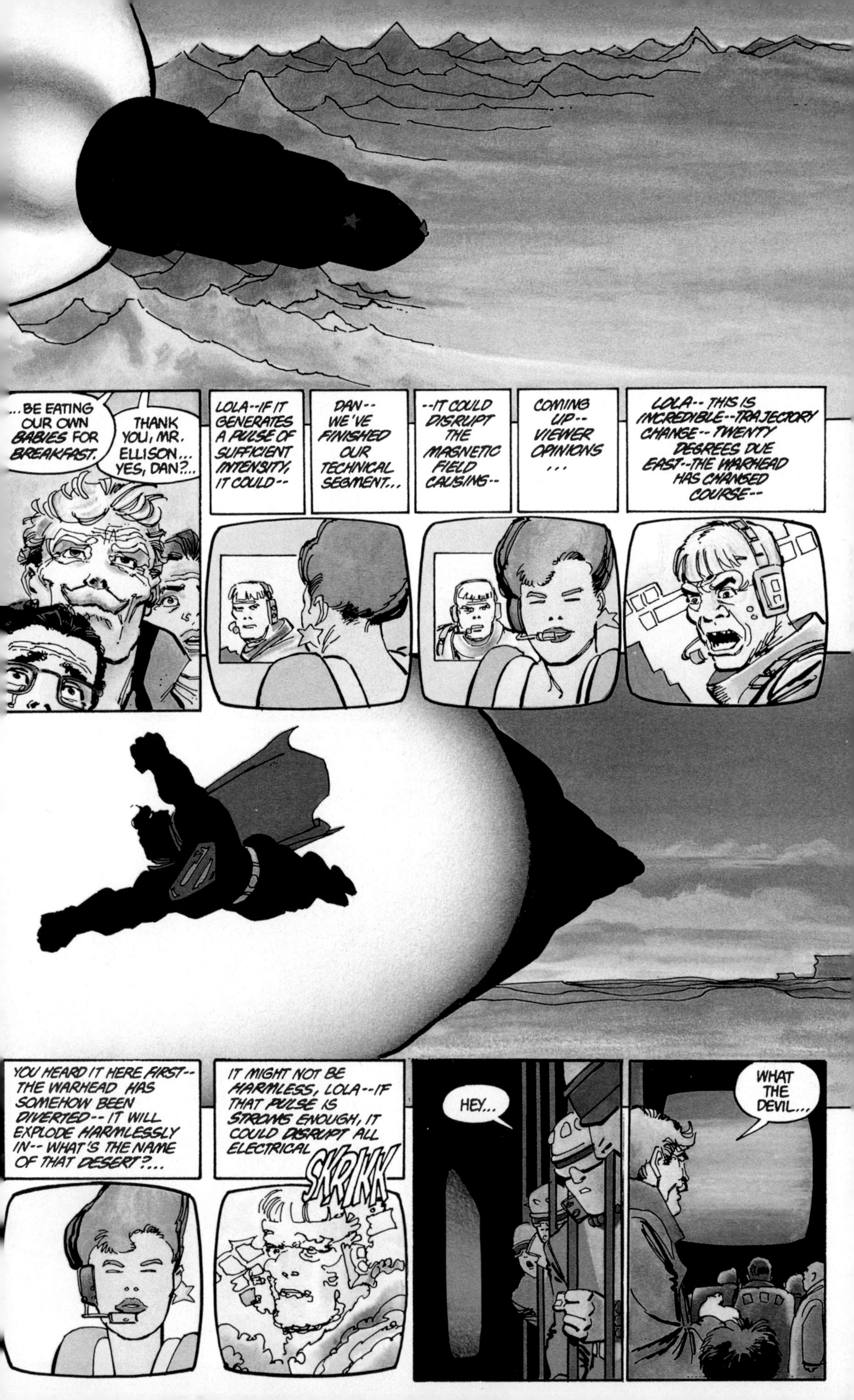

...BE EATING OUR OWN BABIES FOR BREAKFAST.
THANK YOU, MR. ELLISON... YES, DAN?...
LOLA--IF IT GENERATES A PULSE OF SUFFICIENT INTENSITY, IT COULD--
DAN-- WE'VE FINISHED OUR TECHNICAL SEGMENT...
--IT COULD DISRUPT THE MAGNETIC FIELD CAUSING--
COMING UP-- VIEWER OPINIONS ...
LOLA-- THIS IS INCREDIBLE--TRAJECTORY CHANGE--TWENTY DEGREES DUE EAST--THE WARHEAD HAS CHANGED COURSE--
YOU HEARD IT HERE FIRST-- THE WARHEAD HAS SOMEHOW BEEN DIVERTED-- IT WILL EXPLODE HARMLESSLY IN-- WHAT'S THE NAME OF THAT DESERT?...
IT MIGHT NOT BE HARMLESS, LOLA--IF THAT PULSE IS STRONG ENOUGH, IT COULD DISRUPT ALL ELECTRICAL
SKRIKK
HEY...
WHAT THE DEVIL...

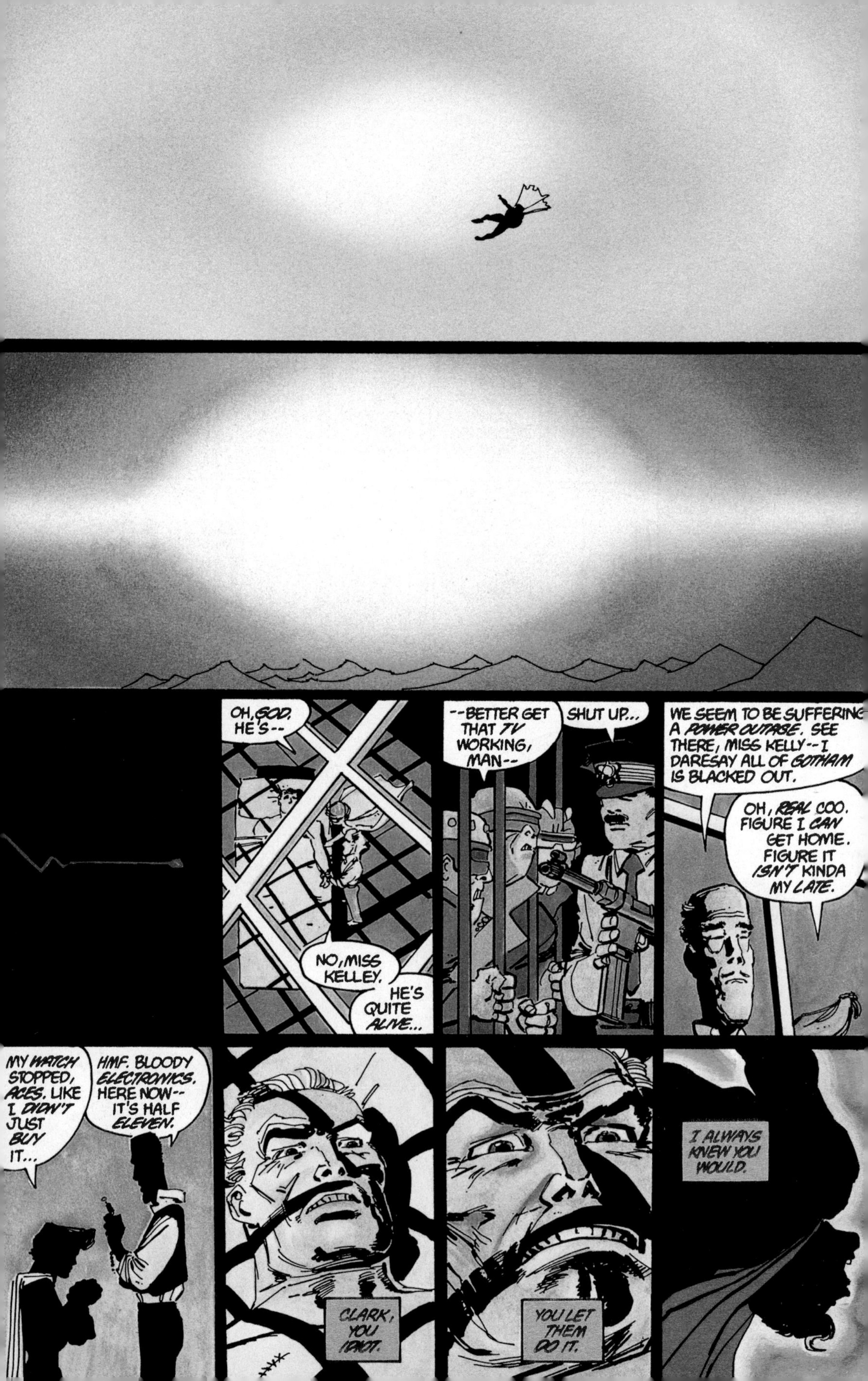

OH, GOD. HE'S--
NO, MISS KELLEY.
HE'S QUITE ALIVE...
--BETTER GET THAT TV WORKING, MAN--
SHUT UP...
WE SEEM TO BE SUFFERING A POWER OUTAGE. SEE THERE, MISS KELLY--I DARESAY ALL OF GOTHAM IS BLACKED OUT.
OH, REAL COO. FIGURE I CAN GET HOME. FIGURE IT ISN'T KINDA MY LATE.
MY WATCH STOPPED, ACES. LIKE I DIDN'T JUST BUY IT...
HMF. BLOODY ELECTRONICS. HERE NOW--IT'S HALF ELEVEN.
CLARK, YOU IDIOT.
YOU LET THEM DO IT.
I ALWAYS KNEW YOU WOULD.

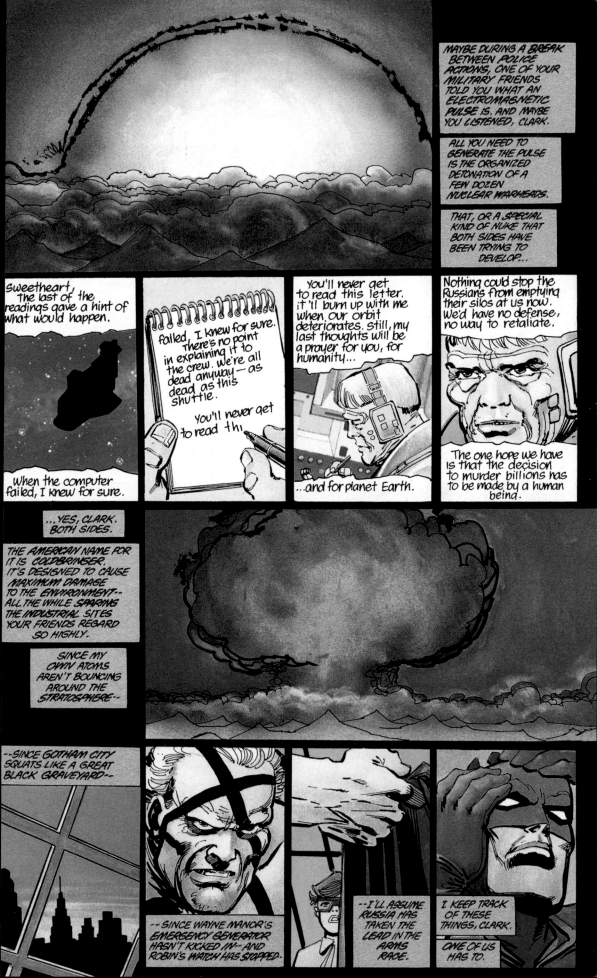

MAYBE DURING A BREAK BETWEEN POLICE ACTIONS, ONE OF YOUR MILITARY FRIENDS TOLD YOU WHAT AN ELECTROMAGNETIC PULSE IS. AND MAYBE YOU LISTENED, CLARK.

ALL YOU NEED TO GENERATE THE PULSE IS THE ORGANIZED DETONATION OF A FEW DOZEN NUCLEAR WARHEADS.

THAT, OR A SPECIAL KIND OF NUKE THAT BOTH SIDES HAVE BEEN TRYING TO DEVELOP...

Sweetheart,
the last of the readings gave a hint of what would happen.

When the computer failed, I knew for sure.

failed, I knew for sure. There's no point in explaining it to the crew. We're all dead anyway — as dead as this shuttle.

You'll never get to read thi

You'll never get to read this letter. it'll burn up with me when our orbit deteriorates. Still, my last thoughts will be a prayer for you, for humanity...

...and for planet Earth.

Nothing could stop the Russians from emptying their silos at us now. We'd have no defense, no way to retaliate.

The one hope we have is that the decision to murder billions has to be made by a human being.

...YES, CLARK. BOTH SIDES.

THE AMERICAN NAME FOR IT IS COLDBRINGER. IT'S DESIGNED TO CAUSE MAXIMUM DAMAGE TO THE ENVIRONMENT — ALL THE WHILE SPARING THE INDUSTRIAL SITES YOUR FRIENDS REGARD SO HIGHLY.

SINCE MY OWN ATOMS AREN'T BOUNCING AROUND THE STRATOSPHERE —

— SINCE GOTHAM CITY SQUATS LIKE A GREAT BLACK GRAVEYARD —

— SINCE WAYNE MANOR'S EMERGENCY GENERATOR HASN'T KICKED IN — AND ROBIN'S WATCH HAS STOPPED.

— I'LL ASSUME RUSSIA HAS TAKEN THE LEAD IN THE ARMS RACE.

I KEEP TRACK OF THESE THINGS, CLARK.

ONE OF US HAS TO.

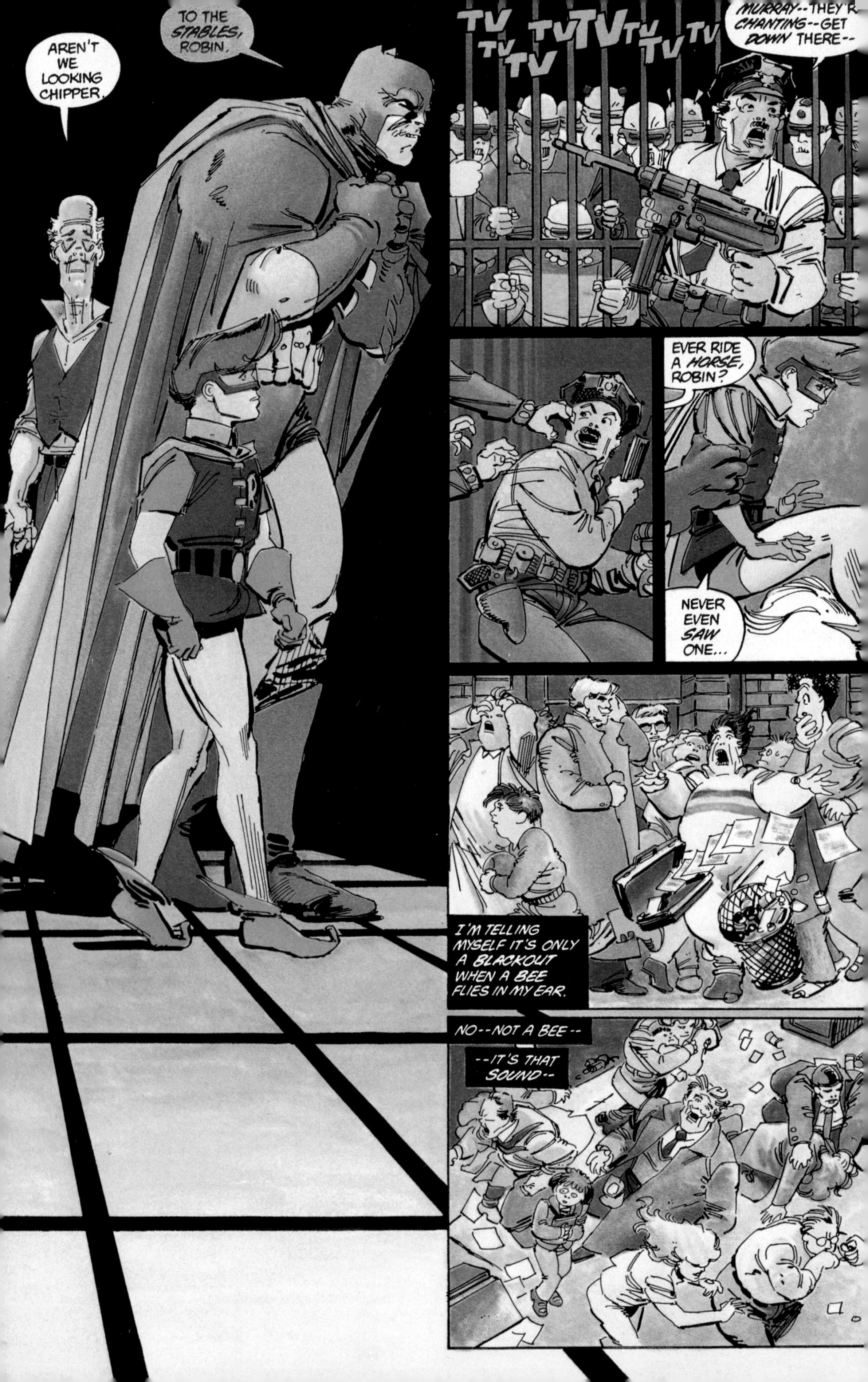
AREN'T WE LOOKING CHIPPER.
TO THE STABLES, ROBIN.
TV TV TV TV TV TV TV TV TV TV
MURRAY--THEY'RE CHANTING--GET DOWN THERE--
EVER RIDE A HORSE, ROBIN?
NEVER EVEN SAW ONE...
I'M TELLING MYSELF IT'S ONLY A BLACKOUT WHEN A BEE FLIES IN MY EAR.
NO--NOT A BEE--
--IT'S THAT SOUND--

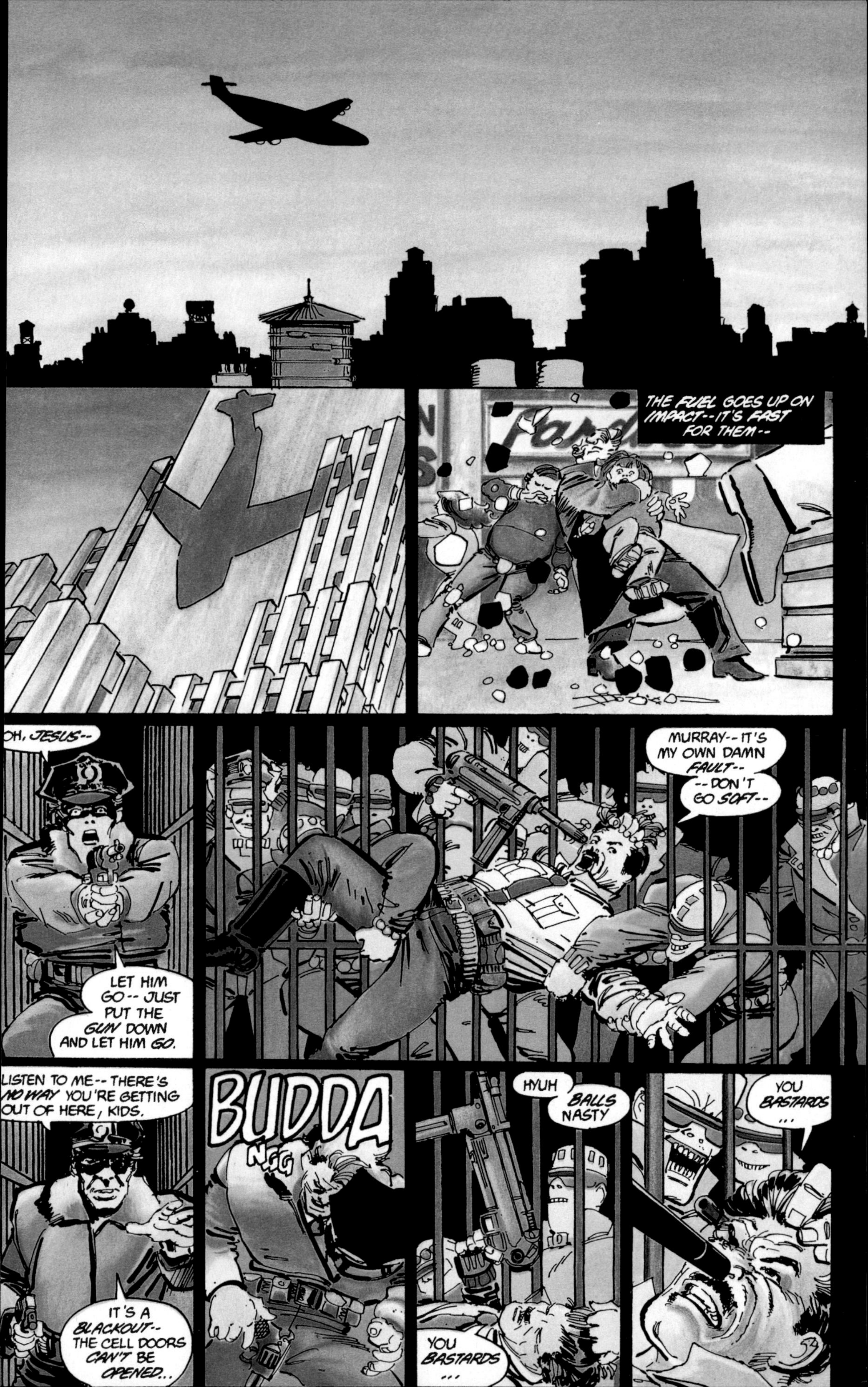
THE FUEL GOES UP ON IMPACT--IT'S FAST FOR THEM--
OH, JESUS--
MURRAY--IT'S MY OWN DAMN FAULT--
--DON'T GO SOFT--
LET HIM GO--JUST PUT THE GUN DOWN AND LET HIM GO.
LISTEN TO ME--THERE'S NO WAY YOU'RE GETTING OUT OF HERE, KIDS.
IT'S A BLACKOUT--THE CELL DOORS CAN'T BE OPENED...
BUDDA
NGG
YOU BASTARDS...
HYUH
BALLS NASTY
YOU BASTARDS...

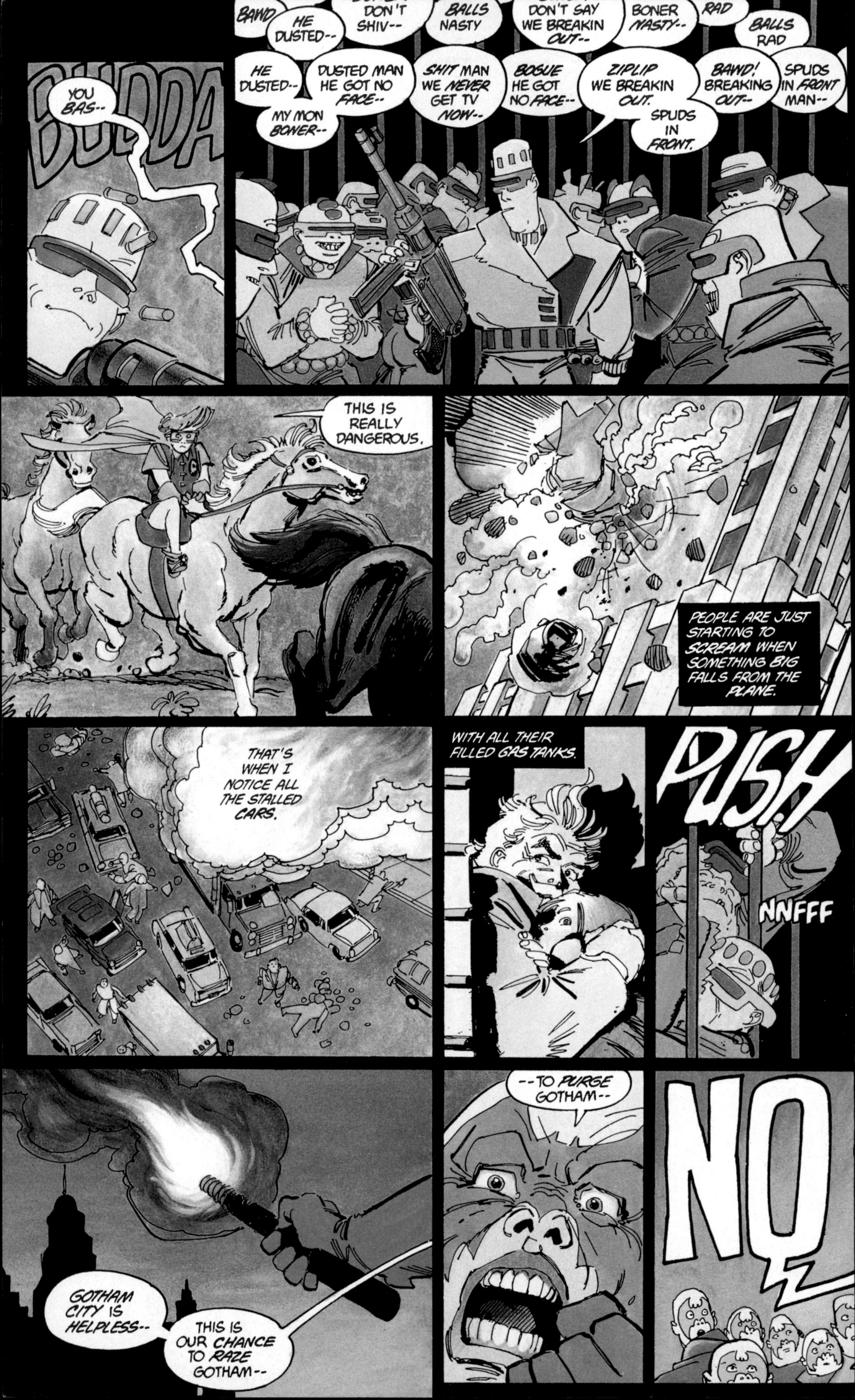
BUDDA
YOU BAS--
BAWD
HE DUSTED--
DON'T SHIV--
BALLS NASTY
DON'T SAY WE BREAKIN OUT--
BONER NASTY--
RAD
BALLS RAD
HE DUSTED--
DUSTED MAN HE GOT NO FACE--
MY MON BONER--
SHIT MAN WE NEVER GET TV NOW--
BOGUE HE GOT NO FACE--
ZIPLIP WE BREAKIN OUT.
SPUDS IN FRONT.
BAWD! BREAKING OUT--
SPUDS IN FRONT MAN--
THIS IS REALLY DANGEROUS.
PEOPLE ARE JUST STARTING TO SCREAM WHEN SOMETHING BIG FALLS FROM THE PLANE.
THAT'S WHEN I NOTICE ALL THE STALLED CARS.
WITH ALL THEIR FILLED GAS TANKS.
PUSH
NNFFF
GOTHAM CITY IS HELPLESS--
THIS IS OUR CHANCE TO RAZE GOTHAM--
--TO PURGE GOTHAM--
NO

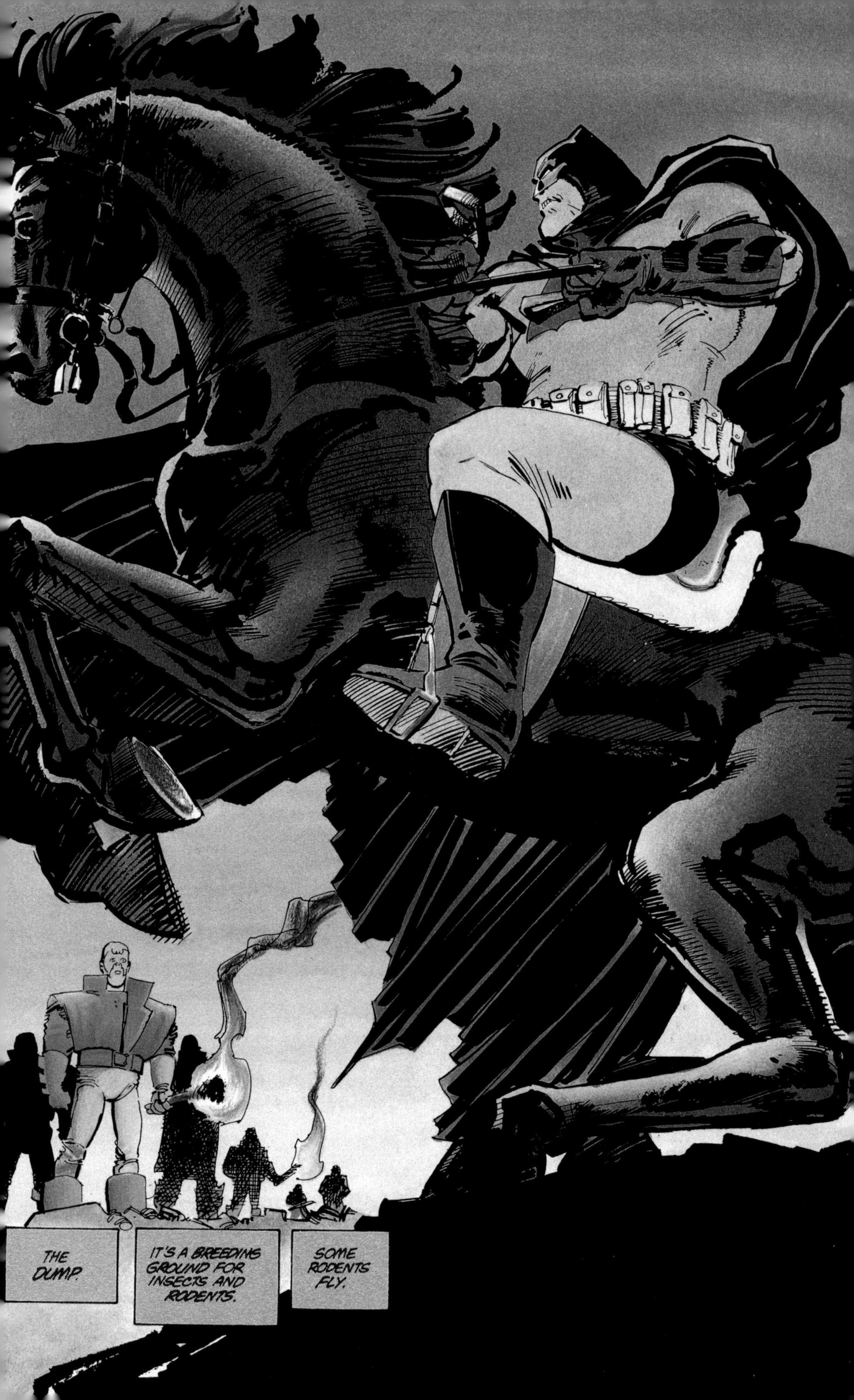
THE DUMP.
IT'S A BREEDING GROUND FOR INSECTS AND RODENTS.
SOME RODENTS FLY.

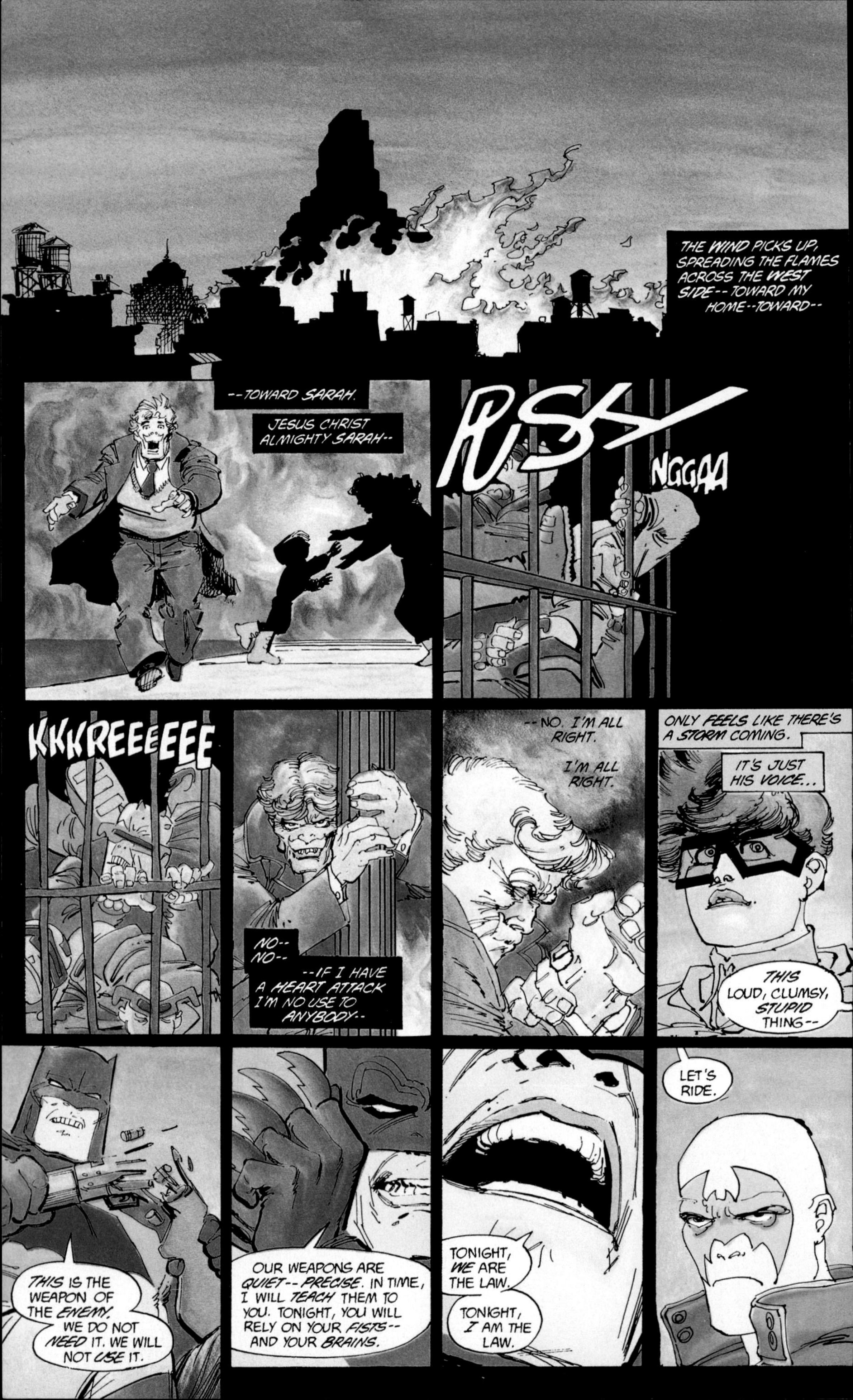
THE WIND PICKS UP, SPREADING THE FLAMES ACROSS THE WEST SIDE-- TOWARD MY HOME--TOWARD--
--TOWARD SARAH.
JESUS CHRIST ALMIGHTY SARAH--
RUSK
NGGAA
KKKREEEEEE
NO--
NO--
--IF I HAVE A HEART ATTACK I'M NO USE TO ANYBODY--
--NO. I'M ALL RIGHT.
I'M ALL RIGHT.
ONLY FEELS LIKE THERE'S A STORM COMING.
IT'S JUST HIS VOICE...
THIS LOUD, CLUMSY, STUPID THING--
THIS IS THE WEAPON OF THE ENEMY. WE DO NOT NEED IT. WE WILL NOT USE IT.
OUR WEAPONS ARE QUIET-- PRECISE. IN TIME, I WILL TEACH THEM TO YOU. TONIGHT, YOU WILL RELY ON YOUR FISTS-- AND YOUR BRAINS.
TONIGHT, WE ARE THE LAW.
TONIGHT, I AM THE LAW.
LET'S RIDE.

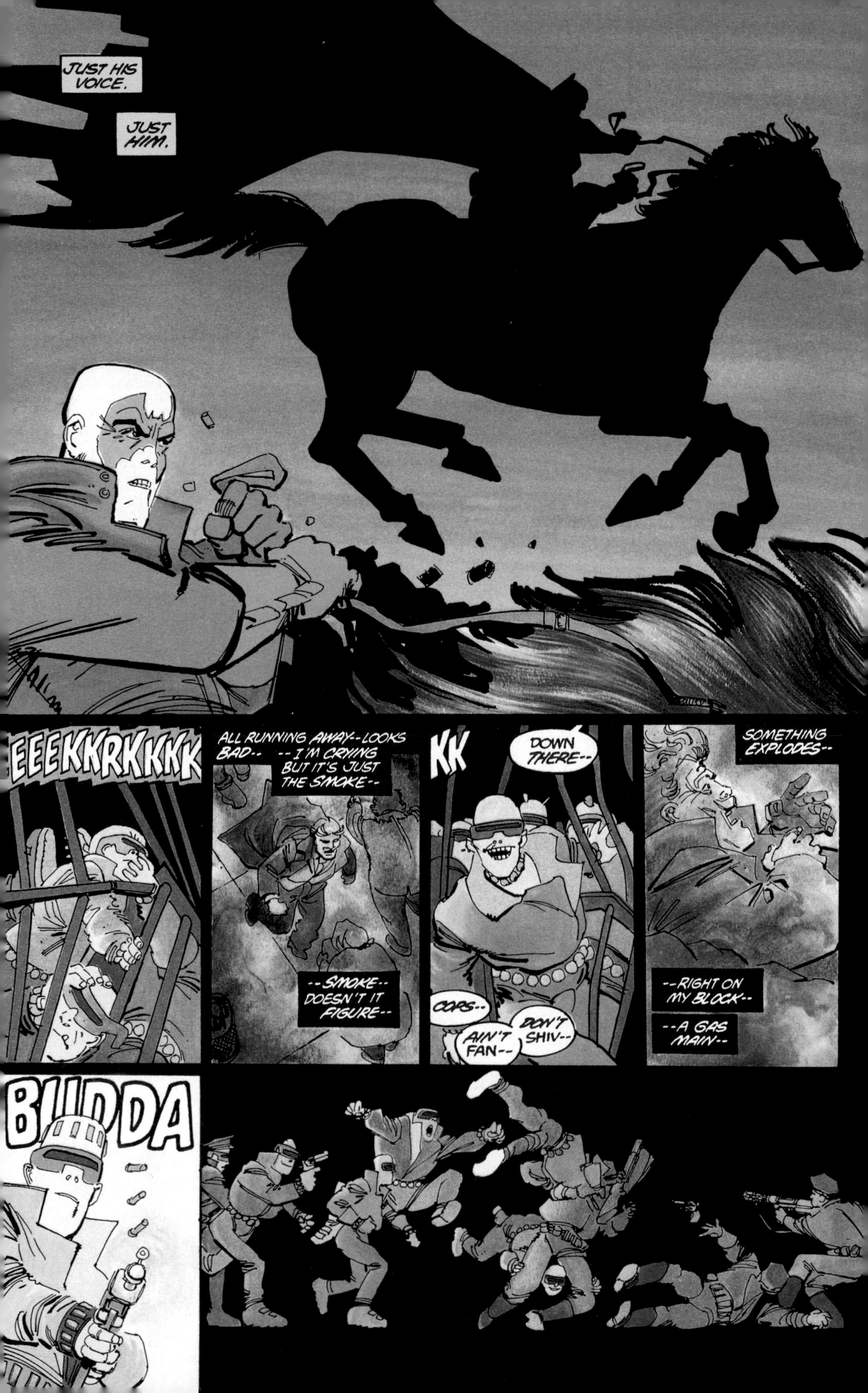
JUST HIS VOICE.
JUST HIM.
EEEKKRKKKK
ALL RUNNING AWAY--LOOKS BAD-- --I'M CRYING BUT IT'S JUST THE SMOKE--
--SMOKE--DOESN'T IT FIGURE--
KK
DOWN THERE--
COPS--
AIN'T FAN--
DON'T SHIV--
SOMETHING EXPLODES--
--RIGHT ON MY BLOCK--
--A GAS MAIN--
BUDDA

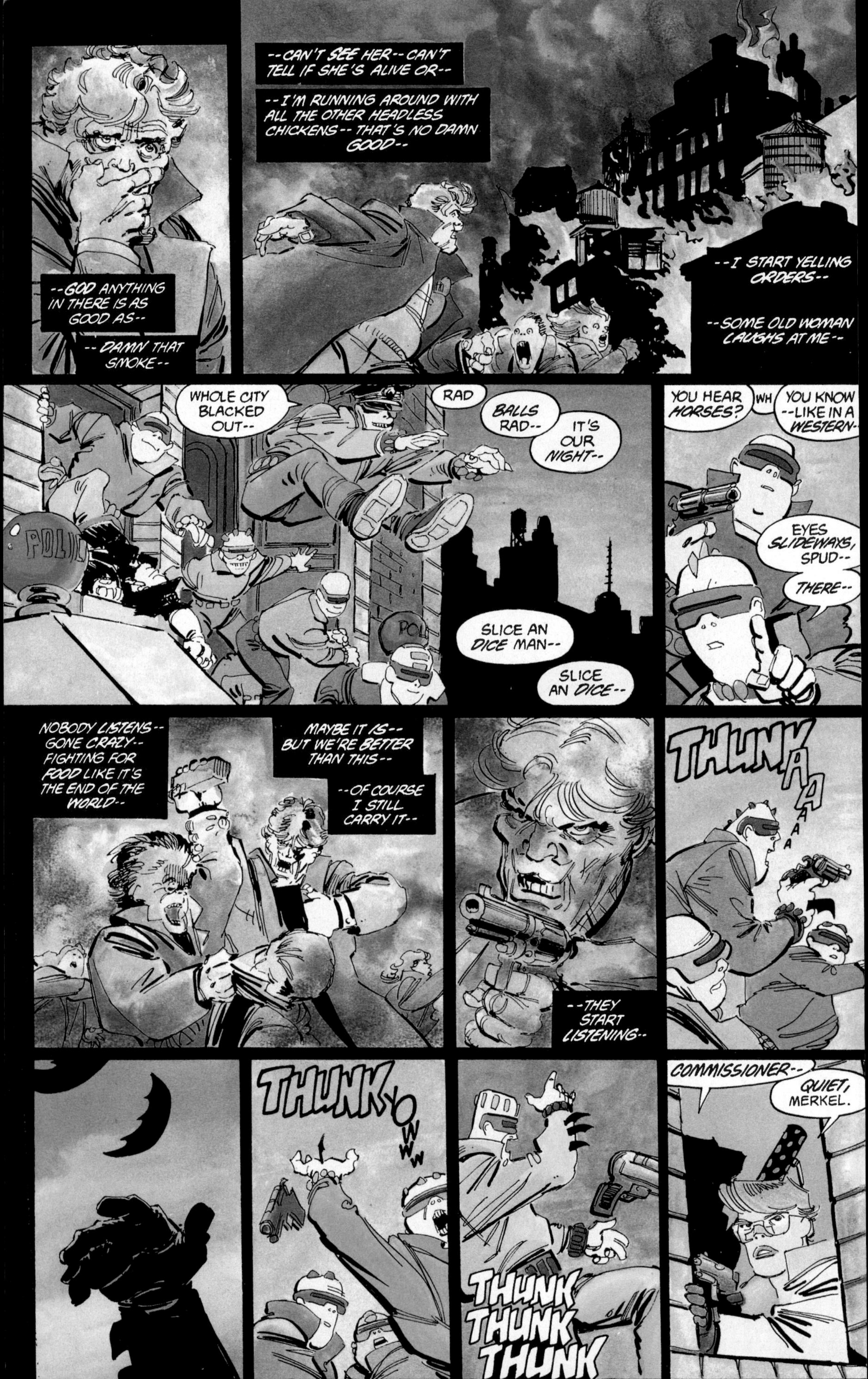
--GOD ANYTHING IN THERE IS AS GOOD AS--
--DAMN THAT SMOKE--
--CAN'T SEE HER--CAN'T TELL IF SHE'S ALIVE OR--
--I'M RUNNING AROUND WITH ALL THE OTHER HEADLESS CHICKENS--THAT'S NO DAMN GOOD--
--I START YELLING ORDERS--
--SOME OLD WOMAN LAUGHS AT ME--
WHOLE CITY BLACKED OUT--
RAD
BALLS RAD--
IT'S OUR NIGHT--
SLICE AN DICE MAN--
SLICE AN DICE--
YOU HEAR HORSES?
WH
YOU KNOW --LIKE IN A WESTERN--
EYES SLIDEWAYS, SPUD--
THERE--
NOBODY LISTENS--GONE CRAZY--FIGHTING FOR FOOD LIKE IT'S THE END OF THE WORLD--
MAYBE IT IS--BUT WE'RE BETTER THAN THIS--
--OF COURSE I STILL CARRY IT--
--THEY START LISTENING--
THUNK
AAAAAA
THUNK
OWWW
THUNK THUNK THUNK
COMMISSIONER--
QUIET, MERKEL.

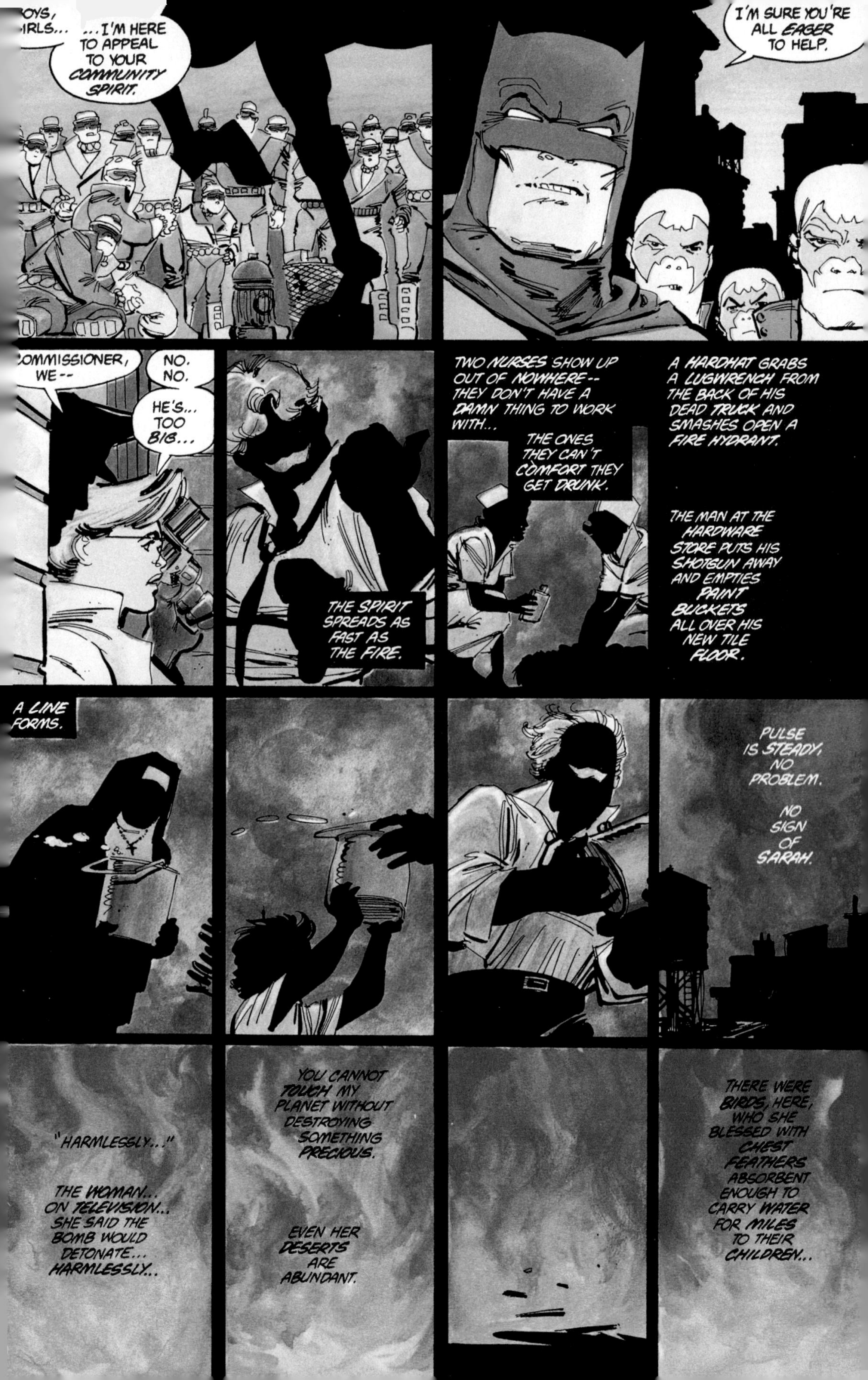

BOYS, GIRLS...
...I'M HERE TO APPEAL TO YOUR COMMUNITY SPIRIT.
I'M SURE YOU'RE ALL EAGER TO HELP.
COMMISSIONER, WE--
NO. NO.
HE'S... TOO BIG...
THE SPIRIT SPREADS AS FAST AS THE FIRE.
TWO NURSES SHOW UP OUT OF NOWHERE-- THEY DON'T HAVE A DAMN THING TO WORK WITH...
THE ONES THEY CAN'T COMFORT THEY GET DRUNK.
A HARDHAT GRABS A LUGWRENCH FROM THE BACK OF HIS DEAD TRUCK AND SMASHES OPEN A FIRE HYDRANT.
THE MAN AT THE HARDWARE STORE PUTS HIS SHOTGUN AWAY AND EMPTIES PAINT BUCKETS ALL OVER HIS NEW TILE FLOOR.
A LINE FORMS.
PULSE IS STEADY, NO PROBLEM.
NO SIGN OF SARAH.
"HARMLESSLY..."
THE WOMAN... ON TELEVISION... SHE SAID THE BOMB WOULD DETONATE... HARMLESSLY...
YOU CANNOT TOUCH MY PLANET WITHOUT DESTROYING SOMETHING PRECIOUS.
EVEN HER DESERTS ARE ABUNDANT.
THERE WERE BIRDS, HERE, WHO SHE BLESSED WITH CHEST FEATHERS ABSORBENT ENOUGH TO CARRY WATER FOR MILES TO THEIR CHILDREN...

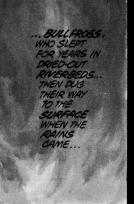

...BULLFROGS, WHO SLEPT FOR YEARS IN DRIED-OUT RIVERBEDS... THEN DUG THEIR WAY TO THE SURFACE WHEN THE RAINS CAME...

NOW... THERE IS ONLY BLACKENED GLASS...

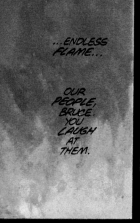

...ENDLESS FLAME...

OUR PEOPLE, BRUCE. YOU LAUGH AT THEM.

THEY CAN DO THIS... AND YOU LAUGH...

...THEY CAN SPLIT THE VERY FABRIC OF REALITY... BLAST A HUNDRED THOUSAND TONS OF SAND INTO THE SKY...

...BLOTTING OUT THE SOURCE OF ALL MY POWER... THE HOPE FOR SCREAMING MILLIONS...

MAGNETIC STORM ...YOU HAVE EVERY REASON TO BE OUTRAGED, MOTHER EARTH... YOU HAVE GIVEN THEM... EVERYTHING...

THEY ARE TINY AND STUPID AND VICIOUS ...BUT PLEASE... LISTEN TO THEM...

PLEASE...I AM SLOW AND DYING...

I NEED ONLY... REACH THE SUN...

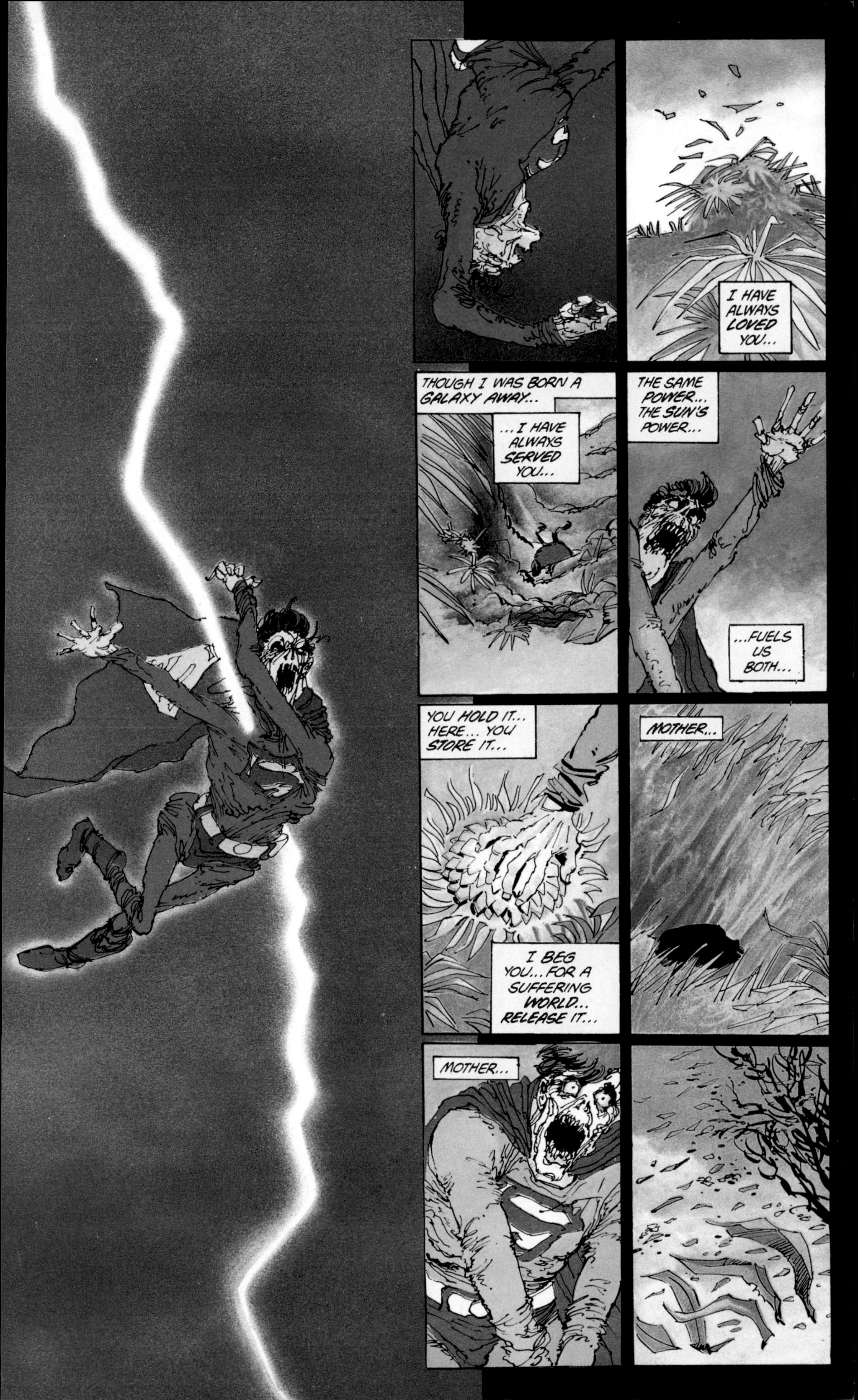
I HAVE ALWAYS LOVED YOU...
THOUGH I WAS BORN A GALAXY AWAY...
...I HAVE ALWAYS SERVED YOU...
THE SAME POWER... THE SUN'S POWER...
...FUELS US BOTH...
YOU HOLD IT... HERE... YOU STORE IT...
I BEG YOU... FOR A SUFFERING WORLD... RELEASE IT...
MOTHER...
MOTHER...

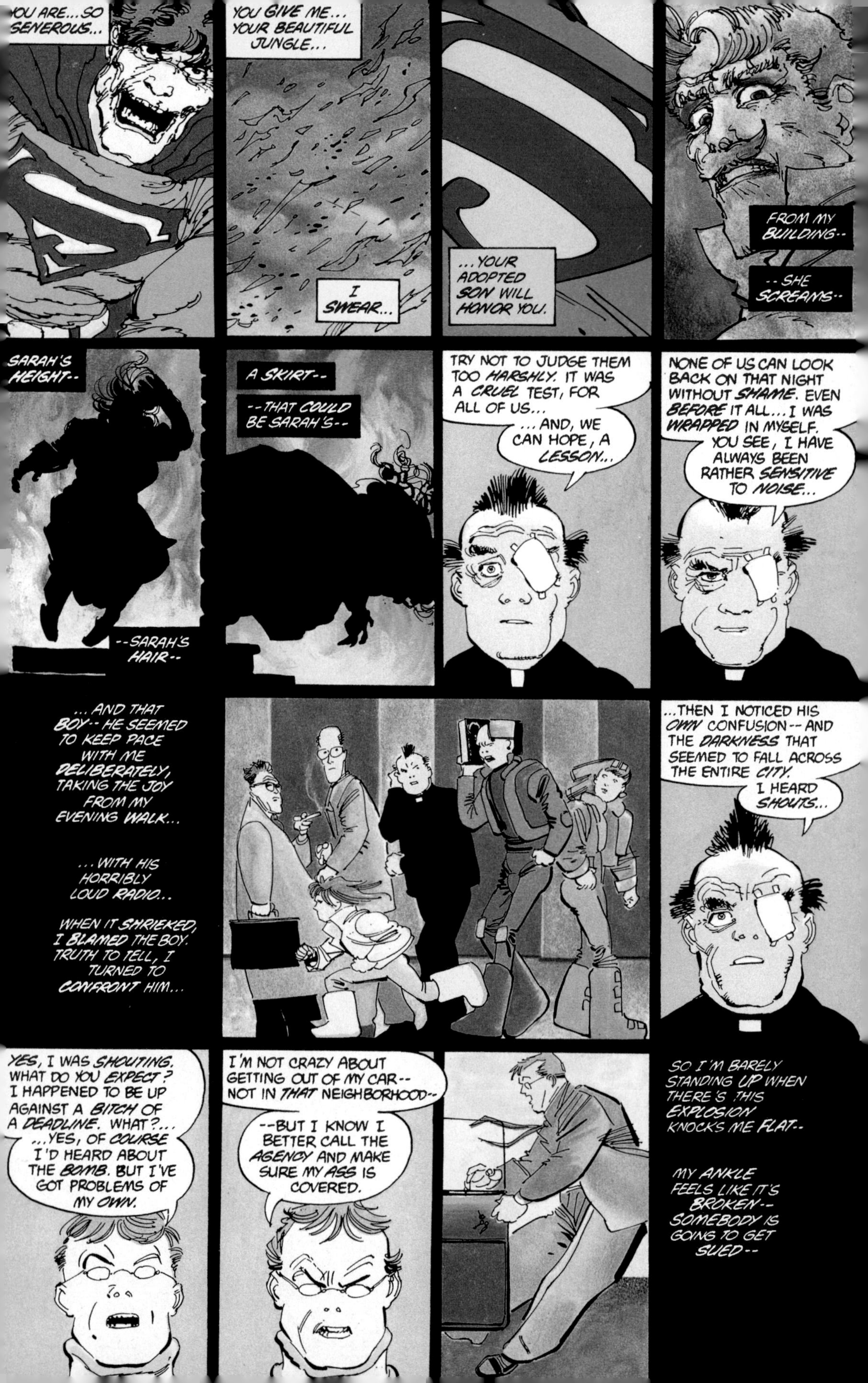
YOU ARE... SO GENEROUS...
YOU GIVE ME... YOUR BEAUTIFUL JUNGLE...
I SWEAR...
...YOUR ADOPTED SON WILL HONOR YOU.
FROM MY BUILDING--
--SHE SCREAMS--
SARAH'S HEIGHT--
--SARAH'S HAIR--
A SKIRT--
--THAT COULD BE SARAH'S--
TRY NOT TO JUDGE THEM TOO HARSHLY. IT WAS A CRUEL TEST, FOR ALL OF US...
...AND, WE CAN HOPE, A LESSON...
NONE OF US CAN LOOK BACK ON THAT NIGHT WITHOUT SHAME. EVEN BEFORE IT ALL... I WAS WRAPPED IN MYSELF.
YOU SEE, I HAVE ALWAYS BEEN RATHER SENSITIVE TO NOISE...
...AND THAT BOY-- HE SEEMED TO KEEP PACE WITH ME DELIBERATELY, TAKING THE JOY FROM MY EVENING WALK...
...WITH HIS HORRIBLY LOUD RADIO...
WHEN IT SHRIEKED, I BLAMED THE BOY. TRUTH TO TELL, I TURNED TO CONFRONT HIM...
...THEN I NOTICED HIS OWN CONFUSION-- AND THE DARKNESS THAT SEEMED TO FALL ACROSS THE ENTIRE CITY.
I HEARD SHOUTS...
YES, I WAS SHOUTING. WHAT DO YOU EXPECT? I HAPPENED TO BE UP AGAINST A BITCH OF A DEADLINE. WHAT?... ...YES, OF COURSE I'D HEARD ABOUT THE BOMB. BUT I'VE GOT PROBLEMS OF MY OWN.
I'M NOT CRAZY ABOUT GETTING OUT OF MY CAR-- NOT IN THAT NEIGHBORHOOD--
--BUT I KNOW I BETTER CALL THE AGENCY AND MAKE SURE MY ASS IS COVERED.
SO I'M BARELY STANDING UP WHEN THERE'S THIS EXPLOSION KNOCKS ME FLAT--
MY ANKLE FEELS LIKE IT'S BROKEN-- SOMEBODY IS GOING TO GET SUED--

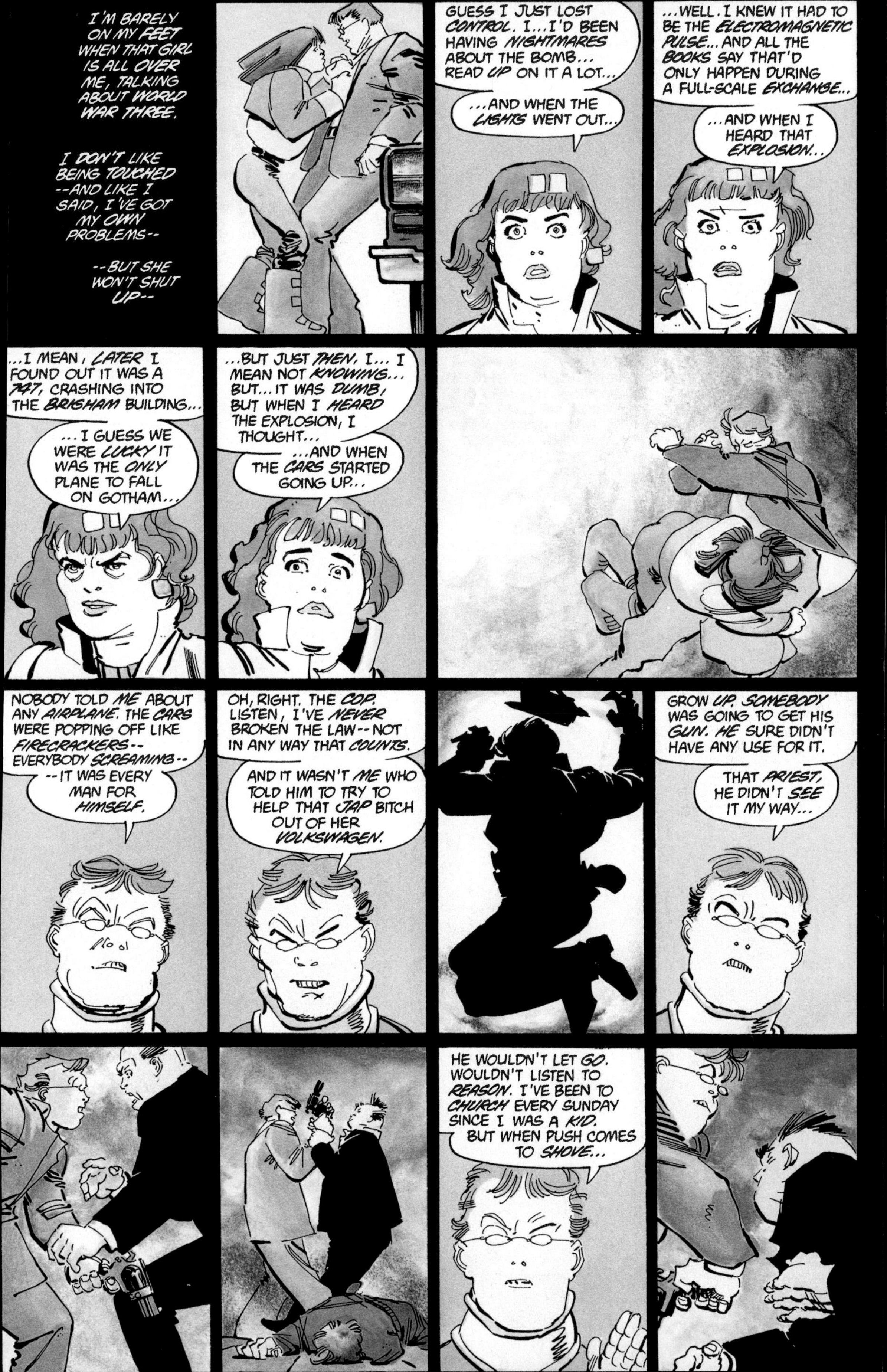

I'M BARELY ON MY FEET WHEN THAT GIRL IS ALL OVER ME, TALKING ABOUT WORLD WAR THREE.
I DON'T LIKE BEING TOUCHED --AND LIKE I SAID, I'VE GOT MY OWN PROBLEMS--
--BUT SHE WON'T SHUT UP--
GUESS I JUST LOST CONTROL. I...I'D BEEN HAVING NIGHTMARES ABOUT THE BOMB... READ UP ON IT A LOT...
...AND WHEN THE LIGHTS WENT OUT...
...WELL. I KNEW IT HAD TO BE THE ELECTROMAGNETIC PULSE... AND ALL THE BOOKS SAY THAT'D ONLY HAPPEN DURING A FULL-SCALE EXCHANGE...
...AND WHEN I HEARD THAT EXPLOSION...
...I MEAN, LATER I FOUND OUT IT WAS A 747, CRASHING INTO THE BRIGHAM BUILDING...
...I GUESS WE WERE LUCKY IT WAS THE ONLY PLANE TO FALL ON GOTHAM...
...BUT JUST THEN, I... I MEAN NOT KNOWING... BUT...IT WAS DUMB, BUT WHEN I HEARD THE EXPLOSION, I THOUGHT...
...AND WHEN THE CARS STARTED GOING UP...
NOBODY TOLD ME ABOUT ANY AIRPLANE. THE CARS WERE POPPING OFF LIKE FIRECRACKERS-- EVERYBODY SCREAMING--
--IT WAS EVERY MAN FOR HIMSELF.
OH, RIGHT. THE COP. LISTEN, I'VE NEVER BROKEN THE LAW--NOT IN ANY WAY THAT COUNTS.
AND IT WASN'T ME WHO TOLD HIM TO TRY TO HELP THAT JAP BITCH OUT OF HER VOLKSWAGEN.
GROW UP. SOMEBODY WAS GOING TO GET HIS GUN. HE SURE DIDN'T HAVE ANY USE FOR IT.
THAT PRIEST, HE DIDN'T SEE IT MY WAY...
HE WOULDN'T LET GO. WOULDN'T LISTEN TO REASON. I'VE BEEN TO CHURCH EVERY SUNDAY SINCE I WAS A KID.
BUT WHEN PUSH COMES TO SHOVE...

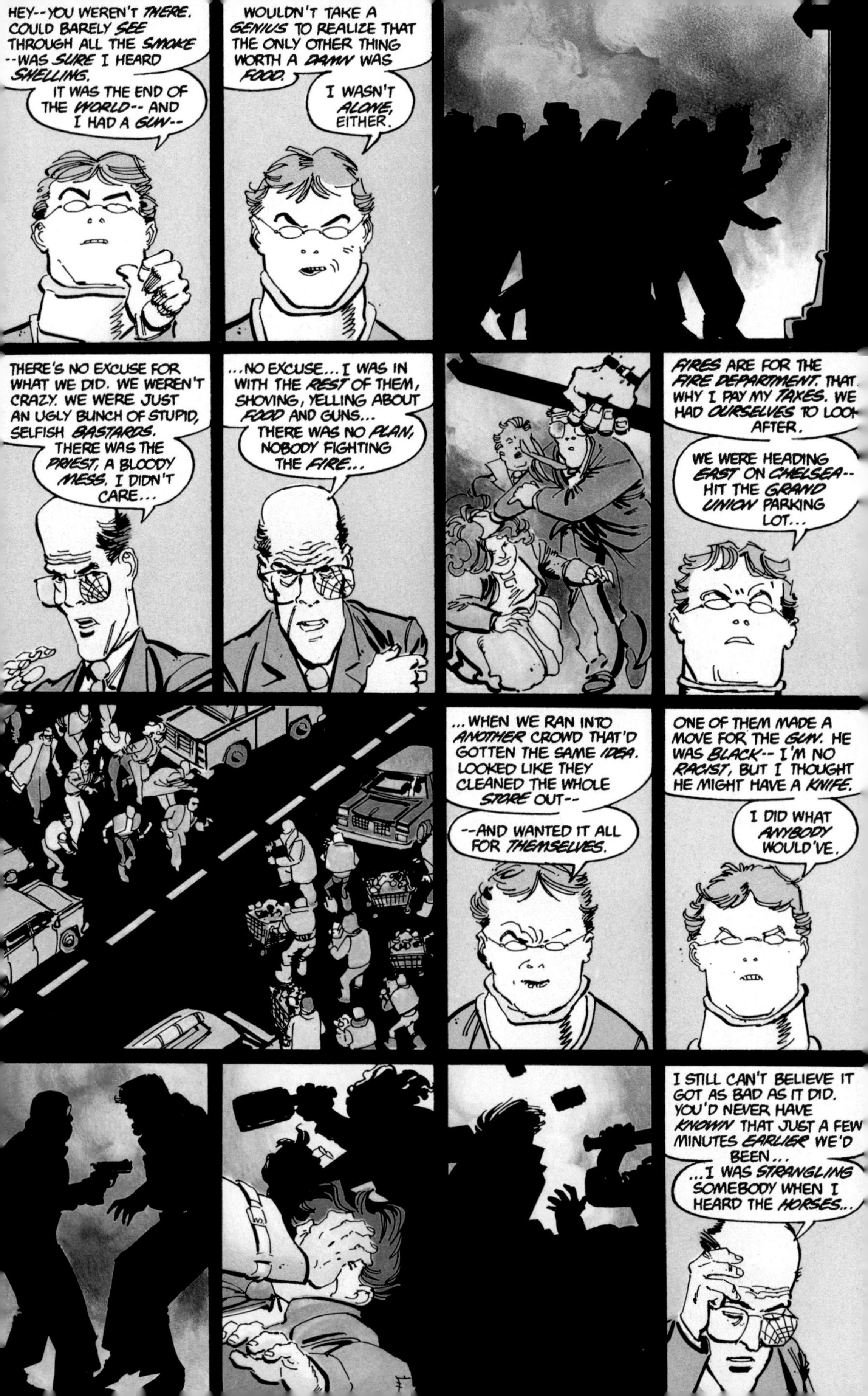

HEY--YOU WEREN'T THERE. COULD BARELY SEE THROUGH ALL THE SMOKE --WAS SURE I HEARD SHELLING.
IT WAS THE END OF THE WORLD-- AND I HAD A GUN--
WOULDN'T TAKE A GENIUS TO REALIZE THAT THE ONLY OTHER THING WORTH A DAMN WAS FOOD.
I WASN'T ALONE, EITHER.
THERE'S NO EXCUSE FOR WHAT WE DID. WE WEREN'T CRAZY. WE WERE JUST AN UGLY BUNCH OF STUPID, SELFISH BASTARDS.
THERE WAS THE PRIEST, A BLOODY MESS. I DIDN'T CARE...
...NO EXCUSE...I WAS IN WITH THE REST OF THEM, SHOVING, YELLING ABOUT FOOD AND GUNS...
THERE WAS NO PLAN, NOBODY FIGHTING THE FIRE...
FIRES ARE FOR THE FIRE DEPARTMENT. THAT WHY I PAY MY TAXES. WE HAD OURSELVES TO LOOK AFTER.
WE WERE HEADING EAST ON CHELSEA-- HIT THE GRAND UNION PARKING LOT...
...WHEN WE RAN INTO ANOTHER CROWD THAT'D GOTTEN THE SAME IDEA. LOOKED LIKE THEY CLEANED THE WHOLE STORE OUT--
--AND WANTED IT ALL FOR THEMSELVES.
ONE OF THEM MADE A MOVE FOR THE GUN. HE WAS BLACK-- I'M NO RACIST, BUT I THOUGHT HE MIGHT HAVE A KNIFE.
I DID WHAT ANYBODY WOULD'VE.
I STILL CAN'T BELIEVE IT GOT AS BAD AS IT DID. YOU'D NEVER HAVE KNOWN THAT JUST A FEW MINUTES EARLIER WE'D BEEN...
...I WAS STRANGLING SOMEBODY WHEN I HEARD THE HORSES...

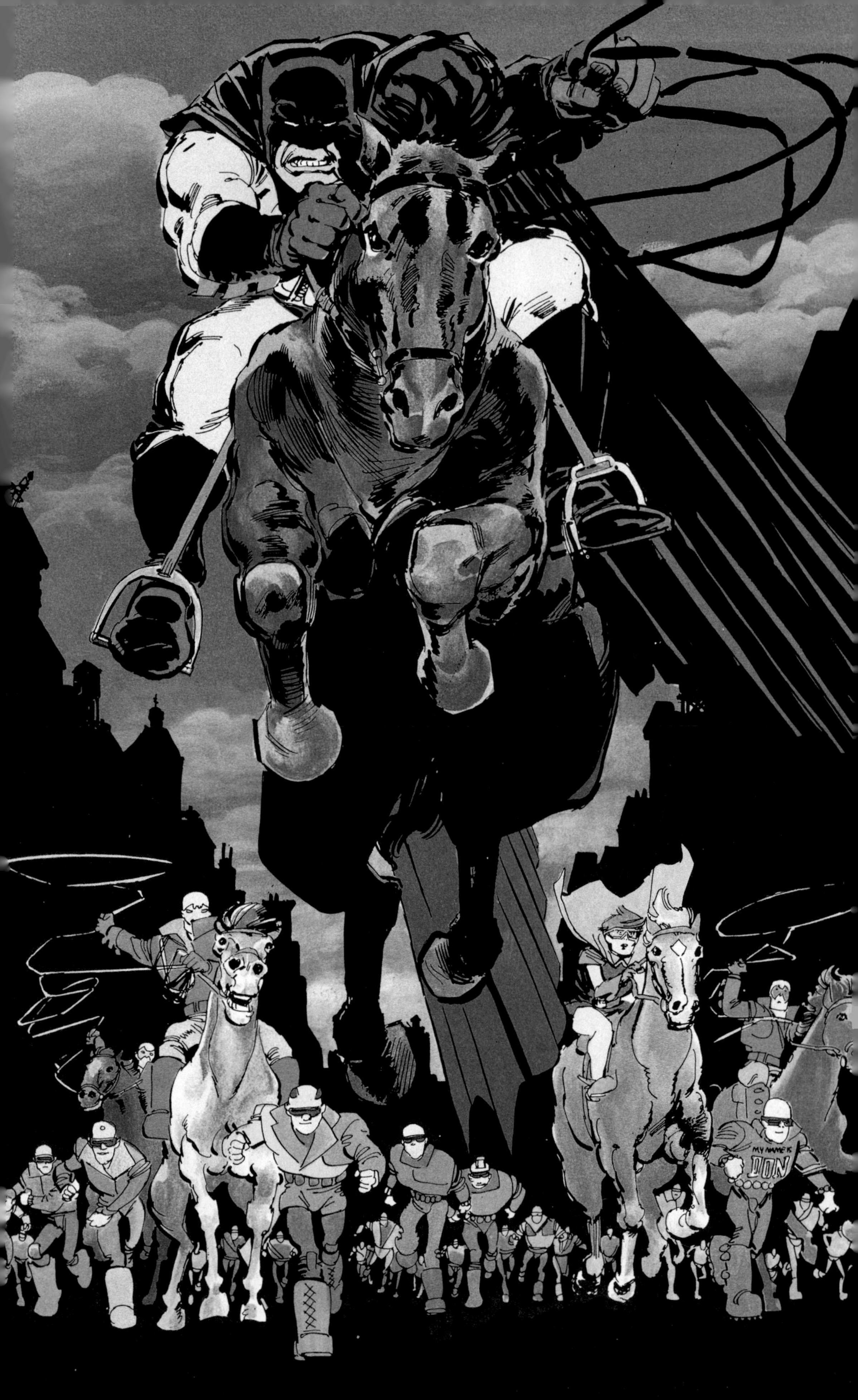
MY NAME IS
DON

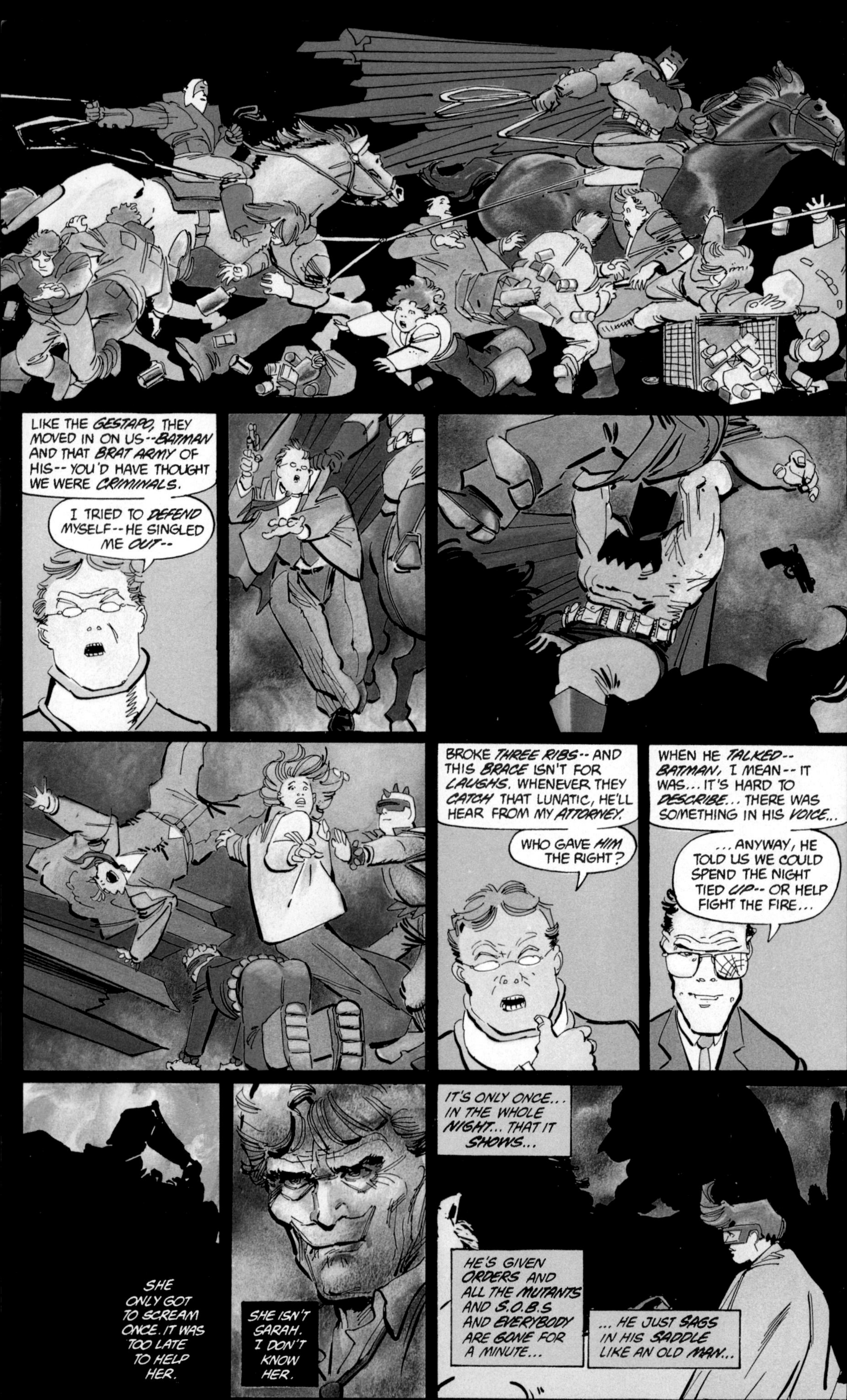

LIKE THE GESTAPO, THEY MOVED IN ON US--BATMAN AND THAT BRAT ARMY OF HIS-- YOU'D HAVE THOUGHT WE WERE CRIMINALS.
I TRIED TO DEFEND MYSELF--HE SINGLED ME OUT--
BROKE THREE RIBS-- AND THIS BRACE ISN'T FOR LAUGHS. WHENEVER THEY CATCH THAT LUNATIC, HE'LL HEAR FROM MY ATTORNEY.
WHO GAVE HIM THE RIGHT?
WHEN HE TALKED-- BATMAN, I MEAN-- IT WAS... IT'S HARD TO DESCRIBE... THERE WAS SOMETHING IN HIS VOICE...
... ANYWAY, HE TOLD US WE COULD SPEND THE NIGHT TIED UP-- OR HELP FIGHT THE FIRE...
SHE ONLY GOT TO SCREAM ONCE. IT WAS TOO LATE TO HELP HER.
SHE ISN'T SARAH. I DON'T KNOW HER.
IT'S ONLY ONCE... IN THE WHOLE NIGHT... THAT IT SHOWS...
HE'S GIVEN ORDERS AND ALL THE MUTANTS AND S.O.B.S AND EVERYBODY ARE GONE FOR A MINUTE...
... HE JUST SAGS IN HIS SADDLE LIKE AN OLD MAN...

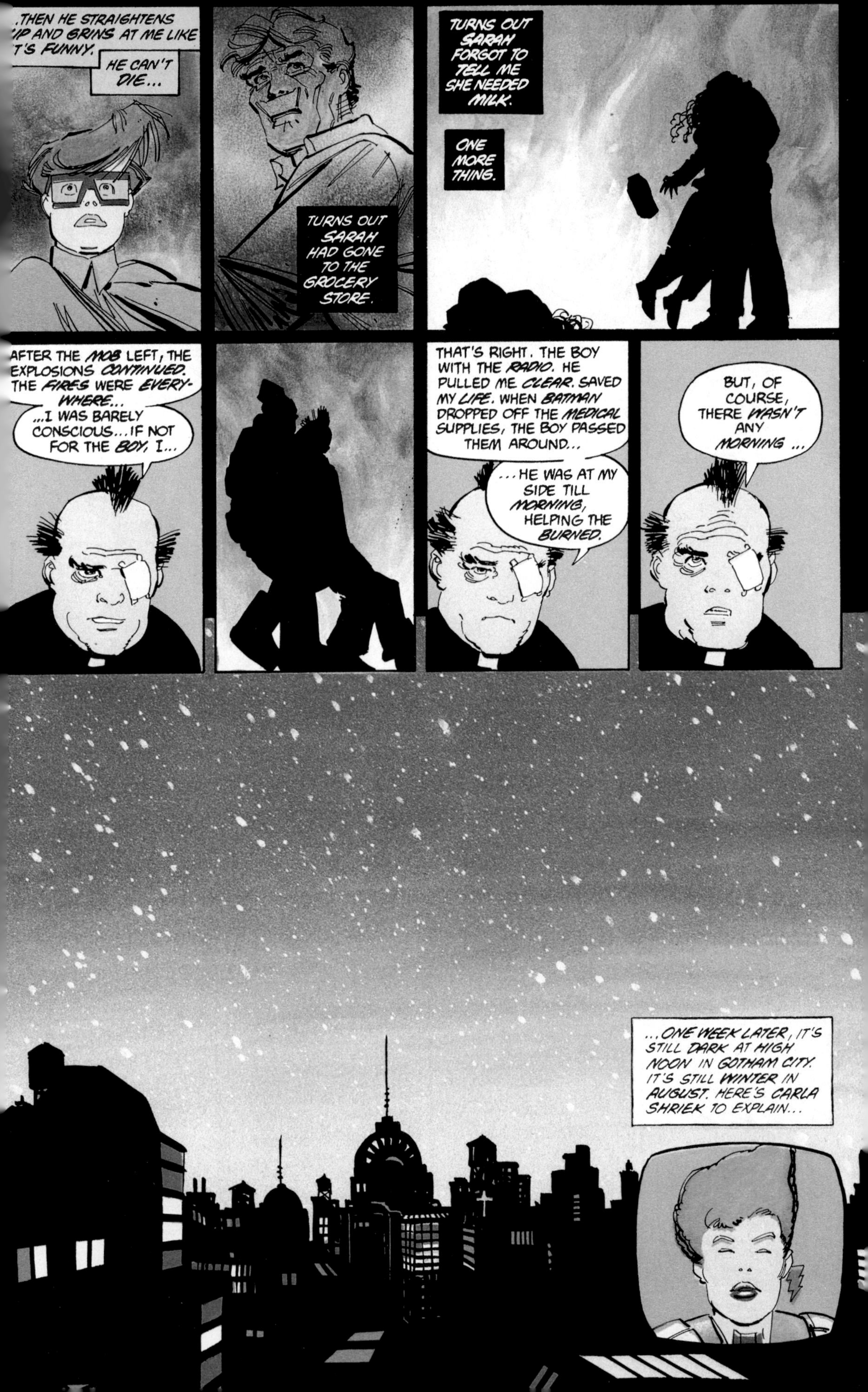
...THEN HE STRAIGHTENS UP AND GRINS AT ME LIKE IT'S FUNNY.
HE CAN'T DIE...
TURNS OUT SARAH HAD GONE TO THE GROCERY STORE.
TURNS OUT SARAH FORGOT TO TELL ME SHE NEEDED MILK.
ONE MORE THING.
AFTER THE MOB LEFT, THE EXPLOSIONS CONTINUED. THE FIRES WERE EVERYWHERE...
...I WAS BARELY CONSCIOUS... IF NOT FOR THE BOY, I...
THAT'S RIGHT. THE BOY WITH THE RADIO. HE PULLED ME CLEAR. SAVED MY LIFE. WHEN BATMAN DROPPED OFF THE MEDICAL SUPPLIES, THE BOY PASSED THEM AROUND...
...HE WAS AT MY SIDE TILL MORNING, HELPING THE BURNED.
BUT, OF COURSE, THERE WASN'T ANY MORNING...
...ONE WEEK LATER, IT'S STILL DARK AT HIGH NOON IN GOTHAM CITY. IT'S STILL WINTER IN AUGUST. HERE'S CARLA SHRIEK TO EXPLAIN...

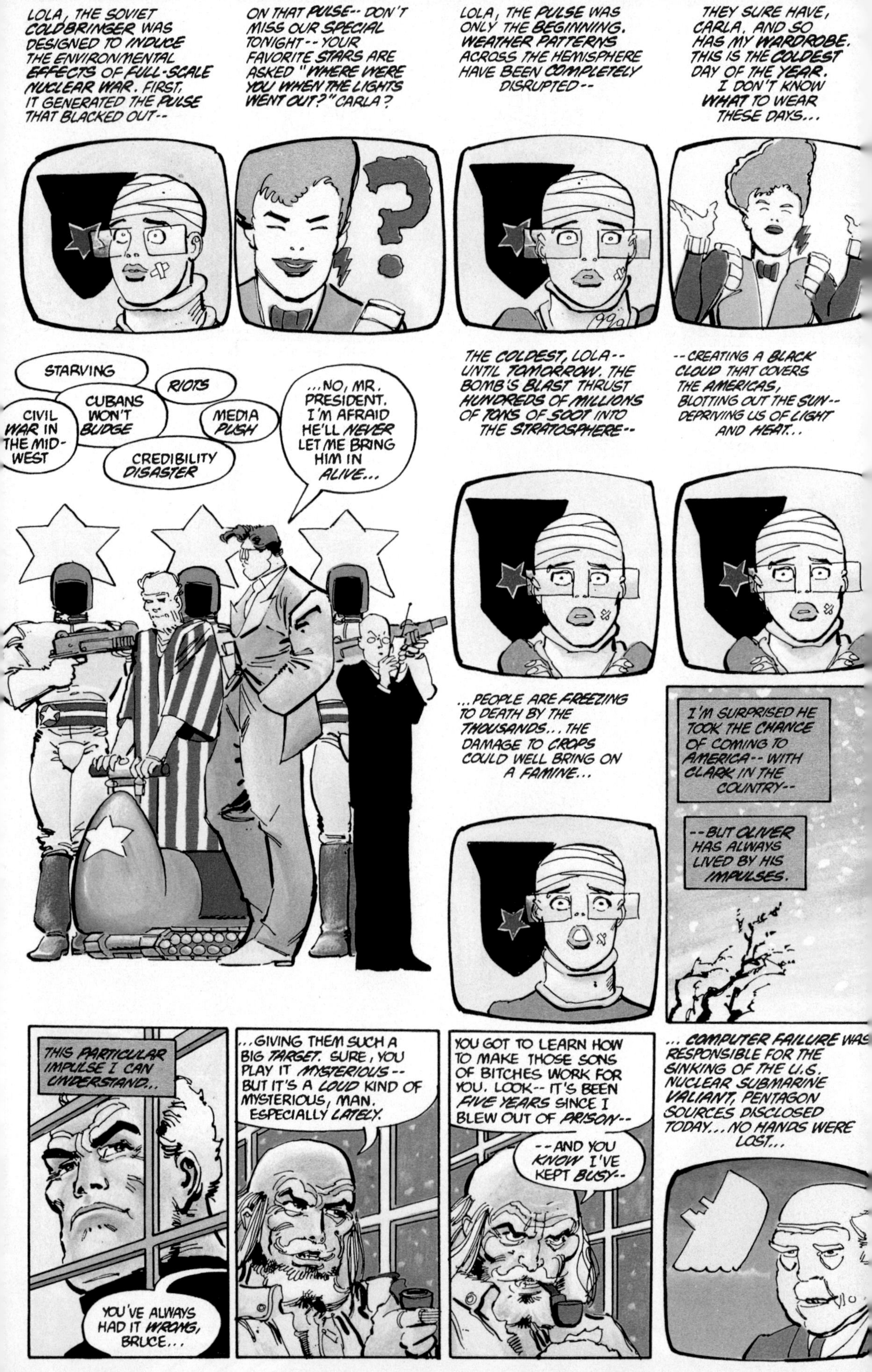
LOLA, THE SOVIET COLDBRINGER WAS DESIGNED TO INDUCE THE ENVIRONMENTAL EFFECTS OF FULL-SCALE NUCLEAR WAR. FIRST, IT GENERATED THE PULSE THAT BLACKED OUT--
ON THAT PULSE-- DON'T MISS OUR SPECIAL TONIGHT-- YOUR FAVORITE STARS ARE ASKED "WHERE WERE YOU WHEN THE LIGHTS WENT OUT?" CARLA?
LOLA, THE PULSE WAS ONLY THE BEGINNING. WEATHER PATTERNS ACROSS THE HEMISPHERE HAVE BEEN COMPLETELY DISRUPTED--
THEY SURE HAVE, CARLA. AND SO HAS MY WARDROBE. THIS IS THE COLDEST DAY OF THE YEAR. I DON'T KNOW WHAT TO WEAR THESE DAYS...
STARVING
RIOTS
CIVIL WAR IN THE MID-WEST
CUBANS WON'T BUDGE
MEDIA PUSH
CREDIBILITY DISASTER
...NO, MR. PRESIDENT. I'M AFRAID HE'LL NEVER LET ME BRING HIM IN ALIVE...
THE COLDEST, LOLA-- UNTIL TOMORROW. THE BOMB'S BLAST THRUST HUNDREDS OF MILLIONS OF TONS OF SOOT INTO THE STRATOSPHERE--
--CREATING A BLACK CLOUD THAT COVERS THE AMERICAS, BLOTTING OUT THE SUN-- DEPRIVING US OF LIGHT AND HEAT...
...PEOPLE ARE FREEZING TO DEATH BY THE THOUSANDS... THE DAMAGE TO CROPS COULD WELL BRING ON A FAMINE...
I'M SURPRISED HE TOOK THE CHANCE OF COMING TO AMERICA-- WITH CLARK IN THE COUNTRY--
--BUT OLIVER HAS ALWAYS LIVED BY HIS IMPULSES.
THIS PARTICULAR IMPULSE I CAN UNDERSTAND...
YOU'VE ALWAYS HAD IT WRONG, BRUCE...
...GIVING THEM SUCH A BIG TARGET. SURE, YOU PLAY IT MYSTERIOUS-- BUT IT'S A LOUD KIND OF MYSTERIOUS, MAN. ESPECIALLY LATELY.
YOU GOT TO LEARN HOW TO MAKE THOSE SONS OF BITCHES WORK FOR YOU. LOOK-- IT'S BEEN FIVE YEARS SINCE I BLEW OUT OF PRISON--
--AND YOU KNOW I'VE KEPT BUSY--
...COMPUTER FAILURE WAS RESPONSIBLE FOR THE SINKING OF THE U.S. NUCLEAR SUBMARINE VALIANT, PENTAGON SOURCES DISCLOSED TODAY... NO HANDS WERE LOST...

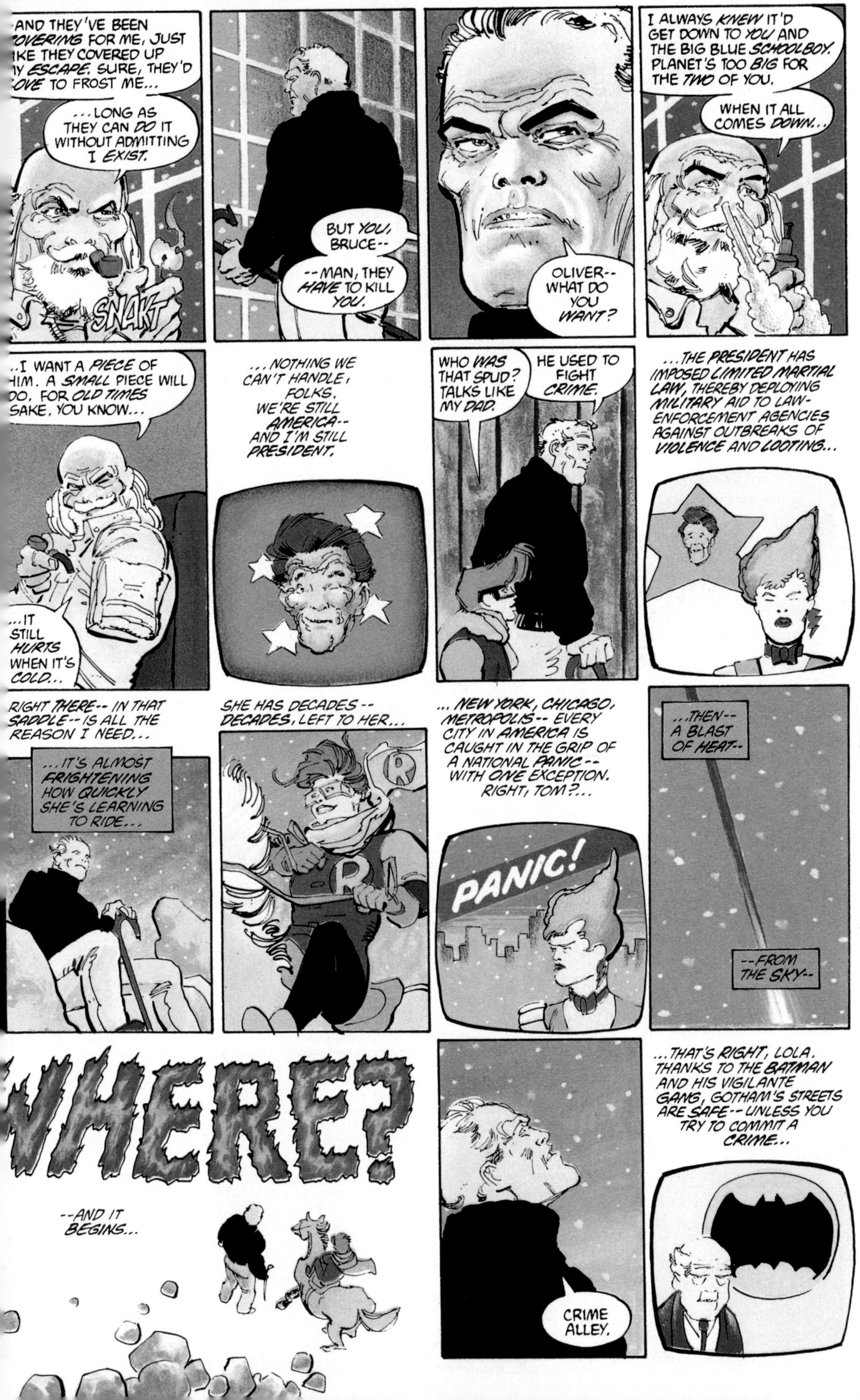
AND THEY'VE BEEN OVERING FOR ME, JUST IKE THEY COVERED UP Y ESCAPE. SURE, THEY'D OVE TO FROST ME...
...LONG AS THEY CAN DO IT WITHOUT ADMITTING I EXIST.
SNAKT
BUT YOU, BRUCE--
--MAN, THEY HAVE TO KILL YOU.
OLIVER-- WHAT DO YOU WANT?
I ALWAYS KNEW IT'D GET DOWN TO YOU AND THE BIG BLUE SCHOOLBOY. PLANET'S TOO BIG FOR THE TWO OF YOU.
WHEN IT ALL COMES DOWN...
...I WANT A PIECE OF HIM. A SMALL PIECE WILL DO. FOR OLD TIMES SAKE, YOU KNOW...
...IT STILL HURTS WHEN IT'S COLD...
...NOTHING WE CAN'T HANDLE, FOLKS. WE'RE STILL AMERICA-- AND I'M STILL PRESIDENT.
WHO WAS THAT SPUD? TALKS LIKE MY DAD.
HE USED TO FIGHT CRIME.
...THE PRESIDENT HAS IMPOSED LIMITED MARTIAL LAW, THEREBY DEPLOYING MILITARY AID TO LAW-ENFORCEMENT AGENCIES AGAINST OUTBREAKS OF VIOLENCE AND LOOTING...
RIGHT THERE-- IN THAT SADDLE--IS ALL THE REASON I NEED...
...IT'S ALMOST FRIGHTENING HOW QUICKLY SHE'S LEARNING TO RIDE...
SHE HAS DECADES-- DECADES, LEFT TO HER...
...NEW YORK, CHICAGO, METROPOLIS-- EVERY CITY IN AMERICA IS CAUGHT IN THE GRIP OF A NATIONAL PANIC-- WITH ONE EXCEPTION. RIGHT, TOM?...
PANIC!
...THEN-- A BLAST OF HEAT--
--FROM THE SKY--
VHERE?
--AND IT BEGINS...
CRIME ALLEY.
...THAT'S RIGHT, LOLA. THANKS TO THE BATMAN AND HIS VIGILANTE GANG, GOTHAM'S STREETS ARE SAFE--UNLESS YOU TRY TO COMMIT A CRIME...

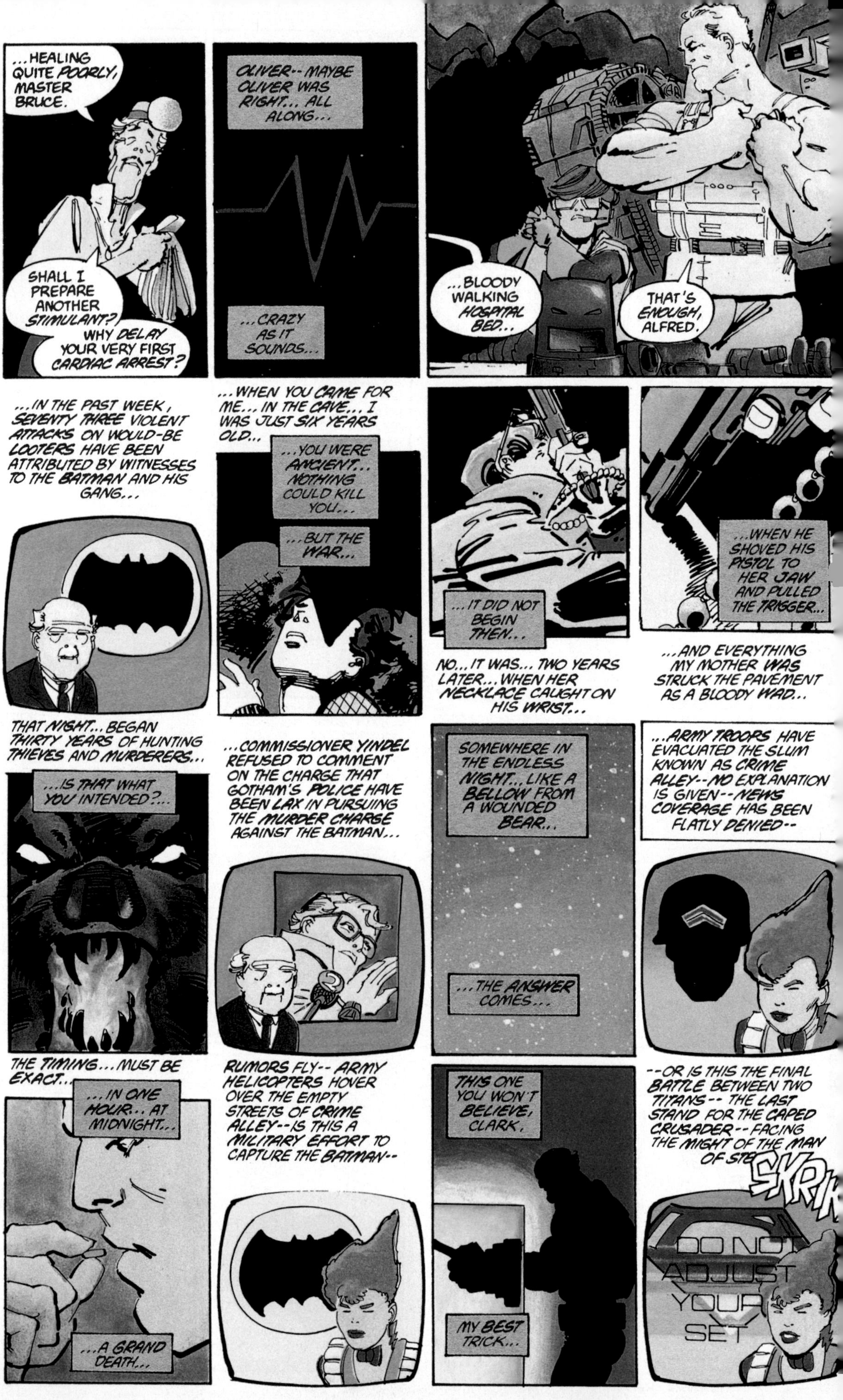
...HEALING QUITE POORLY, MASTER BRUCE.
SHALL I PREPARE ANOTHER STIMULANT?
WHY DELAY YOUR VERY FIRST CARDIAC ARREST?
OLIVER-- MAYBE OLIVER WAS RIGHT... ALL ALONG...
...CRAZY AS IT SOUNDS...
...BLOODY WALKING HOSPITAL BED...
THAT'S ENOUGH, ALFRED.
...IN THE PAST WEEK, SEVENTY THREE VIOLENT ATTACKS ON WOULD-BE LOOTERS HAVE BEEN ATTRIBUTED BY WITNESSES TO THE BATMAN AND HIS GANG...
...WHEN YOU CAME FOR ME... IN THE CAVE... I WAS JUST SIX YEARS OLD...
...YOU WERE ANCIENT... NOTHING COULD KILL YOU...
...BUT THE WAR...
...IT DID NOT BEGIN THEN...
NO... IT WAS... TWO YEARS LATER... WHEN HER NECKLACE CAUGHT ON HIS WRIST...
...WHEN HE SHOVED HIS PISTOL TO HER JAW AND PULLED THE TRIGGER...
...AND EVERYTHING MY MOTHER WAS STRUCK THE PAVEMENT AS A BLOODY WAD...
THAT NIGHT... BEGAN THIRTY YEARS OF HUNTING THIEVES AND MURDERERS...
...IS THAT WHAT YOU INTENDED?...
...COMMISSIONER YINDEL REFUSED TO COMMENT ON THE CHARGE THAT GOTHAM'S POLICE HAVE BEEN LAX IN PURSUING THE MURDER CHARGE AGAINST THE BATMAN...
SOMEWHERE IN THE ENDLESS NIGHT... LIKE A BELLOW FROM A WOUNDED BEAR...
...THE ANSWER COMES...
...ARMY TROORS HAVE EVACUATED THE SLUM KNOWN AS CRIME ALLEY--NO EXPLANATION IS GIVEN--NEWS COVERAGE HAS BEEN FLATLY DENIED--
THE TIMING... MUST BE EXACT...
...IN ONE HOUR... AT MIDNIGHT...
...A GRAND DEATH...
RUMORS FLY-- ARMY HELICOPTERS HOVER OVER THE EMPTY STREETS OF CRIME ALLEY--IS THIS A MILITARY EFFORT TO CAPTURE THE BATMAN--
THIS ONE YOU WON'T BELIEVE, CLARK.
MY BEST TRICK...
--OR IS THIS THE FINAL BATTLE BETWEEN TWO TITANS-- THE LAST STAND FOR THE CAPED CRUSADER--FACING THE MIGHT OF THE MAN OF STE
SKRIK
DO NOT ADJUST YOUR SET

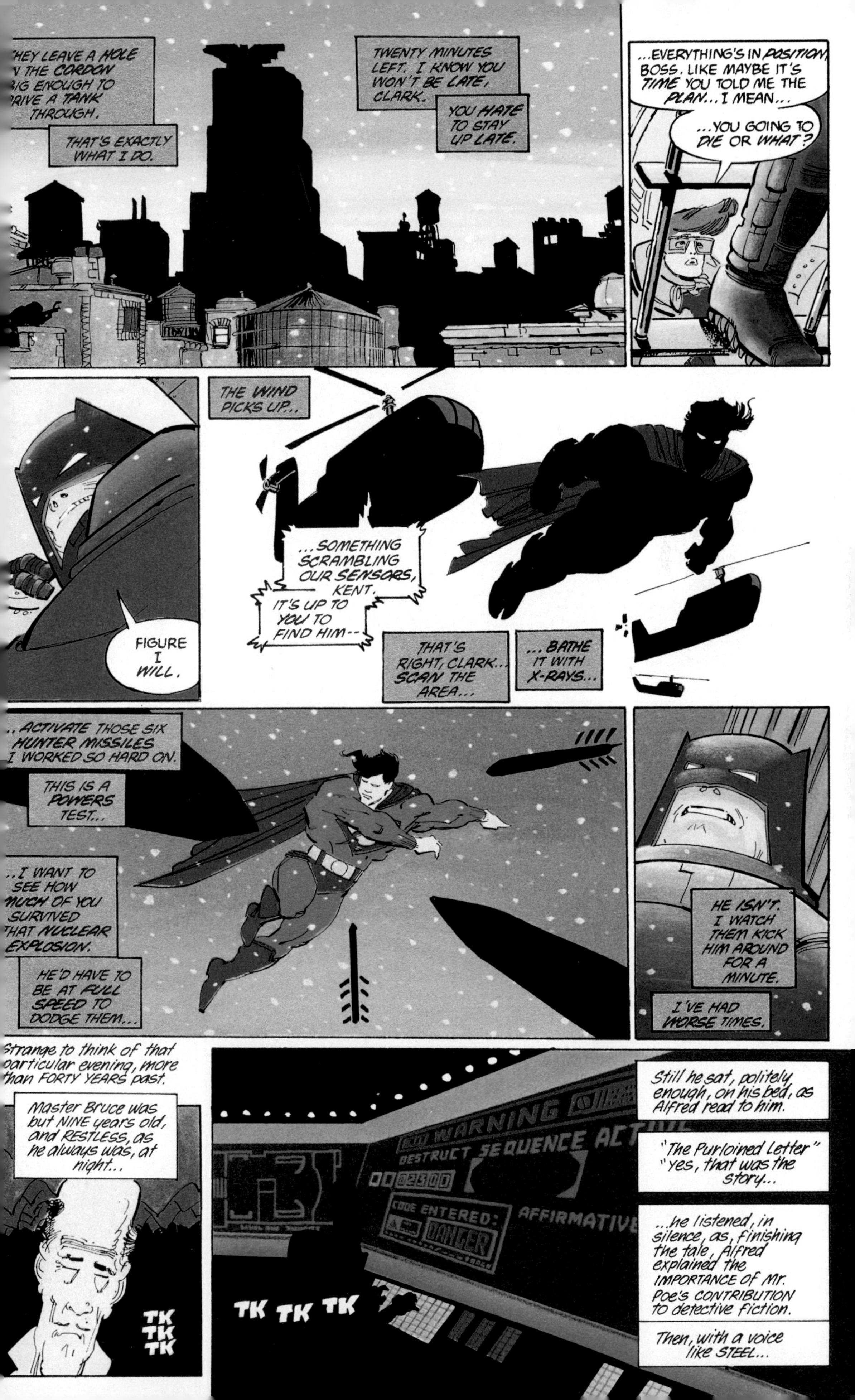
THEY LEAVE A HOLE IN THE CORDON BIG ENOUGH TO DRIVE A TANK THROUGH.
THAT'S EXACTLY WHAT I DO.
TWENTY MINUTES LEFT. I KNOW YOU WON'T BE LATE, CLARK.
YOU HATE TO STAY UP LATE.
...EVERYTHING'S IN POSITION, BOSS. LIKE MAYBE IT'S TIME YOU TOLD ME THE PLAN... I MEAN...
...YOU GOING TO DIE OR WHAT?
FIGURE I WILL.
THE WIND PICKS UP...
...SOMETHING SCRAMBLING OUR SENSORS, KENT.
IT'S UP TO YOU TO FIND HIM--
THAT'S RIGHT, CLARK... SCAN THE AREA...
...BATHE IT WITH X-RAYS...
...ACTIVATE THOSE SIX HUNTER MISSILES I WORKED SO HARD ON.
THIS IS A POWERS TEST...
...I WANT TO SEE HOW MUCH OF YOU SURVIVED THAT NUCLEAR EXPLOSION.
HE'D HAVE TO BE AT FULL SPEED TO DODGE THEM...
HE ISN'T. I WATCH THEM KICK HIM AROUND FOR A MINUTE.
I'VE HAD WORSE TIMES.
Strange to think of that particular evening, more than FORTY YEARS past.
Master Bruce was but NINE years old, and RESTLESS, as he always was, at night...
TK TK TK
WARNING
DESTRUCT SEQUENCE ACTIVE
CODE ENTERED:
DANGER
AFFIRMATIVE
TK TK TK
Still he sat, politely enough, on his bed, as Alfred read to him.
"The Purloined Letter" "yes, that was the story...
...he listened, in silence, as, finishing the tale, Alfred explained the IMPORTANCE of Mr. Poe's CONTRIBUTION to detective fiction.
Then, with a voice like STEEL...

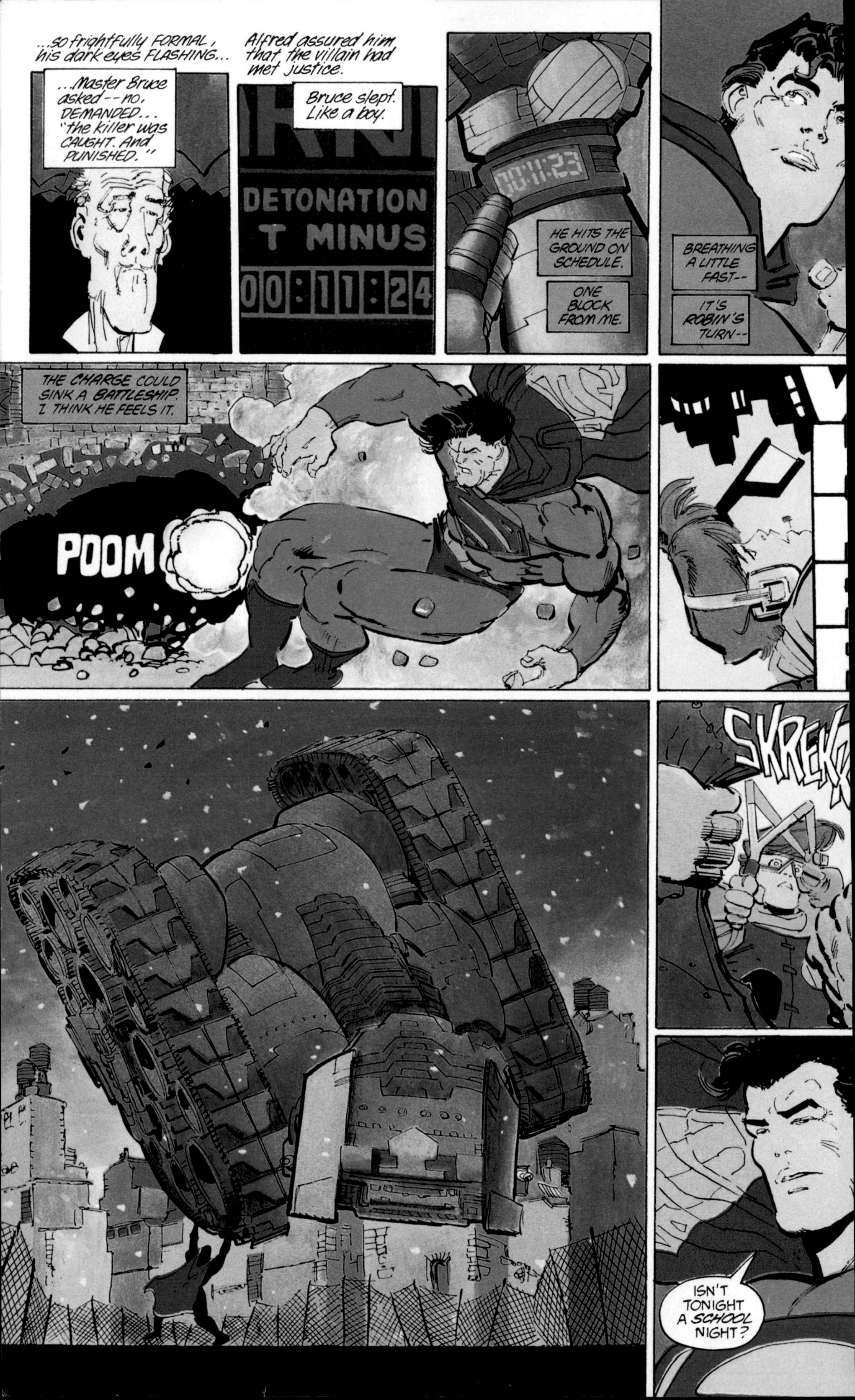
...so frightfully FORMAL, his dark eyes FLASHING...
...Master Bruce asked--no, DEMANDED... "the killer was CAUGHT. And PUNISHED."
Alfred assured him that the villain had met justice.
Bruce slept. Like a boy.
DETONATION
T MINUS
00:11:24
00:11:23
HE HITS THE GROUND ON SCHEDULE.
ONE BLOCK FROM ME.
BREATHING A LITTLE FAST--
IT'S ROBIN'S TURN--
THE CHARGE COULD SINK A BATTLESHIP. I THINK HE FEELS IT.
POOM
SKREK
ISN'T TONIGHT A SCHOOL NIGHT?

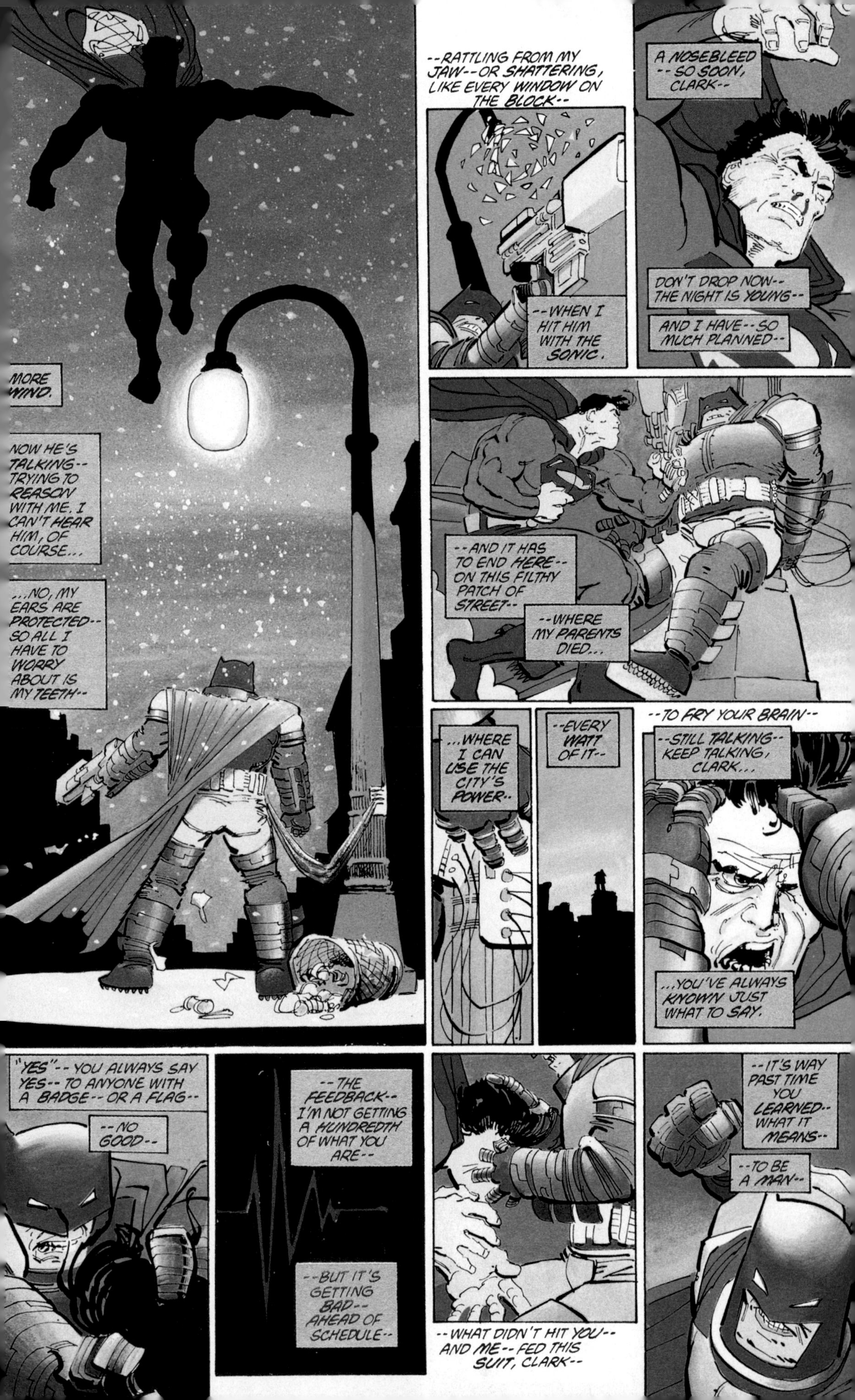
MORE WIND.
NOW HE'S TALKING-- TRYING TO REASON WITH ME. I CAN'T HEAR HIM, OF COURSE...
...NO, MY EARS ARE PROTECTED-- SO ALL I HAVE TO WORRY ABOUT IS MY TEETH--
--RATTLING FROM MY JAW--OR SHATTERING, LIKE EVERY WINDOW ON THE BLOCK--
--WHEN I HIT HIM WITH THE SONIC.
A NOSEBLEED --SO SOON, CLARK--
DON'T DROP NOW-- THE NIGHT IS YOUNG--
AND I HAVE--SO MUCH PLANNED--
--AND IT HAS TO END HERE-- ON THIS FILTHY PATCH OF STREET--
--WHERE MY PARENTS DIED...
...WHERE I CAN USE THE CITY'S POWER--
--EVERY WATT OF IT--
--TO FRY YOUR BRAIN--
--STILL TALKING-- KEEP TALKING, CLARK...
...YOU'VE ALWAYS KNOWN JUST WHAT TO SAY.
"YES"--YOU ALWAYS SAY YES--TO ANYONE WITH A BADGE--OR A FLAG--
--NO GOOD--
--THE FEEDBACK-- I'M NOT GETTING A HUNDREDTH OF WHAT YOU ARE--
--BUT IT'S GETTING BAD-- AHEAD OF SCHEDULE--
--WHAT DIDN'T HIT YOU-- AND ME--FED THIS SUIT, CLARK--
--IT'S WAY PAST TIME YOU LEARNED-- WHAT IT MEANS--
--TO BE A MAN--

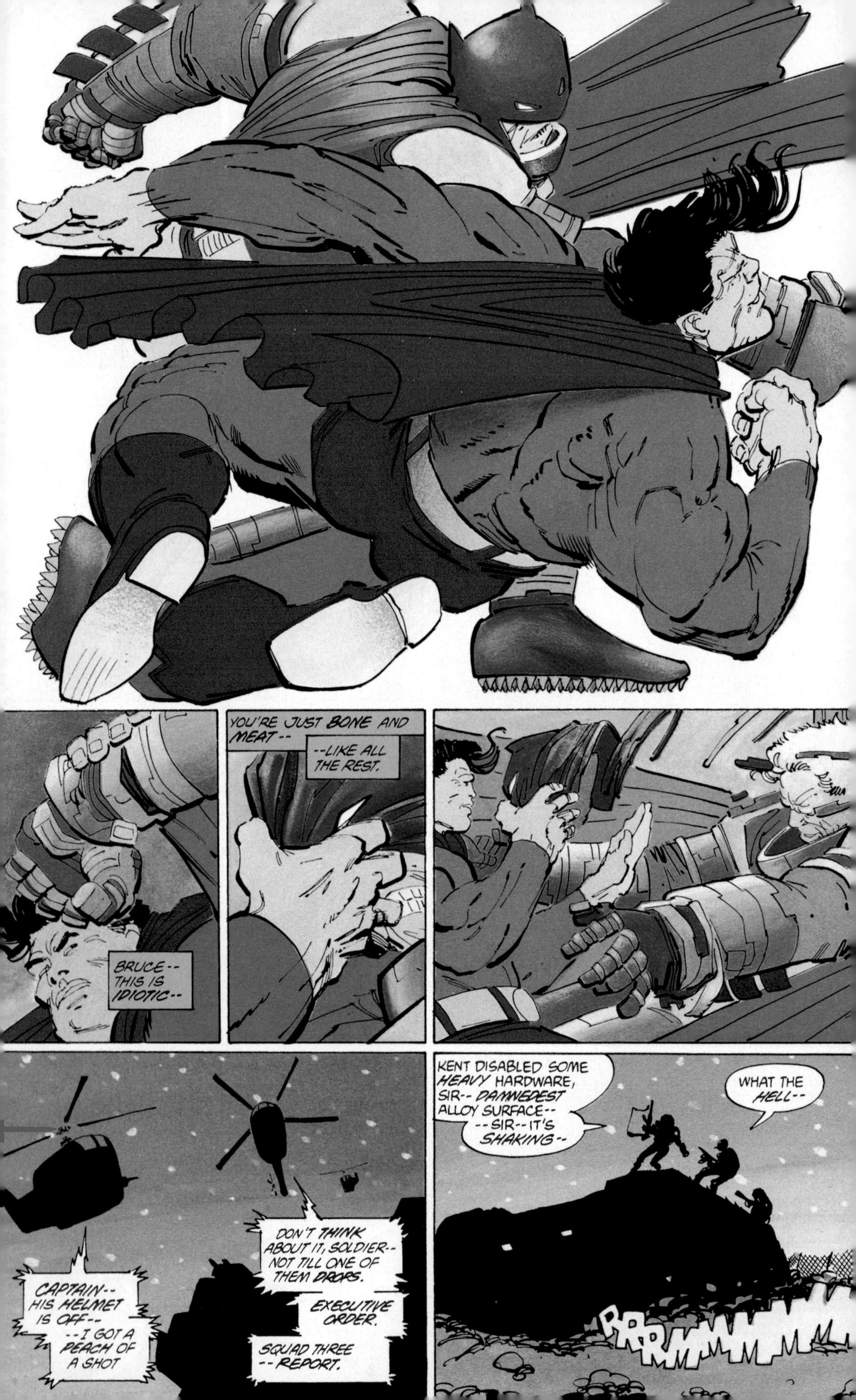
BRUCE-- THIS IS IDIOTIC--
YOU'RE JUST BONE AND MEAT--
--LIKE ALL THE REST.
CAPTAIN-- HIS HELMET IS OFF--
--I GOT A PEACH OF A SHOT
DON'T THINK ABOUT IT, SOLDIER-- NOT TILL ONE OF THEM DROPS.
EXECUTIVE ORDER.
SQUAD THREE --REPORT.
KENT DISABLED SOME HEAVY HARDWARE, SIR-- DAMNEDEST ALLOY SURFACE--
--SIR--IT'S SHAKING--
WHAT THE HELL--
RRRMMMMMMM

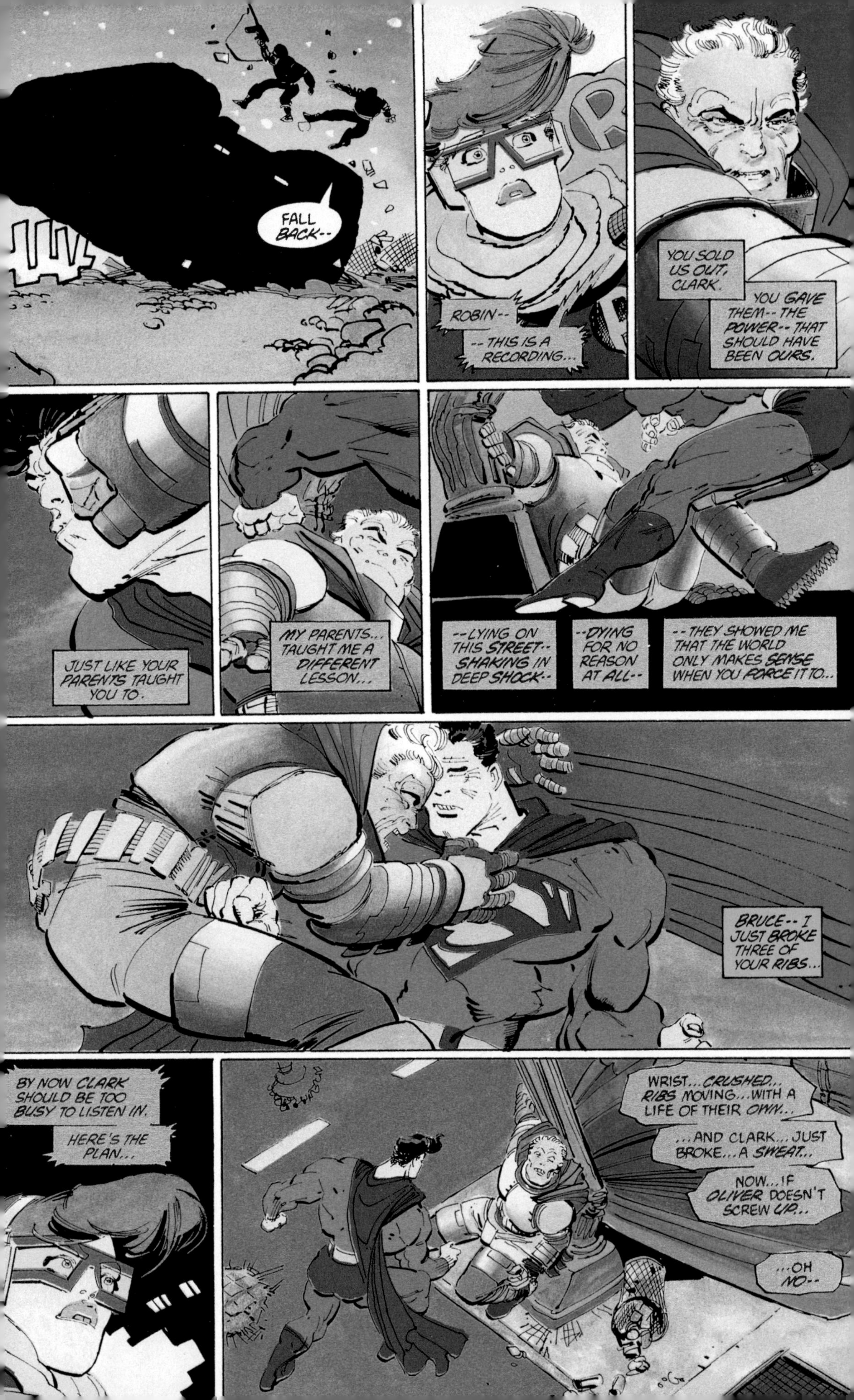
FALL BACK--
ROBIN--
--THIS IS A RECORDING...
YOU SOLD US OUT, CLARK.
YOU GAVE THEM--THE POWER--THAT SHOULD HAVE BEEN OURS.
JUST LIKE YOUR PARENTS TAUGHT YOU TO.
MY PARENTS... TAUGHT ME A DIFFERENT LESSON...
--LYING ON THIS STREET--SHAKING IN DEEP SHOCK--
--DYING FOR NO REASON AT ALL--
--THEY SHOWED ME THAT THE WORLD ONLY MAKES SENSE WHEN YOU FORCE IT TO...
BRUCE--I JUST BROKE THREE OF YOUR RIBS...
BY NOW CLARK SHOULD BE TOO BUSY TO LISTEN IN.
HERE'S THE PLAN...
WRIST...CRUSHED... RIBS MOVING...WITH A LIFE OF THEIR OWN...
...AND CLARK...JUST BROKE...A SWEAT...
NOW...IF OLIVER DOESN'T SCREW UP...
...OH NO--

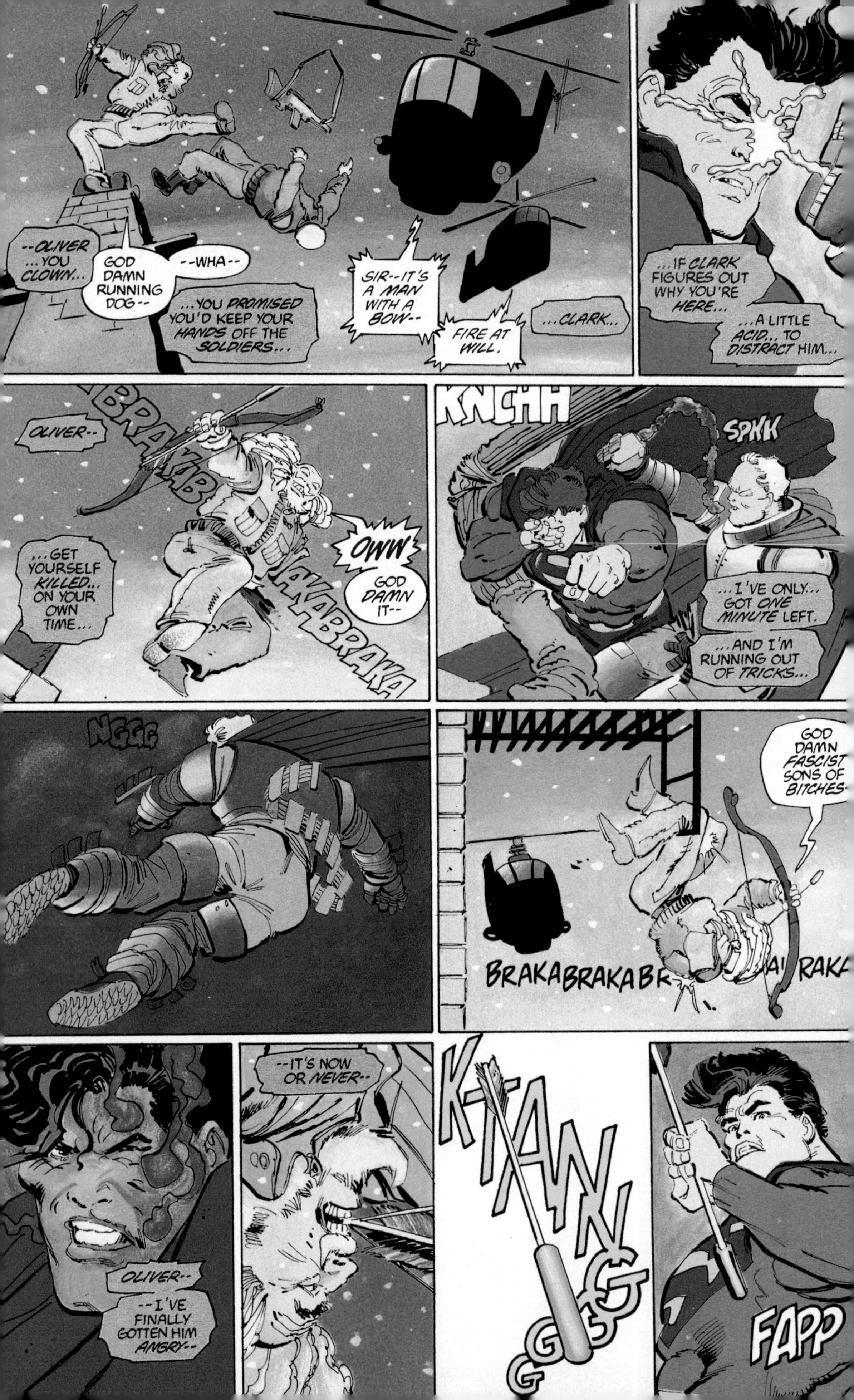
--OLIVER ...YOU CLOWN...
GOD DAMN RUNNING DOG--
--WHA--
...YOU PROMISED YOU'D KEEP YOUR HANDS OFF THE SOLDIERS...
SIR--IT'S A MAN WITH A BOW--
FIRE AT WILL.
...CLARK...
...IF CLARK FIGURES OUT WHY YOU'RE HERE...
...A LITTLE ACID... TO DISTRACT HIM...
OLIVER--
BRAKAB
...GET YOURSELF KILLED... ON YOUR OWN TIME...
OWW
GOD DAMN IT--
AKABRAKA
KNCHH
SPKK
...I'VE ONLY... GOT ONE MINUTE LEFT.
...AND I'M RUNNING OUT OF TRICKS...
NGGG
GOD DAMN FASCIST SONS OF BITCHES--
BRAKABRAKABR
RAKA
OLIVER--
--I'VE FINALLY GOTTEN HIM ANGRY--
--IT'S NOW OR NEVER--
K-TANNGGGG
FAPP

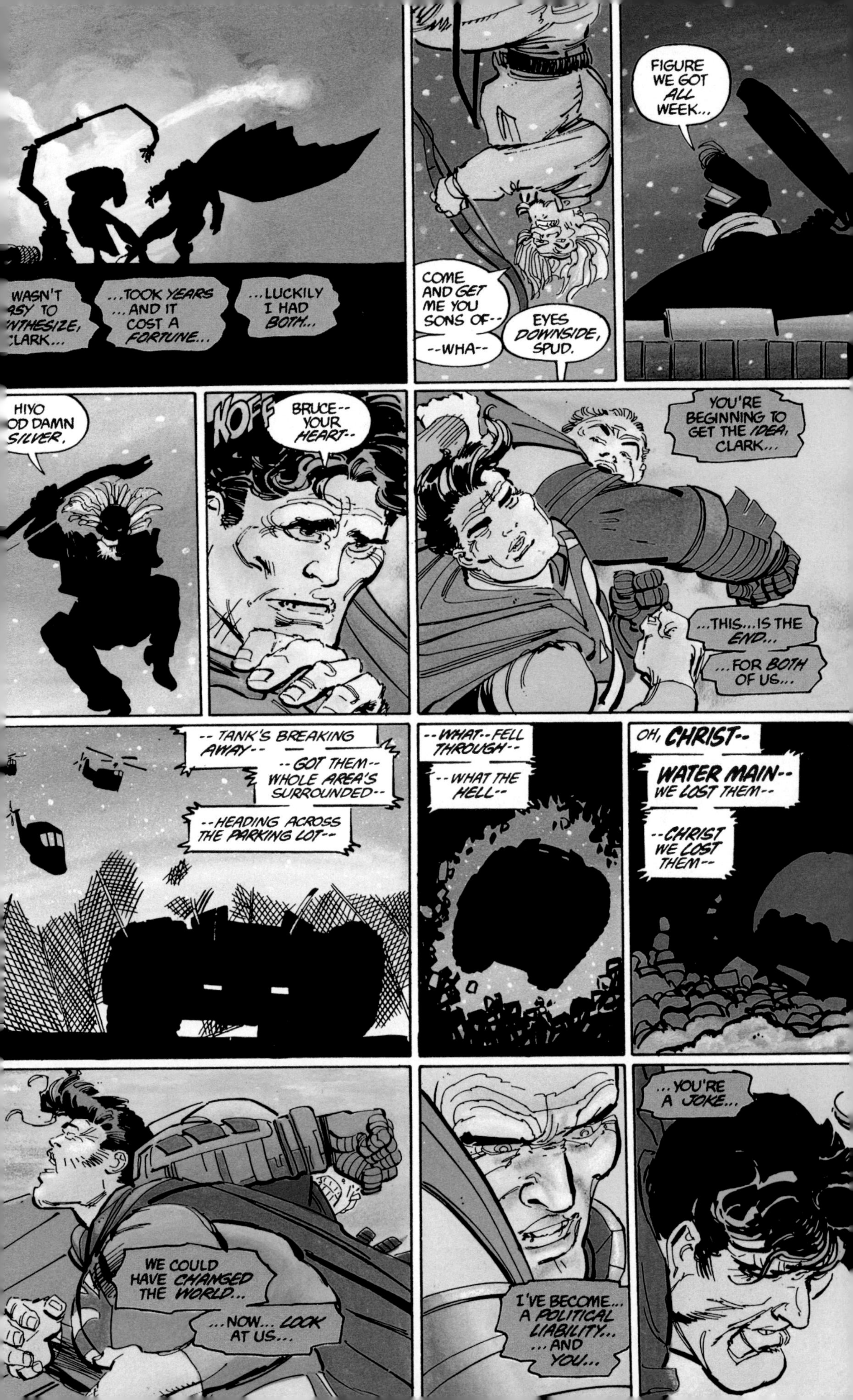
WASN'T ASY TO NTHESIZE, CLARK...
...TOOK YEARS ...AND IT COST A FORTUNE...
...LUCKILY I HAD BOTH...
COME AND GET ME YOU SONS OF--
--WHA--
EYES DOWNSIDE, SPUD.
FIGURE WE GOT ALL WEEK...
HIYO OD DAMN SILVER.
KOFF
BRUCE-- YOUR HEART--
YOU'RE BEGINNING TO GET THE IDEA, CLARK...
...THIS...IS THE END...
...FOR BOTH OF US...
-- TANK'S BREAKING AWAY--
--GOT THEM-- WHOLE AREA'S SURROUNDED--
--HEADING ACROSS THE PARKING LOT--
--WHAT--FELL THROUGH--
--WHAT THE HELL--
OH, CHRIST--
WATER MAIN-- WE LOST THEM--
--CHRIST WE LOST THEM--
WE COULD HAVE CHANGED THE WORLD...
...NOW... LOOK AT US...
I'VE BECOME... A POLITICAL LIABILITY... ...AND YOU...
...YOU'RE A JOKE...

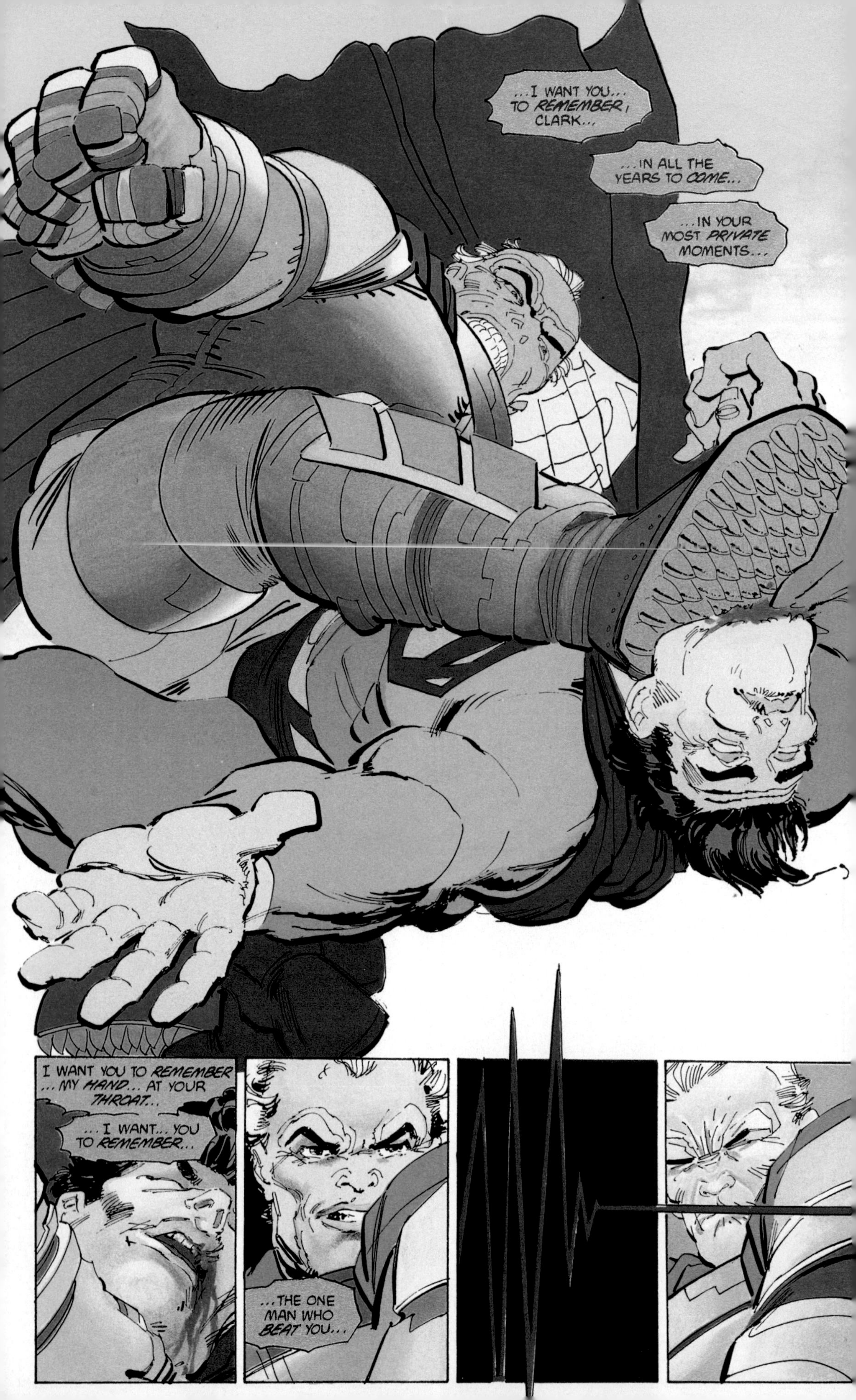
...I WANT YOU... TO REMEMBER, CLARK...
...IN ALL THE YEARS TO COME...
...IN YOUR MOST PRIVATE MOMENTS...
I WANT YOU TO REMEMBER ...MY HAND... AT YOUR THROAT...
...I WANT... YOU TO REMEMBER...
...THE ONE MAN WHO BEAT YOU...

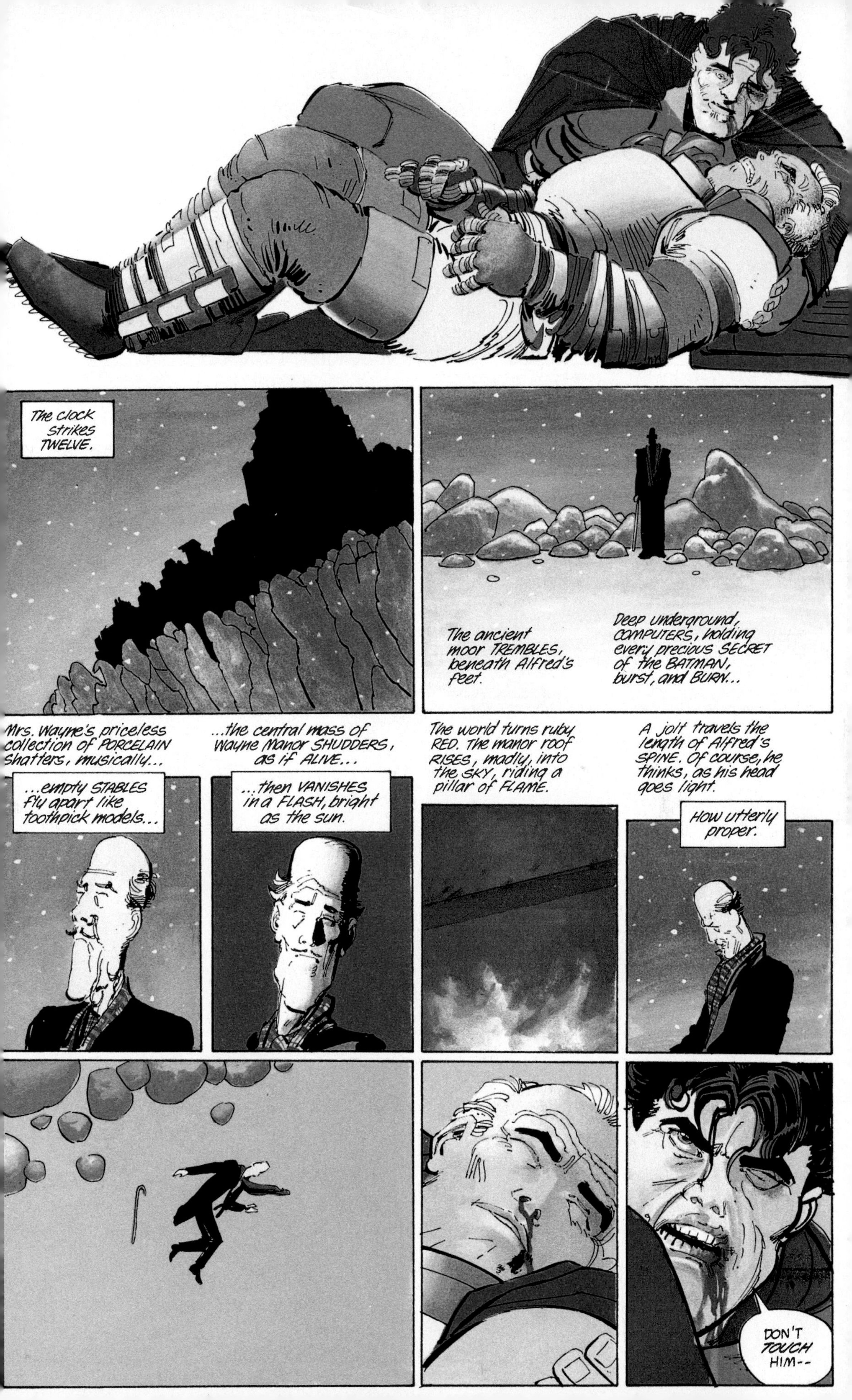
The clock strikes TWELVE.
The ancient moor TREMBLES, beneath Alfred's feet.
Deep underground, COMPUTERS, holding every precious SECRET of the BATMAN, burst, and BURN...
Mrs. Wayne's priceless collection of PORCELAIN shatters, musically...
...empty STABLES fly apart like toothpick models...
...the central mass of Wayne Manor SHUDDERS, as if ALIVE...
...then VANISHES in a FLASH, bright as the sun.
The world turns ruby RED. The manor roof RISES, madly, into the SKY, riding a pillar of FLAME.
A jolt travels the length of Alfred's SPINE. Of course, he thinks, as his head goes light.
How utterly proper.
DON'T TOUCH HIM--

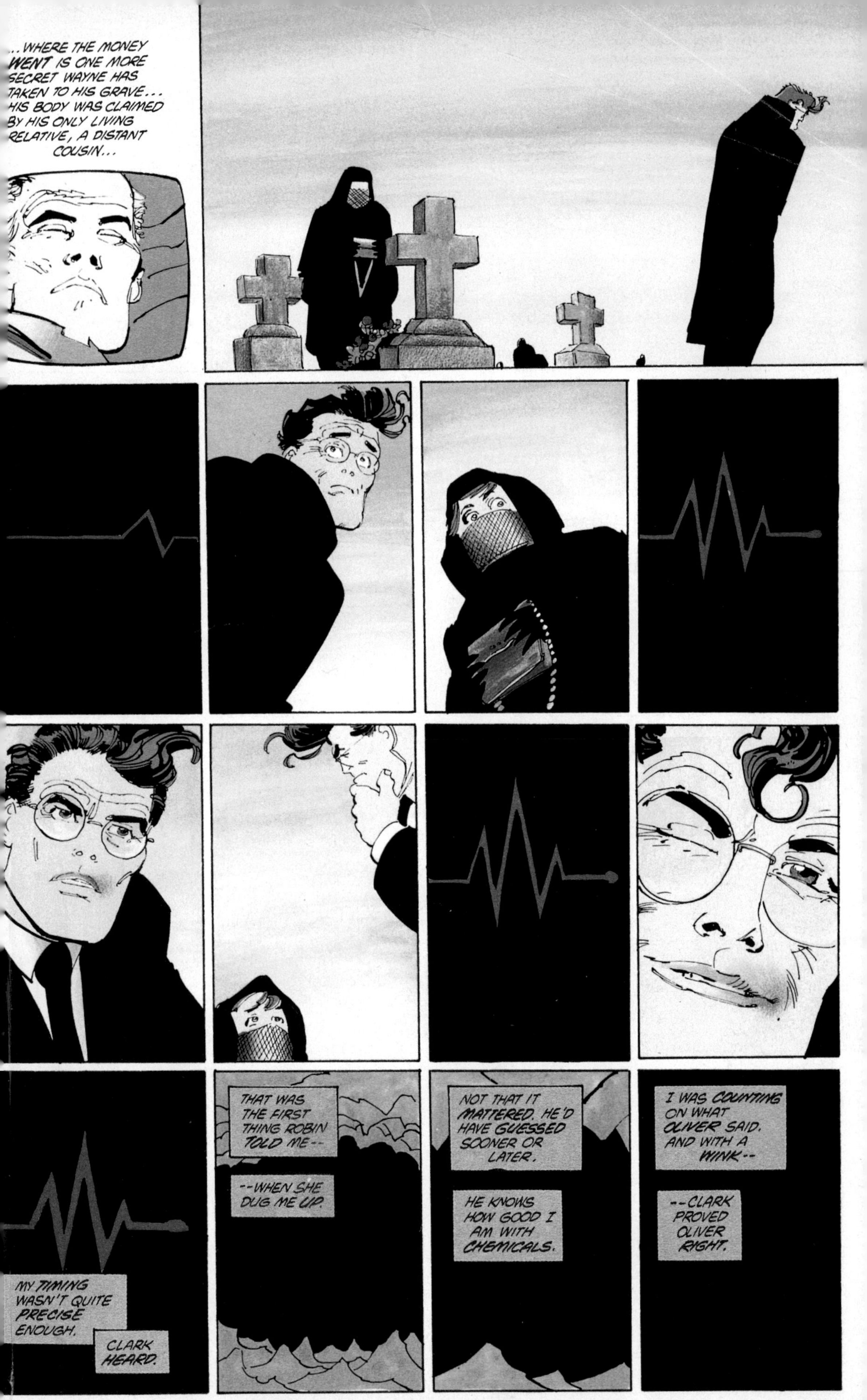

...WHERE THE MONEY WENT IS ONE MORE SECRET WAYNE HAS TAKEN TO HIS GRAVE... HIS BODY WAS CLAIMED BY HIS ONLY LIVING RELATIVE, A DISTANT COUSIN...
MY TIMING WASN'T QUITE PRECISE ENOUGH.
CLARK HEARD.
THAT WAS THE FIRST THING ROBIN TOLD ME--
--WHEN SHE DUG ME UP.
NOT THAT IT MATTERED. HE'D HAVE GUESSED SOONER OR LATER.
HE KNOWS HOW GOOD I AM WITH CHEMICALS.
I WAS COUNTING ON WHAT OLIVER SAID. AND WITH A WINK--
--CLARK PROVED OLIVER RIGHT.

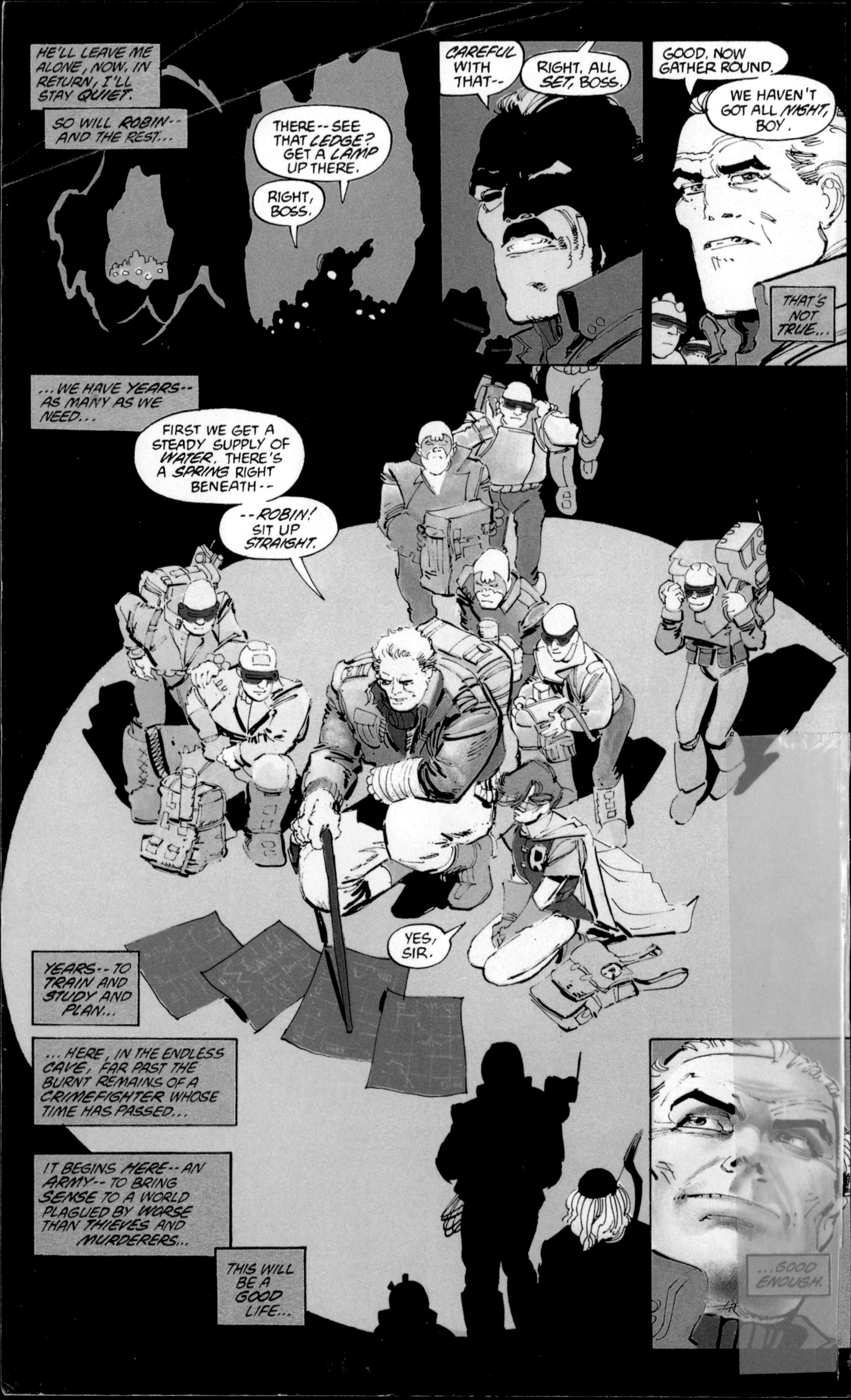
HE'LL LEAVE ME ALONE, NOW. IN RETURN, I'LL STAY QUIET.
SO WILL ROBIN-- AND THE REST...
THERE--SEE THAT LEDGE? GET A LAMP UP THERE.
RIGHT, BOSS.
CAREFUL WITH THAT--
RIGHT. ALL SET, BOSS.
GOOD. NOW GATHER ROUND.
WE HAVEN'T GOT ALL NIGHT, BOY.
THAT'S NOT TRUE...
...WE HAVE YEARS-- AS MANY AS WE NEED...
FIRST WE GET A STEADY SUPPLY OF WATER. THERE'S A SPRING RIGHT BENEATH--
--ROBIN! SIT UP STRAIGHT.
YES, SIR.
YEARS--TO TRAIN AND STUDY AND PLAN...
...HERE, IN THE ENDLESS CAVE, FAR PAST THE BURNT REMAINS OF A CRIMEFIGHTER WHOSE TIME HAS PASSED...
IT BEGINS HERE-- AN ARMY-- TO BRING SENSE TO A WORLD PLAGUED BY WORSE THAN THIEVES AND MURDERERS...
THIS WILL BE A GOOD LIFE...
...GOOD ENOUGH.